HARDPRESS.NET
HOME OF HARD-TO-FIND BOOKS

The Life of Catharine Ii, Empress of Russia
by Jean-Henri Castéra

Address:
HardPress
8345 NW 66TH ST #2561
MIAMI FL 33166-2626
USA
Email: info@hardpress.net

GL

Caste

STANISLAUS AUGUSTUS KING OF POLAND — PAUL PETROVICH EMP

PRINCESS DASHKOFF

PRINCE GREGORY ALEXANDROVICH POTEMKIN — PRINCE GREGORY GREG

J. Chapman sc.

London Published Feb.y 20.1798. for T.N.Longman & O Rees

THE

LIFE

OF

CATHARINE II.

EMPRESS OF RUSSIA.

WITH SEVEN PORTRAITS ELEGANTLY ENGRAVED,
AND A CORRECT MAP OF THE RUSSIAN EMPIRE.

IN THREE VOLUMES.

*Nihil compofitum miraculi causâ, verùm audita scriptaque
senioribus tradam.*　　　TACIT. Ann. lib. xi.

THE THIRD EDITION,
WITH CONSIDERABLE IMPROVEMENTS.

VOL. I.

LONDON:

PRINTED FOR T. N. LONGMAN AND O. REES, PATERNOSTER-
ROW; AND J. DEBRETT, PICCADILLY.

1799.

ADVERTISEMENT.

THE Author being called upon to prepare a third edition for the Prefs, has endeavoured, on revifing the whole, to correct fome inaccuracies which had efcaped
his notice in the former editions; and, in
order to render the work ftill more complete, has added a chapter on the ftate
of literature, arts, and fciences in Ruffia
during the reign of Catharine II. which
he humbly conceives will be deemed an
agreeable and ufeful improvement.

CONTENTS

OF THE

FIRST VOLUME.

PRELIMINARIES.

SECTION I.

EXTENT of the russian empire, Page 1.—Division of Russia into governments, 3. — Population of Russia, *ibid*.

SECT. II. Of the climate of Russia, 7. — Frost and its effects, 11. — Palace of ice constructed by the empress Anne, 14. — Degrees of cold, 16.

SECT. III. Commerce of Russia, 21.—Internal commerce, 23.—Imports, 25. — Exports, 27.—Course of exchange, 30. — Method of trade, 32. — Working-class, 35. — Private manufactories, 37. — Trades, 38. — Weights, measures, and coins, 52. — Genealogical tables, 59.

CHAP. I.

Events previous to the revolution in the year 1762. — Birth and early years of the empress. — Marriage with the grand duke Peter Feodorovitch. — Transactions till the death of Elizabeth. • 63

CHAP.

CHAP. II.

Acceffion of Peter III. — His dethronization and death. — Revolution of 1762. — Catharine affumes the reins of government. - - Page 168

CHAP. III.

Catharine is occupied in fchemes of aggrandifement. — She fupports Biren in Courland. — Panin is defirous of changing the form of the ruffian government. — Beftucheff diffuades the emprefs from it, and wifhes to induce her to marry Gregory Orloff. — A plot concerted at Mofco againft the life of Orloff. — A confpiracy againft the emprefs. — Anfwer of princefs Dafhkoff.—Poniatoffky defirous of coming to Ruffia, &c. — Occurrences of 1762 and 1763. - 335

CHAP. IV.

State of Poland from the time of the kings of the firft race to the death of Auguftus III. — Election of prince Poniatoffky. — Frefh confpiracy at St. Peterfburg. — Journey of the emprefs into Livonia. — Affaffination of prince Ivan in the caftle of Schluffelburg. — Punifhment of Mirovitch, and other events of 1763, 1764, &c. - - - - 390

CHAP. V.

Difcontents at Peterfburg. — Mifunderftanding between the counts Gregory Orloff and Panin. — Viffenfky becomes favourite of the emprefs. — Refignation of the chancellor Vorontzoff. — Prince Radzivil at the head of the confederates. — The bifhop of of Cracow carried off. — The duke de Choiseul incites the Turks to declare war against Ruffia. — Treaty entered into by the emprefs with England. — Tournament at Peterfburg. — Reform of the courts of juftice. —Convocation of deputies from all the provinces of the empire. — Wife reply of the Samoyedes. — Wicked attempt of Tfchoglokoff. — Travels of feveral learned men in the interior of Ruffia. — Academical inftitutions. — Inoculation of the emprefs and the grand duke ; with other events from 1764 to 1768. - - - Page 437

APPENDIX to the FIRST VOLUME.

No. I. Succeffion of the fovereigns of Ruffia, grand princes or grand dukes, tzars, and afterwards emperors ; patriarchs, archbifhops, bifhops, &c. 525

No. II. Ukafe of Peter III. in favour of the ruffian nobility. - - - - - - 534

No. III. State papers relating to the re-eftablifhment of peace.—Declaration delivered by order of Peter III. emperor of Ruffia to the imperial, french, and fwedifh minifters refiding at St. Peterfburg. — Anfwer of the emprefs-queen to the foregoing declaration. — Anfwer given by the french court to the aforefaid declaration. — Anfwer given by the king of Poland, elector of Saxony, to the fame declaration. - - - - - 536
No.

No. IV. Manifesto of the empress Catharine II. on the dethronement of Peter III. - Page 540

No. V. Manifesto of the empress Catharine II. giving an account of her motives for taking the reins of government into her hands. - - 541

No. VI. Declaration of the empress Catharine II. on the recall of count Bestucheff Riumin from banishment. - - - - - 548

No. VII. Translation of a letter from the empress of Russia to M. d'Alembert at Paris, whom she had invited into Russia to educate her son. 550

No. VIII. Declaration of the empress delivered to the foreign ministers. - - 551

No. IX. Substance of a memorial delivered by the chancellor of Russia to the polish resident at St. Petersburg. - - - - 554

No. X. Manifesto published by the court of Petersburg on occasion of the death of prince Ivan. 555

No. XI. Alphabetical list of the towns of the russian empire, shewing in what government they lie, and how many versts distant from the residence, the metropolis, and the government towns. 650

PRE-

PRELIMINARIES.

SECTION I.

Extent, Division, Population, and Revenue of the Russian Empire.

BEFORE we enter on the principal subject of the present undertaking, it will be proper to furnish the reader with some general knowledge of the vast empire to which it so intimately relates.

Russia, in the year 1785, was reckoned to contain within its limits 110 degrees of longitude, and in its breadth 32 degrees of latitude; its superficies was about 305,000 german square miles *, whereof 63,000 are in Europe, and 242,000 in Asia †.

* A german mile is nearly six english miles.

† From Riga to the banks of the Oby in Kamtshatka are reckoned 11,000 versts, or 2200 leagues of 25 to a degree. Three versts make two english miles.

But this empire has been greatly extended since, by the conqueſt of a vaſt territory in the Krimea, by the diſmemberment of Poland, and by the addition of Courland.

Ruſſia actually occupies more than a ſeventh part of the known continent, and almoſt the twenty-ſixth part of the whole globe. The greateſt extent of Ruſſia from weſt to eaſt, viz. from the 39½ to 207½ degree of longitude, contains 168 degrees; and, if the iſlands of the eaſtern ocean be included, it will then contain 185 degrees: ſo that the continental length of Ruſſia, viz. from Riga to Tchukotſkoy Noſs, the eaſternmoſt promontory, will conſtitute about 8500 verſts. The greateſt extent of this empire from north to ſouth, that is, from the 78th to 50½ degree of latitude, contains 27¼ degrees. Hence the breadth of Ruſſia, reckoning it from the cape Taymour, which is the north-eaſtern promontory to Kiakta, will make about 3200 verſts.

To reconcile Ebeling, Krome, Buſching, and the other writers on the population of Ruſſia, this population was eſtimated in 1785 at 24,000,000 of inhabitants, whereof 20,000,000 are in Europe, and only 4,000,000 in Aſia.

Hence it appears, that the mean term of the population of Ruſſia, by the german ſquare mile,

mile, is a little more than 78 inhabitants, but that there are 318 to the fquare mile in european Ruffia, and only 16 per fquare mile in afiatic Ruffia. Now this population feems very trifling in comparifon with that of England and France; where it is calculated that there are 2500 inhabitants per fquare league, that is, nearly five-eighths of a german mile.

Towards the year 1785, Ruffia was divided into forty-three governments, containing in all about 540 towns, 193 whereof were built in the reign of Catharine II. At that period, the emprefs caufed a new divifion of the empire to be made into vice-royalties, which have fince her death been abolifhed by the emperor Paul.

According to the laft revifion, the population of Ruffia amounts to 26,000,000. But it is to be noticed that the nobility, clergy, land as well as fea forces, different officers, fervants belonging to the court, perfons employed under the government in civil and other offices; the ftudents of univerfities, academies, feminaries, and other fchools; hofpitals of various denominations; likewife all the irregular troops, the roving hordes of different tribes, foreigners and colonifts, or fettlers of various nations, are not included in the above-mentioned number: but with the addition of all thefe, the population of

Ruffia, of both fexes, may be fuppofed to come near to 30,000,000.

The revenue of Ruffia is estimated at upwards of 40,000,000 of rubles. The expences in time of peace never exceed 38,000,000; the remainder is employed in conftructing public edifices, making harbours, canals, roads, and other national works.

M. Hermann, in his book on this fubject, in 1790, juftly fays, that the ruffian empire, in its prefent extent, contains a furface, the like of which is not to be found in hiftory. Neither the monarchy of Alexander the great, nor the old roman empire, nor the modern China, are equal to it in magnitude. It comprifes about the feventh part of the firm land of our earth, is as large as the half of all Afia, and more than twice as big as Europe. Its fuperficies contains about 320,000 geographical fquare miles, or above 15,000,000 fquare verfts, whereof 78,000 fquare miles belong to the european, and 242,000 fquare miles to the afiatic part. The two parts confift of 43 vice-royalties, the dimenfions whereof differ from 400 to 140,000 fquare miles. Their magnitude is determinable by an inverted ratio of their population: and in this regard they may be divided into three claffes. The firft includes the moft populous; and

and confequently, according to the circuit of country, the fmalleft vice-royalties ; which are St. Peterfburg, Viborg, Reval, Riga, Polotzk, Mohilef, Smolenfk, Pfcove, Tver, Yaroflaf, Kaftroma, Vladimir, Mofco, Kaluga, Tula, Ræfan, Tambof, Orel, Kurfk, Voronetfh, Kar- kof, Novgorod-Severfk, Kief, Tfchernigof, Penfa, Nifhney-Novgorod, Kafan, Simbirfk. In the fecond clafs follow the vice-royalties, whofe circuit is confiderably larger, but their population not greater, and partly is yet inferior, as, Olo- netz-Novgorod, Tavrida, Viætka ; and in the third clafs, laftly, the moft extenfive, and there- fore the proportionably leaft peopled, are to be placed, Archangel, Vologda, Katarinoflaf, Cau- cafus, Saratof, Ufa, Permia, Tobolfk, Kolyvan, and Irkutfk.

If the difference among authors concerning the territorial extent of Ruffia be great, it is not lefs fo in regard to its population. The author of the " Effai fur le commerce de Ruffie, &c." Amft. 1777, admits it in general to be no more than 14,000,000. Voltaire gives the ruffian empire for the latter years of the reign of Peter I. 18,000,000 of inhabitants, but which is certainly by between 3 and 4,000,000 too many. Marfhall eftimates the population at 18,000,000 ; Williams likewife for 1768, fets it

down

down at only 18,000,000. M. Bufching makes the population of Ruffia amount to 20,000,000; M. le Clerc ftates it at 19,000,000; and M. l'Eveque at 19,050,000; M. de Voltaire, M. Suffmilch, and profeffor Ebeling, about 24,000,000; profeffor Crome and the ftatiftic tables printed at Prague, reckon 25,000,000; and profeffor Albaum, for 1774, 22,000,000. In the hiftorical porte-feuille, part ii. 1786, the population is marked at 27,000,000, and captain Plefcheyef in his Obofrenie roffifkaia imperie, ftates it to be (but for the year 1782 undoubtedly too high) 30,000,000. M. de Beaufobre, fo early as the beginning of the year 1770, gives it at 30,000,000, a number which at that time was almoft a third part too high. Mr. Coxe, on the other hand, ftates the population of the whole empire at 22,838,516 fouls; which, for the time when he vifited the country, was by far too little.

According to the cenfus taken at feveral times, the increafe of the population has appeared to be as follows :

In the year 1722 the number of people was 14,000,000
1742	– –	16,000,000
1762	– –	20,000,000
1782	– –	28,000,000
1788	– –	30,000,000

During

During the reign of Catharine II. then the empire has gained in population not lefs than 10,000,000, whereof, if we deduct (at the ut-moft) for the newly-acquired countries and co-lonifts 3,000,000, there will ftill remain an in-creafe of 7,000,000, arifing from the annual fur-plus of births over the deaths.

SECTION II.

Of the Climate of Ruffia.

THE temperature of the air and the weather in this prodigious empire, are as various as its circuit is extenfive. It comprifes many regions which enjoy the mildeft fky and the pureft air; but ftill more where the weather is extremely rude and cold; and feveral where the exhalations from the earth are not the moft wholefome. The empire, in regard to its weather, and the productions of nature dependent upon it, may generally be divided into three grand depart-ments : 1. The territory which lies above the 60th degree of north latitude, and extends to the 78th ; 2. The territory lying between the 50th and the 60th degree of the fame latitude ; and,

and, 3. The territory which lies more to the south than 50 degrees N. L. and extends southwards from the 50th to the 43d degree. The FIRST is the rudeſt and coldeſt. It contains the greater part of the governments of Irkutſk, Tobolſk, and Vologda : the whole of thoſe of Archangel, Olonetz, and Viborg, with a part of the governments of Perme, Novgorod, and St. Peterſburg. All theſe regions lie in a very cold climate, having a winter, eſpecially Siberia, extremely ſevere. In Uſtiug-Velikiye, in the government of Vologda, ſituate 61 deg. N. L. and 15 deg. more to the north than Peterſburg, quickſilver froze in open air the 4th of November 1786, in a cold of 30¼ degrees by Reaumur's thermometer; the 1ſt of December from 40 degrees; it fell the ſame day to 51, and the 7th of December even to 60 degrees. The quickſilver froze to a ſolid maſs, on which ſeveral ſtrokes of a hammer were ſtruck, before any parts fell off. In Kraſnoyarſk, the quickſilver froze at 235 and 254 by de l'Iſle. (Pallas, Travels, tom. iii. p. 419.) In Solikamſk, the ſame thermometer is ſaid to have fallen in 1761 even to 280. The SECOND department, in regard to fertility, is called the temperate; in one half whereof, namely from the 55th to the 60th degree N. L. though the
                                                          weather

weather is pretty fevere and cold, it yet allows all the fruits of the field and many of the orchard to grow. In the other half, namely from the 50th to the 55th degree, the climate is much milder, and with the ufual products yields ftill others, which in the former do not well fucceed. The whole of this extenfive, beautiful, and important territory of the ruffian empire comprehends the governments of St. Peterfburg, Reval, Riga, Polotzk, Moghilef, Smolenfk, Pfcove, Novgorod, Tver, Yaroflaf, Koftroma, Viætka, Perme, Kolyvan, a good part of Irkutfk and Ufa, the governments of Mofco, Vladimir, Nifhney-Novgorod, Kazane, Kaluga, Tula, Riazane, Voronetfh, Tambof, Penfa, Simbirfk, Kurfk, Orel, Novgorod-Sieverfk, Tchernigof, and the greater part of Kief, Karkof, and Saratof. The THIRD department is the hot, in which products are common, e. g. wine and filk, which do not thrive at all in the former. In this lie Tavrida, Ekatarinoflaf, the greater part of Caucafus, with a part of Kief, Karkof, Voronetfh, Saratof, Kolyvan, and Irkutfk.

Tavrida poffeffes a very agreeable climate. The inhabitants, for three quarters of the year, enjoy fine and warm weather; and Nature here requires but three months at moft to recreate her powers. The fpring feafon commences here

commonly

commonly with March; and from the middle of May to the middle of August generally the greateft heat prevails.   This is ufually fo intenfe, that it rarely happens that winds do not continually blow from ten in the morning till fix in the evening every day, which render it almoft infupportable.   Thunder and ftorms of rain are here alfo not unfrequent, whereby the air is refrefhed.   September and October are, generally fpeaking, the fineft months.   The autumnal weather comes on about the middle of November.   The froft appears in December and January, but is very moderate; feldom lafting for more than two or three days.   Here, however, it is to be remarked, that the level part of this country is in this circumftance to be diftinguifhed from the mountainous; the heat and cold are commonly more intenfe in the former, and rain and fnow lefs frequent.   The air in all the regions of Tavrida, except fome few places on the Sibafh, are reckoned very healthy.——About Kurfk, (in the Ukraine,) all forts of fruit, arboufes*, melons, and apples, are ripe in Auguft; and the corn is already got in. The rivers freeze over at the end of November and in December; and in May they are again free from ice.

* Water-melons.

Thefe

These four several departments, so different from each other, should constantly be kept in view whenever we hear or read of the climate of the russian empire. Hence we see that there are governments which partake in the climate of two; others (for example, Kolyvan) of three; and the government of Irkutsk even of all the four. Whatever Nature produces in these parallels, Russia possesses or might possess; and therefore has advantages of which not one other european state can boast.

The high northern latitude of St. Petersburg, and its situation in a low, marshy, and woody flat, with many large rivers, render its climate cold, rude, and in many respects singular. The imperial academy of sciences has kept a meteorological account, from its foundation in 1725, of the weather of the place; and the freezing of the Neva has been regularly marked annually from the year 1718.

The frost and its effects are here remarkable. The number of frosty days is annually from 150 to 190; and their continuance and severity freezes the ground every winter from 2 to 2¼ and sometimes above 3 feet deep; and the ice of the Neva is from 24 to 36, but generally 28 inches in thickness. Though this body is formed by sheets of ice gliding horizontally upon

upon each other, yet when large square blocks of it stand in the sun upon the ground in spring, they gradually fall to pieces in perpendicular spiculæ of the thickness of one's finger. Likewise in walking over the river in spring, while the ice is still thick, the walking-stick is easily pushed through the ice, by pressing down some of the spiculæ out of their contiguity.

The covering of the Neva with ice, and the breaking-up of it, are remarkable phænomena. At first small distinct flakes of ice are seen floating on the surface, which soon increase into large sheets, of such momentum that the bridges must be removed in all haste to prevent their being carried away by the ice. These sheets of ice drive down the stream for a day or two; during which people pass in boats among them across the river, till at last the ice stops, or the sheets of ice freeze on one another. Immediately the river is passable on foot; and nothing is more common than to see boats rowing over, and in an hour or two afterwards foot-passengers walking to the other side in great numbers.

The breaking-up of the ice come on as suddenly. In spring, at first the snow-water stands on the ice; then the ice becomes spongy, or parts in spikes, admits the water, and assumes a
blackish

blackifh hue.   At length it gives way, but leaves the beaten roads ftill ftanding; in confequence of which foot-walkers are often feen upon the roads, and between them and the floating maffes of ice, boats rowed in various directions. When at laft the roads too break, the ice continues driving for a few days to the gulf, and the river appears with its clear and beautiful current.   In a week or a fortnight afterwards the drift ice comes down from the Ladoga, and continues floating about with the wind for two or three days, making for the time the atmofphere uncommonly cold.

The ice and the cold are made ferviceable in various ways.   Diftances are much fhortened by their means, inafmuch as people, horfes, and carriages of all forts, and of ever fo great burden, can crofs the Neva, and the other rivers, lakes, and canals, in all places and directions: and the Cronftadt gulf fupplies in fome meafure the want of navigation during the winter, by the tranfport of commodities of every denomination over the ice.   As ice-cellars here are a neceffary of life, for keeping provifions of all kinds during the fummer, fo every houfe in every quarter of the town is provided with one filled every year with large blocks of ice cut out of the river.   This operation generally takes place
                                                            about

about the beginning of February.   The ice also administers to the pleasure of the inhabitants, by affording them an opportunity for the diversion of sledge and hore-racing, and for that of sliding down the ice-hills so much admired by the populace.   The weight of these ice-hills, together with that of a multitude sometimes of 5000 or 6000 persons standing about them on holidays, give the spectator a surprising idea of the strength and solidity of the ice.

What may be executed in ice was shewn by the ice-palace which the empress Anna caused to be built on the bank of the Neva in 1740.   It was constructed of huge quadrats of ice hewn in the manner of freestone.   The edifice was 52 feet in length, 16 in breadth, and 20 in height. The walls were three feet thick.   In the several apartments were tables, chairs, beds, and all kinds of household furniture, of ice.   In front of the palace, besides pyramids and statues, stood six cannons carrying balls of six-pounds weight, and two mortars, of ice.   From one of the former, as a trial, an iron ball, with only a quarter of a pound of powder, was fired off.   The ball went through a two-inch board at 60 paces from the mouth of the cannon; and the piece of ice-artillery, with its lavette, remained uninjured by the explosion.   The illu-

9   mination

mination of the ice-palace at night had an afto-
nifhingly grand effect.

In and about Mofco the rivers freeze over in
the middle or towards the latter end of November, old ftyle; and break up in March or the
beginning of April. The buds of the birch-
trees expand in May, and the trees fhed their
leaves in September.——The river Ural ufually
flows, near Gurief, free from ice about the
beginning of March.

The greateft degree of cold finçe the building
of the city of St. Peterfburg was, by Reaumur,
32½, the 6th of January 1760.

The greateft heat, in the fhade, was 28½
degrees, the 23d of July 1757, and the 5th of
July 1758.

By taking the average of all the thermome-
trical obfervations made at the Imperial Academy of Sciences, it is found that the greateft
cold happens in the month of January; and
that its mean intenfity may be eftimated at 22
degrees. Again, that the greateft heat falls in
July; and that its mean force is 23 degrees of
Reaumur.

Months	The mean intensity of the greatest cold.	of the greatest heat.	Mean cold of nights.	cold of days.	Mean heat of nights.	heat of days.
	Degrees.	Degrees.	Degrees	Degrees.	Degrees.	Degrees.
Jan.	22	$\frac{1}{2}$	11$\frac{1}{2}$	8		
Feb.	19$\frac{1}{2}$	2$\frac{1}{2}$	9$\frac{1}{2}$	5		
March	14	7	7	1		
April	6$\frac{1}{2}$	13	1$\frac{1}{2}$			4$\frac{1}{2}$
May	*1	19			5	10
June	*6	21$\frac{1}{2}$			9$\frac{1}{2}$	14$\frac{1}{4}$
July	*9	23			12	17$\frac{1}{4}$
August	*5$\frac{1}{4}$	21$\frac{1}{4}$			10$\frac{1}{4}$	16
Sept.	*1$\frac{1}{4}$	15$\frac{1}{4}$			6	11
Oct.	3$\frac{1}{2}$	10			2	5$\frac{1}{2}$
Nov.	11	4$\frac{1}{2}$	3$\frac{1}{2}$			
Dec.	18	2	7$\frac{1}{2}$	4$\frac{1}{2}$		

The mark * signifies the degree of heat.

In turning over the pages of history, we come to passages where we almost stand astonished at the then climate of Germany, where, for instance, it is said: These countries northward beyond the Danube and the Rhine are covered with vast snows, so that they are uninhabitable from their almost perpetual winters. Virgil and Ovid would not have affirmed, that on the borders of the Danube and in Thrace it was the custom to divide the frozen wine in pieces, if at that time these countries were not subject to so severe a frost. Pliny the elder complains of the immense snows, which will not permit the objects the least remote, in european Scythia, to be seen. Speaking of Thrace, Pomponius Mela tells us, that the clusters of grapes

grapes never come to maturity; and all the antient writers talk of the northern diſtricts of Germany as countries conſiſting entirely of fo-reſts, lakes, moraſſes, ſnow, and ice; complain-ing of the piercing winds that bring from theſe parts tempeſts, ſnows, and froſts. That it is at preſent of a totally different temperature is known to every inhabitant of that country. But from theſe hiſtorical paſſages we might perhaps deduce a cauſe why one part of Ruſſia, though lying under the ſame parallel with Milan, Bour-deaux, and other countries and towns enjoying the moſt agreeable climate, is neverthelefſ of an atmoſpherical temperature entirely different. Thus, for example, Moſco lies under the ſame parallel with England: and yet, on the 14th of April, notwithſtanding the mild winter and an un-commonly early ſpring, the whole country round was covered with ſnow. The ice had begun to break up on many large rivers, while the Volga was yet faſt frozen. The degree of cold, which frequently in Moſco is not inferior to that at St. Peterſburg, and likewiſe reaches to 22 and more below the freezing point, will, on a com-pariſon with the temperature in England, ſhew an extraordinary difference; conſequently, there muſt be ſome material reaſons, occaſioning ſuch conſiderable differences under the ſame degree of

VOL. I. c latitude.

latitude. Considering these countries in this point of view, they are to us what Germany and the countries lying above the 50th and 55th degree were to Italy while they still remained in an uncultivated state. We may therefore partly ascribe this colder temperature to the great number of morasses, lakes, the extraordinarily large forests and tracts of uncultivated land : and the rather, as it cannot be attributed to the high situation or the mountains, which in this region are of no extraordinary height, and the generality of the country is a flat. As it is a well-known observation how much loose heat is absorbed by water when it goes off in vapour, of course those regions which contain such a quantity of water on their surface must be constantly absorbing heat, which, by uniting with that element, is rendered insensible. The alterations in the atmospherical temperature that have been observed in our times, by the draining of morasses and the diminution of forests, likewise shew, that this difference may be attributable to the woods and swamps that are still so numerous. As far as relates to the northern regions, it is very comprehensible how the cold must so extremely increase, as by the flattening of our earth at the poles, they in the same proportion are deprived of light by the southern declination

of

of the fun : fo that, for inftance, in Archangel in
the month of December, when the days are at
the fhorteft, the fun remains above the horizon
only 3 hours and 12 minutes, on the contrary in
the month of June is vifible 20 hours and 48
minutes, and the ftill more northern countries
muft be entirely deprived of it during the winter.
The winds blowing from thefe regions are in this
feafon of an extraordinary drynefs ; as no heat is
let loofe, fo there is no evaporation from ice or
fnow ; whereas, on the other hand, the quantity
of heat that in fummer is fet free, tempered by
the quantity of rain, ice, and fnow, laftly the
water that goes off in vapour, confines a ftill
greater quantity of heat, than was before neceffary to liquefaction, whereby the fenfibility of
the particles of heat muft confiderably decline.

The obfervations made by count Sternberg
during feven months in St. Peterfburg will fhew
the long duration of the cold. The firft fnow
fell the 20th of September, and the furface of
the earth was not feen again till the 25th of
April. The dry ftate of the air, as appeared by
the hygrometer was 95 drought.——The height
of the barometer evinced the low fituation of the
country, and the preffure of the atmofphere.
According to the mean ftation of the barometer,
Peterfburg lay 137—12 lin. lower than Prague.

The

The firſt froſt 1791 was the 14th of September, and the 3d of May 1792 the laſt ; the interval conſequently, was 232 days ; during 119 whereof it never ceaſed to freeze, and 25 on which it did not freeze at all, and 173 when the thermometer ſtood below the point of congelation, 169 days the ſky was partly clouded, and 123 entirely overcaſt. Fogs he reckoned 41. During 69 days it ſnowed, 112 days it rained, and 2 days hailed. Theſe obſervations relate to St. Peterſ-burg ; and we may eaſily conclude from them, that in ſuch a climate but few days remain to the huſbandman for the culture of his field ; and it is abſolutely impoſſible, with ſo few men and ſuch poor implements, to lay out his ground properly in ſo ſhort a ſpace of time. That as well in the higher regions as in thoſe that are at a greater diſtance from the ſea, ſtill fewer days are capable of being employed in culture, is well known ; conſequently ſtill leſs can be performed, until the number of people be larger, the implements better, and they are in poſſeſſion of whatever can facilitate labour; or the atmoſpherical tem-perature be ſoftened by the gradual alteration of the ſurface ; namely, by grubbing up the vaſt foreſts, and draining the ſwamps and moraſſes.

SECTION III.

Of the Commerce of Ruffia.

THE whole of the great and intricate bufinefs comprehended under this head, is naturally reducible to the following branches : Export, import, and the exchange. We will briefly touch on each of them apart.

It is hardly poffible to give a true ftatement of the value, quality, and nature of the exports, without entering into a dry detail of cuftom-houfe lifts. The publicity given to thefe matters here faves a great deal of trouble to the collectors of ftatiftical accounts, in their relations concerning this branch of national affairs. The following ftatements are the refult of a period of ten years, from 1780 to 1790. During that fpace were annually exported,

2,655,038 poods of iron
   19,528   -   -   faltpetre
2,498,950 poods of hemp
  792,932   -   -   flax
2,907,876 arfchines of napkins and linen
  214,704 pieces of fail-cloth and flems
  106,763 poods of cordage
  167,432   -   -   hemp-oil and linfeed-oil

192,328

192,328 poods of linseed
52,645 - - tobacco
129 - - rhubarb
105,136 - - wheat
271,976 - - rye
35,864 - - barley
200,000 - - oats
1456 masts
,193,125 planks
85,647 boards
7487 poods of rosin
9720 - - pitch
37,336 - - tar
81,386 - - train-oil
10,467 - - wax
943,618 - - tallow and tallow-candles
31,712 - - potashes
5516 - - isinglass
8958 - - caviar
5635 - - horse-hair
69,722 horse-tails
29,110 poods of hog's bristles
106,045 Russia mats
292,016 goat-skins
144,876 poods of hides and sole-leather
621,327 pieces of peltry
9982 ox-tongues
73,350 ox-bones.

This

This list, which is complete to the exception of a few articles of inferior consequence, contains, besides napkins, linen, sail-cloth, cordage, tallow candles, pot-ashes, isinglass, caviar, peltry, and leather, no wrought goods; and even some of these have only such a preparation as is necessary for the transport and preservation of the product. The employment of the nation, considerably as it has increased since the time of Peter the great, is still always more directed to production than to manufacture. This is the natural progress of every human society advancing to civilization; and Russia will continue to confine itself to the mere production and the commerce in products, till the quantity of its population and employment be sufficient to the manufacturing of its raw materials.

The buying up of the foregoing articles, and their conveyance from the midland, and partly from the remotest regions of the empire, form an important branch of the internal commerce. The majority of these products are raised on the fertile shores of the volga; this inestimable river, which, in its course, connects the most distant provinces, is at the same time the channel of business and industry. Wherever its water laves the rich and fruitful coasts, industry and diligence have fixed their abode: its course

marks

marks the progress to internal civilization.   But
even from a diftance of from 5 to 6000 verfts,
from the heart of Siberia, rich in metals, St.
Peterfburg receives the ftores of its enormous
magazines. The greater part of them, at leaft the
hardwares, are brought hither from the eaftern-
moft diftricts of Siberia, almoft entirely by
water.   The Selenga receives and transfers them
to the Baikal, from which they proceed by the
Angara to the Yeniffey, and pafs from that along
the Oby into the Tobol ; from it they are tranf-
ported over a tract of about 400 verfts by land
to the Tchuffovaiya, from this into the Kamma,
and then into the Volga ; from which they go,
through the fluices at Vifhney-Volotfhok, into
the Volkhof, and out of that into the Ladoga
lake ; from which they laftly, after having completed a journey through two quarters of the
globe, arrive in the Neva to the place of their
deftination.   This aftonifhing tranfport becomes
ftill more interefting by the reflection that thefe
products conveyed hither from the neighbour-
hood of the north-eaftern ocean, tarry here but
a few weeks, in order then to fet out on a fecond,
perhaps greater voyage ; or after being unfhipped
in diftant countries, return hither under an altered
form, and, by a tedious and difficult navigation,
come back to their native land.   How many
                                            fcythes

ſcythes of the ſiberian boors may have gone this circuitous courſe!

The number of the veſſels which, according to a ten years' average, from 1774 to 1784, came by the Ladoga canal to St. Peterſburg, was 2861 barks, 797 half barks, 508 one-maſted veſſels, 1113 chaloups—in all, 5339. Add to theſe 6739 floats of balks. Sum total, 12,078.

The prodigious value in money of theſe products is, by the want which Ruſſia has of wrought commodities, and by the ever-increaſing luxury, ſo much leſſened, that the advantage on the balance is proportionably but very ſmall. A liſt of the articles of trade with which St. Peterſburg annually furniſhes a part of the empire affords matter for the moſt intereſting economical commentary.

The annual imports at St. Peterſburg for the ſpace of ten years from 1780 to 1790, were

Silken ſtuffs to the amount of 2,500,000 rubles.

Woollen ſtuffs, 2,000,000 rubles.

Cloth, 2,000,000 rubles.

Cotton ſtuffs, 534,000 rubles.

Silk and cotton ſtockings, 10,000 dozen pair.

Trinkets, 700,000 rubles.

Watches, 2000.

Hardware, 50,000 rubles.

Looking-glaſſes, 50,000 rubles.

Engliſh

English stone-ware, 43,800 rubles.
English horses, 250.
Coffee, 26,300 poods.
Sugar, 372,000 poods.
Tobacco, 5000 poods.
Oranges and lemons, 101,500 rubles.
Fresh fruit, 65,000 rubles.
Herrings, 14,250 tons.
Sweet oil, 20,000 rubles.
Porter and english beer, 262,000 rubles.
French brandy, 50,000 ankers.
Champagne and Burgundy, 4000 pipes.
Other wines, 250,000 hogsheads.
Mineral water, 12,000 rubles.
Paper of different forts, 42,750 rubles.
Books, 50,150 rubles.
Copper-plate engravings, 60,200 rubles.
Alum, 25,500 poods.
Indigo, 3830 poods.
Kochenille, 1335 poods.
Glass and glass wares, 64,000 rubles.
Scythes, 325,000, &c.

A very great part of these commodities remain and are consumed in St. Petersburg. The rest is conveyed by land-carriage to various parts of the empire, as to go up the navigable rivers against the stream would be tedious and expensive.

five.   The carts or fledges made ufe of in this
conveyance are moftly drawn by only one horfe,
each having a driver; who all together make up
a caravan of from 25 to 100 carts: fometimes,
on long journies, there is but one driver to every
three carts.

The ftatements of the exports and imports
above given are taken from the cuftom-houfe
regifters.   In order to judge of the worth and
validity of them, it is neceffary to obferve, that
all veffels, on their arrival, undergo a ftrict examination both at Cronftadt and at St. Peterfburg, and are obliged to unload at the cuftom-
houfe.   The proper officers examine the commodities according to the ftatement of the merchants, who are obliged to particularize not only
the nature of them, but, when the duty is to be
paid *ad valorem*, muft alfo fix that value.   If
upon examination it appears, or affords caufe to
fufpect, that the articles are rated below their
proper value, the officer has a right to detain
them, at the price thus fet upon them, with an
additional allowance of 20 per cent. for the
profit.   This method, which is called *under-
writing*, obliges the trader to mark thefe articles
of importation at a value rather too high than
too low: and this practice therefore ftamps a
                                                    great

great authenticity on the custom-house lists. Whether, however, no fraud can be practised in the statement is a question, the solution whereof is only to be had from such as have the greatest interest in denying it. For the rest, it is the general opinion that the prudent precautions are no where in the whole empire so good as at Peterſburg; and that consequently any frauds in the cuſtoms are no where so difficult. That this cannot be said of all cuſtom-house officers is proved from the experience of late years, when thoſe on the borders of Poland were diſplaced. Yet theſe matters do not come properly qualified to the ſtatiſtic till ſeveral years after, as the facts are too recent for obtaining ſure *data* and reſults.

It remains to be mentioned, that the importation of diamonds, books, inſtruments, and the like, is duty-free; and that therefore theſe conſiderable articles either have no place in the entries, or are ſet down at pleaſure.

According to what has been ſeen, we are now enabled to ſtate the value of the imports and exports, and the balance of the trade to St. Peterſburg. By the moſt probable eſtimation, on an average of ten years, from 1780 to 1790, the account is as follows :—

Exports

Exports 13,261,942 rubles.
Imports 12,238,319

Profit 1,023,623 rubles.

In coined and un-
coined gold and fil-
ver, in the three laft
years, were annually
imported   -   -   -   337,064 rubles.

This, added to the
foregoing, makes - 1,360,687 rubles.

The amount of the whole commerce was
therefore in the faid period, from 1780 to
1790, annually 25,837,325 rubles.

The increafe of the commerce appears in a
ftriking progreffion from the following ftatements:—

	IMPORTS.	EXPORTS.
1780.	8,600,000 rubles.	10,900,000 rubles.
1785.	10,000,000	13,400,000
1789.	15,300,000	18,700,000

If we admit, upon the moft probable com-
putation, that the whole commerce of the empire amounts to about 50,000,000 of rubles, it
will follow that St. Peterfburg has more
than

than the half for its share.   The next place in
the commercial scale, after the residence *, is
held by Riga ; the commerce of which collect-
ively may be estimated at about 6,000,000.
This proportion may serve to shew the rank
on this scale that may be allowed to the other
trading towns that come after Riga.

The commerce of St. Petersburg is chiefly
carried on by commission in the hands of factors.
This class of merchants, which consists almost
entirely of foreigners, forms the most respectable
and considerable part of the persons on the exchange. In the year 1790, of the foreign counting
houses, not belonging to the guilds, were eight
and twenty english, seven german, two swiss, four
danish, several prussian, six dutch, four french,
two portugueze, one spanish, and one italian.
Besides these, were twelve denominated burghers, and of the first guild 106, with 46 foreign
merchants and 17 belonging to other towns,
though several cause themselves to be enrolled
in these guilds who are not properly merchants.

In order to form an idea of the exchange and
the course of trade, the following brief account
will suffice.   The russian merchants from the in-

* So St. Petersburg is styled, from being the usual residence
of the later sovereigns.   Mosco is the capital of Russia, as
every reader knows.

terior

terior of the empire repair, at a stated time, to
St. Petersburg, where they bargain with the
factors for the sale of their commodities. This
done, they enter into contracts to deliver the
goods according to the particulars therein spe-
cified, at which time they commonly receive the
half or the whole of the purchase-money, though
the goods are not to be delivered till the following spring or summer by the barks then to come
down the Ladoga canal. The quality of the
goods is then pronounced on by sworn *brackers*
or sorters, according to the kinds mentioned in
the contract. The articles of importation are
either disposed of by russian merchants through
the resident factors, or the latter deliver them
for sale at foreign markets; in both cases the
Russian, to whose order they came, receives them
on condition of paying for them by instalments
of six, twelve, and more months. The russian
merchant, therefore, is paid for his exports
beforehand, and buys such are imported on
credit; he risks no damages by sea, and is ex-
empted from the tedious transactions of the
custom-house, and of loading and unloading.

The clearance of the ships, the transport of
the goods into the government warehouses, the
packing and unpacking, unloading and dispatch-
ing of them,—in a word, the whole of the great

buttle

buftle attendant on the commerce of a maritime town is principally at Cronftadt and that part of the refidence called Vaffilioftrof *. Here are the exchange, the cuftom-houfe, and in the vicinity of this ifland, namely on a fmall ifland between that and the Peterfburg ifland, the hemp warehoufes and magazines, in which the riches of fo many countries are bartered and kept. In all the other parts of the city, the tumult of bufinefs is fo rare and imperceptible, that a ftranger who fhould be fuddenly conveyed hither would never imagine that he was in the chief commercial town of the ruffian empire. The opulent merchants have their dwellings and compting-houfes in the moft elegant parts of the town. Their houfes, gate-ways, and court-yards, are not, as in Hamburgh and Riga, blocked up and barricadoed with bales of goods and heaps of timber; here, befides the compting-houfe, no trace is feen of mercantile affairs. The bufinefs at the cuftom-houfe is tranfacted by one of the clerks, and people that are hired

* The Peterfburg ifland was formerly called Berefovoi-oftrof; the Vaffilioftrof, while Ingria was in poffeffion of the Swedes, bore the name of Givifaari; the Apothecary's Ifland was called Korpofaari; Kammenoioftrof was then Kitzifaari; and the parifh where Peterhof ftands was called Thief.

for

for that purpose, called expeditors; and the labour is performed by artelschiki, or porters belonging to a kind of guild.

The factor delivers the imported goods to the russian merchant, who sends them off, in the above-mentioned manner, or retails them on the spot, in the markets, warehouses, and shops.

There would be no exaggeration in affirming, that it would be difficult to point out a people that have more of the spirit of trade and mercantile industry than the Russians. Traffic is their darling pursuit: every common Russian, if he can but by any means save up a trifling sum of money, as it is very possible for him to do, by his frugal and poor way of living, tries to become a merchant. This career he usually begins as a *rasnoschik*, or seller of things about the streets; the profits arising from this ambulatory trade and his parsimony soon enable him to hire a *lavka* or shop; where, by lending of small sums at large interest, by taking advantage of the course of exchange, and by employing little artifices of trade, he in a short time becomes a pretty substantial man. He now buys and builds houses and shops, which he either lets to others, or furnishes with goods himself, putting in persons to manage them for small wages; begins to

VOL. I.   D   launch

launch out into an extensive trade, undertakes podriads, contracts with the crown, deliveries of merchandize, &c.   The numerous instances of the rapid success of such people almost exceed description.   By these methods, a russian merchant, named Sava Yacovlef, who died not many years ago, from a hawker of fish about the streets became a capitalist of several millions. Many of these favourites of fortune are at first vassals, who obtain passes from their landlords, and with these stroll about the towns, in order to seek a better condition of life, as labourers, bricklayers and carpenters, than they could hope to find at the plough-tail in the country. Some of them continue, after fortune has raised them, and even with great riches, still slaves; paying their lord, in proportion to their circumstances, an *obrok* or yearly tribute.   Among the people of this class at Petersburg are many who belong to count Sheremetof, the richest private man in Russia, and pay him annually for their pass a thousand and more rubles.   It often happens that these merchants, when even in splendid circumstances, still retain their national habit and their long beard; and it is by no means rare to see them driving along the streets of the residence, in this dress, in the most elegant carriages.   From all this it is very remarkable, that

extremely

extremely few ruffian houfes have succeeded in getting the foreign commiffion trade; a ftriking proof that there is *fomething* befides induftry and parfimony requifite to mercantile credit, in which the Ruffians muft hitherto have been deficient.

All the ways of gaining a livelihood among the working clafs have an intimate connection. The raifing the products, their manufacture, and the barter of them, are equally the capital of the nation, and the fource of its profperity and wealth. Among the manufactories the imperial eftablifhments are fo diftinguifhable for the magnitude of their plan, and the richnefs and excellence of their productions, that they may enter into competition with the moft celebrated inftitutions of the fame kind in any other country. The tapeftry manufactory, which weaves both hangings and carpeting, produces fuch excellent work, that better is not to be feen from the Gobelines at Paris. The circumftance that at prefent only native Ruffians are employed, enhances the value and the curiofity of the eftablifhment. No where, perhaps, is the progrefs of the nation in civilization more ftriking to the foreigner than in the fpacious and extenfive work-rooms of this manufactory. The porcelain manufactory likewife entertains, excepting the modellers and arcanifts, none but ruffian workmen, amounting in all to the number of 400, and produces ware that for tafte and fine-nefs of execution approaches near to their beft patterns. The clay was formerly got from the Ural, but at prefent from the Ukraine, and the quartz from the mountains of Olonetz. It is carried on entirely at the expence of government, to which it annually cofts 15,000 rubles in wages, and takes orders. But the price of the porce-lain is high; and the general prejudice is not in favour of its durability. The fayence manufac-tory has hitherto made only ineffectual attempts to drive out the queen's ware of England; but the neat and elegant chamber-ftoves made there, give it the confequence of a very ufeful eftablifh-ment. Almoft all the new-built houfes are provided with the excellent work of this manu-factory; and confiderable orders are executed for the provinces. — A bronze manufactory, which was fet up for the ufe of the conftruction of the Ifaak church, but works now for the court, and private perfons, merits honourable mention, on account of the neatnefs and tafte of its execu-tions.—More remarkable by the mechanifm of their conftruction are the ftone-cutting works at Peterhof. All the inftruments, faws, turning-lathes, cutting and polifhing engines, are worked

9   by

by water under the floor of the building. Fifty workmen are here employed in working foreign, and especially ruffian forts of ftone into flabs, vafes, urns, boxes, columns, and other ornaments of various kinds and magnitudes.—Many other imperial fabrics for the ufe of the army, the mint, &c. are carried on in various places; but the defcription of them would lead us beyond our limits.

The number of private manufactories at prefent fubfifting in St. Peterfburg amounts to about 100. The principal materials on which they are employed, fome on a larger and others on a fmaller fcale, are leather, paper, gold and filver, fugar, filk, tobacco, diftilled waters, wool, glafs, clay, wax, cotton, and chintz. Leather, as is well known, is among the moft important of their manufactures for the export trade; accordingly here are 16 tan-works. The paper manufactories amount to the like number, for hangings and general ufe. Twelve gold and filver manufactories fell threads, laces, edgings, fringes, epaulets, &c. Eight fugar-works. Seven for filk goods, gauze, cloths, hofe, and ftuffs, and feveral others. Here muft not be forgotten the great glafs-houfes fet up by prince Potemkin, where all the various articles for ufe and ornament, of that material, are made; but

D 3 particularly

particularly that for looking-glaffes, where they are manufactured of fuch extraordinary magnitude and beauty, as to exceed any thing of the kind produced by the famous glafs-houfes at Murano and Paris. Among many others which we have not room to particularize, are no lefs than five letter-foundries, one manufactory for clocks and watches, &c.

That in fo large and opulent a city, the refidence of a brilliant court, the neceffary and ufeful trades fhould find employment, may be eafily imagined; but perhaps it is not generally known, that in a city of fo modern a date, that for the fupply of not only the moft neceffary, but alfo of the moft frivolous demands, for the fimpleft not more than for the moft artificial conveniencies, for the moft curious as well as the moft ordinary luxuries, here are artifts and workfhops of all defcriptions. Allured by the numerous wants of a great city, and the profufion of a court, many thoufands of induftrious and ingenious foreigners have been induced to fettle here; by the continual influx of whom, and the communication of their talents, this refidence is become not only the feat of all ingenious trades, but likewife a fource of induftry, which flows in beneficial ftreams through all the adjacent provinces. No country has contributed
in

in so great a degree to effect this salutary change
as Germany; all useful trades, and a great part
of those for the accommodations of luxury, are
carried on by Germans and Russians alone. Next
to the Germans in this respect come the Swedes:
some few French live here in the capacity of
restaurateurs, cooks, friseurs, clock-makers,
and some others. Two or three breweries and
some handicrafts are prosecuted with success by
Englishmen. Germans are dispersed all over
the empire: upwards of 20,000 families dwell
in the Krimea and on the shores of the Volga;
in Mosco, Archangel, and several of the inland
provinces, many, and some of them considerable
families, have been domesticated from the beginning of this century and earlier.

Of the trades which are followed almost exclusively by the Russians, are those of the brick-
layer and carpenter. Besides the bricklayers and
masons that live constantly at St. Petersburg,
above 6000 of them come annually from the
provinces to work during the short summer.
Spacious and handsome buildings are usually
constructed after the plans of an architect, of
whom the court has some of the first eminence
in its service, and under the inspection of a sur-
veyor; but all the rest is performed by russian
builders. These and the masons are for the most

part

part boors, who employ their paffport in working for the ufe and embellifhment of the city.
It is impoffible to refrain from being furprifed at
the talent for imitation that forms the prominent
feature in the character of this nation, on feeing
how quickly thefe clownifh people, deftitute of
all idea of art, attain to the utmoft dexterity and
the niceft judgment in the execution of thefe
works.   The *plotniki*, or carpenters, are equally
expert in the ufe of their axe, which, though fo
fimple in its conftruction, fupplies with them the
place of the hammer, the plane, the faw, and
the chifel.   With this compendium of all tools
they build houfes, make tables, chairs, carts—
in fhort, all the neceffaries of common life that
can be made of wood.   On account of their
dexterity and the cheapnefs of their labour, they
are employed in the conftruction even of brick
and ftone houfes, for executing the coarfer car-
pentry.

The potteries and glazed tile works are all in
the hands of Ruffians.   Befides thefe, the na-
tives are the only butchers and gardeners.   The
latter cultivate every thing which the foil and
climate can produce.   As the greateft advantage of this profeffion is to produce vegetables at
extraordinary feafons, the utmoft endeavours of
thefe people are exerted to that end; and
                                               perhaps

perhaps no where under the fame parallel are all the vegetables of the kitchen-garden produced fo early as here. This trade is moftly followed by boors from Roftof and the adjacent country, who, after a few years ftay, return home with confiderable property, the fruit of their induftry. How profitable this profeffion muft be, from the prevailing luxury of the table, may be eafily conceived.—Prince Potemkin, during his laft fojourn in the refidence, dining one day with count Chernicheff, an experimental *felentfchik*, green-feller, announced himfelf with five uncommonly fine cucumbers, which exactly at that time of the year were extremely rare, and of which the prince was known to be particularly fond. The houfe-fteward took them of the man, and prefented them to his mafter, who was fitting at table with the prince. The cucumbers were devoured in a trice; and the count ordered 100 rubles to be given to the green-feller, as a prefent for the agreeable furprife : but the latter who had already learnt that his goods were irrevocably gone, rejected the prefent, and demanded the payment of 500 rubles; till at length he was with great difficulty perfuaded to be contented with a fmaller fum.

Thefe and a few other lefs important trades are confined folely to the Ruffians. In all the

reft

reft the Germans are as numerous, and often more fo than the Ruffians. This is principally the cafe in all handicrafts that depend on fafhion, as the prejudices here are greatly in favour of foreigners. Thus, for example, there are more german taylors than fhoemakers, in proportion to Ruffians. Among the former are many fub-ftantial and even wealthy perfons, who, befides their houfe in town, have another in the country, keep an equipage, and whofe wives wear dia-monds. Nay, feveral of them give weekly con-certs and routs, and on each of the family feftivals fpend 100 or 150 rubles on the table. People of this fort rife above their trade ; they become artifts ; it is not fo much for the work as for the fafhion that they are paid. One of thefe artifts in drefs, whofe good fortune and reputation have raifed him to opulence, now undertakes nothing more than the cutting out of the clothes, and then gives them to other taylors to few them together ; for this trouble, under the article *pour la façon,* he charges 25 rubles. Many of thefe people too are not merely taylors, but be-long to the clafs called in France *marchands-tailleurs.* Their greateft profit is in buying; they make advances, and give credit to people of rank, of whom they have frequently feveral thoufands of rubles to demand.

Befides

Besides the trades already mentioned, that of the smith is one of the most profitable; as the masters can employ boors in the coarse work, and who, on first coming from the country, are to be had at very low wages. The generality of german smiths succeed very well, build themselves good houses, and leave their children wherewith to begin the world. But in general, the german mechanic, all things considered, lives no where so well as here, as he can no where earn so much with so much ease. The business of the master consists in looking after his workmen, in regulating the day's work, in taking of orders, and getting in his debts. At noon he fits down to a well-furnished table, and the evening he passes in one or other of the numerous clubs in various parts of the town. Far worse fares it with the russian artisan. His work is in some cases (though certainly not in all; for the german master has often only russian journeymen and apprentices) indeed not quite so good; but the price of his workmanship is always far inferior to the value of his labour. In very many of the mechanical trades the Russians already perform all that can reasonably be expected; and from this, and from the insolence of the german masters, their customers increase from year to year.

Most

Moft of the trades that relate to luxuries are here carried on to fuch an extent, and in fo great perfection, as to render it, at leaft for the refidence, unneceffary to import thofe articles from abroad.   The chief of thefe are works in the nobler metals.   Here are 44 ruffian and 139 foreign, confequently·in all 183 workers in gold, filver, and trinkets, as mafters; and befides them feveral gilders and filverers; —— a monftrous difproportion, when compared with thofe employed in the ufeful and indifpenfable bufineffes. The pomp of the court, and the luxury of the rich and great, have rendered a tafte in works of this kind fo common, and carried the art itfelf to fuch a pitch, that the moft extraordinary objects of it are here to be met with.   Several of them are wrought in a fort of manufactory: in one fet of premifes are all the various workmen and fhops for completing the moft elegant devices, ornamental and ufeful, from the rough bullion.   Even the embroiderers in gold and filver, though they are not formed into a company, are yet pretty numerous.   The works they produce are finifhed in fo high a tafte, that quantities of them are fold in the fhops that deal in englifh or french goods, and to which they are not inferior.   This bufinefs, which is a perpetual fource of profit to a great number of
widows

widows and young women of slender incomes, forms a strong objection to the declamations against luxury. Perhaps the remark is not unneceffary, that sham laces and embroidery cannot here be ufed, even on the stage. Next to thefe, may be ranged the hoft of milleners, who are moftly of french defcent; and here, as in Paris, together with their induftry are endowed with a variety of agreeable and profitable talents. Their numbers are daily increafing; and, furprifing! the greater their multitude, the better they feem to thrive. Their work is neat, elegant, and modifh; but they certainly bear an enormous price: a *marchande des modes*, if fhe underftand her bufinefs, is fure to make a fortune. The generality of them, after completing this aim, return to their native country.

The coachmaker's trade is likewife here in a flourifhing ftate. The great concerns in which this bufinefs is carried on in all its parts, from the fimple fcrew to the fineft varnifh; the folidity and durability, the elegance and the tafte of the carriages they turn out, the multitude of people, and, in fhort, the large fums of money that are employed in them, which would otherwife be fent abroad for thefe vehicles, render this bufinefs one of the moft confequential of the refidence. In the judgment of connoiffeurs, and

and by the experience of fuch as ufe them, the carriages made here yield in nothing to thofe of Paris or London; and in the making of varnifh the Ruffians have improved upon the Englifh; only in point of durability the carriages are faid to fall fhort of thofe built by the famous workmen of the laft-mentioned nation; and the want of dry timber is given as the caufe of this failure. With all thefe advantages, and notwithftanding the vaft difference in price of thofe that come from abroad, which is greatly enhanced by the high duties, yet they are yearly imported to a great amount; the blame of which practice is generally laid by the Ruffians on the prejudices of the Englifh merchants, (who lead the fafhions in moft inftances,) in favour of the carriages of their own country. The Ruffians have fucceeded in appropriating the far greater part of this bufinefs to themfelves; the fhape of their carriages is in the height of the mode, the varnifh is excellent, and the outward appearance elegant and graceful; but for durability their reputation is ftill inferior to thofe even of the german workmen here. This cenfure applies to all the ruffian manufactures; their exterior is often not to be found fault with; but they are deficient in the folidity, which fo much recommends the work of other countries. In excufe for the Ruffians, one

one thing ought not to be forgot, that they have to contend with an obstacle that renders it impossible for them to employ so much time, labour, and expence, on their work, as are neceffary for bringing it to the utmost intrinsic perfection; and which, as long as it continues, will confine and impede the progrefs of national induftry. This obstacle is the general prejudice in favour of englifh commodities, which indeed is the cafe, more or lefs, in all countries; but no where in fo high a degree, and with fuch exclusive effects as here. The ruffian manufacturer, therefore, naturally ftrives to impofe his work on the cuftomer for foreign, and to prefs it upon him under foreign names : where this is not practicable, (as with the carriages in the Yæm-fkoi, which every body knows to be ruffian,) he is forced to facrifice folidity to outward appearance, for which he can only expect to be paid. A chariot made by a german coachmaker is not to be had under 6 or 700 rubles ; whereas a ruffian chariot can be bought for half the money ; and it fometimes happens that the latter is even more lafting than the former.

Joinery is practifed as well by the Ruffians as the Germans; but the cabinet-maker's art, in which the price of the ingenuity far exceeds the value of the materials, is at prefent folely confined

fined to fome foreigners, amongft whom the
Germans diftinguifh themfelves to their honour.
The artifts of that nation occafionally execute
mafter-pieces, made at intervals of leifure under
the influence of genius and tafte, and for which
they find a ready fale in the refidence of a great
and magnificent court. Thus not long fince
one of thefe made a cabinet, which for invention, tafte, and excellency of workmanfhip, ex-
ceeded every thing that had ever been feen in
that way. The price of this piece of art was
7000 rubles; and the artift declared, that with
this fum he fhould not be paid for the years of
application he had beftowed upon it. Another
monument of german ingenuity is preferved
in the academy of fciences, in the model of a
bridge after a defign of the ftate-counfellor Von
Gerhard. This bridge, the moft magnificent
work of the kind, if the poffibility of its conftruction could be proved, confifts of 11 arches,
a draw-bridge for letting veffels pafs, diftinct
raifed footways and landing-places, &c. The
beauty of the model, and the excellency of its
execution, leave every thing of the fort very far
behind. The late emprefs rewarded the artificer
with a prefent of 4000 rubles, and he has ever
fince been employed by the court. Among the
more capital undertakers of this clafs are people
who

who keep warehoufes of ready-made goods for
fale; one in particular, who has by him to the
amount of many thoufand rubles, in inlaid or par-
quetted floors of all kinds of wood, patterns, and
colours, that only require to be put together,
which may be done in a few days. Another
confines himfelf to the making of coffins, of
which he keeps a great quantity, of every form
and fize, and at all prices. Several of thefe
dealers on a large fcale have neither fhop nor
tools, nor journeymen, but engage only in podriads; for example, to execute all the timber
and wood-work in a new-built houfe, and then
take on the neceffary workmen, over whom
they act as furveyors.—Before we difmifs this
fubject, a man and his work muft be mentioned,
who does honour to his country, Germany; and
in his line has excelled any thing that the moft
refined induftry of England and France has ever
produced. The name of this man is Rœntgen;
he is a native of Neuwied, and belongs to the
fect of Moravian brethren. He has lived many
years, at feveral times, in St. Peterfburg, and
has embellifhed and enriched the palaces of the
emprefs and the great perfonages of the court
with the aftonifhing productions of his art. In
the imperial hermitage are a great many pieces
of furniture, cabinets, clocks, and other works,

of his invention and execution. They are compofed of the greateft variety of woods, to which
the artift, by a certain preparation, has given a
peculiar hardnefs and durability; and which, by
the moft laborious and extraordinary mode of
polifhing, have received a glofs which needs no
rubbing for its prefervation. The workmanfhip
of thefe pieces is not lefs wonderful than their
invention; not a joint is vifible; all is fitted fo
exactly together as though it were molten at one
caft: fome are inlaid with bronze-work of the
moft beautiful and diverfified gilding; others
with bas-reliefs, gems, and antiques. But the
moft fuperlative production of this artift is a
bureau or writing-defk, which the emprefs prefented to the mufeum of the academy of fciences
about eight years ago. Here the genius of the
inventor has lavifhed its riches and its fertility in
the greateft variety of compofitions: all feems
the work of enchantment. On opening this
amazing defk, in front appears a beautiful group
of bas-reliefs in bronze fuperbly gilt; which, by
the flighteft preffure on a fpring, vanifhes away,
giving place to a magnificent writing-flat inlaid
with gems. The fpace above this flat is devoted
to the keeping of valuable papers or money.
The bold hand that fhould dare to invade this
fpot would immediately be its own betrayer:

3   for,

for, at the leaſt touch of the table-part, the moſt charming ſtrains of ſoft and plaintive muſic inſtantly begin to play upon the ear; the organ whence it proceeds occupying the lower part of the deſk behind. Several ſmall drawers for holding the materials for writing, &c. likewiſe ſtart forward by the preſſure of their ſprings, and ſhut again as quickly, without leaving behind a trace of their exiſtence. If one would change the table-part of the bureau into a reading-deſk, from the upper part a board ſprings forward, from which, with incredible velocity, all the parts of a commodious and well-contrived reading-deſk expand, and take their proper places. But the mechaniſm of this performance of art, as well as its outward ornaments, ſhould be ſeen, as nothing can be more difficult to deſcribe. The inventor offered this rare and aſtoniſhing piece to the empreſs Catharine II. for 20,000 rubles; but ſhe generouſly thought that this ſum would be barely ſufficient to pay for the workmanſhip: ſhe therefore recompenſed his talent with a farther preſent of 5000 rubles.

Several other branches of trade and commerce might be mentioned; but theſe may ſuffice for the information of the readers of the preſent work, eſpecially as in this part of it we muſt neceſſarily conſult brevity.

For

For want, however, of a true statement of weights, measures, and coins, readers justly complain of difficulties in comprehending the authors who treat of foreign countries: we will therefore conclude our Preliminaries with the necessary information on those subjects with regard to Russia.

Throughout the whole russian monarchy, their chronology is kept by the julian calendar with the old style. Accordingly, as is well known, they are 11 days behind us, which, in letters and other writings that pass in correspondence with foreigners, is generally noticed.

Measures and weights are fixed by the government, and are completely the same all over the empire, though some provinces have their own denominations for certain measures and weights. But they are all under the cognizance of the police and the town magistrate, who stamp them, and decide all disputes about them.

Long Measure.——The russian foot is exactly the same with the english, which was adopted by Peter the great for the fleet, and is now become the standard for the whole empire. It is divided into 12 inches; every inch into 10 lines, and every line into 10 scruples.

The russian yard is called arshine. It is in length 28 english, or 26¼ french inches. It is
divided

divided into 16 verſhoks, each of which is therefore $1\frac{3}{4}$ engliſh inches—$93\frac{3}{4}$ arſhines make 100 ells of Berlin—$97\frac{1}{2}$ arſhines make 100 ells of Amſterdam—$80\frac{1}{10}$ arſhines make 106 ells of Hamburgh, &c. At Riga they ſometimes meaſure by the ell, formerly in common uſe there, whereof 100 make only $77\frac{1}{4}$ arſhines.

The ruſſian fathom (ſajéne) is 7 engliſh feet or 3 arſhines; the engliſh and the dutch are no more than 6 feet. A german fathom contains 6 rhenish feet. A french toiſe is 6 french feet. A freyberg lachter is 6 feet 3 inches $10\frac{3}{4}$ lines.

A ruſſian verſt is the length of 500 fathoms (ſajéne), which are equal to 3500 engliſh feet. A geographical mile contains 6 verſts 475 ſajénes, and $7\frac{3}{4}$ arſhines; and a geographical degree $104\frac{3}{4}$ verſts, or exactly ſpeaking, 104 verſts, $131\frac{1}{2}$ ſajénes, and $7\frac{1}{10}$ verſhoks. An engliſh land mile is 2 verſts and 86 ſajénes; an engliſh ſea mile 1 verſt 368 ſajénes and $2\frac{1}{2}$ arſhines; a french league 4 verſts 84 ſajénes; a ſwediſh mile 10 verſts and 17 ſajénes.

Superficial Measure. — Superficies are always reckoned by ſquare verſts, deſættines, and ſquare ſajénes, but moſt commonly by deſættines. A deſættine is 80 ſajénes or 560 engliſh feet long, and 30 ſajénes or 210 feet broad.

broad. It contains therefore 2400 square sajénes or 117,600 ruffian and english square feet. In some provinces a defættine is 60 sajénes long, and 40 sajénes broad, making 2400 square sajénes. A half defættine is likewise called a tfchetvert, which confequently contains 1200 square sajénes. An acre of Berlin contains 180 square rods or 25,920 square feet, a fwedish tonne-land, by which at times they still measure in the governments of Riga, Reval, Viborg, and in the diftrict of Peterfburg, comprifes 46,772 french square feet.

CORN MEASURE.—A garnitza, which is the fame with the ofmuka and ofmufhka, and is the least of corn measures, contains the eighth part of a tchetverik, or a measure holding 5 ruffian pounds of dried rye. It is chiefly used in portioning out oats for horfes.

A kulmit of Œfel and other places, contains 3 garnitza or ¼ tchetverik.

A poltchetverik or half-tchetverik is a measure of 614¼ paris cubic inches. Calculated by dry rye it contains half a pood.

A tchetverik makes two poltchetveriks, and is an eighth of a tchetvert. It contains 1229 paris cubic inches, and holds a pood of dried barley.

A pai

A pai or payok is a quarter tchetvert or 2 tchetveriks, or 16 ofmuki, comprifing 2 pood or 80 pound of dried barley. An exact pai contains 2458 french cubic inches.

A polofmina contains 2 pai or 4 tchetveriks, and comprehends 4 pood of dried rye. The fpace of this meafure is 4916 french cubic inches.

A mefchok or fack is reckoned for 5 pood, and is moft generally ufed for meafuring meal.

A tchetvert, the fourth of an okau, and

An ofmina, are one and the fame meafure. It contains 64 garnbizi, and juft as many ofmuki, 8 tchetveriks, or of dried rye 8 pood; properly 9832 french cubic inches.

A cool or mat-bag weighs, full of barley-meal, 9 pood, and is ufually reckoned equal to 10 tchetveriks.

An okau contains 4 tchetverts, therefore of dried rye 32 pood, &c. It is however, by reafon of its inconveniency, entirely gone out of ufe.

A tonne of corn holds in Reval 5964; in Riga 6570, in Narva 8172, in Sweden 8310 french cubic inches. In Viborg 1 tonne of corn is equal in weight to 6 pood. A bufhel of Berlin contains 2604 french cubic inches.

A lof

A lof in Riga comprifes 3285 french cubic inches, equal to 27 cans. It is therefore fomewhat above $\frac{1}{4}$ of a tchetvert, to which it is commonly reckoned equal.

A laft in Reval holds 24 reval tonns, in Riga 24 riga tonns, or 48 lofs of rye, but of barley only 45 lofs.

LIQUID MEASURE.——A tcharka is the eleventh part of a krufhka or ofmin.

A krufhka or ofmin contains $\frac{1}{4}$ of a vedro.

A tchetvert is $\frac{1}{2}$ of a vedro, or 2 krufhki.

A vedro contains a fpace of 610 french cubic inches, and is equal to 5 riga cans or 10 riga ftoffs.

A botfhka (cafk) holds 4 vedro.

A ftoff in Reval is 60, in Riga 61 french cubic inches.

A fafs in Riga holds 12 ruffian vedro or 120 riga ftoffs.

Nineteen vedro make 1 hogfhead or 6 ankers ; 57 vedro amount to 152 englifh gallons, one of which contains 233 french cubic inches.

WEIGHTS.——The leaft ruffian weight is a folotnik, weighing 68 ; but, according to the ruffian pharmacopœia, 70 medicinal grains. In the common courfe of trade the folotnik is divided into $\frac{1}{2}$, $\frac{1}{4}$, and $\frac{1}{8}$; but the affayers, jewellers,

ellers, and goldfmiths, divide it into 96 parts, and call each a *part*: a diamond, for example, weighs $2\frac{7}{8}$, &c.

A ruffian lote weighs 3 folotniks.

A pound contains 32 lote or 96 folotniks, which make 8512 apothecary grains, or 7452 dutch affe. Five-and-forty ruffian pounds are 38 hamburgh pounds. The parts of a pound are ufually named by folotniks; what, for inftance, weighs 7 lote, is faid to weigh 21 folotniks.

An oka in Tavrida is 3 ruffian pounds.

A dvoinik is 2, a troinik 3, a pæterik 5, and a defæterik 10 pounds, or a quarter of a pood.

A polupood, or half a pood, weighs 20, and a whole pood 40 ruffian pounds, or 3840 folotniks, which, according to riga weight, make $38\frac{1}{4}$, to reval weight 38, to nuremberg weight 35 pound and $2\frac{1}{2}$ lote. A pood is 36 englifh pounds.

A berkovetch is 10 pood or 400 ruffian pounds. A hundred pounds of the weight of Amfterdam are, according to that of Ruffia, $120\frac{7}{11}$ pounds.

100 pounds of Berlin are here $114,\frac{9}{17}$ pounds.

100 pounds of Hamburgh are here $124\frac{31}{33}$ pounds.

100 pounds of Sweden weigh $103\frac{39}{41}$ ruffian pounds.

The

The weight of hay is in many places reckoned by grifta and parms : a grifta is half a pood or 20 pounds ; a parm is 480 grifta or 240 poods.

Coin.	Gold.	Imperial – – –	10 rubles.
		Half Imperial – –	5
	Silver.	Ruble – – – –	100 copecks.
		Half-ruble – –	50
		Quarter-ruble – –	25
		Twenty-copeek piece	20
		Fifteen-copeek-piece	15
		Grievnik – – –	10
		Five-copeek piece –	5
	Copper.	Petaki (5-cop. piece)	5
		Grofch – – – –	2
		Copeek – – – –	1
		Denufhka – – –	½
		Polufhka – – –	¼

⁎ It is neceſſary to mention that the relational value of the ruble to the money of other countries varies with the courſe of exchange ; it will be, however, generally adequate to all hiſtorical purpoſes, if the reader reckons the ruble at four ſhillings. Dividing by five will then give him the ſums ſpecified in pounds ſterling. This may ſerve for the period of this hiſtory : but at preſent, 1798, the ruble is worth no more than two ſhillings.

TABLE I.

ANHALT-ZERBST.

JOHN, prince of Anhalt-Zerbst, born March 24, 1621, died June 4, 1667.
Married Sophia Augusta, daughter of Frederic, duke of Holstein-Gottorp.

John Lewis, resided at Dornburg, born March 4, 1656; died Nov. 1, 1704. Mar. Christiana Eleonora von Zentsch.

Charles William, prince, born Oct. 26, 1664; succ. 1667; died Nov. 8, 1718. Married Sophia, daughter of duke Augustus administrator of Magdeburg.

Christian Augustus, prince, born Nov. 29, 1690; succ. with John Lewis 1742, prussian general, field-marshal, and governor of Stettin; died March 16, 1747.
Mar. Johanna Elizabeth, daughter of Christian Augustus, bishop of Lubeck, Nov. 8, 1727.

John Lewis, prince, born June 12, 1688; succ. conjointly with his brother 1742; died Nov. 5, 1746.

John Augustus, prince, born July 29, 1677; succ. 1718; died Nov. 7, 1742. Mar. 1. Frederica, daughter of Frederic duke of Saxe Gotha.
2. Hedvig Frederica, daughter of Frederic Ferdinand duke of Wirtemberg-Wiltingen.

Frederic Augustus*, last prince of Zerbst, born Apr. 9, 1734; died March 3, 1793. Mar. 1. Carolina Wilhelmina Sophia, daughter of Maximilian, landgraf of Hesse Cassel; died May 22, 1759.
2. Frederica Augusta Sophia, daughter of Victor Frederic, prince of A. Bernburg.

William Christian Frederic, born Nov. 18, 1730; died Aug. 26, 1742.

Sophia Augusta Frederica, born May 2, 1729, afterwards CATARINA ALEXIIVNA.

* There were also three princesses, but who all died in their infancy.

Christian Albert, duke of Holstein-Gottorp, born Feb. 3, 1641, bishop of Lubeck from 1655 to 1666.
Died Dec. 27, 1694.
Married Frederica Amelia, daughter of Frederic III. king of Denmark.

Frederic IV. born Oct. 18, 1671; died July 19, 1702. Mar. Hedwig Sophia; daughter of Charles XI. of Sweden,

Charles Frederic, born April 30, 1700; died June 18, 1739. Mar. Anna Petrowna, daughter of tzar Peter the great.

Charles Peter Ulric, born Feb. 21, 1728, afterwards Peter III. emperor of Russia, and husband of Catharine II.

Christian Augustus, born Jan. 11, 1673, bishop of Lubeck; died Apr. 25, 1727. Mar. Albertina Frederica, daughter of Frederic Magnus, margraf of Baden-durlach.

Adolphus Fred. king of Sweden; died 1771. Mar. Luisa Ulrica princess of Prussia.

Gustavus III. king of Sweden, assassinated 1792.

Gustavus Adolphus, present

Frederic Augustus, bishop of Lubeck, died 1785;

Hedwig Elizabeth Charlotte, married to the duke of Sudermania.

Johanna Elisab. born Oct. 24, 1712; died May 30, 1760. Mar. Christian Aug. prince of Anhalt-Zerbst.

Sophia Augusta Friderica, afterwards wife of Peter III. and empress Catha-

George Lewis, born March 1, 1719; died Sept. 7, 1763.

Peter Frederic Lewis, present prince bishop of Lubeck.

R U S S I A.

Tzar Alexey Michailovitch succeeded in 1645, died 1676.
Married 1. Maria Illitichna Miloslauffkaia.
2. Natalia Kirilovna Narishkina.

1. Tzar Feodor III. Alexieyvitch, succ. 1676, died 1682.

1. Tzar Ivan III. Alexieyvitch succeeded with his brother Peter 1682, abdicated 1689, died 1696. Mar. Procopia Feodorovna Solticova.

2. Tzar Peter I. Alexieyvitch the great, succ. with Ivan 1682, reigned alone from 1689, first emperor 1721; died 1725. Mar. 1. Evdokia Feodorovna Lapoukina, died 1699. 2. Catharina I. Alexievna, reigning emprefs 1725; died 1727.

Catharina Ivanovna, died 1733. Mar. Charles Leopold, duke of Mecklenburgh, 1716; died 1747.

Anna Ivanovna, emprefs 1730; died 1740. Mar. Frederic William, duke of Courland, 1710; widow 1711.

1. Alexey Petrovitch, put to death 1718. Married: Charlotta Chriftina Sophia, princefs of Brunswic-Blankenburg; died 1725.

2. Anna Petrovna, Mar. 1725 to Charles Fred. duke of Holftein-Gottorp; died 1718.

3. Elisaveta Petrovna, emprefs 1741; died Jan. 5, 1762.

Anna Carlovna (Elisabeth Catharina Christina), regent of Ruffia 1740, pulled down and imprifoned 1741; died 1746. Mar. Anthony Ulric, prince of Brunfwic - Wolfenbuttel, 1739. Put into prifon 1741. Died 1776.

Peter II. Alexieyvitch, emperor 1727, died 1730.

Peter III. Feodorovitch (Charles Peter Ulric,) emp. Jan. 5, 1762, dethroned July 9; died July17. Mar. Catharine II. Alexierna (Soph a Augufta Frederica), reigning emprefs, July 9, 1762; died Nov. 17, 1796.

Ivan IV. (III. VI.) Antonovitch, born Aug. 23, 1740; emp. Oct. 28, 1740; depofed Dec. 6, 1741; put to death July 16, 1764.

Catharina Antonovna, born Jul. 26, 1741.

Elizabeth, born Nov. 1743, died Oct. 1784.

Peter, born 1745.

Alexei, born 1746; died Oct. 1787.

Paul Petrovitch, Born Oct. 1, 1754; emperor Nov. 17, 1796. Mar. 1. Natalia Alexierna (Wilhelmina), princefs of Heffe Darmftadt, died 1776. 2. Maria Feodorovna, (Sophia Corothea Augufta Louifa,) princefs of Wirtemberg. Iffue fix children, all alive.

Anna Petrovna, born Dec. 20, 1757; died March 19, 1759.

L I F E

OF THE

EMPRESS CATHARINE II.

C H A P. I.

*Events previous to the Revolution in the Year
1762.—Birth and early Years of the Empress.
—Marriage with the Grand Duke Peter Fedo-
rovitch.—Transactions till the Death of Elizabeth.*

IT is now scarcely possible for any great events
to escape the pen of history; and those which it
seems to record with most delight are the sanguinary catastrophes that shake empires to their
base, or cause the reins of government to pass
from one hand to another. Vain then would be
the attempt to conceal or disguise the causes of
that revolution which, in 1762, brought the
throne

throne of Ruffia under another fovereign.
Many will, doubtlefs, be the writers who will
endeavour to unveil them: and therefore it is
of confequence that pofterity fhould faithfully be
made acquainted with that tranfaction.

In order to form a true judgment of the character of Peter III. of his failings and misfortunes, we muft firft caft an eye over the reign of
Elizabeth, to difcover the intrigues that were
formed againft her nephew by the ambitious and
faithlefs courtiers of that princefs.

Elizabeth Petrovna was the daughter of Peter
the great and the firft Catharine ; who, notwithftanding her great power, was obliged, at her
death, to leave the throne to the young Peter II.*
fon of the unfortunate tzarovitch Alexius, deca-
pitated by order of his father.

Peter II. reigned only three years, and was
followed † by the emprefs Anne, daughter of the
tzar Ivan, elder brother of Peter the firft.

To Anne, in 1740 ‡, fucceeded Ivan III.
her nephew, being yet in his cradle ; and who,
by a confpiracy headed by a german furgeon
of french extraction, named Leftoc, was dethroned, thirteen months afterwards §, for the

* May 18, 1727.   † February 1, 1730.
‡ The 28th of October.   § December 7, 1741.

purpofe

purpose of raifing Elizabeth to the fovereign power *.

Elizabeth, it is faid, bore a likenefs to the handfome Catharine, her mother, and even tranfcended her in beauty. She was of an advantageous height, and of a figure remarkably well proportioned; and though her features were rather large, her countenance difplayed an inexpreffible fweetnefs, which fhe increafed ftill further by the charms of a converfation, often gay, and almoft always flattering. But if fhe equalled her mother in thofe advantages which render the fociety of a woman fo agreeable; if fhe furpaffed her in the immoderate love of pleafure; fhe was very far from poffeffing, like her, that ftrength of mind which gives to them to whofe fhare it falls, the irrefiftible afcendant over all that fur-

* Leftoc became, in his turn, the victim of a cabal that was formed againft him. The chancellor Beftucheff, and feveral other courtiers, accufed him to the emprefs Elizabeth of holding a dangerous correfpondence with the ambaffador of Pruffia; and the deluded princefs facrificed to their animofity the man to whom fhe owed her crown. Leftoc was deprived of all his property, and exiled to a miferable village in the province of Archangel, where he was abandoned to the extremeft indigence. Peter III. recalled him; but a part of his property was loft, which he did not regret, any more than the court, where he ceafed to appear, as he was now apprifed of its dangers. He died at Peterfburg in 1767.

round them. Inftead of having the art of commanding, Elizabeth fubmitted herfelf continually
to the guidance of others ; and this weaknefs was
a primary caufe of the misfortunes of Peter III.

That fhe might fecure her independence,
Elizabeth conftantly refufed to take a hufband,
with whom fhe muft have fhared the empire;
but fhe did not the more abftain from volup-
tuous gratifications, or even tafting the pleafures of the maternal ftate ; and as, with her other
infirmities, fhe had that of being a bigot, the
field-marfhal Alexey Gregorievitch Razumofffky,
her grand-veneur, fucceeded in determining
her privately to give him her hand. The counts
Tarrakanoff and their fifter * were the fruit of
this clandeftine union. Razumofffky †, however,

---

* We fhall hereafter relate the unhappy end of this young
princefs, and the cruel treatment fhe experienced from
Catharine II. and Alexius Orloff, when fhe was brought off
by the latter from Rome, whither fhe had been conducted
by prince Radzevil.

One of the brothers, Tarrakanoff, is ftill alive. The
other died miferably at Peterfburg. Being defigned to be
admitted into the college of Mines, he attended a courfe of
chemiftry under profeffor Lehmann : and in fetting on the
furnace a veffel filled with poifonous ingredients, he broke
it, and was fuffocated.

† The emprefs Elizabeth loaded Alexius Razumofffky
with benefits. She made him a prefent of the palace An-
nitakoi,

ever, was not the only lover of Elizabeth; she found it agreeable to make frequent changes; but the crafty favourite permitted none to be prefented to her view, except fuch as he thought to have too little underftanding or ambition to attempt a competition with him.

To her propenfity to voluptuoufnefs, Elizabeth firft added the love of good cheer, and then gave herfelf up to the pleafures of wine. Banquets, balls, mafquerades, the moft frivolous amufements, were preferable in her mind to the perplexities and troubles of bufinefs; and therefore confumed the days fhe had promifed to employ for the profperity of the empire.

The perfon who, after Alexey Razumofffky, had the moft influence on the mind of Elizabeth, was the grand chancellor Alexey Beftucheff Riumin*, the boldeft and the ableft m anof all
that

---

nitzkoi, which, after the death of that favourite, lapfed back to the domains of the crown: and it is a remarkable circumftance, that Catharine II. afterwards beftowed this palace on prince Potemkin.

* The grand chancellor was the fon of a fcottifh officer, named Beft, whom Peter the great brought with him at his return from England. Beft, which in the ruffian language fignifies *beaft*, is a horrid term of abufe, when applied to a man or woman; therefore Peter familiarly told him to

change

that attended the imperial court.   He governed
at once the emprefs, her favourite, and the minifters of ftate ; he in a manner directed the
affairs of the empire both at home and abroad.

Count Ivan Ivanovitch Shuvaloff was alfo one
of the favourites of Elizabeth ; but he made no
other ufe of his influence than as a means of augmenting his wealth, which was already enormous ; leaving the arts of intrigue to his coufin
Peter Ivanovitch Shuvaloff*.   Skilled in the
ways of flattery, Ivan Shuvaloff made humanity
and glory the chief fubjects of his difcourfe with
the emprefs.   He extorted from her, by various
means, prefents of immenfe value, and infpired
her with the defire of caufing the hiftory of
Ruffia to be compofed ; a defire which he was
artful enough likewife to turn to his advantage,
by attracting to himfelf the praifes of Voltaire.

In the mean time, Elizabeth, being determined to deprive the family of Anna Ivanovna

---

change it.   " If your majefty does not approve of my
name," faid the lieutenant, " I befeech you to alter it to
your own mind."—" Well then," returned the tzar, " let
it be Beftucheff, and thou art a Ruffian at once."

· * Peter Ivanovitch Shuvaloff had conceived the hope of
feizing the throne to the prejudice of the grand duke ; but
this project appeared fo extravagant, that Elizabeth herfelf
only made it a fubject for laughter.

of

of all hope of re-afcending the throne, in the
year 1742 nominated for her fucceffor Charles
Peter Ulric, fon of the duke of Holftein Gottorp, by Anne daughter of Peter the great.
This young prince might by his birth have
fooner preferred his claim to the imperial
crown; but the law enacted by Peter I. concerning the freedom of choice in naming a fucceffor *, and feveral revolutions, had been againft

* Peter I. pufhing defpotifm to its utmoft extremity, had
made a law, which authorized the fovereign to defignate for
his fucceffor whom he would.   This law was eafily eluded in
a country where the exifting monarch confiders what has
been enacted by his predeceffors as obligatory only when it is
his intereft to do fo, where the conftitution and the form of
government have no fecurities.   However, the law was
made and adopted; and it was not for the legiflator to be
the firft to infringe it.   Peter died without defignating his
fucceffor, without even knowing who fhould fill his throne.
That monarch put his fon to death, that his fceptre might
not fall into hands which he thought not able to wield it;
thus ftifling the fentiments of paternal affection from attachment to the empire he had formed.   Though apprehenfive
that his painful and glorious labours would not be continued,
that prince, inftead of naming his fucceffor, and thereby
declaring to his people him on whom he founded his hopes,
died without forefeeing the troubles, the incalculable mif-
fortunes, fuch a neglect might produce.   What an error in
a legiflator! what inconfiftency in the conduct of Peter! So
true it is, that the greateft man is fometimes guilty of faults
which an ordinary perfon would have avoided.

F 3

him,

him.   On the death of Peter, in 1725, his widow Catharine I. got poffeffion of the throne,
more, by the boldnefs of Mentchicoff, than in
confequence of her hufband's will.   After her
death, which happened in 1727, the defcendants
of Peter recovered the fucceffion.   His grandfon, the fon of the unfortunate Alexey Petrovitch, inherited the throne, which had been be-
queathed him by his ftep-grandmother; but
with this condition, that in cafe he fhould die
without an heir, then her children by Peter
the great fhould fucceed.   By the premature
death of Peter II. in 1730, the male line of the
ruffian tzars of the houfe of Romanof became
extinct: the female fucceeded of courfe.   But,
during the laft reign, a council of its own erection, affuming the ftyle of the high privy council, and taking upon itfelf the defpotic decifion
in all matters of ftate; in order to fecure its authority, found it neceffary to circumfcribe that
of the princes.   This council juftly imagined,
that the family of Peter the great would never
fubmit to any binding capitulation, and arbitrarily paffed by his daughters.   Anna Petrovna,
the eldeft, already deceafed in 1728, was the
mother of Charles Peter Ulric, duke of Holftein Gottorp, who, therefore, for this time, loft
the fucceffion.   The fecond daughter, Elizabeth,

was

was likewise paffed over : and the views of the nation were turned to the female pofterity of the emperor Ivan Alexieyvitch. But that elder brother of Peter the great, and for a time his partner in the empire, had voluntarily relinquifhed the government, and left it to the latter alone : accordingly the offspring of the latter fhould of right fucceed to the fovereigns their progenitors, even if no regard were to be paid to the teftament of Catharine. But in refpect to the family of Ivan, the council now purfued a like arbitrary conduct, by excluding the eldeft daughter Catharina and her pofterity from the throne, becaufe they dreaded the impetuous temper of her hufband, Charles Leopold, duke of Mecklenburg. The fecond daughter Anna Ivanovna became emprefs in 1730, under a very limiting capitulation, which in a fortnight afterwards fhe tore in pieces. The pofterity of Peter was farther and farther removed from the fucceffion. Anna named her nephew, the infant fon of her elder fifter Catharina, who in the mean time died, to be her fucceffor : and this child was called to be emperor, under a regency, upon the demife of his aunt in 1740. Three weeks after, a revolution difplaced the guardian Biron, duke of Courland ; and from that event a year had fcarcely elapfed when a fecond revolu-

F 4   tion

tion depofed the infant emperor, the regent-mo-
ther, and the whole family. Elizabeth Petrovna
was raifed to the throne in December 1741, who
immediately, as was before obferved, called Peter,
the only fon of her deceafed elder fifter Anna, in
order to nominate him grand duke, and heir to
the imperial throne. —— Thus then, though late,
the fucceffion was recovered by the rightful
heirs, according to the law of primogeniture
obferved in all the reft of Europe. And now,
according to the cuftom introduced univerfally
in modern times among fovereigns, the next grand
concern was to unite the heir apparent in marriage with fome european princefs, as hitherto
the tzars and emperors of the family of Romanof
had taken their wives from the daughters of the
ruffian magnates.

Peter had been already duke of Gottorp fince
the year 1739, on the death of Charles Frederic
his father. In December 1741, Elizabeth recalled him to the ruffian empire, which he had
quitted when a child : he arrived at St. Peterfburg in February of the following year, and in
March accompanied his aunt to her coronation
at Mofco. Queen Ulric Eleonora, the fifter of
Charles XII. who brought her hufband Frederic
of Heffe-Caffel to the throne of Sweden, having
lately died, the eftates of that kingdom were con-

fulting on the nomination of a prince who fhould hereafter be their king. The 16th of November they fixed their choice on the nephew of the deceafed queen, the duke of Gottorp, of which they fent him notice by a folemn embaffy; but precifely two days after his election in Stockholm, in Mofco he was declared heir to the ruffian throne.

Peter now, on the 18th of November 1742, in the chapel of the imperial palace, being 14 years of age, having publicly adopted the greek religion, and received at his confirmation the name of Peter Feodorovitch *, was folemnly proclaimed grand duke, with the title of imperial Highnefs, and declared fucceffor to the throne; at the end of which ceremony all prefent took the oath to maintain his fucceffion.

In the year 1743, when he had attained his 16th year, the emprefs refolved to provide him

* The ruffian nobility always add to their own chriftian name the chriftian name of their father, with the termination *ovitch* or *evitch*, which denotes the fon, as *ovna* or *evna* implies the daughter. By this means foreigners, on coming into this country, drop the name they have hitherto borne, and are known by another. Thus a Mr. John Jennings, if his father's name were John, on his arrival here is Ivan Ivanovitch, and his fifter Anne will be Anna Ivanovna.— Theodore, in ruffian orthography, is Feodor, and is alfo adopted for Frederic.

a fpoufe.

a spouse. Elizabeth and the great Frederic of Prussia were still upon amicable terms. They took up the affairs of Sweden; and the empress first made the proposal, in 1744, to marry the new heir-apparent with Louisa Ulrica, the king of Prussia's sister. For, it is said in the contemporary accounts, that Elizabeth proposed to the king a connection between his youngest sister, Anna Amelia *, and her nephew. But Frederic, who was not fond of the changes of religion required in this country on such occasions, declined the offer; the acceptance of which might perhaps have occasioned him one formidable foe the less in the seven years war. In his turn he amicably proposed the princess Sophia of Zerbst, as a relation of the grand duke †; and this proposal met her full approbation. The important events of the last fifty years it was certainly impossible for any one to foresee; yet Frederic was too wise to turn his thoughts on any princess but one whom he knew to be worthy of so mighty an empire. He therefore prepared for Catharine the way to the russian throne; and to be introduced to fortune by such a judge of talents, made her success more honourable.

* She died abbess of Quedlinburg in 1787.
† Their grandfathers were brothers.

The

The father of Sophia Augusta Frederica was Chriftian Auguftus, prince of Anhalt-Zerbft-Dornburg, at that time major-general in the pruffian fervice, commander in chief of the regiments of infantry, and governor of the town and fortrefs of Stettin. Her mother, a woman of parts and beauty, a friend and correfpondent of Frederic prince royal of Pruffia, of about the fame age with herfelf, was born princefs of Holftein, and therefore nearly related to the three great families of the north. — On the death of John Auguftus, reigning prince of Zerbft, the 7th of November 1742, without iffue, he was fucceeded by his two coufins conjointly in the government, John Lewis and Chriftian Auguftus. The eldeft of thefe brothers died, unmarried, the 5th of November 1746; the now fole prince Auguftus furvived him not long, only to the 16th of March 1747, when he died a general feldt-marfhal in the pruffian fervice, and governor of Stettin. Befide his daughter, he left behind him only one fon, who had not yet completed his 13th year. The dowager princefs was called to the regency, and governed in his name till July 31, 1752, when the young prince, on being declared of age by the emperor, took the government upon him. The mother, as in fimilar cafes had often been done by the

princes

princes of Germany, retired to Paris, where she died the 20th of May 1760.   The son Frederic Augustus bore no resemblance, either in mind or dispositions, to his illustrious sister.   He died in 1793, in foreign parts, where he had latterly lived, lamented by none.   He had been twice married, but was always childless: the branch Zerbst of the house of Anhalt became extinct with him.

The princess Sophia, of whom we are now to speak, and whom fortune early called to act a part upon a higher stage than that of Zerbst, was born at Stettin the 2d of May 1729*; consequently

* This year, 1729, given in all the almanacs and genealogical tables, is now, and was even during the life of the empress, called in question.   Some affirm her to have been older by two years; though the marriage of her parents was only consummated a year and a half before.   It is pretended that she was afterwards stated to be younger, probably from a piece of gallantry by no means unusual towards ladies; or, according to another phraseology which we meet in the Moniteur, (which abruptly pronounces the year of her birth uncertain,) that she might appear younger than her husband, as the contrary is even prohibited by the canons of the greek church.   But her husband, as we learn from the family pedigree, was her elder by a year and a quarter.   Others, on the contrary, declare her to be younger; and that on her transition to the greek church, it was objected to her, that she was not, by several years, competent to this religious

quently four years after the death of Peter the great, and two years after that of the first Catharine, and in the territory of Frederic, with whom she afterwards shared the renown of the present century. Her mother took the care of her education on herself. Burghers are still living in Stettin, who remember in their childhood to have played with the princess; for she was brought up in the simplest manner, and was called by her parents, in the common diminutive of her name, Fiékè. Good-humour, intelligence, and spirit were even then the striking features of her character. Whatever was the

religious act.—Her age at that time was fifteen years and two months.

The whole of this report, which has been far enough spread to deserve a refutation, is entirely unfounded. As a proof, we will only refer to a little book, which, though of itself insignificant, yet on this occasion, in regard to the time, and as there is no reason to suspect it of incorrectness, must be held valid;—the Berlin Calendar of the year 1731. (It is well known that a calendar is printed in the year before that for which it is to serve; and its accounts are therefore of the second year previous to that of the date it bears on its title-page.) In this we read the following article:

" Illustrious births from 1 Jan. to ult. December 1729.

" Soph. Aug. Friederika, daughter of the prince of Anhalt-Zerbst, gen. major in the service of the king of Prussia, and command. at Stettin, the 2d of May."

play,

play, she always took upon herself the principal part, and made her little companions know theirs, sometimes with the full emphasis of command. A lady of quality, who frequently saw her, describes her in the following manner: " Her deportment from her earliest years was " always remarkably good; she grew uncom- " monly handsome, and was a great girl for her " years. Her countenance, without being beau- " tiful, was very agreeable: to which the pecu- " liar gaiety and friendliness which she ever dis- " played gave additional charms. Her educa- " tion was conducted by her mother alone, who " kept her strictly, and never suffered her to " shew the least symptoms of pride, to which " she had some propensity; accustoming her, " from her earliest infancy, to salute the ladies " of distinction, who came to visit the princess, " with the marks of respect that became a child; " an honour which my mother on all such oc- " casions enjoyed, and which she was obliged " never to omit, by the express command of " the princess."

These days, which Sophia passed in easy se- clusion, were always recollected by Catharine with pleasure. While arbitrary sovereign of the russian empire, she still retained sentiments of affection for the place of her birth, and for

several

feveral perfons of her former acquaintance. She annually fent to the magiftrate of Stettin the medals fhe caufed to be ftruck in commemoration of the events of her reign, as well in gold as in filver. Shortly after her coming to the crown, fhe fent to the fociety of markfmen of the town a prefent of 1000 ducats. In her youth fhe had frequently attended the amufements of thefe burghers, and at times even fhot at the mark. Soon after her arrival in Peterfburg, fhe fent the lady who waited upon her, and gave her the firft leffons in the french language *, fome beautiful furs; and to her writingmafter†, a fum of money. In the very late years of her life, fhe tranfmitted her picture, accompanied with the moft flattering expreffions of efteem, to a lady formerly her playmate. This lady, who has permitted herfelf to be named as the communicator of thefe anecdotes of the early life of Catharine, is the countefs von Mellin, at Gartz. The particulars, though trifling in themfelves, yet, as authentically relating to the illuftrious fubject of thefe memoirs, are of confequence enough to be inferted here.

* A demoifelle Quardel, then married to a burgomafter of Demmin.

† Laurent, the fchoolmafter belonging to the french congregation in Stettin.

She

She lived till her fifteenth year alternately in Stettin and in Dornburg or in Zerbst; but she always accompanied her mother on several little journies, which contributed much to the forming of her mind and manners. The princess often made some stay at Hamburg with her mother, the widow of the bishop of Lubeck, at whose court was a M. von Brummer, who filled the post of a gentleman of the bed-chamber*, who communicated to the young princess the most instructive works of the then living authors, which had a beneficial effect on her mind and heart. She was always addicted to reading, to reflection, to learning, and to employment. Still oftener was the princess at Brunswick, with her relation and former preceptress, Elizabeth Sophia Maria, dowager duchess of Wolfenbuttel, born princess of Holstein-Norburg. Here she used sometimes to pass the whole summer; she was there also in December 1743, and caused her daughter Sophia to be daily instructed in the doctrines of the lutheran religion, by the court-preacher Dovè, who at that time little thought that his illustrious disciple would so suddenly afterwards adopt the very different faith of an-

* Afterwards an oberhof-marshal von Brummer went from Holstein with the grand duke Peter to Russia. *Query,* whether the same?

other

other church.   The vifits to Berlin were likewife not unfrequent; for example, in January 1742, on occafion of the marriage ceremony of the prince of Pruffia, father of the prefent king; and for the laft time about the beginning of the year 1744, whence the journey was farther continued to Ruffia.

In the fpring of the year 1742, fhortly before her departure from Stettin, the young princefs wrote the following fhort note to the countefs von Mellin :

    " MADAME,   à Stettin, ce 20 Mars 1742.

   " Je ne manquerai pas de vous envoyer mon
" portrait, puifque vous me faites l'honneur de
" me le demander; & je vous prie, madame, de
" l'accepter comme un gage de mon amitié, &
" vous prie en même tems de me conferver auffi
" la vôtre.   Je me recommande à l'honneur de
" vôtre fouvenir, & fuis,

        " Madame,
    " Votre fidele amie & fervante,
      " SOPHIE AUGUSTE FRIDERIQUE."

As, fo far as it appears, Catharine afterwards never returned to Stettin, thefe lines were moft probable intended as an affectionate farewel*.

                           Three

* With the mother of the princefs the countefs always continued an epiftolary correfpondence, but with the latter

Three years after Peter had been called to Ruffia, it was therefore agreed to marry him with

---

it dropped, who feemed likewife to have forgotten the promifed portrait. After fhe had afcended the throne as emprefs, the countefs von Mellin fought various opportunities of reminding her of it; but probably the letters never reached her hand, as no anfwer enfued. The hope of obtaining the picture was therefore abandoned.

At the inftance of her fon, however, to whom fhe fhewed the note, the countefs wrote once more to the emprefs in 1789, inclofing the lines in her own hand-writing, and delivered it to the care of her nephew, count Auguftus von Mellin, prefident in Riga, who has made himfelf fo famous by his excellent maps of Livonia. Very foon afterwards fhe was agreeably furprifed at receiving, by the hands of count Neffelrode, ambaffador from Ruffia at the court of Berlin, not only an exceedingly fine miniature of the emprefs, richly fet with diamonds, accompanied with a golden *fouvenir*, alfo fet with brilliants, with the cypher E. II. (Ekatarinà the fecond), but alfo this very gracious letter:

" Madame la comteffe de Mellin. Vous m'avez fait
" plaifir de me rappeller la promeffe que je vous avois laiffée
" par écrit, en partant de Stettin, de vous envoyer mon
" portrait. Il eft vrai que les nombreufes diftractions dans
" lefquelles je fus dès lors entrainée, me firent perdre cet
" engagement de vue; mais il n'en a pas été de même de
" votre fouvenir, celui-ci ne s'eft point effacé de mon
" efprit, & je me fuis fouvent retra _ les momens agréables
" que j'ai paffés en votre fociété. Vous m'avez donné de
" votre côté une preuve bien convaincante de votre attache-
" ment pour moi, en confervant un fi grand nombre d'an-
" nées

with Sophia Augusta of Anhalt-Zerbst*, who was about one year younger than himself, and who, on embracing the greek religion, changed her name to that of Catharina Alexievna, a name which she has rendered so illustrious since.

All Europe was deceived on the causes of this alliance, which was attributed to the intervention of the king of Prussia. It is true that Frederic was desirous of seeing it brought to effect, but, without a motive unconnected with politics, the sollicitations of that monarch would have fallen to the ground.

" nées mon billet que vous venez de m'addresser en original.
" Je vous le renvoye conformément à vos désirs, en y joi-
" gnant le portrait dont je suis restée votre débitrice. Vous
" n'y reconnoitrez plus les traits sous lesquels vous m'avez
" autrefois connue, mais je vous prie de croire que mes sen-
" timens pour vous sont encore les mêmes, que je prendrai
" toujours beaucoup d'intérêt à ce qui vous concerne, &
" que je vous souhaite un bonheur constant jusqu'à la fin de
" vos jours. Si ces assurances de ma part peuvent ajouter
" quelque chose à votre contentement, je vous les donne de
" bien bon cœur, étant très parfaitement, Madame la com-
" tesse de Mellin,

" Votre bien affectionnée,

" A St. Petersbourg,   " CATHARINE.
" ce 31 Mars 1789."

* She was born April 25, 1729.

G 2   Long

Long ere she mounted the throne of the tzars, Elizabeth had been promised to the young prince of Holstein-Eutin, brother to the princess of Anhalt-Zerbst, mother of Catharine; but at the instant when the marriage was about to be celebrated, the prince fell sick, and died. Elizabeth, who loved him to excess, became inconsolable; and in the bitterness of her grief made a vow to renounce the nuptial tie: a vow which, as we have already observed, was, at least as to the public, religiously kept. Even if Elizabeth was seen afterwards to yield to the gallantries of several of her courtiers, she nevertheless retained a lively tenderness for the object of her first affection. She paid a sort of worship to his memory, and never mentioned him without tears.

The princess of Anhalt-Zerbst, not ignorant of the tender remembrance preserved by Elizabeth for her brother, resolved to take advantage of it for securing a throne to her daughter. She trusted her plan to the king of Prussia, who applauded her for it, and shortly after supported it with all his might.

The princess of Zerbst repaired to Petersburg, where Elizabeth received her with friendship. Her daughter, who was handsome, and endowed with all the graces of youth, immediately made

a pretty

a pretty forcible impreffion on the heart of the young grand duke; and as he himfelf was at that time well made, and of a very good figure, the attachment became reciprocal; and it was foon the fubject of the converfations at court.   Elizabeth herfelf remarked them without feeming to be difpleafed.   The princefs of Zerbft, who fpied the favourable moment, loft no time, but ran and threw herfelf at the feet of the emprefs, reprefented to her the inclination of the two young lovers as an unconquerable paffion; and calling to her mind the love fhe had herfelf borne to the prince of Holftein, her brother, fhe conjured her to promote the happinefs of the niece of that fo much regretted prince.

There was, doubtlefs, no need of all this for determining the emprefs to confent to their union.   She mingled her tears with thofe of the princefs of Zerbft; and, embracing her, promifed her that her daughter fhould be grand duchefs.

The day following the choice of Elizabeth was announced to the council and to the foreign minifters.   The marriage was fixed for a day fhortly to arrive; and preparations for its celebration were arranged with a magnificence worthy of the heir of the throne of the Ruffians.

o 3   But

But fortune, which had hitherto feemed fo favourable to the grand duke, now began to change its courfe; and Catharine was threatened with the lofs of her lover, as Elizabeth had been deprived of hers. The grand duke was attacked with a violent fever; and a fmall-pox of a very malignant nature foon after made its appearance. The prince, however, did not fall under the violence of this difeafe, though he retained the cruel marks of it. The metamorphofis was terrible. He not only loft the comelinefs of his face, but it became for a time diftorted, and almoft hideous.

None were permitted to approach the young princefs from the apartment of the grand duke; but her mother regularly brought her tidings of the turns of the prince's diftemper. Obferving how much he was altered, and defirous of weakening the effect the firft fight of him might have upon her daughter, fhe defcribed him as one of the uglieft men imaginable; recommending her, at the fame time, to diffemble the difguft fhe muft naturally feel at his appearance. Notwithftanding this fage precaution, the young princefs could not revifit the grand duke without feeling a fecret horror; fhe was artful enough, however, to reprefs her emotion, and running to meet him, fell upon his neck, and embraced him with
marks

marks of the moſt lively joy. But no ſooner was ſhe retired to her apartment than ſhe fell into a ſwoon; and it was three hours before ſhe recovered the uſe of her ſenſes.

The uneaſineſs which the young princeſs had juſt experienced, was however no inducement to her to endeavour at deferring the period of her union with the grand duke. The empreſs contemplated this alliance with pleaſure; the princeſs of Zerbſt was paſſionately deſirous to ſee it concluded; and the ſuggeſtions of ambition acting more powerfully on the heart of Catharine than even the will of her mother, and that of the empreſs, permitted her not a moment's heſitation.

The nuptials were accordingly ſolemnized; but, notwithſtanding the attachment which was ſo manifeſt between the grand duke and the princeſs from the firſt moment of their meeting, their love was fated not to be of long duration; however, they lived ſome time in an apparently good underſtanding, which Catharine ſupported as long as ſhe conceived it to be neceſſary.

This princeſs, brought up with all poſſible care under the eye of a prudent mother, and at no great diſtance from the court of the great

Frederic,

Frederic, where reigned such a taste for the sciences and the fine arts, added to the beauty, and to the quickness of understanding which she had received from nature, a very extensive knowledge, and the facility of expressing herself with elegance in several languages.

Peter too had sense; but his education had been totally neglected. He possessed an excellent heart; but he wanted politeness. He was of a good stature, but ugly and almost deformed. He frequently blushed at the superiority of his wife, and his wife often blushed at seeing him so little worthy of her; the alteration that had taken place in the features of the prince's visage was not the sole cause of the indifference of his young consort: in short, he was not capable of making her happy *. Hence

---

* Il avoit une imperfection qui, quoiqu' aisée à détruire, sembloit bien plus cruelle: la violence de son amour, ses efforts réitérés ne purent le faire réussir à consommer le mariage. Si ce prince étoit confié à quelqu'un qui eut un peu d'expérience, l'obstacle qui s'opposoit à ses désirs eut été vaincu. Le dernier rabin de Petersbourg ou le moindre chirurgien l'en auroit délivré. Mais telle étoit la honte dont l'accablé ce malheur qu'il n'eut pas même le courage de le révéler, & la princesse, qui ne recevoit plus ses caresses qu'avec répugnance, & qui n'étoit pas alors moins inexpérimentée que lui, ne songea ni à le consoler, ni à lui faire chercher des moyens qui le ramenassent dans ses bras.

arose

arofe that mutual diflike which the people
of the court were not long in finding out,
and which was vifibly augmenting from day to
day.

By one of thofe ftrange perverfions of judgment, which often appear in the uncultivated
mind, Elizabeth pretended to think that her nephew was too well informed, and that he was in
danger of becoming too amiable by his manners,
and too enviable by his knowledge. From the
very moment of her choofing him for her fucceffor, fhe regarded him as a rival. For this
reafon it probably was, that fhe took him from
under the tuition of the enlightened Brumner,
who had begun his education in Holftein ; and
placed about him Tfhoglokoff, a man of mean
talents and a narrow mind. In vain did a few
difinterefted perfons at the court of Peterfburg,
for there are fome fuch in all courts ; in vain did
fome eftimable women, for there were fome
fuch even about Elizabeth ; in vain did thefe
perfons, lamenting the ignorance and the fort of
defertion in which the young Peter was left, endeavour to reprefent to his aunt the danger
he incurred : the emprefs was deaf to their remonftrances, and even on fome occafions repulfed
them with harfhnefs.

Among

Among many examples one only need be mentioned, that of a woman of the bed-chamber named Johanna, who had the spirit to ask this princess why she kept the grand duke from all the deliberations of the council. " If you permit " him not to know any thing of what is ne- " cessary for governing the country," added she, " what do you think will become of him, and " what do you think will become of the empire?" All the answer she got, was, that Elizabeth, look- ing at her angrily, said, " Johanna, knowest " thou the way to Siberia ?"——However, the generous Johanna escaped with only the fright, and took care for the future to make no more remonstrances on that head to her mistress.

But, if some few dared to lift up their voice in favour of Peter, a great many others made themselves heard against him. The principal families had beheld him with jealousy from the instant of his arrival, as a man who would share with them the power they had now long en- joyed, or perhaps entirely deprive them of it. Among those who strove the most to injure him, we may reckon the great chancellor Bestu- cheff. From the very day of the grand duke's marriage, he had formed the design of excluding that prince from the throne ; and though his

plan

plan was fo bold and dangerous, he was perpetually employed about the means of bringing it to effect. His forefight was too great to allow him to flatter himfelf with the expectation of feeing Peter completely difinherited, but he hoped at leaft to banifh him to the camps and armies, and to place Catharine at the head of affairs.

No fooner had Beftucheff matured his plan, than he communicated it to feveral of the courtiers whom he knew to have imbibed the fame rancour with himfelf. Even women were admitted into the confidence, and they were not the leaft ferviceable in promoting the chancellor's plan. This minifter conducted his intrigue with the utmoft addrefs. He every day wrote the inftructions which he gave to the perfons of his party, on fmall fcraps of paper, and in terms which could be underftood by none but themfelves; then fhutting thefe papers in a fnuff-box with a double bottom, under pretence of offering fnuff, he diftributed them to the individuals for whom they were defigned. By this means his confidants were informed of all they were to fay or to do throughout the day. Their principal employment was to blacken the grand duke in the eyes of Elizabeth. They magnified his flighteft defects, they aggravated his moft venial faults, they imputed to him vices which

which he had not as yet, and which they wanted
to make him contract. They even went so far
as to alarm the emprefs with fears that her
nephew might become dangerous to her authority.

The feeble-minded Elizabeth was but too
prone to lend an ear to thefe vile infinuations.
Naturally timid and fufpicious, fhe at length ab-
horred him whom fhe had no reafon to diftruft for
a fingle moment.

But to what caufe are we to afcribe this conduct in the ambitious Beftucheff? Keen and
crafty, this minifter had long perceived the
grand duke's character to be feeble and unfettled. Doubtlefs, with equal perfpicacity, he
had obferved that the grand duchefs was the
very reverfe of her hufband. Ought he not
then reafonably to have expected, that if they
mounted the throne, it would be more eafy for
him to govern the prince than the princefs?
No; he cherifhed no fuch expectation; for
he knew that Peter entertained a ftrong refentment againft him for over-reaching the duke
his father, in relation to his hereditary eftates in
Holftein.

Beftucheff, who had applied himfelf to bufinefs
and intrigue for more than forty years; Beftucheff, who, after having accompanied the ruffian
ambaffadors

ambaffadors at the congrefs of Utrecht, had formed his mind in England under the minifters of George I. and who, at his return to Peterf-burg, had been appointed minifter to the court of Copenhagen, and thence went to Ham-burgh in quality of envoy extraordinary to the circle of Lower Saxony ; Beftucheff, paffing through Kiel, had had the impudence and dexterity to carry off from the archives of the dukes of Holftein the teftament of the emprefs Catharine I. and the original acts relating to the connections of thofe dukes with Ruffia.—This it was that Peter could never forgive ; and Beftu-cheff feverely felt it.

Peter likewife on another account entertained a diflike to the chancellor ; he always fupported the interefts of the houfe of Auftria with his aunt, againft the king of Pruffia, to whom this young prince had devoted himfelf with a fort of idolatry.

The grand chancellor had had the addrefs to bring into his party almoft all thofe for whom Peter feemed to have an inclination, and who only approached him as fpies upon his actions in order to injure him. Of this number was Cyril Razumofffky, who had made one of thofe fortunes which are regarded as prodigies in other countries, but which are very frequent in Ruffia.

Cyril

Cyril was a peafant who, immediately on being informed of the favour which the field marfhal his brother enjoyed with the emprefs, fet out from the Ukraine, his native place, and arrived with his balalaika * at Peterfburg. Cyril was prefently created count, commander of the ifmailof guards, hetman of the Kozaks of Little Ruffia, and even prefident of the academy of fciences †. Though of an extraction fo grofs, and without education, Cyril Razumoffky, cunning and pliant, infinuated himfelf into the good graces of the grand duke ‡; and, though but lately come to court, he betrayed the prince with an effrontery and bafenefs worthy of an experienced courtier.

To the defire of promoting the aims of the grand chancellor, were foon added, in the heart of Cyril Razumoffky, the motives of perfonal vengeance. In proportion as his honours in-

* A rude fort of guitar, with only three ftrings, in common ufe among the ruffian boors.

† He was in the fequel knight of the orders of St. Andrew, of St. Alexander Nefski, of St. Anne, and of the white eagle of Poland.

‡ The grand duke called him *his brother, his friend*, which is not extraordinary, as *drug moi* and *bratitz* are common terms of familiar addrefs and falutation from fuperiors as well as equals: but Peter would have Cyril Razumoffky to give him the fame appellations.

creafed,

creafed, he only bore with impatience the humours of the grand duke; who, to fay the truth, in the orgies to which Cyril himfelf would excite him, frequently recalled to his mind, in too coarfe a manner and too publicly, his birth, his balalaika, and the fervile occupations of his youth.

The grand duke had another favourite, who did not betray him; but who unhappily had neither the forefight nor the addrefs to prevent the reft from betraying him: this was his aide-de-camp general Gudovitch. A native of Little Ruffia, Gudovitch wifhed to become its hetman, and Peter favoured his pretenfions, even in the fight of Cyril Razumofffky. Thenceforward Cyril vowed in his heart an implacable hatred to the prince.

He offered the grand chancellor a country-houfe which he poffeffed not far from Kamennoi-nofs, as a place where they might deliberate more at their eafe on the project of ruining the grand duke; and it was at that very houfe that afterwards were held all thofe traitorous councils, at the head whereof were at firft Beftucheff, Cyril, and afterwards Shuvaloff, the young princefs Dafhkoff, and Maria Simeonovna Tfhoglokoff, lady of honour to the emprefs, and one of her moft dangerous confidants. The confpirators con-fulted concerning the perfons whom they wanted

3

to

to affociate with them. They gave an exact account of all the fteps they had feverally taken, prepared new projects of attack, and concerted the fureft meafures to deprive of the throne the laft fprout from the ftem of Peter the great.

They wanted, for example, to perfuade the emprefs that her nephew was addicted to drunkennefs, even long before he was in the habit of drinking to any degree of excefs, a habit which he contracted at firft, without doubt, merely from the want of employment, from the irkfomenefs of his fituation, and from the bafe fuggeftions of thofe that furrounded him. The method they adopted was the following:

Simeonovna Tfhoglokoff, difcourfing one day with Elizabeth, and perceiving that the monarch was difcontented with the grand duke, fhe told her with an afflicted air, that it was a great misfortune that this prince, who was ftill fo young, fhould give himfelf to drinking. Elizabeth, who now for the firft time heard the grand duke accufed of that vice, confidered it as mere calumny, and defied Simeonovna to make good her affertion. "Nothing is eafier," returned the impudent Simeonovna. "Your majefty "may be convinced of it by your own eyes." A few days afterwards, knowing that the grand duke was a little out of order and kept his room, fhe she went to visit him; when, watching her opportunity, she asked him permission to keep him company at dinner. Peter good-naturedly consented, and bid her place herself at table with him. During the repast, Simeonovna putting on a humour uncommonly gay and fond, told the prince that she would cure him with a bottle of champagne. The bottle was called for; the artful Simeonovna seized it, slily threw into it some narcotic or inebriating ingredient, and, making the grand duke repeatedly drink bumpers of it to the health of his aunt, she completely intoxicated him. The perfidious lady of honour immediately ran to acquaint the emprefs. Elizabeth came; and, not knowing the particulars of the scene that had just passed, beheld with grief and indignation the sad condition of her unhappy nephew. Already too much disposed to take up prejudices against him, she thenceforward more readily believed all that Simeonovna Tshoglokoff and her accomplices were desirous of imputing to the prince; and, emboldened by this success, the conspirators proceeded in their insolence to propagate against him the most scandalous reports.

To all this, it must be added that the state of inactivity and loneliness in which Peter was left to languish, and the unhappy pliancy of his character, tended infallibly to favour the designs of his enemies.

When the empress was persuaded that he delivered himself up to excess, she not only suppressed the gratification of fifty thousand rubles, of which she customarily made him a present on the anniversary of his birth, but she gave orders so far to diminish the expences of his table, that the prince and his guests had not always sufficient to eat. Peter on these occasions would suffer some complaints to escape him not entirely free from expressions of petulance and ill-humour; and these complaints were carefully preserved, exaggerated, and delivered to the empress.

Shortly after the marriage of the grand duke, his aunt had made him a present of Oranienbaum; a country-palace that had formerly belonged to the famous Mentchikoff; and as soon as the fair weather permitted him to leave Petersburg, where he lived more like a state prisoner than the heir to the throne, thither Peter used to retire. There, freed from the presence of his aunt, and throwing off all constraint, he amused himself with dressing his people in a german uniform, and making them perform the prussian exercise.

exercife. Elizabeth feemed highly to approve of this occupation, thinking it might preferve her nephew from getting a tafte for dangerous pleafures, and even from a difpofition to political intrigues, which fhe confidered as far more dangerous ftill. At the fame time fhe gave orders that, from feveral regiments, a fufficient number of foldiers fhould be drafted and fent to the garrifon at Oranienbaum, in addition to thofe of the grand duke; but this attention, which wore the femblance of a favour conferred on the prince, was perhaps nothing more than an additional precaution againft him. However this might be, he received it with tranfport, and gave himfelf up, with renovated ardour, to his military and pruffian inclination.

It has long been the cuftom for numbers of Germans to go and feek their fortunes in Ruffia. The elevation of a holftein prince to the rank of grand duke drew them thither in ftill greater multitudes. The foldiers whom Peter kept at Oranienbaum were almoft all of that nation. Befides thefe, he had made a felection of many others who underftood mufic or difplayed talents for acting of plays; and of thefe he formed a company, whom he made to reprefent the beft pieces of the german theatre.

However,

However, neither the theatre nor military exercises could employ the whole time of the prince; and the void was but too often filled up with the habits he had begun to contract in the indolence of the palace of Petersburg.

The party formed against him, knowing his extreme propensity to every thing that was prussian, had found means to persuade him that in Prussia every officer had continually his pipe in his mouth, and was as constantly employed in drinking and gaming. The young people who surrounded him added, if not from malice, at least from libertinism, example to precept; and, in conformity to it, he became smoaker, drinker, gamester.

Catharine all this time was pursuing a conduct diametrically opposite to that of her husband. Directed by her vigilant mother, she was solely employed in gaining partisans from among the most powerful persons of the court. Her violent disposition to pleasure was mute at the calls of ambition; and if she did not succeed so far as to captivate the friendship of the empress, she at least extorted her esteem.

In the mean time, what will perhaps seem difficult to be believed, the princess of Zerbst was neglectful of that circumspection, with regard to herself, which she inspired into her daughter.

daughter. Elizabeth confidered her as a friend or a fifter, and repofed an unlimited confidence in her. Proud of her influence, the princefs of Zerbft feemed in hafte to abufe it. She mixed in the intrigues of the courtiers, made herfelf the difpenfer of imperial favours, in fhort, fhe pryed into the fecrets of the moft important concerns. Her arrogance difgufted the favourites, her curiofity was vexatious to the minifters. They united together to roufe the jealoufy of the emprefs, and to free her from a yoke under which fhe had infenfibly bowed her neck. Their efforts were not in vain. Elizabeth almoft immediately withdrew the confidence fhe had granted to the mother of Catharine.

The princefs of Zerbft, diftreffed at this reverfe of fortune, turned on every fide for a remedy. She afked advice of the king of Pruffia and of the king of Sweden; but fhe was obferved with a watchful eye. It became extremely difficult for her to maintain correfpondences. She was fain to have recourfe to the refinements of artifice to get a letter conveyed to the king of Sweden. On one occafion fhe adopted the following method : A ball was given at court ; the princefs of Zerbft was there with the grand duchefs her daughter. All at once the grand duchefs advanced towards the aged

H 3   Leftoc,

Leftoc, who, according to his custom, was amusing himself in chatting with the women; and, throwing a glove at him, she said she would dance with him. On taking up the glove, Leftoc perceived that it contained a paper. On this the artful courtier, smiling to the grand duchess, said, " I accept the challenge, madam: " but, instead of restoring you your glove, I " beseech you to give me the other, that I may " present them both, from you, to my wife; " the favour will then be complete." The country dance being finished, Leftoc stole away, hiding the gloves under his waistcoat, fearing left the empress might have some intelligence of what had passed, and should cause him to be searched at the door.

All the stratagems put in practice by the princess of Zerbst were not so successful. Every day brought with it some complaint against her, or discovered some fresh intrigue. The resentment of the empress was now at its height; she ordered the princess to quit the empire.

The princess of Zerbst, at parting from her daughter, experienced the most poignant sorrow. Catharine herself could not, without great regret, see her mother depart; but the hope of the throne which had fortified her against other misfortunes, supported her under this; and love
soon

foon brought its confolations to mingle them with thofe of pride.

The young men that furrounded the grand duke did not all, like the prince, refign themfelves entirely to the pleafures of the table, to play, and to military parade. There was efpecially one who diftinguifhed himfelf as much by his tafte for the amiable arts, as he was admired for the graces of his perfon : it was Soltikoff, the prince's chamberlain. He made one in all his parties : but he was afhamed of his company. He was tolerably well verfed in french literature ; he knew by heart the fineft paffages of Racine and Voltaire, and in the recitation of them his voice feemed to heighten their beauties. Though fcarcely outgrown the boy, he had already the reputation of having obtained the favours of feveral belles of the court ; and his fuccefs made him proud. Soltikoff, it is true, was held rather deficient in courage with the men, but he was not the lefs prefumptuous nor lefs bold with the women. Perhaps he would have trembled at the fight of a naked fword ; but for extending the number of his conquefts in gallantry, he had often been thought to brave the deferts of Siberia. In fhort, the hufbands of Peterfburg regarded him as the moft agreeable and the moft dangerous man in town.

Soltikoff

Soltikoff was not long ere he lifted his eyes even to the fpoufe of his mafter ; and vanity yet more than love led him to conceive the temerarious defign of captivating her heart.   He began by feduloufly ftudying the inclinations of the prin-cefs.   He perceived that, notwithftanding the conftraint in which fhe lived, Catharine had always a propenfity to pleafure ; and that the folitude of Oranienbaum rendered diffipation neceffary to her.   He accordingly procured her fome new amufement with every returning day. He engaged the grand duke to give frequent entertainments, he took upon himfelf the tafk of inventing and directing them, fecretly giving the grand duchefs to underftand that fhe was the fole object for which they were made, and that it was to him alone fhe was indebted for them. Catharine was not infenfible to fuch gallant, fuch continued attentions.   The feducing figure of Soltikoff, and the vivacity of his wit, had made impreffion on her mind.   His affiduities made him mafter of her affections ; but Soltikoff, fenfible that the heart of the grand duchefs was no ordinary conqueft, was afraid of betraying himfelf by an imprudent explanation.   It is even not impoffible that at firft he meant only to feign a paffion which in the fequel grew up into a real attachment.   In fhort, for a confiderable time

paft,

paſt, their fondneſs had been mutual, without any declaration on the part of either.

An unfortunate event was the occaſion of accelerating this declaration. Soltikoff loſt his father. His duty obliged him to repair to Moſco. He obtained the grand duke's permiſſion to depart, and at taking leave of Catharine he was not ſufficiently maſter of his feelings to prevent his diſcovering how much this parting coſt him. The princeſs, who ſaw his tears, was no leſs touched herſelf at the cauſe whence they flowed; and fixing her eyes, with a look of extreme ſignificance, on Soltikoff, ſhe conjured him to ſhorten his abſence as much as he could, and to return and forget his grief in the midſt of a brilliant court, where without him there could be no ſuch thing as pleaſure.

The character of Soltikoff renders it eaſy to judge what effect theſe words muſt have produced. He thought he perceived that he was beloved; and his conſcious pride redoubled. His journey took him up but a few days. What were domeſtic concerns when balanced with the felicity he expected? What was Moſco to him in compariſon of Peterſburg? He abandoned all for the ſake of returning to ſecure his triumph.

However, on approaching again the grand ducheſs, all the flattering ideas with which he
had

had regaled his delighted imagination began súddenly to diffolve and vanifh. His audacity forfook him. He found himfelf a prey to the moft ferious and gloomy reflections. He faw at once all the danger of his amour. He could no longer prefume to flatter himfelf that Catharine would fo far forget what fhe owed to her rank, to her fpoufe, as to accept the affiduities of a fimple chamberlain. But if he were fo happy as to fee her vouchfafe to correfpond to his paffion, could he imagine that he fhould deceive the penetrating eyes of the jealous and humiliated courtiers, by whom fhe was furrounded? In a word, how rifk a confeffion which might be repaid by a perpetual imprifonment, or even with the lofs of his life! He fhuddered, he trembled, he refolved to renounce the fallacious hopes his unbounded arrogance had made him cherifh.

In this ftate of perturbation and defpondence, Soltikoff no longer difplayed that brilliant gaiety for which he had hitherto been always diftinguifhed. In vain did he fometimes affect an air of eafy elegance which he now no more poffeffed. A fettled melancholy corroded his heart, and was depicted on his face ; his health was vifibly declining. The grand duchefs took the alarm ; and one day, on finding herfelf alone with him, defired him to reveal the caufe of fo fudden an alteration.

alteration. Soltikoff, unable at that moment to ftifle or refift a paffion thus preying on his vitals, avowed it in expreffions of the tendereft emotion. Catharine heard him without anger; fhe feemed even to pity him; but, with a collected air, fhe counfelled him to renounce an inclination, of the irregularity and danger whereof he ought to be fenfible. Although ftill very young, Soltikoff knew but too well the female heart to be ignorant, that fhe who allows herfelf to liften to a lover has already begun to approve him. He took courage. He threw himfelf at the knees of the grand duchefs, and embraced them with boldnefs. The princefs was agitated; fhe let fall fome tears; and retiring precipitately from the tranfports of Soltikoff, to go and fhut herfelf in her cabinet, fhe addreffed to him that verfe which Monimia fpeaks to Xiphares in the tragedy of Mithridates :—

"Et méritez les pleurs que vous m'allez coûter*."

From that moment the chamberlain refumed his wonted gaiety with returning hope; and the happy alteration in his behaviour was felt by all around him.

While the grand duke and the grand duchefs were paffing the fummer at Oranienbaum, the

* And merit thofe tears you are about to coft me.

I 5   empreſs

emprefs Elizabeth remained at Peterhof, though
not without fending, from time to time, for the
imperial couple to fhare in the pleafures of her
court.   On thefe little expeditions Soltikoff
never failed to make one of the party.   In order to avoid being prefent at the entertainments
and feftivities of the palace, where the prying
eyes of indifcreet obfervers would throw too
great a reftraint on her conduct, Catharine
feigned an indifpofition.   The grand duke was
fo infatuated in regard to his chamberlain, that
he even engaged him himfelf to fhare in the folitude of his wife, and to exert all the talents of
his capacity to amufe and to cheer her.   This
was exactly what the two lovers defired ; and it
is not difficult to imagine that they turned the
moments to profit.   This tide of fuccefs feemed
now at its height ; and the young chamberlain
experienced a fignal turn of affairs.   The grand
duchefs was not always fufficiently on her guard
for concealing the inclination fhe entertained for
him.   The courtiers, always artful, always en-
vious, began by remarking the preference that
wounded their pride, and were not long in
tracing it to its fource.   The ruin of Soltikoff
was now pretty certain.   The very men who
fhewed him the moft marks of friendfhip, and
who of courfe had the moft means of doing him
                                  differvice,

differvice, fecretly found the method of conveying to the emprefs their fufpicions of an amour between the chamberlain and the grand-duchefs. Of an amorous difpofition herfelf, Elizabeth perhaps was not bound to take great offence at the intrigue : but fhe was haughty ; and in the firft burfts of her indignation, fhe declared that Soltikoff fhould pay for his temerity by an exile into Siberia.

Soltikoff, informed of the dangers that menaced him, immediately fet about the means of avoiding them. He faw that the beft method of preventing the ftorm from burfting upon him was boldly to brave it. Affuming, therefore, a look of affurance, and putting on the air of affronted innocence, he ran to the grand duke to complain of the calumnies that had been fo audacioufly fpread. He reminded the prince that he had only prefented himfelf to the grand duchefs in confequence of exprefs orders received from himfelf ; and that he had never beheld her but with all the refpect that was due to her rank. He remarked to him, that thefe invidious flanders, though outwardly lanced againft him, were intended as a clandeftine, but certain attack on the heir of the empire, fince in thefe infamous reports the honour of the crown was infinitely more implicated than the

reputation

reputation of an individual like him. He concluded by adding, that, in order to furnish no
farther pretence to the jealousy of his enemies,
and to calm the mind of the empress, he prayed
the grand duke for permission to retire to
Mofco.

The speech of Soltikoff not only imposed on
the credulous prince, but persuaded him that
for his own honour he should keep the chamberlain about the person of his spouse. He ordered him to remain ; then asked for an audience of the empress, in which he complained of
the insolent reports that had been industriously
sent abroad : he defended Soltikoff with so much
vehemence, and with such specious arguments,
that Elizabeth began to believe herself, that the
reports which had been raised about him might
possibly be no more than the fabrication of envy.

While this scene was transacting in the apartment of Elizabeth, the grand duchess did not
remain idle : she was more interested than any
one in putting a stop to these injurious reports,
and to preserve her lover. Indeed, who was
more capable than herself of undertaking her
own defence ? Informed by madame Narish-
kin of the pains the grand duke had taken in
the justification of Soltikoff, and of the success
he had just obtained, she immediately presented

herself

herfelf to the emprefs.   Forgetting the air of
meeknefs fhe had hitherto always put on in the
prefence of the fovereign, fhe broke forth into
reproaches on the credit that could be given to
fuch odious fufpicions.   She reprefented how
much the proofs demanded by the emprefs of her
innocence muft be fallacious and uncertain, and
how all public inquiry muft infallibly be attended
with difgrace, as on-all occafions of this nature
the fmalleft doubt always left an indelible blot.
Grief, vengeance, rage, by turns gave fo much
force to her eloquence, that Elizabeth was unable to refift it : fhe appeared moved, melted,
perfuaded ; and the victory of Catharine was ftill
more complete than that of the grand duke.

In the evening, as is the cuftom at the court
of St. Peterfburg, there was a circle at the
palace, and the emprefs with eagernefs embraced
the opportunity for teftifying in the eyes of the
court, that Soltikoff had nothing to apprehend
from her.   The chamberlain was engaged at
play: Elizabeth advancing to the back of his
chair, afked him, with that grace which fhe had
the art of throwing into all that fhe faid, whether
he was happy ? — " Never madam," returned
Soltikoff. — " I am forry for it," fhe replied ;
" but perhaps that may be partly by your own
" fault.   It is faid that you intend to quit
" the

" the grand duke? I cannot believe it; and I
" invite you to remain about him: be assured
" that if your enemies should attempt again to
" injure you, I shall be the first to defend
" you."

Though it had been true that Soltikoff had
seriously formed the design of retiring from
court, these words would have been enough to
have detained him; and even though his enemies
might have acquired the most convincing proofs
of his audacity, they would have stopped their
mouths for ever.

In the mean time the grand duke cohabited
with his spouse; and thenceforward Soltikoff
thought he had no longer any danger to prevent;
he now tasted without disturbance or remorse
those pleasures from the consequences of which
he had nothing to dread. Catharine herself
had no need to be so severe in her precautions;
her first success had given her additional boldness. Besides, the example of the empress
Elizabeth, whose manners were growing more
and more corrupt, and who engaged in new
follies from day to day, seemed to afford some
excuse for her passion. The empress questioned
nothing of an intrigue which she might easily have
perceived; or, if she observed it, she at least no
longer evinced either anger or suspicion.

Time,

Time, which enfeebles and often extinguifhes the moft ardent paffions, diminifhed not that of Catharine. That princefs expected fhortly to become a mother; Soltikoff was daily acquiring a greater afcendant over her heart; but his happinefs was at its ultimate term; he became himfelf the artificer of his ruin.

The grand chancellor Beftucheff, with the reft of the courtiers, had been filent on the favour enjoyed by Soltikoff; but he was not on that account the lefs vigilant and attentive. Inceffantly occupied with the project of difplacing the grand duke from his fucceffion to the throne, the veteran minifter perceived that the fureft means for fucceeding was to gain over the favourite of the prince himfelf.

Beftucheff, whom the title of grand chancellor, united with the general adminiftration of affairs, his influence, and his profound policy, rendered one of the moft powerful perfons of the empire, became the humble fycophant of Soltikoff. He lavifhed on him the marks of deference, praifes, careffes, in the greateft profufion. He revealed to him the fecrets that were of the utmoft importance; he frequently confulted him, or feigned to confult him; he at length fo completely gained his confidence, that the chamberlain, blinded by pride, thought he had no firmer a friend than the wily minifter: while he, who now faw what authority he had acquired over Solti-koff, and thought of nothing but to free himfelf from fo dangerous a rival, induced him to take the moft fatal meafures. He told him, that, for augmenting the afcendancy he had gained, and to render himfelf entirely mafter of the grand duke's mind, it was neceffary to put away from the prince all perfons of birth, of ambition, or talents, and to let him have none about him but vile and obfcure people, or who, being placed by Soltikoff himfelf, would be fervilely devoted to his intereft. Soltikoff perceived not the fnare. He was moreover incapable of penetrating into the motive of fo perfidious an advice. His favour made all things poffible to him; his ambition increafed; he attempted to fecure to himfelf an abfolute fway; and he was eager to put in prac-tice what the old chancellor had told him. Thus one moment of imprudence demolifhed a triumph of feveral years.

This new tempeft raifed againft the favourite, blackened all at once. The young courtiers feeing themfelves removed from the heir of the throne, broke out into murmurs, and joined their efforts to thofe of the friends of Beftucheff. The chancellor rekindled the audacity of Tfchog-lokoff, of Razumofffky, and thofe of their party;
who

who at length all united together to caufe their complaints to reach the ears of Elizabeth. Beftucheff perceived that it was time for him to fpeak to the emprefs himfelf. He accordingly had a fecret conference with her; in which he recalled to her mind all that fhe already knew of the weaknefs of the grand duke, of his extravagancies, and the riot to which he was addicted. He told her that thefe extravagancies and this riot took their origin from Soltikoff; who, that he might the more effectually fubject the prince to his will, fuffered none to approach him but abject flatterers and vile debauchees. He revived the fufpicions, but too well founded, and for fo long time fpread, on the criminal intercourfe carried on by the chamberlain with the grand duchefs. He concluded by reprefenting him as a perfidious favourite, whofe ambition threatened Ruffia with an odious reign.

The emprefs, incenfed at what fhe heard, refolved once more to punifh Soltikoff; but, directed by the aged chancellor, fhe took at this time furer meafures than before. The fecret was kept, and the difgrace of the chamberlain was covered by the pretext of an honourable embaffy. Elizabeth commiffioned him to repair to Stockholm with the title of envoy extraordinary, to notify to the king of Sweden the

birth

birth of Paul Petrovitch, of whom the grand duchefs had juft been delivered *. The prefumptuous Soltikoff at firft confidered this employ as a new mark of the emprefs's favour. He accepted it with gratitude, repaired haftily to Sweden, and left it with equal fpeed. But fcarcely had he quitted Stockholm to return to St. Peterfburg, when he was ftopped on the way by a courier, who put into his hands the order for him to go and refide at Hamburgh, in quality of minifter plenipotentiary from the court of Ruffia.

Soltikoff now opened his eyes. He faw that he had been cruelly deceived. He wrote to the grand duchefs, and engaged her to follicit his recall. That princefs, not lefs fenfible than he to this feparation, wifhed at firft to employ her influence and her eloquence with the emprefs, to induce her to command his return; but the chancellor, who had forefeen all that happened, went to her with fpeed, to convince her of the danger of this propofal. He told her plainly that the fteps fhe hazarded in favour of Soltikoff would corroborate the fufpicions that were already excited againft her, and would effectually tend to her ruin. She was entirely convinced

* The 1ft of October 1754.

by

by his arguments.   Ambition impoſed ſilence on love.

Catharine, however, preſerved for ſome time the paſſion ſhe had conceived for the chamberlain.   She wrote to him, and frequently received letters from him.   Misfortune ſeemed even to augment her tenderneſs, when all at once, the preſence of a ſtranger whom fortune had brought to the court of Ruſſia, cauſed her to forget the lover whom ſhe no longer ſaw.

The young count Staniſlaus Poniatofsky, whom Catharine firſt raiſed to the throne of Poland, and afterwards hurled him indignantly from it, was the happy ſucceſſor of Soltikoff.   Born a ſimple nobleman, and deſtitute of fortune, but endowed with a handſome figure and full of ambition *, Poniatofsky amuſed for ſome time in Germany and France his anxiety and his vague

* The father of Poniatofsky was an adventurer; who, from the condition of domeſtic in the family of Michielky in Lithuania, went into the ſervice of Charles XII. and obtained the confidence of that prince. He afterwards attached himſelf to king Staniſlaus Lechinſky, whom he betrayed by conveying from him the abdication which Auguſtus II. had formerly given him in preſence of Charles XII.   Provided with this important record, Poniatofsky repaired to Warſaw, where Auguſtus rewarded his perfidy by giving him in marriage the princeſs Chartorinſky, a deſcendant of the houſe of Yagellon.   Staniſlaus Poniatofsky was the fruit of this marriage.

expect-

expectations.   He met with tolerable fuccefs at
Paris, where the friendfhip of the fwedifh ambaffador procured him diftinguifhed connections:
but his mother, who dreaded the influence which
the too bewitching pleafures of that city might
have upon him, wrote to him her commands
to leave it.   Poniatofsky immediately quitted
France and repaired to England, where he found
fir Charles Hanbury Williams, whom he had
formerly known at the court of Warfaw; and
who, being appointed by the cabinet of London
to the embaffy of Peterfburg, engaged him to
accompany him thither.   Without bearing any
title that attached him to the embaffy, the young
Pole employed himfelf in the cabinet of the ambaffador, and ferved him in the office of fecretary.   He even determined at firft to confine
himfelf to diplomatic affairs; but the tafte for
diffipation to which he had long been accuftomed,
his youth, the feducing opportunities which daily
prefented themfelves, foon brought him back to
the purfuit of pleafure.   He was by nature of a
gay, witty, and fpirited difpofition, and therefore
adapted to fucceed at a court where amufement
feemed to be the moft important concern.   Accordingly it was not long before he perceived
the impreffion he had made upon the heart of
Catharine.

Poniatofsky,

Poniatofsky, bold and even audacious, was yet awed by the high rank of the grand duchefs ; and the obfervant eyes of the numerous courtiers obliged him to reprefs his ardour. For fome time the two lovers converfed only by their looks; but to thefe mute converfations at length others fucceeded in which they reciprocally declared their attachment, and confulted on the means of indulging their inclinations without conftraint.

Led by the feveral motives of intereft and vanity, fome perfons of the court, who watched the motions of the grand duchefs only to thwart and cenfure her views, loft no time in informing the emprefs Elizabeth of the new intrigue of her adoptive niece.

Elizabeth had no efteem for her nephew; fhe cared but little for the honour of the grand duchefs ; fhe was in general not more fevere towards the conduct of others, than careful of her own ; in fhort, fhe was always afraid to punifh : but the extreme facility with which fhe followed the counfels of the perfons about her, made her often act with a rigour entirely abhorrent to her general character. She gave orders to Poniatofsky to quit Ruffia without delay. Poniatofsky obeyed.

I 4

By continuing to cabal against the grand duke, and by removing Soltikoff from the court, the chancellor Beftucheff had neglected nothing for ftrengthening his party with that of the grand duchefs. His devotion to this princefs appeared to increafe from day to day. He flattered her inclinations; he even miniftered to them; he made her at length forget that he had been the chief caufe of the ruin of her firft lover. She thought fhe might make ufe of him in recovering the fecond. The old minifter promifed his return, and haftened his endeavours to fulfil it. Poniatofsky he thought far lefs to be dreaded than Soltikoff. He knew that the heart of Catharine could never remain in a ftate of inaction: he therefore preferred feeing a foreigner rather than a Ruffian, the object of her choice.

The grand chancellor was intimately connected with the count de Bruhl, prime minifter of the king of Poland. He acquainted him by letter with a paffion the grand duchefs entertained for Poniatofsky, and the advantage to be derived of fending the young Pole to Ruffia, invefted with a character that would ferve as a plaufible pretext for his return. The count de Bruhl immediately perceived the importance of the project;

project; some embarrassment, however, attended its execution: two positive laws in direct opposition to his views on the favourite must be infringed in their behalf.

Every Pole, in possession of a starosty, was prohibited by the former from quitting the republic.

The other enjoined, that a Pole could never be charged at a foreign court with the management of the affairs of Saxony, nor a Saxon with those of Poland.

But Bruhl had often the art of making the laws subservient to his will. The necessity of gaining the ascendant at the court of Russia, and the desire of further conciliating the favour of the russian minister, whom the Saxon regarded as one of his chief supports, obviated every objection. Poniatofsky was publicly decorated with the order of the White Eagle; and soon after a secret council was held, in which he was named minister plenipotentiary of the republic and king of Poland to the empress Elizabeth. The customary convocation of the *senatus concilium* was even neglected on this occasion.

The indignation of all patriot Poles was excited at this transaction. But they were not aware that the new plenipotentiary was the crea-

4   ture

ture of Chartorinſky, and devoted to the politics of England and Pruſſia.

Durand, a man of perſpicacity and courage, charged with the concerns of France in the abſence of the count de Broglio, repaired to count Bruhl, to remonſtrate with him on the choice he had made, at a moment when it was of ſo much importance to Poland to keep on good terms with the courts of Vienna and Verſailles. The count by a falſehood attempted to impoſe on the agent of France; he proteſted that he had exerted no influence in the nomination of Poniatofsky; and in the meanwhile haſtened his departure with the greater zeal.

Bruhl, become now the patron of Poniatofsky, omitted nothing on his part to enſure a ſucceſs that might juſtify his choice. He well knew the uneaſineſs that pervaded the ruſſian court, while it affected an exterior of oriental magnificence. He was not ignorant that Elizabeth was laviſhing on her minions, and the inventors of ſumptuous and fantaſtical feſtivities, the ſums that ſhould have been applied to the wants of the empire; in ſhort, he knew that the grand duke and grand ducheſs were languiſhing in a penury unworthy of their rank. He therefore remitted to Poniatofsky 6000 ducats, that, on preſſing preffing emergencies, he might advance them to the prince and his confort, and thereby conciliate their entire concurrence. Poniatofsky dexter-oufly profited by the counfels and benefactions of Bruhl. He was already fure of the grand duchefs's heart; he fucceeded foon after with the fpoufe. He talked englifh and german with him; he drank, fmoked, fpoke ill of France, abufed the French, and extolled the king of Pruffia with unlimited praife. In addition to fo many recommendations, he affected an immo-derate purfuit of pleafure. But the Poles, and even the Ruffians, foon penetrated his ambitious defigns, and pretended that he was facrificing the interefts of his mafter and the Chartorinfkys to his own private views. Time has fince fhewn that they were not deceived.

What indeed might not a man of penetration and addrefs have done in thofe days at the court of Peterfburg? What were the principal perfon-ages at that luxurious, intriguing, and profligate court?

The emprefs Elizabeth had infenfibly pro-ceeded from moderate pleafures to the extrava-gance of fenfuality; and her tafte for devotion augmented with her voluptuoufnefs. She con-tinued whole hours on her knees before the picture

ture of some saint*, to which she spoke, which
she even consulted, and passed alternately from
acts of bigotry to the intemperance of lust, and
from scenes of lasciviousness to the opiates of
prayer.   She would frequently drink to excess;
and at such times, too sensual, too impatient for
the delays of unlacing, her women used to effect
the same purpose by means of the scissars.   In
what manner such nights were passed, it becomes
not the historian to undraw her curtains to
reveal.

* The worship of the pictures of saints is in universal
practice in the orthodox greek church.   The decalogue, it
seems, forbids only *graven* images.—Notwithstanding the
unbounded toleration which prevails in Russia, there is still
what is called a predominant religion, and to which, as
John James observes, the prince and the executioner always
belong.   The system of faith adopted by the tzar and the
native Russians is that denominated by divines the *greek*
religion, which in some particulars differs from the latin.
Without tiring the reader with a circumstantial exposition of
these idle distinctions, to say nothing of their several notions
about the procession of the holy ghost, and of the quality
of the bread in the sacrament, it will be sufficient to observe
that the Greeks deny the supremacy of the roman pontiff in
church matters, and condemn the worship of carved images.
Accordingly they have no images in their churches, but
multitudes of pictures, representing thousands of saints, to
which they pay almost the same divine honours as to the
deity himself.

The

The grand duchefs, blinded by her paffion, and confequently unmindful of the leffons of prudence which her mother had left her, but which she afterwards took for the guides of her conduct, betrayed a faint imitation of the irregularities of her aunt. She followed no counfels but thofe of Beftucheff, the englifh ambaffador Williams, and the gallant Poniatofsky : on which occafion, a foreigner then at Peterfburg obferved, in allufion to thefe three perfonages, that fhe could not fail of being badly conducted, fince fhe took for her guides men fo confummate in knavery, madnefs, and folly. Poniatofsky was never from her; fhe devoted to him the whole of her time; and fhe made fo little fecret of this intimacy, that public report was very loud to her prejudice. The grand duchefs was after fome months delivered of the princefs Anne *, who lived only fifteen months.

The grand duke was the only man at court that knew nothing of what was paffing. Nor ought this to excite our furprife. Peter, though, as we have feen, apparently marked out for particular exploits, by having at once two diftinct offers of a crown, yet the people among whom he was thrown did not co-operate with the finger of

* In the month of February 1758.

fortune,

fortune, but feemed rather anxious to fruftrate her views.   His education had been entirely neglected in Holftein ; his naturally good underftanding was not enriched with fcience ; his vehement temper was undirected to ufeful exertion, unfoftened by culture to the tender affections, and by love to the fine arts.   In Ruffia his fituation afforded him but little opportunity, awed as he was by the chanceller Beftucheff Riumin, for improving his qualities or extending his knowledge.   He was young, and had no honeft friend. The image of his illuftrious grandfather might prefent itfelf to his imagination: but he found no guide to affift him in the emulation of his great example.   Kept at a diftance from all bufinefs of public concern, he confined himfelf almoft folely to the company of his Holfteiners, and to the exercifes of his german foldiers. His enemies had even robbed him of the affection of his aunt, and ftrove to fow difcord between him and his fpoufe.   Diftruft and apprehenfion muft frequently have got poffeffion of his foul ; and in thofe moments he had recourfe to artificial exhilarations that were unworthy of him.

What wonder then that he was blinded to what fo nearly concerned him ? Befides, being always a great admirer of the king of Pruffia, he now devoted himfelf entirely to copy, with a
                                              fervile

fervile affectation, the air, the manners, the tone of that monarch. He dreffed his little army at Oranienbaum in the pruffian uniform, and wore it himfelf; he fatigued his foldiers in ufelefs manœuvres and painful exercifes: from thefe he fat down to the exceffes of the table, and in the delirium of intemperance would declare, that he would one day be the conqueror of the north, and the rival of the pruffian hero. But how great was the difference between the imitator and the model!

The grand chancellor inceffantly occupied in his project of vilifying and calumniating the prince, and of favouring the inclination of Catharine, in the hope that when fhe fhould have afcended the throne fhe would keep him in his place, forgot the intereft of the empire in attending to his own. The other minifters, who for the moft part were creatures devoted to his views, followed the fteps of their mafter.

The Razumofffkys, the Schuvaloffs, the Tfhoglokoffs, the Narifhkins, the Vorontzoffs, and the whole herd of courtiers, while they faw the depravity of their patrons, meanly fuppreffed their contempt, or ftifled it with flattery.

The people, who could eafily fee the diforders of the court, feemed afraid to lift their eyes on Elizabeth. They revered in her the blood of

Peter

Peter the great, without taking umbrage at her vices. Such force has still the impulsion given by the legislator of Russia! So far is the Russian addicted to obedience, and hardened to the yoke!

The empress Elizabeth had ordered general Apraxin to march, with 40,000 Russians, to assist Maria Theresa in re-conquering Silesia from the king of Prussia. The grand duke, lamenting to see these succours dispatched against a monarch whom he admired to idolatry, applied to Bestucheff to induce him to recall the troops. The count entertained no violent affection for Frederic; on the contrary, he was a warm partisan of the court of Vienna. Above all, he had no desire to do any thing that would please the grand duke. But Elizabeth was just fallen sick, the grand duke might presently be called to the throne; and Bestucheff, wishing at any price to preserve his authority, sacrificed his hatred, his affections, and the honour of the empire, to his unbridled ambition. He sent orders to general Apraxin to abandon his conquests, and to hasten his return: but for this once he was the dupe of his own cunning.

This retreat, so unaccountable to Elizabeth, gave her ground to suspect that she had been betrayed by her ministers or her generals.

Marshal

Marſhal Apraxin was removed from the command, and put under arreſt. He juſtified his conduct by producing the orders from count Beſtucheff. Beſtucheff was removed from his office, and alſo put under arreſt. Count Vorontzoff ſucceeded Beſtucheff in his employment, and the generals Brown * and Fermer took the command of the army in the place of Apraxin.

The

* General Brown was a native of Ireland, and was born in the beginning of the preſent century. Being a roman catholic, he was compelled to ſeek his fortune in foreign countries by the exertion of thoſe talents which he would willingly have dedicated to the ſervice of his own. He firſt entered the auſtrian, and afterwards the ruſſian ſervice. While acting under count Munich againſt the Turks, in the campaigns of 1737 and 1738, he diſtinguiſhed himſelf at the ſiege of Otchakof : being ſent with a corps of troops into Hungary, he was taken priſoner by the Turks, ſold as a ſlave, and transferred to four different maſters. At one time he was bound back to back with another priſoner for eight-and-forty hours, and expoſed almoſt naked at the various places where ſlaves are brought for ſale. He had then borne the rank of colonel in the ruſſian ſervice, but gave out that he was only a captain, in order to leſſen the price of his ranſom. Having been accidentally met by a gentleman to whom he was perſonally known, he ſent an account of his ſituation to the french ambaſſador, who found means to purchaſe him for 300 ducats. But his turkiſh maſter diſcovering that he was of higher rank than he had pretended, re-claimed his priſoner, and threatened to

uſe

The affair was thus.   Though Beftucheff had
got a great number of partifans, and a ftill
greater number of creatures, he had alfo many
enemies; and thefe enemies had a glimpfe of a
means for effecting his ruin, which they eagerly
feized.   They perceived that it would be no
difficult matter for them to caufe hatred and
quarrels to fucceed to the coldnefs which for a
long time had been vifible between Peter and
his fpoufe, and that they might then bring Beftucheff to punifhment, as the primary caufe, not
only of thefe difagreements, but even for the
eftrangement which the emprefs evinced to her
nephew.

This plan once concerted, the firft ftep was
to call the prince's attention to the frequent
converfations of Poniatofsky with the grand
duchefs.   Their geftures were watched; every
little word that efcaped them, which might ferve
as a pretext for fome allufion, was carefully laid
hold of.   One evening in particular, when the
grand duchefs was at table with a numerous

---

ufe force in order to recover him.   The french ambaffador,
however, applied to the grand vizir, who decided in his favour.
Count Brown recovered his liberty, and returned to Ruffia,
where he was gradually promoted, and died governor of
Riga in 1789, at the age of 88.——See *Coxe's Travels*, 8vo.
vol. ii. p. 417, 418.

company,

company, and feated facing Poniatofsky, the
difcourfe fell upon the dexterity with which
fome women managed a horfe, and the dangers
to which they expofed themfelves in that exercife.   Catharine, who had her eyes fixed on her
lover, anfwered in her lively manner: " There
" are few women fo bold as I am.   I am of an
" unbounded courage."   Thefe words were
immediately reported to the grand duke, accompanied with fuggeftions that might occafion fome
finifter application to arife in his mind.

The jealoufy of Peter being thus alarmed,
they loft no time to fofter thefe furmifes of
the hufband into proofs of the infidelity of the
wife, in her love for the Polander, and the criminal correfpondence they mutually entertained.
The prince was overwhelmed with grief and
confternation.   He bewailed his misfortune, and
condemned his imprudence.   He no longer
obferved the confideration and refpect he had
hitherto fhewn the grand duchefs, and forbad
her to be feen with Poniatofsky.   He then
haftened to the emprefs, and befought her to
avenge the affront he had received; telling her,
at the fame time, that the chancellor had not
only favoured the mifconduct of the grand
duchefs, but had repeatedly betrayed the confidence of his imperial aunt.   He concluded this

K 2   addrefs,

address, by shewing her the order sent by that minister to marshal Apraxin, to make him retreat from Silesia.

Elizabeth, moved at the sorrows of her nephew, and incensed at the treachery of Beftucheff, gave orders to arrest him on the spot. The chancellor was at once deprived of his place, tried, pronounced guilty of high treason, and sentenced to death. But the empress contented herself with banishing him to an estate 120 versts beyond Mosco. Thus passed all at once, from the pinnacle of power into bondage, that man who could make Russia tremble at his word, and controlled the fortunes of a great part of Europe! Such were the explanations universally believed at the time; and the consequence was, as said above, that count Voront zoff succeeded Beftucheff in the office of grand chancellor.

Catharine, who thought she had every thing to apprehend from the resentment of her husband, now saw herself abandoned on all sides. The courtiers who had been the most assiduous in their flatteries, were now the first to forsake her. Great minds rebound from error with a force proportionate to that which impelled them to it: the grand duchess was sensible to the extent of her imprudence; but her courage never forsook her. Resolved to employ that eloquence
which

which had formerly fucceeded fo well with the emprefs, fhe demanded an audience; which Elizabeth refufed. She then thought it advifable to apply to the ambaffador of France[*], becaufe, as well from his fituation as his perfonal talents, that minifter had confiderable influence at court. She intreated him to ufe his intereft on her behalf, and to reprefent to the emprefs how extremely fhe was diftreffed at the lofs of her favour; and that if it were poffible fhe could difpleafe her, the fincerity of her contrition, with fuch a heart as Elizabeth's, could not plead in vain for pardon.

The ambaffador was not deficient in marks of refpect for the princefs; he gave her fuch confolations and advice as his prudence fuggefted; but he thought it not confiftent with propriety to attempt to effect a reconciliation which appeared to him impoffible.

Catharine therefore remained for fome time in this diftreffing fituation. She had at once to fupport the averfion of the grand duke, the indignation of the emprefs, the infulting difdain of a court which, a few days before, was lavifh of its affiduities and fmiles; and, what afflicted her much more, the dread of lofing for ever her favourite Poniatofsky.

* M. de l'Hôpital.

K 3   The

The young Pole was not less a prey to disquietude than herself.   He had just received from Warsaw letters of recal; and yet he could not resolve upon quitting Ruffia.   Feigning an indifpofition, he confined himfelf all day to his hotel, and in the obfcurity of the winter evenings repaired to Catharine's apartments.   But the ever-waking eyes of fufpicion and malice were continually upon them.   Their places of affignation were difcovered; and the emprefs, whofe ears were open to every tale, was foon made acquainted with thefe tranfactions.

The return of fummer threw frefh difficulties in the way of thefe interviews.   The grand duchefs was obliged to accompany her hufband to Oranienbaum; and Poniatofsky was reduced to the neceffity of having recourfe to all manner of difguifes for gaining admiffion to this palace. One day, having put on a convenient habit, and fauntering in one of the walks of the grounds where Catharine had appointed to meet him, he was recognized by one of the domeftics, who prefently ran to acquaint the grand duke.   The prince, willing to humiliate Poniatofsky, ordered one of the moft athletic of his ruffian officers to be fetched; and after having given him the characteriftic defcription of the Pole, commanded

him

him to go up to him unawares in the grounds, and bring him either voluntarily or by force.

The officer was not long in coming up with the man who anfwered the defcription he had received; when he roughly interrogated him, Who he was? and what he would have? Poniatofsky, thus taken by furprife, fcarcely knowing what anfwer to make, ftammered out the firft thing that occurred: that he was a german taylor, and that he was come to Oranienbaum to take meafure of a holftein officer for a fuit of clothes. " I have " orders to bring you to the grand duke," replied the Ruffian.—" I muft decline the honour, though " my fortune may depend upon it: I have not a " moment of time," returned the Pole.—" Oh, " as to the matter of time, whether you have " time or not, you muft follow me," anfwered the officer. Having faid this, on feeing fome figns of reluctance on the other, he made a flip-knot in his handkerchief, which he threw over his neck, and thus led him captive to the feet of the prince.

The grand duke, feeing Poniatofsky brought like a malefactor before him, affumed an angry air, and in a feigned paffion foundly rated the officer for making fuch a miftake; but afterwards amufed himfelf with the adventure at the expence of the

count, and affected chiefly to relate it in the prefence of Catharine.

It was about this time that, whether in compliance with an involuntary paffion, for paffions
are involuntary in fuch characters as Peter, or
whether he thought to avenge himfelf for the infidelities of his wife, the grand duke formed an
attachment with one of the three daughters of
the fenator Vorontzoff, brother of the new chancellor. The eldeft of thefe fifters, madame
Boutturlin, was juftly reckoned one of the handfomeft ladies of Ruffia. The youngeft, who has
fince played fo active and refolute a part, under
the name of the princefs Dafhkoff, was equally
handfome, and moreover endowed with extraordinary talents; but as for the third, Elizabeth
Romanovna Vorontzoff *, of whom Peter was
fo paffionately enamoured, fhe was neither witty
in converfation, graceful in behaviour, nor
beautiful in perfon †. Her good-humour, fo

* The french author here adds, " to whom the grand
duke gave the title of countefs," by miftake. She was a
countefs by birth.

† Notwithftanding this affertion, fhe was faid to have
been very handfome at that time; latterly, it is true, fhe
grew corpulent. As madame Pofianfki, fhe was an excellent wife to the admiral of that name, a good mother,
and a charitable and worthy woman.

congenial

congenial to his own, feduced him, her caprices amufed him, and the habit of living with her foon gained her an imperious afcendant over him. The fenator Vorontzoff, an infipid and ambitious courtier, with abject complaifance, connived at the commerce of the prince with his daughter.

In the mean time the health of Elizabeth began vifibly to decline; and the neceffity of indulging repofe, in addition to her natural indolence, rendered her more negligent than ever of the affairs of government. It was with difficulty the new grand chancellor Vorontzoff could prevail on her to fet her fignature to the official difpatches; fhe could only fummon up the fcattered remains of her fpirits for her cuftomary diffipations. Feftivities, balls, mafquerades, and brilliant fhows ftill yielded a faint amufement; and dreading to lie down upon a reftlefs pillow, fhe went to the opera or the play at eleven, paffed the reft of the night at table, and went to bed at five in the morning. Bufineffes of the graveft import appeared now as trifles to her. Acquainted with the paffion of her nephew for the young countefs Vorontzoff, to whom fhe fcornfully gave the nick-name of la Pompadour, fhe liftened with avidity to the idle tales that were brought her of the particulars of their
amorous

amorous revels; feeming to feek in fuch anecdotes fome palliation for her own infirmities,
But fhe neverthelefs continued to meet the looks
of the prince with a face of indifference, and often
of coldnefs.

Catharine, who waited with impatience for a
favourable opportunity of reconciliation with the
emprefs, now that a fufficient interval of filence
had elapfed, thought it her duty to renew her
efforts. She threw herfelf at her feet, and implored her forgivenefs; but the irritated monarch would liften to no accommodation, except on the moft mortifying conditions. It was
afterwards propofed to her, by meffage, to con-
fefs her guilt, and to fubmit to the clemency of
her hufband and the emprefs.

From this moment Catharine fummoned up
all her pride. She purpofely avoided appearing
at court, kept clofe to her apartments, and
afked leave of the emprefs to retire into Germany; a permiffion which fhe was very fure of
being refufed; becaufe, knowing the extreme
fondnefs of Elizabeth for the young Paul Petrovitch, fhe had no reafon to apprehend that that
princefs would confent to fee the departure of the
mother of a child which would thereby be expofed to the hazard of being hereafter declared
illegitimate. The ftratagem fucceeded: an

accom-

accommodation fhortly after enfued. At the very moment when fhe was thought on the brink of irremediable difgrace, to the great aftonifhment of the court, fhe made her appearance at the theatre, by the fide of the emprefs, who carefully drew upon her the notice of the fpectators by the particularity of her attentions.

It is true that, in the private converfation which the grand duchefs had with the emprefs, fhe promifed no longer to permit the vifits of Poniatofsky; and thenceforward fhe actually held a greater referve in her conduct. Poniatofsky almoft immediately demanded his audience of leave. But as his attachment to Catharine was founded more on ambition than love, and, determined to neglect nothing that might add frefh fuel to a paffion which afterwards elevated him to the throne of Poland, he found new pretences for ftill prolonging his ftay in Peterfburg.

In the mean time the cabal formed by Beftucheff had not been annihilated by the difgrace of that minifter; and the enemies of the grand duke continued on all occafions to blacken him in the eyes of his aunt. They gladly took advantage of the ficknefs and infirmity of that princefs, to make her believe that Peter openly rejoiced in her approaching diffolution, and manifefted his impatience to enter into his

9   heritage.

heritage.   The mind of the empreſs, already too incenſed againſt her nephew, was cruelly wounded by theſe reports.   In the firſt emotions of reſentment, ſhe ſuffered ſome menaces to eſcape her of depriving him of the ſucceſſion.   At firſt it was thought by ſome that ſhe intended to reſtore the inheritance to prince Ivan, dethroned by her twenty years before, and whom ſhe ſtill kept languiſhing in a dungeon.   Others ſuppoſed, with greater reaſon, that ſhe had formed the deſign of cauſing the infant Paul Petrovitch to ſupplant his father.   Not many days after *, while the grand duke was at Oranienbaum, ſhe unexpectedly gave orders to have a play got ready ; and, contrary to uſual cuſtom, ſhe had neither the foreign miniſters nor the perſons of her court invited.   The grand ducheſs, her ſon, and the moſt intimate favourites were her only attendants.   No ſooner was ſhe ſeated in the imperial box, than ſhe began to complain of the thinneſs of the houſe, and concluded by ſaying that the ſoldiers of her guard muſt be admitted. In an inſtant the theatre was full.   Then, taking in her arms the little Paul Petrovitch, ſhe preſented him to the view of thoſe veteran warriors to whom ſhe was indebted for the throne ; and,

* In the month of December 1761.

praiſing

praifing his winning fmiles, his ftriking phyfiog-
nomy, his endearing qualities of heart and
mind, fhe feemed to afk of them the fame attachment for him which they had fhewn to her.
The foldiers replied by reiterated fhouts of applaufe.   If Elizabeth had proceeded to explain
herfelf farther, Peter had been excluded from
the throne for ever; but, notwithftanding the
enthufiaftic vociferations of her guards, the
emprefs ftopped fhort in her encomiums, fat
down in her feat, and the piece went on.   It is
probable that fhe thought it neceffary `firft to
found their difpofitions, in order to execute her
project with greater folemnity and precaution ;
it may be likewife, that fhe meant only to intimi-
date the grand duke by fhewing him how dependent he was on her will.

The news of this fcene was prefently fpread
abroad, and gave rife to many reflections.   On
this occafion the public recollected an old
opinion, undoubtedly falfe, but which, circulated in whifpers, had gained fome credit, at
the time of the birth of Paul Petrovitch.   It
was pretended, that the emprefs Elizabeth
had gained over by bribes the nurfe of the
grand duchefs's child, and caufed a fon fhe
had had by Razumofflky to be fubftituted in
its place.

Yet,

Yet, whatever were the defigns of the emprefs Elizabeth, the execution of them was prevented by the hand of death. A few days after the tranfaction in favour of the infant prince, fhe perceived her health to be fenfibly declining from day to day. Tormented with violent pains in her bowels, which no medicines were found to affuage, for procuring fome refpite to fuffering nature, fhe had more frequent recourfe to her cuftomary means of ftifling fenfibility in the ftupefactions brought on by the ufe of ftrong waters. In vain did her phyficians reprefent to her that fhe herfelf was contributing to fruftrate their efforts, and accelerating the period of her days. In vain did her attendants, by facrificing obedience to affection, fecretly remove or deftroy the intoxicating beverage : fhe would conftantly have a cafe of it in her chamber, of which the key was always kept within reach. It was now clearly feen that her end was rapidly approaching. The interefted and ambitious, who had feverally been contending for honours or wealth, now formed into bands in order to ftrengthen their forces, and prefently divided into two very oppofite parties.

The former was made up of the remains of the friends of Beftucheff, whofe cabals all tended in favour of Catharine, and of which,
after

after the exile of the old chancellor, count Ivan
Ivanovitch Schuvaloff had been confidered as
chief. Schuvaloff, whofe rapacity made the
ruffian merchants tremble, and whofe infolent
peculations incenfed the grand duke ; Schuvaloff,
convinced that his power and his profperity ran
great hazard of becoming extinct with the life of
Elizabeth, and feeing no other means of efcaping
the vengeance of the prince than by cutting him
off from all hopes of the crown ; fteadily adhering to the plan that had been, twenty years
before, chalked out by Beftucheff, and refting
on the well-known intentions of the emprefs,
confented fo far that Peter fhould be elected
fovereign of Ruffia, but was for giving the regency to the grand duchefs, under the authority
of a council, in which he modeftly offered himfelf to prefide.

Though fecretly irritated at feeing Ivan Schuvaloff appropriating to himfelf fo great a fhare
in this partition, yet the grand duchefs feconded
with all her efforts the plan of the favourite.
To this fhe was animated by the twofold motive
of ambition and fear. But the more fhe was
defirous of obtaining the fovereign power, the
more carefully fhe concealed that defire. Towards thofe who, from the nature of their
employment or ftation, approached her but
feldom,

feldom, fhe covered her fchemes with an apparent indifference, and fhe perpetually repeated
to her moft intimate confidants, that " the title
" of the mother of the emperor fhe fhould
" always think preferable to that of his fpoufe."
On the other hand, fhe could not diffemble that,
fince her infidelities were known to the grand
duke, fhe had every thing to dread from the refentment of that prince. He did not conceal
the animofity he bore her, of which fhe had
evident proofs at various times.

The other party into which the court was
fplit, and which defended the rights of Peter to
fucceed to the throne, was headed by the fenator
Vorontzoff, brother of the new grand chancellor.
This Vorontzoff was more ambitious, and at the
fame time more fordid than any of his competitors for power. He was not deftitute of
fagacity and courage ; but the former he only
employed in feeking means of intrigue, and his
courage in braving contempt. His daughter
was publicly the miftrefs of the grand duke ; and
the fenator, who, as before obferved, had himfelf prepared and formed this connection, now
neglected nothing for drawing it clofer. The
accefs which he had to the grand duke, furnifhed
him with frequent opportunities of exafperating
him more againft his wife, and of difcourfing on
what

what it would be advisable to do on ascending the throne. He succeeded so well in gaining his confidence, that the prince determined on nothing till he had consulted the count, or previously informed him of his intention through his daughter. In short, according to the instigations of Vorontzoff, and some other courtiers at the devotion of that senator, the grand duke resolved to assemble the troops at the instant the empress should close her eyes, to cause himself to be proclaimed emperor, to repudiate the grand duchess, to declare the young Paul Petrovitch illegitimate, and publicly to marry his mistress Elizaveta Romanovna Vorontzoff.

All things seemed to concur to the success of this enterprise. The grand duke, it is true, was not agreeable to the courtiers, but he was still respected by the people, who looked up to him as the offspring of Peter the great. Vorontzoff had, moreover, far greater address than Schuvaloff, and he laid his account that England would furnish him with considerable sums.

In the midst of this train of things, the perpetual intrigues and agitations with which the two parties filled the court of the dying monarch, and whose animosities were augmenting from day to day, there started up all at once a man who undertook to calm their tempers, compromife their differences, and even reconcile their opinions. This man was Nikita Ivanovitch count Panin, who afterwards for many years filled the place of prime minifter to Catharine, and was then juft returned from Stockholm, where he had long refided in a diplomatic capacity.

Count Panin was of an obfcure family, and fet out in life as a foldier in one of the regiments of horfe guards*. Under the patronage of prince Kourakin

---

* Count Nikita Ivanovitch Panin, minifter of the department for foreign affairs, was born the 15th of September 1718. His family was originally from the republic of Lucca, whence they came to Ruffia fome time in the 15th century. His father ferved under Peter the great, and was fo fortunate as to obtain the particular favour of his fovereign. He was promoted to the rank of lieutenant-general, and died in 1736 of the confequences of the wounds he had received in feveral battles, leaving behind him two fons. The elder was entrufted with the moft important concerns of the empire, and educated the heir of the crown; the fecond gave many proofs of courage and military fkill in the pruffian war, governed as ftadtholder the whole of the country conquered from Pruffia, afterwards led his army againft the Turks, ftormed Bender, effectuated the independency of the Krim Tartars; laftly, after he had for fome years retired from the fervice at his own requeft, quelled a great infurrection; and, by this important fervice rendered to his country, obtained the appellation of defender of the nobles, againft whom the attacks of the rebels were chiefly directed. Nikita Ivanovitch, by his good conduct,

Kourakin he became gentleman of the bed-
chamber.   The emprefs foon noticed him from
the people of the palace, and thought he might
be employed in confidential affairs.   Accordingly
fhe fent him in 1749 to Sweden, with the title
of minifter plenipotentiary at the court of Stockholm.   On his return he had been appointed
governor to prince Paul Petrovitch.   Panin had
received but little help from education; in natural talents he did not rife above mediocrity;
but, as is often obfervable in minds of that
ftamp, he found nothing arduous or difficult,
but thought always that cunning was equal to
wifdom.   Obftinate and inflexible in his opinions, which being neither founded on judgment
nor derived from experience, were not always

---

duct, and the intereft of his relation prince Kourakin, who
had married his fifter, procured him accefs to the court on
all occafions.   The emprefs Elizabeth Petrovna, at her acceffion, made him a gentleman of the bed-chamber; and the
particular favour fhe fhewed him prefently made him an
object of jealoufy and envy, two vices that are faid to be no
ftrangers in courts.   His enemies engaged in feveral intrigues
in hopes of removing him from the palace; but, as in all his
behaviour they could find no handle for calumny, they
were reduced to the neceffity of employing his merits to
further their aim.   They reprefented to the emprefs his
dexterity in political matters, and he was fent in 1747 as
minifter plenipotentiary to the danifh court.

the moſt juſt, he ſeemed to imagine that what he knew and what he thought was always the beſt. However, in the latter years of his life, after he had done with all public affairs, he has often confeſſed to his friends, that during the whole courſe of his miniſtry he made it the baſis of his conduct in all negotiations, either foreign or domeſtic, to gain time, and truſt chiefly to the chapter of accidents : and he had ſeldom been miſtaken in the event. Indeed the face of human affairs is in ſuch perpetual fluctuation, and is ſubject to ſuch an endleſs variety of changes, that the chances attending on what a day may bring forth are frequently, both in private and public life, ſeen to favour the maxim of this conceited politician. His reſidence in Sweden had taught him to believe that an ariſto-cratic conſtitution, with the forms of a ſenate, was the maſterpiece of governments. To theſe notions he pertinaciouſly adhered. The reſt of his character was made up of indolence, inaccuracy, and a paſſion for goſſiping.

In accepting the poſt of preceptor to the young prince, he had now to determine his choice between the grand duke and his conſort. Panin did not allow himſelf a moment's heſitation. He devoted himſelf entirely to Catharine. Being admitted into her confidence, and informed of

4

her

her defign to fnatch the fceptre from the hand of her hufband, he eafily perceived the extent of the danger to which fhe was expofed. He was fenfible that fhe might fail in the attempt, and be covered with ruin; that fhe might fuddenly be hurled from the throne and the bed of the emperor, and that her fon would partake in her fall. It was this that the governor dreaded the moft.

The firft thought that occurred to him for avoiding this misfortune, was to engage the two oppofite parties to abate of their extravagant pretenfions; and he could no otherwife hope to gain their confent to this mutual furrender, than by employing thofe fears they reciprocally entertained of each other. He accordingly refolved to bring about a coalition, thereby to pave the way for Peter to be feated on the throne, and in order that he might be proclaimed emperor, not by the troops, but by the fenate, who at the fame time would limit his power, and fecure the authority to his wife and his fon.

This project once conceived, Panin fet himfelf ferioufly about the means of its execution. Ambition all at once gave a momentary turn to his character. His indolence gave place to activity, difcretion fucceeded to his temerity, and referve to his ufual babble. He diftrufted even Catharine

L 3

tharine herfelf, and never imparted to her a
fhare in his fecret. He went farther: he affected
no longer to frequent, and feigned to have abandoned his party. But, no fooner did he think
himfelf fafe from all fufpicion of his intentions,
than he reforted in fecret to the houfe of Ivan
Schuvaloff.

Ivan Schuvaloff had given himfelf up to the
moft pungent anxieties. He fhuddered, he even
fhed tears at the thoughts of being the leader
of a party, and at feeing the dangerous honour
afcribed to him of a project conceived by Peter
Schuvaloff, his ambitious coufin*; who, confined
at this time to his bed by a ficknefs that laid
him foon after in the grave, could not fupport
the infolence he had for fome time infpired into
the haughty and pufillanimous favourite of
Elizabeth.

The circumftance was favourable to Panin.
He failed not to turn it to his advantage. He

---

* Count Peter Schuvaloff was of a bold and romantic
turn, and the oppofite in all things of his coufin Ivan,
whofe only propenfity was to fordid intrigue. Peter Schuvaloff made himfelf famous in Ruffia for his ambition, and
in Europe for the invention of the cannons that bear his name.
He fancied himfelf alone able to prevent the grand duke
from reigning, and only made ufe of his coufin Ivan as an
ordinary inftrument.

dexteroufly

dexteroufly employed his ingenuity in augmenting the horrors of Ivan Schuvaloff, by exaggerating the dangers to which he was expofed.——
" How can you venture," faid he, " to contend
" with unequal forces, againft the grand duke,
" bringing upon yourfelf an irreparable ruin and
" a certain death, by endeavouring to fet afide
" from the throne a prince who is called to it
" by the choice of the fovereign, and who, by
" his birth is the only legitimate heir ? But
" even fuppofing you could fucceed in prevent-
" ing the fceptre from paffing into his hand,
" have you any reafon to hope to preferve your
" influence for any confiderable time, during a
" minority, the weaknefs whereof will embolden
" your rivals, and raife up a hoft of malcontents,
" inceffantly plotting your difgrace ? If you are
" victorious over one faction, can you equally
" flatter yourfelf with efcaping the other ? If the
" firft blow that is ftruck at you falls fhort of its
" aim, by the fecond, more fuccefsful, you may
" be eafily overthrown. If you would follow the
" advice of a friend, and the dictates of prudence,
" you will feduloufly frequent the levées of the
" grand duke and conciliate his favour. Time
" ftill is yours. He himfelf is well informed of
" the obftacles to be thrown in his way, and he
" will think himfelf happy enough, if, at the

L 4 " expence

" expence of some sacrifices, he deprives them
" of the power to hurt him.　Let us leave him
" then the quiet possession of the throne; but
" let us oblige him to purchase it on conditions
" that will thenceforward dispel our fears, and
" for ever disable the prince from abusing his
" power.　It would be unnecessary at present
" for me to specify those conditions: but if you
" comply with my advice, I have not the least
" doubt but the grand duke will easily be brought
" to agreement, and I promise to furnish you
" with a plan adapted to reconcile the several
" parties that divide the court."

Count Ivan Schuvaloff answered not a single word; but, convinced of the wisdom of Panin's advice, he immediately repaired to his cousin Peter, and imparted to him in whispers the counsels he had just received.　Disease had abated the courage of Peter Schuvaloff, and relaxed the springs of his ambition.　But, though he easily yielded to the persuasion of the reality of all the formidable apprehensions that terrified Ivan, yet, in relinquishing his project, he was determined to play the principal part.

He sent an humble message to the grand duke, acquainting him, that, having to communicate to him secrets of the utmost importance, and being prevented from quitting his bed by a painful

disease,

difeafe, he was his fubmiffive petitioner for the honour of a vifit. The prince went directly to his chamber. Being feated by his couch, Peter Schuvaloff addreffed him with the energy and awful folemnity of a man, who, trembling on the brink of the grave, knows of no artifices for concealing the truth, and has nothing any longer to defire or to fear.——" My prince," faid he, " you are not ignorant of the prepoffeffions that " are abroad againft you. The people imagine " that you incline more to the Germans than to " them ; the clergy dread you ; the principal " nobility hate you. The clouds that are ga- " thering round, feem to threaten you with a " tempeftuous reign. All circumftances concur " to demonftrate that for preventing the alter- " ations you are thought to intend, your enemies " will proceed to extremities. I pretend not, " my prince, to know what are the defigns you " really meditate ; I cannot forefee whether you " will triumph over thofe who are feeking your " ruin, or whether they will get the better of " you. But if you carry into effect what it is " fuppofed you are determined to do : if you " repudiate the grand duchefs, to elevate to her " place a woman fo vile and contemptible as the " countefs Vorontzoff, be affured that you will " draw upon yourfelf a feries of calamities, to
" which,

" which, fooner or later, you will fall a victim,
" and that you and your memory will be dif-
" honoured for ever."

As he liftened to this difcourfe, the grand duke
was obferved at feveral times to change colour;
and on perceiving that Peter Schuvaloff had left
off fpeaking, he affured him, that the charge of
any defign to diffolve his marriage was a falfe
imputation, and that nothing fhould ever perfuade him to it.   But what might lead to a fufpicion of the fincerity of thefe proteftations, is,
that the prince added thefe remarkable words:
" Romanovna herfelf may perhaps give credit to
" reports that flatter her vanity: fhe is a fimple-
" ton, whom I never promifed to marry, but in
" cafe the grand duchefs fhould die; and fhe is
" ftill alive."

However, as Peter Schuvaloff was fincerely defirous of an accommodation with the grand duke,
he omitted to give this laft avowal all the interpretation of which it was fufceptible, and was fatisfied with the promife given him by the prince,
that he would blot from his memory all the
machinations that had been fo daringly formed
againft him.

This reconciliation was effected without
trouble, but one other ftill remained, not lefs
important, and far more difficult to obtain.   We
                                                    have

have seen what odious fuspicions the enemies of the grand duke were continually pouring into the ears of the emprefs. That princefs was alarmed with the apprehenfion that her nephew might be led to get rid of her by poifon, and thefe fears augmented her weaknefs, and filled her with averfion for him that had raifed them. Ever fince her illnefs had prevented her from appearing in public, fhe had ordered the grand duke to be denied admittance to her apartment; and that this order might appear the lefs extraordinary, fhe had caufed it in like manner to be fignified to the grand duchefs. The fecret of thefe divifions, of thefe difturbances in the imperial family, was ftill confined within the walls of the palace; but it might eafily get vent, and be fpread through the town; and if this fhould be the cafe, if the emprefs fhould have died without feeing the prince and his fpoufe, the populace, always implicitly credulous, would have thought the unjuft fufpicions of Elizabeth to have been founded in truth, and would have eagerly attributed to the nephew the death of the aunt. Something was therefore to be done to induce that princefs to call the grand duke to her prefence.

Count Ivan Schuvaloff was grand chamberlain, and the principal perfon about the emprefs. Panin

Panin thought him the propereſt man to ſollicit the reconciliation he wanted ; but whether it was that Schuvaloff was afraid of troubling the empreſs too much in her preſent infirm condition ; whether he was willing to keep the grand duke longer in an anxious ſuſpenſe, and avoid an explanation of the uttermoſt danger to all thoſe who had endeavoured to injure that prince ; or whether, in a word, he reckoned on the ſurreptitious teſtament it was propoſed to bring to light ; however it be, he abſolutely refuſed to make this requeſt.

Panin, on ſeeing the failure of his firſt attempt, addreſſed himſelf now to the confeſſor of Elizabeth. He frankly acknowledged to him, that the commiſſion with which he was charged was of a nature extremely delicate ; and that though his ſollicitude for the ſalvation of the ſovereign might bring upon him remedileſs misfortune, yet the glory and comfort that would accrue to him from the ſucceſs of his aim, ſhould make him ſcorn diſgrace, and expect his recompenſe in a better world. He aſſured him likewiſe of the gratitude of the grand duke and grand ducheſs ; and the monk, not leſs wiſhing, it may be ſuppoſed, to cheriſh the favour of the heir to the throne, than zealous for the eternal repoſe of the empreſs, promiſed to deliver his exhort-
ations

ations to her with all the energy of facred eloquence.

Every needful precaution was taken. A moment was chofen when Ivan Schuvaloff was abfent, and then the confeffor approaching the
bed of Elizabeth, difcourfed to her of heavenly
things, of the fupreme and immortal Sovereign
by whom earthly monarchs reign, of his juftice,
of his clemency, of his tribunal, before which
only they who forgive can obtain forgivenefs,
and of that kingdom of God, of which the terref-
trial paradife was but a faint adumbration, but
where only the charitable can obtain admiffion,
but where only the merciful can hope for mercy:
which ended, he obtained of her a fign of confent. At this inftant the grand duke entered,
leading Catharine by the hand, who both fell on
their knees by the bedfide, and Elizabeth pronounced in an indiftinct tone of voice, and as if
no more than the animal machine was concerned
in the utterance, whatever was dictated to her
by the prieft. She faid to the prince and princefs :—" That fhe had always loved them ; and
" that with her dying breath fhe wifhed them all
" kinds of bleffings." ·

All that were witneffes of this fcene faw
clearly, that the pardon came only from her lips;
but appearances fufficed the prince ; and his partifans

tifans did not fail emphatically to repeat through the city the affectionate words pronounced by the emprefs, with feveral additions of their own.

On the other hand, Ivan Schuvaloff, who had not been able to make a merit of the reconciliation with the grand duke, but refolved not to furnifh an occafion for irritating that prince againft him, ftudioufly omitted to contradict whatever they pleafed to publifh on the matter.

Proud of the important fervice he had rendered the grand duke, Panin imagined he had thenceforward acquired fuch a confequence with him as to make him confent entirely to the plan he had marked out. According to which, Peter, as foon as the emprefs had departed this life, was to repair to the fenate, and there receive the crown by a folemn decree.

Panin therefore demanded an audience of the grand duke. This the prince granted without hefitation. He began by telling the prince, that what he had to deliver was worthy of all his attention. He then addreffed him to the following effect :——" It is on the firft ftep you fhall " take on afcending the throne, that the pro- " fperity of your reign and the glory you will " merit chiefly depend. There are two me- " thods, my prince, of invefting yourfelf with
" the

" the sovereign power; the former, by causing
" yourself to be proclaimed emperor by the
" army; the second, by receiving the crown at
" the hands of the senate.   The former is more
" prompt; the latter more sure.   The eyes of
" all Europe and a great part of Asia are fixed
" upon you.   Reflect then on the honour you
" will acquire among the numerous nations in
" subjection to your sovereignty, and even fo-
" reigners too, when they behold you so gene-
" rous as to wish to hold, from the free choice
" of the representatives of the russian empire,
" an authority which your predecessors owed
" only to the force and venality of the troops.

" You know how frequent revolutions have
" been in this empire; you know with what
" facility a seduced or mutinous soldiery have
" crowned or dethroned their monarchs.   The
" method that I propose is the only one adapted
" to the prevention of dangerous machinations.
" The senate, having once elected you, will
" feel itself interested in supporting the work of
" its hands; and the people, regarding your
" person more sacred, will always be ardent in
" your defence."

The grand duke was moved; he was yielding
to the impression, when suddenly two of his
courtiers entered.   He communicated to them
                                        the

the propofal of Panin, and afked their opinion. One of them, who prefently perceived the infidious nature of the meafure propofed to the prince, advifed him to fubmit his decifion to the judgment of the old prince Trubetſkoï, whofe long experience and confummate wifdom rendered him a proper guide. Prince Trubetſkoï had indeed been witnefs of feveral revolutions, and was a perfect mafter of the ufages and cuftoms of his country.

He was fent for. The grand duke repeated to him all that he had juſt been hearing from the mouth of Panin, and did not conceal his inclination to follow the advice of the count. But Trubetſkoï expreffed himfelf of a different opinion, and delivered it with all the boldnefs of a veteran foldier, jealous of the honour of his fovereigns.

" My prince," faid he, " the ftep you have
" been advifed to take is not only attended with
" far greater danger than that you areinftructed to
" dread, but in direct oppofition to the cuftoms
" of the empire. The ruffian conftitution is
" purely military; and the fenate has never pre-
" tended to interfere in the election of the tzars.
" And what is that imaginary glory in preferring
" to be crowned by a juridical affembly rather
" than by a victorious army? Chofen by a diet or
                                                      " by

" by a fenate, will the kings of Poland and of
" Sweden ever take precedence of the emperor
" of all the Ruffias? The true, the only glory
" of a monarch is to reign worthily. Make it
" your endeavour then to merit that glory with-
" out difquieting yourfelf about a vain formality,
" and putting yourfelf under the tutelage of an
" ambitious fenate, who will foon make you re-
" pent the confidence you have repofed in it.
" But if unhappily your throne fhould fhake,
" will that fenate have the force to eftablifh it?
" and if you fhould fet out with rendering the
" army diffatisfied by difdaining to follow their
" ancient ufage, will you not, fooner or later,
" have reafon to dread their vengeance ?"

This fpeech caufed the grand duke to waver
in his refolution. He was flattered by the brilliant novelty of the counfels of Panin; but the
dread of affronting the army deprived him of
courage to follow them. In this perplexity of
mind, not knowing what determination he ought
to adopt, he difpatched one of his chamberlains
to confult the grand duchefs.

Catharine, whofe ambition was roufed by
Elizabeth's approaching diffolution, and who
felt the neceffity of conciliating the popular favour by an exterior of piety, which, by thofe

VOL. I.   M   who

who beſt knew her, was ſuppoſed not to proceed
from her heart; Catharine was punctual in fre-
quenting the churches at the ſtated times of
public devotion; but more particularly at the
prayers that were now daily put up for imploring
the re-eſtabliſhment of the health of the empreſs.
Panin had imprudently neglected to inform her
of his project.   She was ſtill in the dark concerning the advantages to accrue from it to her.
Beſides, ſhe had been employed ſeveral days in
framing herſelf the form of the proclamation
acknowledging the emperor, as well as that of
the oath to be taken by the troops: and as ſhe
plumed herſelf on writing in a ſtyle of peculiar
elegance, and imagining that theſe two pieces
would be received with admiration by the people
at large, ſhe would not ſacrifice a labour, that
would be loſt if the prince ſhould cauſe himſelf
to be elected by the ſenate, as that body would
itſelf, in that caſe, preſcribe the new form of the
oath, and dictate the new proclamation.   She
therefore returned an abrupt anſwer to the grand
duke, "that he ought to conform to eſtabliſhed
"cuſtom."

Almoſt at the moment the grand duke received
this anſwer, word was brought him, that his aunt,
the empreſs Elizabeth, "commanded him to
"live

" live long*;" in other words, that fhe was dead.
The tzarina expired on Chriftmas-day 1761 †,
after a long illnefs, and in excruciating pains, in
the 52d year of her age, and the 22d of her
reign.   This princefs was fecond daughter to
Peter the great; and, from being little better
than a prifoner, became in a moment a defpotic
fovereign, holding in her feeble and negligent
hands the reins of this gigantic empire, the moft
extenfive on the globe of the earth; one part
whereof alone, the ruffian Afia, is (as has already
been obferved in our preliminaries) far greater
than all Europe taken together: nay, of which
part only, one province, Siberia, greatly exceeds
an empire of the firft magnitude, namely China,
with all its adjacent territories.   For Elizabeth
poffeffed neither the abilities nor the inclination
for being an active fovereign : and the illuftrious
family of this mighty monarch was more than
once difturbed by intefine revolutions.   In

* The ufual form of announcing to another the death of
fome perfon, in practice among all claffes and conditions of
people.   Procopy Kirillitch prikazal jeel: Procopius the
fon of Cyril, or perhaps Procopius Fitz-Cyril, " orders you
" to live," is the fame as to tell you that he is dead : or
as often, Afanafi Vaffillievitch, Athanafius the fon of Bafil,
prikazal dolgo jeet, orders you to live long.

† Or the 5th of January 1762, N. S.

M 2.   dungeons

dungeons at various diftances from the refidence, were languifhing, in her reign, a dethroned emperor, exiled princes and dukes, vanquifhed magnates, banifhed commanders, ftatefmen, courtiers, and women.

The reign of Elizabeth may be defervedly termed peaceful and tranquil; yet, without reckoning the grand tumult at her acceffion to the throne, there were not wanting revolutions of an inferior kind. In the year 1743, not long before the arrival of Catharine, a court confpiracy againft the emprefs was detected: which, though it coft none of the accomplices their lives, yet the minifter for the marine, Lapoukin, his very beautiful lady, his fon, the countefs Beftucheff, fifter-in-law to the chancellor of the empire, feveral gentlemen of the chàmber, and officers, received the knoot, had the fore-half of their tongues cut out, and were fent to Siberia. In the year 1748, count Leftoc, formerly bodyfurgeon to the emprefs, and the principal inftrument of her elevation to the throne, was difgraced by the chancellor Beftucheff, whom he himfelf had promoted to that office, and by general Apraxin: he was firft imprifoned in the caftle, and afterwards exiled to fome obfcure and folitary place in the government of Archangel.

Ten

Ten years afterwards the chancellor's own turn came; being in 1758 accufed of high treafon, and fent off to one of his eftates 120 verfts beyond Mofco. — Of more confequence to the country was Elizabeth's participation in the formidable league againft Frederic of Pruffia, at the inftigation of Beftucheff, and which the grand duke beheld with extreme difcontent. During the ever-memorable war of 1757—1762, that monarch was cruelly haraffed by the ruffian arms, though at times fuch glorious victories were gained over them by his own; but what benefit could accrue from all this to the enormous empire? What was to compenfate the thoufands of lives and the prodigious fums of money that it coft to Ruffia?

The eafinefs and indolence of Elizabeth's character fubjected her to the humours of favourites, who made a bad ufe of her authority. Her devotion often rendered her impious, and her clemency cruel. At the commencement of her reign fhe made a vow never to punifh a malefactor with death: the judges therefore, who could not decapitate criminals, deprived them of their lives by the barbarous punifhment of the knoot; and never were there more tongues cut out, and more wretches fent to Siberia, than

M 3   under

under the reign of this princefs, fo unjuftly extolled for her clemency *.

It is fuppofed that her government coft every year to the empire at leaft 1000 of her fubjects by private imprifonment, which, during the 20 years and upwards that fhe reigned, makes the number amount to above 20,000. Nothing was more eafy than to obtain a fecret order for this purpofe by the flatterers of all ranks that fwarmed about her perfon. It was fufficient for one of the maids of honour to think herfelf flighted, for

* The panegyrifts of Elizabeth (fays Mr. Coxe) would certainly have entertained fome doubts concerning her boafted clemency, if they had recollected that fhe did not abolifh, but retained, the following horrid procefs for the purpofe of extorting confeffion from perfons charged with treafonable defigns. The arms of the fufpected perfon being tied behind by a rope, he was drawn up in that pofture to a confiderable height in the air; whence being fuddenly lowered to within a fmall diftance of the ground, and the motion being there as fuddenly checked, the violence of the concuffion diflocated his fhoulders, and in that deplorable fituation he underwent the knoot. To this dreadful engine of barbarity and defpotifm, Elizabeth, amidft all her imputed lenity, gave unlimited fcope; and, during her whole reign, it was ordinarily applied even at the difcretion of inferior and ignorant magiftrates; nor was it abolifhed until the acceffion of the prefent emprefs (Catharine II.), who has prohibited the ufe of torture in all criminal cafes. *Coxe's Travels,* 8vo. edit. vol. iii. p. 130.

getting

getting an order to have a person taken out of bed in the night, carried away blindfolded, and gagged, and immured under ground, there to drag out the remainder of life in a solitary and loathsome dungeon, without ever being charged with any crime, or even knowing in what part of the country he was.   On the disappearance of any such person from his family, from his relatives, from the circle of his acquaintance, it was highly dangerous to make any inquiries after him.   " He has disappeared," was held a sufficient answer to questions of that nature.   Many of these were known to be still miserably wearing out existence under the bastions and towers of Schluffelburg and other fortresses, so lately as the winter of 1780, not to mention the exiles to Siberia.   To all this it may be added, that her reign was never marked by a single act that could justify the revolution that placed on her head the crown of Russia.   In a word, she was fitter to have vegetated in the sloth of a convent, than to be seated on the throne of one of the largest of the chief empires of the world.

M 4

C H A P. II.

Accession of Peter III.—His Dethronization and Death. — Revolution of 1762. — Catharine assumes the Reins of Government.

THE part taken by Elizabeth in the seven years' war, though it might in some measure have been dictated by resentment, might at the same time have passed for the result of the soundest policy. No power but that of the king of Prussia was capable of checking hers. He was, not only from his strength and character, but from the situation of his dominions, the only prince in Europe from whom it could be materially her interest to make conquests.

By the capture of Colberg on one hand, and Schweidnitz on the other, the king of Prussia's dominions were entirely at the mercy of his enemies; his forces were worn away, and even his efforts had gradually declined: a complete victory, though this was an event not at all probable, could not have saved him. The Russians, by wintering in Pomerania, and, by the possession of Colberg, which insured them supplies by a safe and expeditious channel, were in a condition

dition to commence their operations much earlier than ufual, as well as to fuftain them with more fpirit and uniformity. No refource of policy could be tried with the leaft expectation of fuccefs. After fuch a refiftance for five years, of which the world never furnifhed another example, the king of Pruffia had nothing left, but fuch a conduct as might clofe the fcene with glory ; fince there was fo little appearance of his concluding the war with fafety.

In the midft of thefe gloomy appearances, his inveterate and inflexible enemy, the emprefs of Ruffia, died ; and he was extricated by that event, alone from the diftreffes by which he was actually furrounded, and the greater miferies that feemed to await him.

With regard to her own dominions, Elizabeth, for her perfonal conveniency, had created a government by favourites ; and by her paffion for pomp and fenfual gratifications, had incurred enormous debts.

No fooner had the emprefs clofed her eyes, than the courtiers preffed in crowds to the grand duke. This prince, laying afide at once his weaknefs and indecifion, accofted them with dignity, and received the oaths of the officers of his guard.

In

In about an hour he got on horseback, and traversed the ftreets of St. Peterfburg, diftributing money to the multitude. As he went, the foldiers flocked about him, crying, " If thou " take care of us, we will ferve thee as faithfully " as we ferved our good emprefs." The people mixed their fhouts of joy with the acclamations of the foldiers ; and, though the enemies of the grand duke had long fince fucceeded in their attempts to bring odium and contempt upon him, yet his acceffion to the throne was not attended with the leaft mark of difcontent or ill-will.

As for himfelf, delivered on a fudden from the long and fervile conftraint in which he had been kept by his aunt, he negligently let his fatisfaction appear, but without betraying an indecent joy. He took the name of Peter III.

It was eafy for him to efface the memory of his predeceffor; yet it was obfervable that there was little appearance of thofe cheerful fentiments which ufually take poffeffion of the hearts of the fubjects on the acceffion of a young prince to the throne. All tempers feemed out of tune : the emperor neither found nor felt any more affection in the larger circle of the court, than in the fmaller one of his family.

The

The Ruffians were at that time, generally speaking, indifpofed towards foreigners, though numbers of them, fince the time of Peter the great, had always held places at the court, in the army, in the fleet, and in the civil departments. Elizabeth had flattered this old ruffian prejudice; and, in order to ingratiate herfelf with the people, on her coming to the crown, had promifed to remove the foreigners: but in the opinion of many of the nobility, and efpecially of the army, fhe came very far fhòrt of her word. During her reign, in the year 1740, an infurrection broke out on this account; the foldiers in the camp near Viborg, during the fwedifh war, began 'on a fudden to maltreat their foreign officers, and were threatening to proceed to very dangerous extremities, when difcipline and order were prefently reftored by the great prefence of mind of the intrepid Keith. Even in Peterfburg a fimilar mutiny, fhortly after the former, broke out, which, though at firft only an attack on a german officer, yet proceeded to fo great a height as to fill the whole city with alarm and confternation. It was chiefly on account of this national humour, that generals Lœvendal, Keith, Manftein, and other deferving foreigners, afterwards took leave of the fervice.

Indeed

Indeed the grand duke Peter could not properly be deemed a foreigner ; he had rather a juft claim on the, national love, as the grandfon of Peter the great.   But he was after all an Holfteiner ; he had not long been refident in Ruffia ; and lived there almoft like a foreigner.   Neither in manners, nor in language, nor in religious profeffion, did he feem a complete and genuine Ruffian.   His confidence and familiarity were confined to the Germans from his dukedom ; all his affections feemed to centre in Holftein alone, while he fhewed only coldnefs or even repugnance to the concerns of his future empire.   Nor was this at all furprifing, as the fituation in which he was held, by keeping him at a diftance from the deliberations of the cabinet, naturally diminifhed his attention to public affairs ; and as he juftly difapproved of the violent participation with which his aunt and her miniftry engaged in the great german war. —— Both parties, if they had not yet proceeded to intemperate meafures, had, however, already concerted their plans, or rather had begun to put them in play.   The grand duke, according to fome, ought to be deprived of the fucceffion ; and then they could caft their eyes on no perfon fo proper for it as his confort ; who, though a foreigner likewife, had yet in her whole behaviour affimilated herfelf more with the

the nation, and might reign as the guardian of her son. On the other hand, the grand duke wanted, as was said by others, or perhaps by the same, entirely to new-model the whole system of Ruffia, to put every thing on a german footing, to employ the force of the empire only in the aggrandisement of Holstein; and, in order to enable himself to act with perfect freedom, and to annihilate the opposite party at a stroke, to detach himself from his family, and to secure to a paternal relation the expectative of the crown.

Such was the temper of the times when Peter acceded to the imperial dignity. In the manifesto by which he proclaimed this event to the empire, he mentioned neither his consort nor even his son; and interpreters were not wanting, who clearly perceived in this omission the overthrow of the hereditary succession. A circumstance that operated with greater impression was, that he made no preparations for his coronation at Mosco; a solemnity of the utmost importance, as a practice of high antiquity, and as conferring an awful sanction on the authority of the sovereign in the minds of the people. Instead of this he pushed his blind passion for imitating the king of Pruffia so far, that he made

pre-

preparations in this immature ftate of his government to quit Ruffia, and go into Germany, for the fake of an interview with that great monarch, whofe genius, principles, and fortune he fo extravagantly admired.

The impartial hiftorian cannot withhold the tribute of praife from his conduct at the beginning of his reign. To fay that he revenged himfelf on no one, though he very well knew who had taken pains to injure him with the late emprefs, would be but flight commendation, in comparifon of the acts of beneficence and juftice with which he fignalized his firft acceffion to the fupreme command, to the aftonifhment of thofe who knew him only by his vices. The transformation appeared as complete as it was fudden. Gentlenefs and humanity took the place of violence, and reflection fucceeded to paffion. The grand duke had been inconfiftent, impetuous, and wild: Peter III. now fhowed himfelf equitable, patient, and enlightened. He exercifed kindnefs towards all who had been attached to the late emprefs his aunt. He continued in their pofts almoft all the great officers of ftate. He pardoned his enemies. He raifed to the rank of field-marfhal Peter Schuvaloff, who had been long confined to his bed, and who died fhortly after.

after.   He left the place of grand-veneur to
Alexey Gregorievitch Razumoffſky*, the favourite of Elizabeth.   He even conferred benefits on Ivan Schuvaloff, though he had frequently
made an unworthy uſe of his influence.

Prince Shaſuſkoï, advocate of the ſenate, of
whom Peter III. had great reaſon to complain,
was the only perſon he removed from his employment; but he exacted of him nothing more
than a ſimple reſignation, leaving him both his
liberty and his poſſeſſions.   At the ſame time a
certain Gleboff, who from being but a common
attorney, was appointed to tranſact the affairs of
Holſtein, and in that adminiſtration had obtained
the good-will of the prince, was put into the
place of Shaſuſkoï.   Gleboff afterwards but ill
requited ſo ſignal a mark of the confidence of his
maſter.

The grand ducheſs, who could not think without dread of the moment when her huſband
ſhould be inveſted with the ſovereign power,
and expected nothing ſhort of a very ſevere
animadverſion upon herſelf, received from him

* Alexey Razumoffſky had often injured the grand duke
with the empreſs Elizabeth.   The grand duke one day ſent
him an axe upon a red ſatin cuſhion, as a hint of the cata-
ſtrophe that awaited him ; but when this prince was ſeated on the throne, he diſdained every idea of revenge.

the

the moſt flattering ſalutations, and marks of the
greateſt confidence.   He ſeemed to forget the
wrongs he had ſuffered, in the elegancies of her
mind, and the force of her genius.   He paſſed
a great part of the day in her apartments : diſ-
courſed with her on the moſt friendly footing,
and conſulted her on all delicate and important
affairs.   The courtiers, ſurpriſed at this conduct,
felicitated Catharine on the happineſs of her lot.
Catharine was almoſt the only perſon who was
not deceived.   She eaſily ſaw that her huſband
was not capable of governing by himſelf, and
ſhe was too well acquainted with his character, to
miſtake that for benevolence which was only
weakneſs.

    With regard to the government of his coun-
try, nothing could be more popular and auſpi-
cious than his firſt meaſures.   The earlieſt uſe
the new tzar made of his abſolute power, was to
ſet the ruſſian nobility and gentry free, and to
put them on the ſame footing with thoſe of their
rank in the other more moderate governments
of Europe.   He recalled that multitude of ſtate
priſoners with whom the ſuſpicious temper of
Elizabeth, and the jealouſies of her ſervants, had
peopled the deſerts of Siberia *.   Among theſe

* It is ſaid that Peter III. recalled to the number of
17,000 exiles.

                                           unfortunate

unfortunate wretches was the famous Biren *, who had long been the haughty lover and the cruel

* Erneft John Biren, become fo famous by his great advancements, and his not lefs extraordinary reverfes of fortune, was born in Courland, of a family of mean extraction. His grandfather had been head groom to James the third, duke of Courland, and obtained from his mafter the prefent of a fmall eftate in land. His fon accompanied prince Alexander, youngeft fon of the duke, in a campaign into Hungary againft the Turks, in quality of groom of his horfe, and with the rank of lieutenant. Prince Alexander being killed before Buda, in 1686, Biren returned into Courland, and was appointed mafter huntfman to the duke. Erneft John his fecond fon was born in 1687, received the early part of his education in Courland, and was fent to the univerfity of Konigfburg, where he continued till fome youthful imprudencies compelled him to retire. In 1714, he made his appearance at St. Peterfburg, and follicited the place of page to the princefs Charlotte, wife of the tzarovitch Alexey; but being contemptuoufly rejected as a perfon of mean extraction, retired to Mittau, where he chanced to ingratiate himfelf with count Bettucheff, mafter of the houfehold to Anne, widow of Frederic William, duke of Courland, who refided at Mittau. Being of a handfome figure and polite addrefs, he foon gained the good-will of the duchefs, and became her fecretary and chief favourite. On her being declared fovereign of Ruffia, Anne called Biren to Peterfburg, and the fecretary foon became duke of Courland, and firft minifter or rather defpot of Ruffia. All now felt the dreadful effects of his extreme arrogance, his bafe intrigues, and his horrid barbarity. The cruelties he exercifed on the moft illuftrious perfons of the country

eruel minifter of the emprefs Anne.   Peter III.
reftored him only to liberty; but Catharine
fince gave him back the duchy of Courland;
and Biren, inftructed in the fchool of adverfity,
paffed the reft of his life as a practical philofo-
pher, and became the father of a people whom
he had formerly oppreffed.

Peter III. brought alfo from Siberia marfhal
Munich *, at the age of 82, upon which one
of

---

almoft exceed belief: and Manftein conjectures, that
during the ten years in which Biren's power continued, above
20,000 perfons were fent to Siberia, of whom fcarcely 5000
were ever heard of more.   It is affirmed that the emprefs
has often fallen on her knees before him, in hopes of moving
him to clemency, but neither the prayers nor the tears
of that princefs were able to affect him. — On the death
of Anne, which happened in 1740, Biren being declared
regent, continued daily increafing his vexations and cruelties,
till he was arrefted on the 18th of December, only twenty
days after he had been appointed to the regency, and at the
revolution that enfued he was exiled to the frozen fhores of
the Oby.

* Chriftopher Burchard, better known under the name
of marfhal Munich, was fon of an officer in the fervice
of Denmark.   After having received a good education, he
entered at the age of 17 into the fervice of the landgraf of
Heffe-Darmftadt, and diftinguifhed himfelf in his firft campaign under prince Eugene and the duke of Marlborough.
He afterwards went into Poland, and thence paffed on to
Ruffia,

of his fons who was yet alive, and thirty-two of his grandchildren and great-grandchildren, went to accoft him on his approach to the fuburbs of the refidence. The old foldier prefented himfelf before the emperor with his numerous family, and dreffed in the fame fheepfkin pelice which he had worn in the deferts of Pelim; but the prince haftily reftored him the badges of the order of St. Andrew, together with his rank of field-marfhal, and faid to him, in a friendly tone of voice: " I hope that, notwithftanding your " advanced age, you may ftill ferve me." — Munich replied: " Since your majefty has " brought me from darknefs to light, and called

***

Ruffia, where his bravery and his talents obtained him the rank of field-marfhal. His capital defect was being too circumftantial and over-nice in matters of fmall import: accordingly the flighteft inftance of forgetfulnefs, the leaft inattention of a fubaltern, threw him into a rage, though he was prefently after afhamed of his violence. When Elizabeth had afcended the throne, fhe fought to avenge herfelf on Munich, for having formerly caufed one of her lovers to be put into prifon. Being brought to an iniquitous trial, he was condemned to be quartered; but his fentence was changed by the emprefs into perpetual banifhment in Siberia. He was followed into exile by his wife and feveral domeftics. He was allowed but 12 copeeks per day for the maintenance of them all, but he procured fome addition to this allowance by felling milk, and giving leffons in geometry to the young people that came to his folitude from the neareft towns.

" me

" me from the depths of a cavern to admit me
" to the foot of the throne, you will find me
" ever ready to expofe my life in your fervice.
" Neither a tedious exile, nor the feverity of a
" fiberian climate, have been able to extinguifh,
" or even to damp the ardour I have formerly
" fhewn for the interefts of Ruffia and the glory
" of its monarch *."

Leftok, to whom Elizabeth in a great meafure
owed her elevation to the throne, and whom fhe
afterwards bafely facrificed to the intrigues of his
enemies, who only coveted his property, was alfo
recalled by Peter III.†, and, by living afterwards
at Peterfburg contented with an humble mediocrity, proved that he had fhewn no lefs
docility to the leffons of adverfity than Biren
and Munich.

Thus every day was feen arriving at Peterfburg fome of the victims of the foregoing reign;
and their return prefented an affecting fcene
to the people, and a fubject of benedictions to

* Munich enjoyed the favour and patronage of Peter III.
and Catharine II. and died on the 16th of October 1767,
in the 85th year of his age.

† Leftok was a furgeon; by birth a German. He was
favourite to Elizabeth, and was a principal in planning
the revolution of 1742. But that ungrateful princefs forgot
this favour, and banifhed and detained him in prifon till fhe
died.

the

the tzar. The whole empire refounded with the praifes of its new fovereign ; and it is impoffible to defcribe the admiration, the tranfports of joy, that it occafioned on his going in ftate to the fenate, and reading a declaration, by which he permitted the nobility either to bear arms or not, at their own difcretion, and to travel abroad, a liberty not allowed them before. He affranchifed them at the fame time from the fervitude in which they had been held by his predeceffors. The nobility, in the excefs of their gratitude, would do no lefs than erect to him a ftatue of gold: but this enthufiafm lafted not long *.

A benefit more effential which Ruffia owes to Peter III. is the abolifhment of that inquifition, that terrible tribunal, or, as his fucceffor, when fhe confirmed the emperor's ukafe, very juftly

---

* See the Appendix at the end of the volume. Catharine, not willing to difoblige the nobility, and being moreover very fure that this ordinance would only be executed as far as fhe pleafed, left it to fubfift ; in fuch manner, that if the nobles would travel, they might do fo of right, but not of fact, fince they muft afk permiffion of the fovereign; and that princefs did not always grant it. Of this count Stroganoff was a proof. For more than three years he was defirous of making the tour of Europe ; but it was in vain that he follicited the confent of the emprefs ; who always gave him for anfwer, that fhe could not difpenfe with him ; and he remained at home.

N 3

named it, the secret inquisition chancery, a persecuting court that shunned the light, in which every cruelty of indefinite accusation, and an examination without judicial forms prevailed, and which perpetrated so many horrors under the reign of the suspicious and timid Elizabeth. Alexey Michailovitch, the father of Peter the great, was the institutor of this tyrannical tribunal, under the name of the secret committee, which was busied in judging or rather in condemning all such as were accused of high treason, in other words, whoever was displeasing to the prince or his informers. Persons of all ranks and sexes were liable to be arrested upon the slightest suspicions, and tortured in the most dreadful manner. There was a by-word; " Slovo i delo, " words and deeds ;" which if any one only pronounced against another, was sufficient cause for the latter to be immediately apprehended, and sent to the secret committee.

But it ought to be noticed how Peter III. came to utter these two declarations, dictated by the most enlightened notions of justice, and the most generous confidence. It should be explained how it happened, that in the conduct of this prince was to be seen such an extraordinary mixture of foresight and forgetfulness, of dignity and weakness. His defects, his vices, were the

7

unhappy

unhappy and neceſſary effect of his education; his worthy actions might charitably be ſuppoſed to proceed from the noble ambition of doing good: but this ambition was often in need of being rouſed.

The tzar had, in quality of his general aid-de-camp, an intimate friend, a young Ukrainer, named Gudovitch *, of whom we have before made mention, and who, of all his courtiers, was the only one that loved him ſincerely. It was Gudovitch, who, when Peter was on the point of coming to the throne, induced him to follow the advice of the old prince Trubetſkoï, rather than implicitly to rely on that of Panin; it was he likewiſe who prompted him to all thoſe prudent and dignified meaſures which ſignalized the firſt days of his reign. But the emperor, ſurrounded by his corrupters, ſoon fell back into his indolence, and more than ever abandoned himſelf to his cuſtomary habits. Shut up for ſeveral days ſucceſſively with his miſtreſs and ſome of his table-companions, he was in a ſtate of almoſt continual intoxication, when Gudovitch preſented himſelf before him, and, with a countenance of ſtudied ſeverity, ſaid to him: " Peter Feodoro- " vitch, I now plainly perceive that you prefer

* The ſame whom the tzar, while only grand duke, would have made hetman of the Koſaks, in the room of Cyril Razumoffſky.

" to

" to us the enemies of your fame. You are
" irrecoverably subservient to them ; you ac-
" knowledge them to have had good reason for
" saying that you were more addicted to low and
" degrading pleasures, than fit to govern an em-
" pire. Is it thus that you emulate your vigilant
" and laborious grandsire, that Peter the great
" whom you have so often swore to take for your
" model ? Is it thus that you persevere in the
" wise and noble conduct, by which, at your ac-
" cession to the throne, you merited the love and
" the admiration of your people ? But that love,
" that admiration, are already forgotten. They
" are succeeded by discontent and murmurs.
" Petersburg is anxiously inquiring whether the
" tzar has ceased to live within its walls ? The
" whole empire begins to fear that it has che-
" rished only vain expectations of receiving laws
" that shall revive its vigour and increase its
" glory. The malevolent are alone triumphant ;
" and soon will the intrigues, the cabals, which
" the first moments of your reign had reduced
" to silence, again raise their heads with re-
" doubled insolence. Shake off then this dif-
" graceful lethargy, my tzar ! hasten to shew and
" to prove, by some resplendent act of virtue,
" that you are worthy of realising those hopes that
" have been formed and cherished of you."

Peter

Peter liftened to this difcourfe with a mixture of confternation and fhame ; and when Gudovitch had left off fpeaking, he afked what he would have him to do to compenfate the empire for the days he had been fpending in riot. Gudovitch inftantly prefented him the two declarations that had been put into his hands by the grand chancellor Vorontzoff—one for reftoring the nobility to their rights, and the other for abolifhing the fecret committee. Peter took thefe papers without ftaying to confider of them, and putting them under his arm, went and read them to the fenate.

All thofe who were apprized of the contents of thefe new declarations made their difcontentment give place to joy, and fondly imagined that the emperor had been folely employed, during his late retreat, in framing thefe wife and falutary laws.

Peter III. undertook alfo to correct the numerous abufes that had crept into the adminiftration of juftice, and to eftablifh fome forms of jurifprudence more prompt in deciding, and lefs favourable to the arts of chicane ; but as an alteration attended with fo many difficulties was not the work of a day, it was neceffary for him to begin by gaining a thorough knowledge of the

courts,

courts, and a clofe inveftigation of their practice. He repaired to the fenate at an inftant when he was not expected; and finding it nearly deferted, he fent for the fenators, and reprefented to them with fharpnefs, but with dignity, how fenfible he was of their negligence *.

Commerce, the fcienees, the arts, were equally the objects of attention to the new tzar. In Ruffia almoft every department of the adminiftration is confided to a certain number of perfons, who form a board, to which is given the title of College: thus it is faid, the College of Commerce, the College of Juftice, the College of War, the College of Foreign Affairs, and the like. Peter III. frequently vifited thefe colleges; he affifted at their deliberations; he even fummoned them together; and though he might not enlighten them by his fagacity, he at leaft animated them by his encouragements.

He feemed to have it at heart to induce the people to put confidence in him. But this was no eafy tafk, for the people by the fuggeftion of

* On a fimilar occafion, Peter I. behaved with fomewhat lefs moderation. He gave each of them a fhower of blows with his *doubine* — a ftaff that he always carried with him, and which in fize was not one of the fmalleft.

the

the popes *, knew that this prince preferred
lutheranifm to the orthodox greek religion, and
the Germans to the Ruffians.   Neverthelefs the
tzar, docile to the advice of his friend, and fe-
dulous to imitate the example of the king of
Pruffia, gave eafy audience to all who came,
received their petitions, and took the pains himfelf to fee that juftice was done them. His very
enemies, therefore, could not forbear to extol a
popularity that reminded them, in fome refpects,
of that of Peter the great.

Peter III. on his firft acceffion to the crown,
invited the foreign minifters to his audience, and
received their congratulations with dignity.
This noble and becoming behaviour, in entire
oppofition to the idea they had almoft all formed
of this prince, exceedingly furprifed them : but
what aftonifhed them ftill more was, that in a
fplendid repaft which he gave them, he was very
referved in his difcourfe, and drank with moderation †. In fhort, the Ruffians and foreigners vied
with each other in admiring a change which they

---

* All the parifh-priefts in Ruffia are called popes. The
pope of fuch a church, village, &c.

† His enemies, always faithful to their plan of calumny,
ftudioufly propagated, both within and without the empire,
the report that this prince was almoft perpetually in a ftate
of inebriety.

could

could fcarcely credit.   Even the court of Vienna
for fome time fecurely repofed in the intentions
of the new tzar.   Maria Therefa flattered herfelf that the death of Elizabeth would not totally
diffolve the alliance that fubfifted between the
two empires; but fhe was deceived in her expectations.

It was impoffible for Peter III. to diffemble;
and of all the fentiments he entertained, that
which he was leaft able to conceal was his enthufiafm for the king of Pruffia.   He fet at
liberty all the pruffian prifoners that were confined at Peterfburg, and admitted them to his
table.   One of them, whom he treated with the
greateft deference, was the count de Hordt, a
fwedifh officer, who had entered into the fervice
of Frederic, and whom Elizabeth had detained
three years in exile *.   The tzar took him into

* Count de Hordt, lieutenant-general of the pruffian
troops, was made prifoner by the Ruffians after the battle
of Cuftrin.   Elizabeth fent him into banifhment in revenge
for the treatment of a ruffian officer, whom the king of
Pruffia had caufed to be broke alive on the wheel, for forming a plot of revolt, and meditating to maffacre the garrifon of Cuftrin, where he was kept prifoner.   When Hordt
appeared before Peter III. and related to him, that, independently of the ill-treatment he had received in prifon, he
had been denied the ufe of books; Catharine, who was
prefent, exclaimed; " That was very barbarous."

                                                                his

his confidence, made him his friend, and the king of Pruſſia was almoſt always the topic of their converſation.

He but rarely invited the foreign miniſters to his court, excepting the pruſſian envoy and Mr. Keith, the britiſh ambaſſador; which rendered his coolneſs the more diſagreeable to the reſt. Peter had long kept up a cloſe correſpondence with Frederic, whom he addreſſed in his letters under no other ſtyle than his dear brother or his worthy maſter. He reminded him in one of them, that previous to his being elected grand duke, he had had the honour of ſerving in his army; and went ſo far as to pray him to grant him a higher rank.

The king of Pruſſia very dexterouſly took advantage of the friendſhip of the tzar. He gave him not immediately the rank he ſollicited, that he might increaſe his avidity for it: but after ſome time had elapſed, wrote him word, that he had appointed him major-general, not on account of his quality as a prince, but ſolely becauſe of the military ſkill he knew him to poſſeſs. This pretended favour filled Peter with joy. His faſcination for the king of Pruſſia became now more ſtrong. He cauſed the portrait of that monarch to be placed in his chamber,

ber *, and celebrated this inauguration, and the glory he had acquired in being admitted to a rank at Berlin, by a splendid repast, in which he forgot that temperance which he had for some time observed.

If Peter's infatuation for the king of Prussia had not been complete, he might have been corrected of it by some lessons he received from his own subjects. To mention but one. " Do " you know," said he one day to the hetman Razumoffsky, " do you know that, before I was " grand duke, I was lieutenant in the service of " the king of Prussia?"—" Well!" replied the kozak, " your majesty may now make the king " of Prussia a field-marshal."

The prussian ascendant was not only displeasing to the generality of the courtiers and to some of the foreign ministers, but the alterations introduced by the tzar did not meet with universal approbation. Some of them even created him

* It was a portrait which count Totleben had made a present of to the empress Elizabeth, who had dismissed it into an obscure corner of the palace; and during the whole of her reign nobody might keep a portrait of the king of Prussia. The grand duke alone had a miniature, which he wore on his finger in a ring, and which he took care to conceal when he was in the presence of his aunt.

a great

a great number of enemies, and evinced that if
he had sometimes good intentions, he was deficient in judgment, and especially in that energy
of character so necessary for the ruler of a nation.
Together with the wisest plans he often adopted
such as were useless, and others that were even
dangerous.   The desire of making improvements made him imprudently hazard premature
reformations.

Peter took the vast possessions of the church,
and made them into domains of the crown,
putting the clergy on yearly salaries, but forming
a very decent income, of 5000 down to 150
rubles.   It was, undoubtedly, just and beneficial
to diminish the wealth of the monks, and to attack
prejudices injurious to the state; but at the
commencement of a reign against which pre-
possessions had long been formed, in a nation sunk in superstition, and just beginning
to emerge from barbarism, was it expedient to
irritate a numerous class of men, who by their
situation had so much influence over the rest?
Was it expedient to take from the churches the
figures of the saints, which to the Russians are
the objects of profound veneration ? Was it
expedient to excite the sacred rage of the devo-
tees by banishing the archbishop of Novgorod,
who stood forth against this violation? Surely
not: and yet this was what Peter did; but he
found

found himself suddenly obliged to recal this prelate : and by this fresh instance of weakness he revived the hopes of his enemies, and 'did not pacify the offended popes. They spread a report from one end of the empire to the other, that the emperor had only feigned to embrace the greek communion to qualify himself for filling the throne, but that he was still a lutheran at heart, of which he was every day giving fresh proofs by shewing a profound contempt for the rites, the ceremonies, and the religion of the Russians.

To corroborate these reports, the people were reminded, that he had caused to be built, in his palace at Oranienbaum, a lutheran chapel, at the consecration whereof he himself had assisted, distributing with his own hands hymn-books among his holstein soldiers, though he had not deigned to set his foot in a greek church that was constructed about the same time. It was said that he had again insulted the saints, in naming two of his newly-constructed ships, the one after his uncle, the Prince George, and the other the Frederic, after the king of Prussia *.

* Catharine, who knew how to flatter the people, changed the names of these two ships. The one was called the St. Nicholas, the other the St. Alexander. Their holy patrons, however, did not save them from the Turks in the war of 1768 : they were both taken.

It

It was induſtriouſly propagated, that he never ſpoke but with diſdain of the ruſſian empire and only with reſpect of the Germans. All theſe reports, circulated with artifice, ſoon alienated from the prince thoſe hearts which the firſt days of his reign had won him.

While his adverſaries were thus eaſily rendering him ſo ſuſpected of the people, he himſelf was ſeemingly taking pains to offend the army. He was continually ſhewing preferences to the german ſoldiers over the ruſſian troops: He diſbanded the noble guards, who had formerly placed Elizabeth on the throne ; he deprived the horſe guards of the ſervice they performed at court, and ſubſtituted his holſtein guards in their place. He introduced the pruſſian exerciſe, which was undoubtedly better than that to which they had been accuſtomed, but which diſpleaſed becauſe it was ſtill to be learned ; he excited diſcontents in the regiments of Iſmaïloff and Préobajenſky, by ordering one part to leave St. Peterſburg, and march into Pomerania, to join the army he had deſtined to act againſt Denmark. He raiſed his uncle, prince George of Holſtein, an officer of but little experience, to the rank of generaliſſimo of the ruſſian armies, giving him at the ſame time the particular command of the horſe guards—a command which

had hitherto never belonged to any one but the
supreme head of the empire.   In short, he so
far prejudiced his troops against him, that the
most beneficial alteration occasioned a general
discontent.   It was even made a subject of
murmur, that he designed to distinguish the
regiments by different facings and collars *.—It
was said to be a german fashion, not proper for
Russia.

The king of Prussia, whom Peter III. informed, with scrupulous care, of all that he was
doing, frequently gave him advice.   His first
step was to dissuade him from the plans of hos-
tility he was meditating against Denmark, in
order to recover his dukedom of Holstein : but
seeing that he could not induce him to alter his
resolution, he advised him, previous to his
entering on the war, to go and be crowned at
Mosco, with all the customary pomp and ceremony, and not to set out on his march for the
army without taking with him the foreign ministers, and all the Russians whose fidelity he had
reason to suspect.   He also recommended him
not to begin too soon to touch the possessions of

* It has been falsely asserted that Peter III. wanted to
introduce in Russia the blue colour instead of green in the
clothing of the troops: he changed nothing but the trim-
mings and the facings of the dress of the infantry.

the

the church, and not to meddle with the drefs of the monks, as all thefe minute particulars are of the utmoft confequence in the eyes of a bigoted race.   In fhort, he ufed every argument to per-fuade him to keep up that deference and refpect which he owed to his fpoufe, and efpecially for his own fecurity *.

It is not to be doubted that Frederic, who was well acquainted with the character of Peter and that of Catharine, had long forefeen what happened afterwards. Accordingly, writing to his minifter to continue to live in intimacy with the tzar, he gives him orders to pay great at-tentions to the emprefs.

However, Peter unhappily thought it not neceffary to follow in all things the leffons of the monarch whom he ftyled his mafter. He in-fenfibly refumed his vicious habits; frequently

* Peter III. was fo remote from all miftruft, that he anfwered the king of Pruffia:—" In regard to the concern " you take in my fafety, I befeech you to give yourfelf no " uneafinefs. The foldiers call me their father; they fay " that they had rather be governed by a man than a wo-" man. I take my walks alone about the ftreets of Peterf-" burg; if any one defigned to do me harm, he would " have executed his purpofe long ago: but I am continually " doing good on all occafions that offer, and I truft in the " protection of God alone; with that I have nothing to " fear."

paffing the whole day in drinking and fmoaking amidft a company of bafe courtiers, who, for the moft part, were eagerly feeking his ruin, and perfidioufly applauding his fantaftical humours and his moft dangerous innovations.

His behaviour to his fpoufe was equally in—confiftent.   At the very moment when he was doing homage to the fuperiority of her mind, he would let flip fome plain intimations of the indignation his wrongs had infpired into his breaft. In the moft facred and pompous ceremonies of the ruffian church, fuch, for example, as the benediction of the waters *, he made her appear
adorned

* The greek church has fome fimilarity with the latin in point of ceremonies, but exceeds it, which is not faying a little, in fuperftitious rites.   Among others, for example, annually on the 6th of January, Twelfth-day, as it is called with us, a fingular feaft is folemnized, denominated by the Ruffians the bleffing of the waters.   For this ceremony at St. Peterfburg, a fort of wooden chapel or tabernacle, painted green and ftuck about with boughs of fir, is conftructed on the ice of the Neva, between the Admiralty and the imperial palace.   This little building is covered with a dome, refting on eight fmall columns, on which ftands the figure of John the baptift with the crofs in his hand, amidft bulrufhes; the infide of the edifice being decorated with paintings reprefenting the baptifm of Jefus, his transfiguration, and other tranfactions of his life.   From the centre of the dome is fufpended by a chain a monftrous large holy-ghoft
of

adorned with all the marks of imperial dignity, while he was content to follow her train as a

---

of wood over the aperture in the ice, round which are spread rich carpets. This little temple is entirely surrounded with palifadoes, which are alfo ornamented with fir-branches: the fpace within being likewife covered with carpets. A fort of gallery round the building communicates with a window of the palace, from which the imperial family come forth to attend the ceremony. (For feveral years paft the emprefs and her grandchildren only faw the folemnity from the windows of the palace.) The ceremony begins immediately when the regiments of guards have taken their ftation on the river. Then the archbifhop appears amid the found of church bells and the firing of the cannon of the fortrefs, and proceeds along the carpets, attended by his train of bifhops and other ecclefiaftics, into this little church, where, ftanding at the hole in the ice, he dips his crucifix three times in the water, at the fame time repeating prayers, and concludes with a particular one to the great faint Nicholas; which done, the water is accounted bleffed. The prelate then fprinkles with it all the furrounding multitude, and the banners of all the regiments which are at that time in Peterfburg. The confecration ended, he retires; and now the people prefs in crowds to the hole in the ice, where they drink it with pious avidity: mothers, notwithftanding the cold, dip their naked babes in the ftream, and men and women pour it on their heads; every one holds it a duty to take home a veffel of the water, in order to purify their houfes, and for the cure of certain difeafes, for which it is affirmed to be a powerful fpecific. During which four popes, one at each corner of the aperture, chant a fort of litany for the occafion.

O 3   fimple

simple colonel, as if he intended to shew to his people, that she was born to reign, and he to obey. Even at court he would often leave her to ` execute the whole of the reprefentation ; while he, dreffed in the uniform of his regiment, refpectfully came and reprefented to her his officers, whom he called his comrades. Peter the great had formerly done the like with Catharine I. and his minifter Mentchikoff: but Peter the great knew how, whenever he had occafion to difplay the emperor, to employ means which Peter III. had not.

In the mean time the apparent favour of the emprefs was not of long duration. No fooner did the tzar think himfelf well fettled on the throne, than he no longer concealed his indifference, and fometimes even made her experience it in a very humiliating manner. At the time of the celebration of the peace that had juft been figned with the king of Pruffia, Peter, who, during the exhibition of the fireworks, was feated by the fide of Catharine, on feeing the countefs Vorontzoff, his miftrefs, pafs by, called to her, and made her fit down befide him: Catharine immediately retired, without any endeavour to detain her being vouchfafed on the part of her hufband.

The fame evening, at fupper, he drank the health of prince George of Holftein; at which all the company rofe up, excepting Catharine, who pretended to have got a hurt in her foot. Peter, irritated that the emprefs fhould affect to fail in the refpect which fhe owed to her uncle, launched at her an epithet, which, whether or not fhe deferved, the emperor ought to have fpared his fpoufe. Catharine was fo mortified that fhe could not refrain from weeping, and fpoke for fome time, in a low voice, of this affront to her chamberlain Stroganoff *, whom fhe had again the vexation to fee almoft immediately put under arreft. But her tears interefted the fpectators, as the harfhnefs of Peter excited their indignation.

It was by fcenes of this nature that the emprefs felt her hopes revive. She faw that fhe fhould foon get the better of the tzar, by oppofing to his flights and imprudent rudenefs, great circumfpection and the arts of addrefs. She now made it her fole employment to gain thofe hearts which he was lofing. Inftructed from her infancy in the arts of diffimulation, it was not difficult for her to affect, in the fight of the multitude, fentiments the moft foreign to her mind. The pupil of the philofophers now put on the air of a bigot : fhe feduloufly repaired

* Count Stroganoff paffed for one of the favourites of Catharine.

every

every day to the churches of Peterſburg, praying
with all the ſemblance of a ſincere and fervent
devotion, punctual in the moſt ſuperſtitious
practices of the greek religion, accoſting the
poor with benignity, and treating the popes with
reverence ; who failed not afterwards to go proclaiming her praiſes from houſe to houſe.

In the apartments of the palace, the way of
life purſued by this married couple was not leſs
different.   While Peter III. was ſhut up with
the counteſs Vorontzoff, Mr. Keith, ſome pruſſian officers, and others of his favourites ; while
he was ſo far forgetful of his rank as to live familiarly with buffoons, and to make them at
times ſit at table with him *, the empreſs kept
her court with ſuch a mixture of dignity and
affability as charmed all thoſe that approached
her ; ſhe particularly made it her ſtudy to attract
to her ſuch perſons as, by their reputation, their
courage, or their intrigues, might become uſeful
to her.

By theſe acts of imprudence the tzar diſpleaſed
not only the greater part of the Ruſſians, but al-

* One evening among others, after the play, at the
counteſs Nariſhkin's, he cauſed the comedians to ſit down
promiſcuouſly with the ladies and grandees of the court,
and ſeated beſide him a dancer, whom he called his little
wife.

moſt

moft all the agents from the foreign courts.
The minifter of Denmark never appeared before
him, but he was fure to meet with fome difagreeable behaviour; that of Auftria was always accofted with coolnefs; and even the ambaffador
of France *, who had enjoyed fuch high confideration during the late reign, was prefently
made to perceive that the intentions of Peter III.
were not more favourable towards the court of
Verfailles than to that of Vienna †.

Peter

* It was M. de Breteuil, who fucceeded M. de l'Hôpital.
When Peter concluded a treaty of peace and amity with
Frederic, there was certainly nothing blameable in his en-
thufiaftical attachment to one of the moft extraordinary characters of modern biftory; only in many difplays of this
attachment and admiration we do not difcern the autocratic
monarch of a mighty empire. If Peter, on one hand, put
a ftop to the flaughter and ravages of war, and in their
ftead reftored tranquillity and the bleffings of peace; yet,
on the other, he only began with more violence, and contrary to the advice of all experienced perfons, his long concerted hoftilities againft Denmark, which, according to his
plan, were to proceed to a real war of extermination, as it
was his determination to drive Frederic V. out of all his
european territories, and confine him to the dominion of
Tranquebar.

† Peter gave proofs of this on every occafion. When
the model of the new rubles was fhewn him for his approbation, perceiving that the artift had reprefented him with
a large wig of monftrous curls flowing down his fhoulders,
he

Peter III. had already come to the refolution of putting an end to hoftilities againft Frederic; and,

---

he exclaimed that he would not have fuch a head-drefs as that; it would make him look like the king of France. Supping one evening with the grand chancellor Vorontzoff, where the foreign minifters were invited, the tzar kept inceffantly talking of the king of Pruffia all fupper-time. He was acquainted with all his campaigns, even to the minuteft particulars. He harangued upon them with delight, always accompanying the encomiums he lavifhed on his hero with farcaftical and ironical invectives againft his enemies. He rofe from table after having drank greatly too much; then the punch that he took, and the tobacco that he fmoaked, completed his intoxication. A party at cards was propofed; the emperor accepted it, and was one of the firft who loft againft the french ambaffador. Then, feeing the fpanifh minifter, M. d'Almodovar, who had taken his place, he went up to the former and faid in his ear, alluding to the war againft the Englifh: " Spain will lofe."— " I think not," returned the Frenchman; " we are on her " fide, and fhe has fhewn herfelf formidable even when " alone."—The emperor, with a fhrug and a fneering fmile, only faid: " Ah! ah!"—" However, fir," anfwered the ambaffador gravely, " France and Spain are very eafy " on that fcore: and if they retain the alliance of your " majefty, they will be equally fo in regard to the war on " the Continent and with Germany."—Peter paufed for a moment, and then anfwered in a high tone of voice: " I " will have peace."—" We wifh for it as much as your " majefty," replied the ambaffador; " but we would have " it and, being of a character little fitted to wait the slow produce of a joint negotiation, gave way to his ardent desires for peace, and to the sentiments of that extravagant admiration which he had conceived for the king of Pruſſia. A ſuſpenſion of hoſtilities was concluded between them on the 16th of March; and it was followed not long after * by a treaty of peace and alliance. Nothing was ſtipulated by the tzar in favour of his former confederates, whom he entirely abandoned. He even agreed to join his troops to thoſe of the king of Pruſſia to act againſt them. In a little time a ruſſian army was ſeen in conjunction with one of Pruſſia, to drive out of Sileſia thoſe Auſtrians who had been a few months before brought into that province by the ruſſian arms.

This was a miraculous revolution. Fortune, who had ſo long abandoned the king of Pruſſia to his genius, after having perſecuted him for near five years, and overpowered him with the

---

" it ſafe, honourable, and in concert with our allies."—
" Juſt as you pleaſe," exclaimed the tzar: " for me, I
" will have peace: do afterwards as you think proper."
This anecdote was related by M. de Breteuil himſelf; but
it does not prove, it ſhould ſeem, that the tzar was quite ſo
drunk as that miniſter pretended.

* May the 5th.

whole

whole weight of her anger, at length made amends by a sudden turn, and did for him, at one stroke, the only thing by which he could possibly be saved.

Sweden, who after she recovered her liberty, lost her political importance, and for a long time acted entirely under the direction of russian councils, followed, on this, as on other occasions, the example of the court of Petersburg, and signed a treaty of peace with the king of Prussia on the 22d of May.

In order to account for whatever was not the result of mere personal character in this extraordinary revolution of politics in Russia, it will be necessary to remind the reader, that the tzar Peter the Third was duke of Holstein; and that the dukes of Holstein had pretensions to the duchy of Slefwick. These pretensions were compromised by a treaty in 1732. But as the cession made by the house of Holstein in this treaty was the effect of necessity, it had been always apprehended that she would make use of the first safe opportunity of reclaiming her ancient rights. The tzar seized eagerly on the great one, which the possession of the whole russian power afforded him, and he resolved to enter into an immediate war for this object, to which his predilection for his native country gave in his eyes a far greater importance

portance than to all the conquefts of his predeceffor. As long as this war with the king of
Pruffia fubfifted, it was impoffible that his defigns againft Denmark could be profecuted with
any hope of fuccefs. Wholly indifferent therefore to all others, and paffionately fond of this
object, as foon as he came to the throne, without any difpute or negotiation, he offered the
king of Pruffia, in his great diftrèfs, every thing
he could have hoped from a feries of victories,
and whilft he joined his arms to thofe of that
monarch in Silefia, he caufed an army to march
towards Holftein.

Accordingly, fome few days afterwards, he
difpatched his orders to general count Chernicheff, who commanded the 30,000 ruffian auxiliaries in the auftrian army, which had taken up
their winter-quarters in Moravia, to march
them into Poland through Silefia. A fecond
meffenger followed clofe at the heels of the
former, with orders to the fame general to act
with his troops in concert with thofe of the
king of Pruffia, and to conform in all things to
the pleafure of that monarch. The tzar did
not even deign to communicate thefe meafures
either to the courts of Vienna and Verfailles, nor
to the minifters from thofe courts, who were then
refident at Peterfburg. The firft intimation they
had of them was through the gazettes.

Some

Some time afterwards, the ruffian ambaffador at Vienna declared to prince Kaunitz, " that the " tzar, finding the method of a congrefs too " tardy, had preferred a direct negotiation with " the king of Pruffia ; that he was on the eve of " making a peace with that monarch ; that he " advifed the court of Vienna to imitate his ex- " ample ; and that it would be aftonifhing if it " fhould take in ill part what he had done, fince " the war of Germany was not only foreign to " him, and prejudicial to himfelf, but burden- " fome to his people."

This declaration was immediately followed up by the treaty which he concluded May 5, 1762 : and was dictated by the baron de Goltz, fent by the king of Pruffia to St. Peterfburg in quality of minifter plenipotentiary, and Mr. Keith, the englifh ambaffador.

Peter III. caufed the peace to be celebrated with the greateft magnificence. The rejoicings lafted feveral days ; he himfelf was prefent at them, dreffed in a pruffian uniform, decorated with the order of the black eagle which had been fent him by Frederic : and as if he had been re- folved to feize the opportunity afforded by thefe feftivities, for inflicting a greater infult on Auftria, he caufed the ambaffador * from Maria Therefa

* The count de Merci, who was afterwards ambaffador in France.

to

to be invited; but that minister indignantly rejected the invitation.

During all the time that these entertainments
lasted, scarcely a day passed that Peter did
not finish by drinking to excess, and his excesses
were always followed by some dangerous in-
discretion. One evening, according to custom,
he turned the conversation on Frederic; then,
fixing the eyes of the councillor of state Volkoff,
he suddenly exclaimed: " You must agree that
" he is a magician, a sorcerer, that king of
" Pruffia! He knew all our plans for the
" campaign, as soon as we had resolved on
" them." Volkoff reddened with embarrassment.
Peter said to him, " Why that embarrassment?
" you have no longer any need to fear Siberia.
" Is it not true, that, notwithstanding the dread
" you had of it, you communicated to me all the
" plans and projects that were resolved on in the
" council, and that I sent them off to his majesty
" the king*?"

Towards the termination of the rejoicings
that were made for celebrating the peace between
Ruffia and Pruffia, the tzar, who guessed how
much the ambassador of Vienna must be incensed, and doubtless was inclined more deeply

* It was thus he styled Frederic, II. unless when he
called him his preceptor, his friend, his brother.

to affront him, fent him word, " that, fince the
" emprefs-queen alone threw obftacles in the
" way of a general pacification, from a fpirit of
" unbounded ambition, and the unjuft defire of
" recovering Silefia and the county of Glatz, fo
" folemnly ceded to Pruffia, he had refolved to
" fend 20,000 men more into Germany, in order
" to force Maria Therefa to relinquifh her ille-
" gitimate pretenfions."

Every thing feemed to announce that this
would not end in an empty menace. The king
of Pruffia already began to flatter himfelf that
frefh fuccours would foon be added to the
Ruffians, who were marching under his banners ;
and fuch, in fact, were the intentions of the tzar.
But a fudden cataftrophe fruftrated the expectations of Frederic, and wrought a change in the
court of Ruffia.

In the midft of thefe warlike preparations,
of thefe reformations undertaken, but feldom
effected, and of thefe ufelefs feftivities, Peter III.
was not unmindful of the countefs Vorontzoff;
he allowed her, on the contrary, daily to gain
over him additional influence. This young
woman, not fhrewd, but ftupidly proud, and directed by an ambitious and crafty father, found
means to induce the tzar, one while by flattering,
at another by fcolding, and fometimes by carrying

ing her frowardnefs fo far as to dare to beat him,
to renew the promife he had made, while yet only
grand duke, that he would marry her, and place
her in the room of Catharine on the throne of
Ruffia.

Proud of this hope, fhe had the imprudence to
boaft of it, and this imprudence brought on her
ruin.   While her father and fome of the courtiers
who were devoted to him, were labouring at
paving her way to the throne, the jealoufies without number that her prefent influence and her
apparently approaching grandeur had created,
the enemies of the tzar and the partifans of the
emprefs, were all ftriving, as if by confent, to
find means for excluding her from it.

Peter III. not a whit lefs indifcreet than the
countefs Vorontzoff, feemed to authorife by his
conduct the reports that fhe fpread, and he even
no longer feemed to take any pains to conceal his
intention to repudiate Catharine, and to declare
the illegitimacy of Paul Petrovitch.   However,
he had refolved to cover this act of defpotifm
with an appearance of juftice; fondly imagining,
that, on publifhing to the world the proofs of
the infidelities of Catharine, his conduct would
meet the approbation of all his fubjects and the
reft of Europe.

VOL. I.   P   The

The countefs Vorontzoff, informed by the aged fenator her father of the firft amours of the emprefs with Soltikoff, had long fince taken care that the tzar fhould have no reafon to complain that fhe kept the fecret from him: fhe apprized him of it; and this it was that prevailed on the prince to refolve on declaring the illegitimacy and the exheridation of his fon. In confequence of this determination, he recalled Soltikoff from Hamburgh, where he had conftantly refided fince Elizabeth had appointed him her minifter. He loaded him with careffes and benefits, and put every ftratagem in practice to draw from him the authentic avowal of the criminal commerce he had formerly held with Catharine. It was vifible to all the court, that Soltikoff, incited by the hope of glorious rewards, or intimidated by the dread of ferious chaftifements, would do whatever the tzar defired, and the tzar himfelf was not deceived in his expectations that his worthy chamberlain would favour his inclinations. He was now only reftrained by the difficulty in the choice of a fucceffor.

Although this prince lived openly with the countefs Vorontzoff, though he held frequent affignations with a handfome ftage-dancer of Peterfburg, though he gave reafon to think that he he had various adventures of gallantry, he was not perhaps therefore the fitter for obtaining an heir. By an operation in a small degree similar to that of the judaical rite, which he had undergone in the first years of his marriage, he was freed from an obstacle without procuring greater means. Nature had inspired him with an ardent passion for women; his desires were impetuous, but all seemed to prove that his efforts were doomed to be fruitless. Thinking himself well assured of his misfortune, and, wishing notwithstanding to raise some one to the place of Paul Petrovitch, he conceived all at once a very singular project. He determined to adopt prince Ivan, who had been dethroned by Elizabeth, to declare him his successor, and to unite him in marriage with the young princess of Holstein-Beck, who was then at St. Petersburg, and whom he cherished as his daughter.

Peter III. then with a very few attendants, went privately to the fortress of Schluffelburg, in the design of making a visit to Ivan*, without discovering

---

* It has already been seen that Ivan III. was still in his cradle when the revolution that placed Elizabeth on the throne, in 1741, occasioned him to be shut up, with the regent Anne, his mother and all his family, in the fortress of Schluffelburg. In the first moments of that revolution, the soldiers who entered the apartment of the

young

discovering himself to him, in order that he might form a judgment whether he was worthy of the elevated station he intended to give him.

young emperor found him asleep, and waited respectfully till he should awake, to carry him to Elizabeth. That princess took him up in her arms and fondly caressed him; when, perceiving him to smile at the shouts of "Hourra Eliza-veta!" which resounded from the gates of the palace, she could not restrain her pity, saying: "Unhappy child! thou knowest not, alas! that they are the cries of joy of those that hurl thee from the throne!" From Schluffelburg Ivan was transported, together with his family, to the fortress of Riga, where they remained 18 months. From Riga they were conveyed to Dunamunde, and afterwards to Oranienburg, a town built by Mentchikoff, in the cold province of Voronetch. There Ivan was separated from his family, who were transported to Kolmogor. A monk who had access to the prison where Ivan was detained, carried him off from Oranienburg, in the design to conduct him to Germany: but he was arrested at Smolensk. Ivan was then shut up in a monastery, situate in the Valdaï, not far from the road that leads from St. Petersburg to Mosco. The empress Elizabeth having a desire to see him, in 1756, caused him to be brought back to Schluffelburg, where he had been put immediately on his dethronement. He was led very secretly to St. Petersburg, in the house of Peter Schuvaloff, where Elizabeth had a pretty long conversation with him, but without making herself known to him. Ivan was then about 16: he was of a good height, of an interesting figure, with fine hair, and a voice of much sweetness. Elizabeth shed many tears as she talked with him: but that did not save Ivan from being led back to his dismal dungeon, where Peter III. six years after went to see him.

The

The emperor, on this expedition, was only attended by count Leof Alexandrevitch Narish-kin, his grand-ecuyer, baron Ungern-Sternberg, one of his general aides-de-camp, baron Korff, master of the police at St. Petersburg, and the counsellor of state Volkoff. He was himself furnished with an order signed in his own hand, in which he enjoined the commandant to give the bearers free leave to walk about the whole for-tress, without even excepting the place where Ivan was confined, and to leave them to converse alone with that prince. Peter moreover took care to conceal the ensigns of his dignity, and to recom-mend Leof Narishkin, who was tall and of a portly figure, to act so as that he should be taken for the emperor. But Ivan was not thus de-ceived. After having contemplated for some time the strangers that entered his cell, he threw himself all at once at the feet of the tzar. " Tzar!" said he, " you are the master here. " I shall not importune you by a long petition; " but mitigate the severity of my lot. I have " been languishing for a number of years in this " gloomy dungeon. The only favour I entreat " you to grant, is, that I may be permitted, " from time to time, to breathe a freer air." Peter was extremely affected at these words: " Rise, prince!" said he to Ivan; and, gently

flapping

flapping his shoulder; " be under no uneasiness
" for the future.　I will employ all the means in
" my power to render your situation more tole-
" rable.—But tell me, prince, have you any re-
" collection of the misfortunes you have ex-
" perienced from your earlier youth ?" —" I
" have scarcely any idea of those that befell
" my infancy," replied Ivan; " but, from the
" moment that I began to feel my misery, I
" have never ceased from mingling my tears
" with those of my father and my mother, who
" were miserable solely because of me: and my
" greatest distress proceeds from the thoughts of
" the ill treatment they received, as we were
" transported from one fortress to another." —
" Hah ! whence came that ill treatment ?" interrogated the tzar. " From the officers who
" conducted us, and who were almost always the
" most inhuman of mankind," returned Ivan.
" Do you recollect the names of those officers ?"
said Peter.—" Alas !" replied the young prince,
" we were not very curious to learn them.
" We were content to return thanks to heaven
" on our bended knees, when these monsters
" were relieved by officers of a less savage dispo-
" sition."—" What !" said the emperor, " you
" never fell into the hands of such as had any
" humanity ?" — " Only one deserved to be dis-
　　　　　　　　　　　　" tinguished

"tinguished from that pack of tigers," answered Ivan. "He gained our esteem, and we lamented the loss of him. His good nature, his generous attentions will never depart from my remembrance."—"And you know not the name of that worthy man?" eagerly asked the tzar.—"Oh, as to him, I remember him very well," replied Ivan: "he was called Korff."

This same baron Korff, as we have already seen, was one of those who accompanied Peter. He melted into tears as he heard these particulars; and the tzar, who was no less affected than him, took him by the arm, and said in a broken voice: "Baron, you see how a good action is never lost!"

That he might have time to recover from his emotion, Peter went out with Korff, Narishkin, and Volkoff, leaving baron Ungern-Sternberg alone with Ivan. "How then did you come hither, prince?" said Ungern-Sternberg. "Who," returned Ivan, "can be guarded and secured against razboïniks*? One day, an order from I know not who was brought to the prison where I was with my parents. The razboïniks fell upon my family, and tore me from the only persons I knew in the world, and

* Robbers.

P 4

" w

" who alone had gained my affection and my con-
" fidence : I mean my father and my mother, and
" my brothers and my fisters. Oh how I did cry!
" and how they themfelves, if they are yet alive,
" muft lament the death of their fon and their
" brother !"——" What do you think will be the
" lot of our new emperor ?" afked the baron.
" If I may judge from my idea of the Ruffians,
" it will not be more happy than mine. My
" father and my mother have often repeated to
" me, that foreign princes will always be hated
" and dethroned by the treacherous and haughty
" Ruffians."

The tzar now re-entered, with Narifhkin,
Korff, Volkoff, and accompanied this time by
the commandant, to whom he faid, in the prefence
of Ivan : " I order you to give the prince from
" this moment, all the fuccours he fhall afk, and
" to allow him at all times to walk and divert
" himfelf within the precincts of the fortrefs. I
" will fend you written orders containing more
" particulars, by which you are henceforward to
" regulate your conduct in regard to his facred
" perfon."

On coming out of Ivan's chamber, the emperor went over the infide of the fortrefs*; and,
                                        after

* The fortrefs of Schluffelburg, while in the poffeffion of
the Swedes called Nœteborg, occupies a fmall ifland, fituate
                                        juft

after having examined a fpot that feemed to him
proper for the conftruction of an edifice for con-
veniently lodging the prifoner, he gave orders to
the commandant to fet the proper workmen
about it, and added: " Let it run in a ftraight line
" from one wall to the other of this angle of the
" fort, fo as to form nine rooms in front, and
" the reft of the fpace, to the extremity of the
" angle; may be made into a little garden,
" with which he may amufe himfelf in the
" air, and find fome alleviation of the feverity
" of his confinement. When the building fhall
" be finifhed, I will come myfelf and put the
" prince in poffeffion."

Probably the tzar only fpoke in this manner to
the commandant of Schluffelburg as a blind, to
prevent him from furmifing his real intentions;
for otherwife what need had he to give orders
for the conftruction of a new prifon for him
to whom he meant to give the throne? Befides,
this prifon had a quite different object. It is not

---

juft where the Neva flows out of the lake Ladoga, in 59° 50'
N. L. It is in the antique form, with high walls and vaulted
ramparts, and being ufed for the confinement of ftate-prifoners, is only inhabited by the garrifon. Schluffel in german fignifies *a key*. Its prefent name was given it by Peter I.
as being the key to his new city.

to

to be doubted that it was Catharine for whom it was defigned by her hufband *.

Before he quitted Schluffelburg, Peter went once more into the prince's dungeon; after this, he returned to St. Peterfburg; where no one entertained a fufpicion of the extraordinary interview he had juft had, and much lefs of what he was meditating in favour of Ivan.

When the prince of Holftein, the emperor's uncle, was informed of the vifit this monarch had made to Ivan, he advifed him to fend that unfortunate prince into Germany, together with duke Anthony of Brunfwic, his father, and the reft of the family. Peter, to avoid raifing any fufpicion of his plan in the mind of his uncle, pretended to approve his advice, but for the prefent he refted fatisfied with caufing Ivan

* Though it is currently taken for granted, that it was the emperor's plan to caufe his wife to be arrefted, and to be fhut up in Schluffelburg, yet it is very far from being fatiffactorily made out, even by the evidence arifing from this new houfe erected in the fortrefs, defigned, it is faid, for the emprefs. It is thought by numbers of people, that it was really intended for prince Ivan, inftead of the difmal and inconvenient hole in which he was lodged. Peter, by having him removed to Kexholm, brought him more within his reach, in order perhaps to produce him whenever occafion might offer. This may eafily be fuppofed an after-thought.
to

to be conveyed to the fortress of Kexholm, built on a little isle in the Ladoga lake, and much nearer to the residence than Schlusselburg. It is impossible on this occasion to forbear remarking that a sort of adverse fate seemed every where to pursue the unfortunate Ivan; for, as he was rowed from Schlusselburg, to get on board the galleot that was to convey him to Kexholm, the skiff in which he was, narrowly escaped being lost, by one of the tempests that suddenly rise in summer, and dangerously agitate that stormy, and, in many places, unfathomable lake *.

In the mean time the indiscretions of the tzar revived from day to day the hopes of Catharine; and the designs he had formed against her, a part whereof were but too well known, emboldened

* To secure the barks coming with goods from the Volkoff acrofs the Ladoga, from the dangerous storms and whirlpools of this boisterous lake, was the view of Peter I. in digging the Ladoga canal; and this design is fully attained. This canal, which Peter began in 1719, and which the emprefs Anne finished by count Munich in 1730, follows, through a morafs, the southern shore of the Ladoga, and, 10 fathom broad, and from 7 to 10 feet deep, extends its course of 104 verfts, to Schlusselburg, where it enters the left bank of the Neva. The Ladoga receives the waters of the rivers Rœbona, Lava, Schaldica, Nafia, and Lipka, to which the only outlet is the Neva.

her

her to run all hazards in order to prevent them. Difmiffed to Peterhof, and lodged in one of the apartments the moft retired, and leaft apparent of the palace, fhe paffed her days in meditating the project for precipitating her hufband from the throne, and her evenings in the company of a peculiar intimate, whom fhe had made the moft intrepid of the confpirators.

The power of the tzars, though abfolute and uncontrollable in its exercife, is extremely weak in its foundation. There is not perhaps in Europe a government which depends fo much on the good-will and affection of thofe that are governed, and which requires a greater degree of vigilance and a fteadier hand. The regular fucceffion which has been fo often broken, and the great change of manners, which in lefs than a century has been introduced, have left in Ruffia a weaknefs amidft all the appearance of ftrength, and a great facility to fudden and dangerous revolutions.

Peter III. paid little attention to thofe difficulties, which to him were the greater, as he was a foreigner born. They were augmented by the fuperior and invidious regard he feemed to pay to foreign interefts, and foreign perfons.

Since

Since the removal of count Poniatofsky,
though the emprefs had the addrefs to appear, in
the eyes of the moft attentive of the courtiers,
faithful to her attachment to him, yet in the
intimacy of this friend fhe found the means of
compenfating his abfence.   Thus, to encourage
the miftake of her prying obfervers, fhe had
the twofold motive of interefting them in behalf
of a difappointed paffion, and of averting their
looks from her obfcurer indulgences.   Her very
friends were deceived.   M. de Breteuil, who
imagined himfelf a perfon of great difcernment,
and that he was in the entire confidence of
Catharine, thought her fo conftant to Poniatoffky, that he degraded his quality of ambaffador
fo far as to deliver into her hand all the letters
from the count, and to forward her anfwers.
Princefs Dafhkoff herfelf was ignorant that fhe
had any other love than that of ftudy and of
Poniatofsky; and fhe had long been plotting
in concert with Orloff, without once fufpecting
that Orloff was even known to the emprefs.
In fhort, the only perfon that was in the fecret,
and was the manager of the piece, was one of
her women, named Catharine Ivanovna, the moft
ingenious of confidantes, and the leaft fcrupulous
of duennas.   She behaved with fo much addrefs,
that thofe whom fhe prefented to Catharine

3   enjoyed

enjoyed almoſt always the favours of that princeſs, without knowing who ſhe was *.

Gregory Orloff poſſeſſed neither the advantages of birth nor thoſe of education ; but he had received from nature what are often found more uſeful, courage and beauty. He had a poſt in the artillery, while his two brothers were only common ſoldiers in the regiments of guards†. Count Peter Schuvaloff, grand maſter of the artillery, a vain and pompous man, was deſirous of having the handſomeſt of his officers for aide-de-camp, and he ſelected Gregory Orloff. He had alſo for his miſtreſs one of the moſt illuſ-

* M. de Rulhiere tells us it was by chance that "Orloff deſcried, in the pomp of a public ceremony, the "miſtreſs whom he adored." But it is very difficult to believe that the aide-de-camp of count Peter Schuvaloff ſhould not know the grand ducheſs, as Peter Schuvaloff went frequently to court, and as in Ruſſia an aide-de-camp always attends his general.

† Alexius and Vladimir. The Orloffs were five brothers : Gregory, the favourite; Alexius, ſince become admiral, who, in the war againſt the Turks, in 1768, commanded the Ruſſian fleet in the Archipelago, was latterly at Moſco, led thither on account of ſome affairs of trade, having large tanneries on his eſtate, but was driven out of that capital by an order from Paul Petrovitch ; Vladimir, made ſenator after the revolution ; Feodor, chamberlain ; and Ivan, likewiſe chamberlain, but who came very rarely to court.

trious

trious and the handsomeft women of the court,
the princefs Kourakin, who was not long in
giving the aide-de-camp to underftand that fhe
preferred him to his general. But unfortunately
the general, who furprifed them together, forbad Orloff any more to appear in his prefence,
and threatened to exert all his intereft to get him
banifhed to Siberia. This adventure made a
noife : it was for a time the fubject of converfation both in town and country ; and the ftory
found its way even into the retreat in which Catharine was forced to do penance. Curiofity,
pity perhaps, led her to wifh for an acquaintance
with the young officer whofe difafter was the
topic of public difcourfe. Ivanovna, with the
cuftomary precautions, procured her a fight of
him ; and Orloff, at firft unable to guefs who
the fair-one might be that took fuch concern in
his lot, found her to poffefs more charms and a
fonder affection than the princefs Kourakin.
This firft and myfterious converfation was fucceeded by feveral interviews, in which Catharine
was only obliging ; but when fhe thought herfelf
well affured of the boldnefs and the difcretion of
her new acquaintance, fhe unveiled to him her
ambitious defigns. Orloff now entered into a
confpiracy with her, in which he fhortly after
engaged his brothers, his companion Bibikoff,
                                    lieutenant

lieutenant Paſſik, with other officers ; by means of whom he won over ſome companies of guards, but without imparting to them his real deſign.

Catharine was as yet but grand ducheſs when her connection with Orloff began ; and her correſpondence with him was not the only one that ſhe carried on with no leſs art than ſucceſs. Several other officers, ſeveral courtiers even participated in her favours ; but as ſhe did not expect to find in them the devotedneſs and the genius that was neceſſary to her, ſhe was ſatisfied with making them her friends, and never diſcloſed her ſecret to them. Lieutenant-general Villebois* was one of thoſe whom that princeſs had diſtinguiſhed; and when he obtained the command of the artillery, on the death of the general that had diſplaced Orloff, ſhe induced him to give the latter the place of captain-treaſurer of his corps. Villebois did as he was requeſted by Catharine, without entertaining the ſmalleſt ſuſpicion that he was ſerving a rival preferred to himſelf.

Being ſeated on the throne, Catharine continued not leſs the inviſible and powerful inſtigatrix of the faction of the great, the remainder of thoſe conſpirators at the head of whom Beſ-

* An officer of conſiderable merit, ſon of a french refugee.

tucheff

tucheff and the Schuvaloffs had fucceffively appeared, and whereof the hetman Kurilli Razumoffſky, the prince Volkonſky, nephew of the exiled Beſtucheff, and major-general of the guards, together with count Panin, were the moſt powerful fupports.

In a word, ſhe had been able to form a third confpiracy, contrived by the young princeſs Daſhkoff *, who always appeared, if not the moſt formidable, at leaſt the moſt active and impetuous. The accomplices in theſe three factions acted, moreover, without the knowledge of each other; and Catharine, who was the animating ſpirit of them all, feemed to have no ſhare whatever in the plot.

Princeſs Daſhkoff, lately returned from Mofco, where her huſband had kept her in a kind of exile, was prevented from concurring with the aims of her relations, who were defirous of feeing her fupplant her fifter in the favour of the tzar. That fifter was more fuitable to the military taſte of Peter; and madame Daſhkoff would never be fatisfied with a lover addicted only to drinking and the fumes of tobacco. She then formed an intimate connection with Catha-

* Princeſs Daſhkoff was born in the year 1744; confequently this extraordinary woman was no more than 18 at the time of the revolution.

rine. They paſſed whole days together in the purſuits of literature and intrigue ; and when the empreſs was diſmiſſed to Peterhof, princeſs Daſhkoff remained at Peterſburg, in order to ſerve her the better. She kept up a correſpondence with the empreſs, in which ſhe gave her the account of all that was paſſing at the court or in the city, and the means which ſhe ought to employ for preventing the deſigns of the tzar.

The attachment which princeſs Daſhkoff had vowed to Catharine was not the ſole motive for exciting her zeal. She was principally jealous of the glorious elevation that awaited her ſiſter ; and neither the menaces of that ſiſter and of her father, nor the authority of the chancellor her uncle, in whoſe houſe ſhe had been brought up, were able to detach her from a party of which ſhe fondly made it her pride to be the prime mover. She had ſtudied the languages, and read many of the works of foreign authors, during her ſojourn at Moſco ; which augmented her natural vanity, and taught her to deſpiſe the ignorance of the nation to which ſhe belonged. In the hopes of arriving at the ſlippery honour of directing a conſpiracy, ſhe openly braved the reſentment of her family ; ſhe would have braved every danger, and even boldly looked death in the face.

Princefs Dafhkoff had for fome time kept about her a Piedmontefe named Odart, whom penury and the hopes of making his fortune had brought to St. Peterfburg, and who had confirmed the tafte of that lady for french literature, by making her acquainted with the beft writers of that nation. Odart was become the more valuable to the princefs, as like her, with an aptitude at witty conceits, he poffeffed a turn for intrigue. She was ever extolling a man to whom fhe thought herfelf indebted for her fuperiority; and fhe fpoke of him to the emprefs in fo advantageous a manner, as to induce that princefs to defire his attachment, and to give him the title of her private fecretary.

It was not long ere this artful and infinuating fecretary became one of the confidents, not in the delicate connections of Catharine, but in her ambitious defigns. A witnefs to the grievances of this princefs, and foreboding the humiliation that awaited her, he eafily perceived that there was no other way of efcape, both for the prefent and the future, than by the fall of the emperor. But how to accomplifh this fall? How dare to attempt it? Odart faw all the difficulties, all the dangers with which it was attended; but he alfo knew, that if punifhment and death were on one fide, honours and riches prefented them-

felves

felves on the other.   Riches were the only deities of Odart: he was not long in determining his choice.   He directly addreffed himfelf to princefs Dafhkoff; who, anticipating his bold and afpiring ideas, was elated to excefs at finding in a man, whom fhe efteemed for his talents, an accomplice in atchievements worthy of herfelf.   What flattering hopes now intoxicated the minds of thefe vain and conceited confpirators! What did they not promife themfelves, if they could but overthrow the fovereign of one of the greateft empires of the world? Odart expected that an immenfe fortune would be the reward of his fervices : the princefs imagined that the whole univerfe would be inceffantly talking of her, and that her glory would afcend far fuperior to hers on whofe head fhe fhould place the crown.

But the execution of fo great a project demanded more efficacious inftruments than vain imaginations and barren defires.   More was wanting than a woman of eighteen, and an adventurer whom nobody knew.   Accordingly, when Odart and madame Dafhkoff had fufficiently entertained themfelves with the magnificent recompences they hoped to obtain, they began to think of procuring foldiers, and money, which always propagates foldiers, and in Ruffia

more

more than elfewhere; and a chief, whofe name
and authority might command refpect; and efpecially a man who, accuftomed to direct courtiers,
to manage intrigues, was neither to be embarraffed
by obftacles, not difmayed by difappointments.
They then turned their eyes on the hetman
Cyril Razumofffky and count Nikita Ivanovitch
Panin.

The great influence the hetman * had enjoyed
during the reign of the emprefs Elizabeth, and
the familiarity of Peter III. which he had had
the art of preferving, ftill gave him confiderable
intereft at court, and his immenfe riches, which
enabled him to exercife continual liberalities
towards a multitude of neceffitous officers and
foldiers, fecured him a great number of friends
among the troops. He filled one of the firft
pofts in the empire. He had no efteem for
Catharine, of whofe talents he did not think
much, and whofe miftakes he had feen; he
knew the danger of attempting to dethrone the
tzar, but was true in his adherence to his former
party. When princefs Dafhkoff communicated
her defigns to the hetman, he applauded the

* It has been imagined by fome, that though the devout
Elizabeth had married the grand-veneur Alexey Razumofffky, brother of the hetman, the latter was neverthelefs
a lover of that emprefs.

Q 3   fcheme;

scheme; and, without seeming to take a direct part in the business, assured her that, in case of need, she might rely upon his concurrence. Therefore when Orloff came to him a few days after, in order to sound his disposition, he encouraged him to oppose the designs which the emperor was meditating against his consort, telling him, at the same time, that they who should defend that princess might depend upon his joining them. The hetman kept Orloff's secret as he had kept madame Dashkoff's; and happy in the contemplation of two new rising factions, he resolved in his mind to support them with all the power of his own.

Razumoffsky went yet farther. He assembled his friends on the spot; and without disclosing to them precisely the twofold plan with which he had been entrusted, informed them that he knew with certainty, that among the troops a plot was hatching to dethrone the tzar; and if they neglected for a moment to declare themselves its leaders, no other alternative would be left them than to submit to become the forced instruments of the soldiers, or probably their victims. They then asked him what he thought it necessary for them to do. " Join me at the instant the " conspiracy breaks out," answered the hetman; " and I will take care to assign to each of you " the

" the rank to which his birth, his fortune, and
" his talents, give him a right to aspire.   The
" blind intrepidity of some obscure conspirators
" is now meditating to make the first blow.
" Let us diligently watch the moment.   If they
" succeed, it is for our dexterity to reap the
" fruits of their success.   Do you feel yourselves
" heartily resolved to follow my example ?"
All swore they were ; and the meeting broke up
in expectation of the terrible event that flattered
either their hatred or their ambition.

Thus certified of the assent of Razumoffsky,
princess Dashkoff and Odart now made it their
business to bring over count Panin to their
party ; and Catharine earnestly recommended it
to them to let nothing escape them that might
conduce to that end.   She very well knew that if
the name and the presence of the hetman would
be of great weight in the first openings of the
revolt, the experience and the ability of Panin
were still more necessary for leading it to success.
It was he alone who, by the arts of soft insinua-
tion, could moderate the impetuous vanity of
the princess Dashkoff, excite, inflame the hatred
and revenge of Razumoffsky, direct the covetous
and servile ambition of Odart, and justify in
appearance the conspiracy by annexing to it the
name of the young Paul Petrovitch, his pupil.

Princess

Princess Dashkoff then commissioned Odart to
propose to Panin his uniting with them; and
Panin, prompted by a motive more dear than
that of serving the empress and the grand duke,
promised all that the princess desired.

All this did not yet suffice madame Dashkoff.
She made direct application to prince Volkonsky, major-general of the guards. Volkonsky, well taught in the arts of intrigue by his
kinsman Bestucheff, and the inheritor of his
hatred against Peter III.; Volkonsky, whose
ambition was waiting for a change in the government, and who flattered himself with having
shortly to act the principal part in the new
faction, was not more difficult than Panin and
Razumoffsky.

The archbishop of Novgorod was in like
manner brought over. They had made themselves sure of this prelate even before they dif-
closed their design. The emperor had just recalled him from exile, to which he had some
months before been condemned; but the prelate,
more irritated at the severity of the prince than
affected by his clemency, waited only for an
opportunity for signalizing his sacred fury. In-
ventive superstition furnished him with numerous
means. He knew the blind zeal of the Ruffians for whatever belongs to the orthodox
greek

greek religion; and the swarms of monks whom
he had at command continued, under pretence of
defending that religion, to disseminate in all hearts
their hatred towards the prince who imprudently
seemed to have declared himself its enemy.

The princess wanted also to secure a part of
the troops. She knew several of the officers;
these she went to see under pretence of a mere
visit of politeness, and repaired to the barracks.
There she was met by Orloff. The explanation
was not difficult to either. They immediately
agreed; and, still ignorant that Orloff was
known to Catharine, the princess Dashkoff
found in him more than an accomplice.

Having apparently gained over only Gregory
Orloff, the princess Dashkoff flattered herself that
she had also won, by his means, the two brothers
of that conspirator, in person not less handsome,
in temper not less bold than he, and of a bodily
strength and a brutality that rendered them formidable even to their friends. She added at
the same time to her party many other officers
or soldiers, whom Orloff had long been preparing for the rebellion; and when Odart
thought to make the empress acquainted with all
this success, that dissembling princess, whose
lover brought her accounts of all in their noc-
turnal interviews, was careful neither to unde-
ceive

ceive the secretary, nor affront the vanity of madame Dashkoff.

One alone of all the factious stood in no need of artful prepossession: it was that very Gleboff whom the tzar had raised from the lowest forms of chicane to the important place of procureur-general to the senate*.   The traitor, judging that his master would prove unable to resist the united attacks of such a host of foes as were plotting his destruction, and adding cruelty to ingratitude, resolved to contribute what he could to his ruin, in order to profit by the change it would produce.   He accordingly looked about for a band of conspirators with whom he might join; and having discovered that of Odart and princess Dashkoff, he went to them with the offer of his services.

The aim of all those who severally conspired against Peter III. was to dethrone him; but they were not disposed to set about it in the same manner.   Panin, Razumoffsky, Orloff, thought it best to begin by seizing on his person at Peterhof†, at the conclusion of one of those
orgies

* When, on his accession to the throne, this prince demanded the resignation of prince Schasuskoï.

† The imperial palace of Peterhof, situate on the shore of the Cronstadt gulf, is 25 versts from St. Petersburg,
8 versts

orgies which could not fail to take place on his
coming thither to celebrate the anniversary of
St. Peter and St. Paul. Panin, with some
others of the conspirators, had even been to
gain an accurate knowledge of his apartment, in
order the more easily to seize him on the fittest
occasion. Lieutenant Passick, the most ferocious, the most barbarous of his countrymen,
insisted on assassinating him with a poignard in
the midst of his court: and in spite of all that

---

8 versts below Strelna, and 8 versts above Oranienbaum.
Peter the great employed the architect Le Blond to build it,
and to direct the laying out of the gardens; and its deco-
rations have been increased by all the succeeding monarchs.
Here annually a grand festival is given in honour of the
patron saints of the imperial house, Peter and Paul. It
consists in masquerades, to which from 3000 to 4000 persons of both sexes repair from Petersburg, so that there is
scarcely a horse left in the town. At night the palace, with
all the gardens, walks, terraces, canals, cascades, and fountains, as well as the yachts that lie off the shore, are all
grandly illuminated; which, especially the vast cascade, roll-
ing its sheets of water over the lamps, have a surprisingly
brilliant effect. In some of the apartments are refreshments
of every kind, accessible to all. About ten in the evening
long tables are set out with a variety of choice dishes in
great abundance, at which as many as can find room pro-
miscuously take their places, and are sumptuously entertained; as each is satisfied, he retires, and others succeed;
for which purpose the tables are constantly replenished by
an uninterrupted succession of dishes.

Panin

Panin could do, by intreating and forbidding, he went, with one of his comrades, named Baſchkakoff, to lie in ambuſh two days ſucceſſively, waiting for this prince on one ſide of the ſmall wooden houſe inhabited by Peter while he was laying the foundations of Peterſburg : theſe two days Peter III. did not appear. But if the conſpirators differed about the means of dethroning the tzar, they were ſtill leſs agreed on the manner of ſupplying his place. Catharine aſpired to the ſole poſſeſſion of the ſupreme authority. Orloff and princeſs Daſhkoff ſupported this pretenſion. Panin, on the other hand, propoſed, that ſhe ſhould govern only under the name of regent; and that the title of emperor ſhould devolve on the young grand duke, Paul Petrovitch. The hetman Razumoffſky was of the ſame opinion.

At a long conference held by the principal conſpirators, in which theſe ſeveral propoſals were diſcuſſed, Panin had the courage to ſay to Catharine :—" I know, madam, what you " would have, and what you are able to do ; " but I know alſo where your ambition ſhould " ſtop. You have repeated it a hundred times, " while as yet grand ducheſs, that you were only " deſirous of the title of mother of the emperor. " Does that title at preſent ſeem too diminutive

" to

" to you? You would now remove your son
" from the throne of Ruffia; but what right
" have you to feat yourfelf upon it alone? Are
" you of the blood of the tzars? Are you even
" a native of the empire? Think you that this
" ancient and warlike nation will acknowledge
" for their fovereign a countefs of Anhalt?
" Think you that they will not be inceffantly
" plotting in favour of the defcendants of Peter
" the great, while one of them lies languifhing
" at the foot of the throne, and others continue
" to groan in dark and loathfome dungeons?
" Ah, madam, give up your pretenfions to what
" you can never obtain.   Think it your greateft
" happinefs to be able to efcape the extreme
" danger that preffes upon you; and that the
" only means of juftifying our violent under-
" taking, is to convince the world that your
" fon is, more than yourfelf, the object of your
" concern."

The confpirators, ftruck with the firmnefs
and propriety of this difcourfe, for a time remained mute.   Orloff fhuddered.   Catharine
herfelf kept a momentary filence.   At length,
turning to Panin: — " Count," faid fhe, " your
" arguments are full of force; but they are not
" fufficient to produce any alteration in my fen-
" timents.   I know the Ruffians, and you your-
" felf

" felf are fo well acquainted with them as to
" know, that, provided they are governed, they
" care but little about the origin of them by
" whom the government is adminiftered. This
" nation knows of nothing but obedience, even
" when the hand that rules it leans heavily on it.
" Mentchikoff, Biren, Munich, may ferve as
" proofs of this truth. But it is not thus that I
" defign to reign: far from it; I fhall act with
" lenity, with juftice, and in fuch manner as not
" to give the flighteft pretext to difcontent.
" But you, who tell me of murmurs and rebel-
" lions, do you forget that it is moftly under
" regencies that rebellions break out? Nay,
" fhould we ever have had a thought of that we
" have now been contriving, if Peter III. were
" capable of guiding with firmnefs the reins of
" government? You are alarmed for my fon;
" but had you rather abandon him to the fantaftic
" humours of a father, by whom he is already
" difowned, than truft his fortune to a mother
" who loves him? and, if I afpire to the fupreme
" command, is it not for the welfare of that
" child? is it not that I may be the better able
" to recompenfe thofe who, like you, affift me
" to defend him? Doubtlefs, they may all rely
" on my everlafting gratitude; but in order to
" prove it to my heart's content, I muft have
                                        " the

" the power; and that power is what I expect
" from you."

Panin was not in the least shaken; opinions
were divided, and the conspirators came to no
fixed determination.

It was easy to perceive that Panin only wished
to set his pupil on the throne, in the hope of occupying himself the second place in the empire,
and to govern in his name. Catharine had too
much discernment not to have discovered this
motive long before; accordingly she had given
private assurances to Panin that she would appoint him prime minister; taking care, however,
not to confirm this promise in presence of the
other conspirators, for fear of offending the ambition of any of the party.

Princess Dashkoff, Orloff, Odart, those who
wanted to bestow the supreme power on Catharine, vied with each other in seeking some
means for inducing count Panin to alter his
mind; but it was long to no purpose, and they
would certainly not have been able to succeed, if
a passion less terrible, but more powerful, had
not come into conflict with ambition. Love
had already enlisted in the service of Catharine
the boldest and most intrepid of her conspirators:
love granted another lady the boon of subduing
him.

him, whofe ftubborn mind was not to be moved
by majefty itfelf.

The neceffity into which the plot had led
Panin of converfing frequently with the princefs
Dafhkoff; the wit, the vivacity, the petulance
of this young woman; her whole character, in
fhort, infpired him with a lively tendernefs for
her. He was not long in making her an open
declaration of his paffion: fhe received it with
coldnefs, and afforded him no hope of fuccefs.
It was not however virtue in madame Dafhkoff,
that impelled her to reject the profeffions of
Panin. Many other known fuitors had already
experienced that it was not invincible. But the
age, the heavy air of Panin, his equivocal reputation in his attachments; and, above all, the
deep and lively fentiment fhe had vowed to
another, prevented her from yielding to the perfuafions of the preceptor, who, dumb from that
moment on the fubject of his paffion, feemed to
take pleafure in contradicting the author of its
difappointment.

The fubtle and vigilant Odart alone difcovered the fecret motive of Panin's refiftance,
and immediately promifed to overcome it. He
haftened to the princefs; and, after having heard
her confirm what he had only fufpected, converfed
                                    with

with her in all the familiarity of a zealous confidant and an accomplice, who was daily in
concert with her, braving exile and death.
Exempt from all prejudices, or rather incapable
of an esteem for virtue, Odart had the effrontery
to ridicule that which seemed to be a check on
princess Dashkoff.　Then, putting on a graver
look, he represented to her that if she thought
it a fault to yield to the follicitations of Panin,
that fault would be ennobled by the motive that
impelled her to commit it.　He reminded her
of the union of sentiment that attached her to the
empress; and, friendship being the principal
virtue, no sacrifice should seem too dear, when
we were called to the service of a friend: and
concluded with representing to her, that it would
be the triumph of heroism to brave the disgrace
of making her charms subservient to her ambition.
The princess Dashkoff, whose romantic imagination was easily elevated, gave implicit credit to
all that was told her by Odart, consented to
whatever Panin proposed, and Catharine had no
more obstacles to apprehend on the part of the
count *.

The

* It is but justice to observe in this place, that many
persons who attended successively the courts of Elizabeth,
Peter III. and the late empress, have uniformly affirmed,

The conspirators therefore being brought to agreement, thought no longer of any thing but of putting their plan in execution. Of chiefs there was no want; but soldiers were to be obtained. The first thing to be done was to gain over those of the guards, as well for depriving the emperor of their defence, as for a support to the cause. The Orloffs, Bibikoff, and Passick had already seduced three companies of the regiment of Ismaïlof; but this number was not sufficient, and it was only by money that they could hope to corrupt others. The empress had it not in her power to furnish any, as she had scarcely wherewith to defray the daily expences of her household. She therefore, in concert with princess Dashkoff, commissioned Odart to make application to M. de Breteuil for a supply. That minister, long the confidant and the dupe of the empress, was preparing to quit Petersburg. He was not ignorant that a conspiracy was on foot, but he knew neither the

---

that, of all the imputations thrown out on princess Dashkoff concerning certain peculiarities in her disposition and temper, they never once heard the slightest suspicion cast on her chastity : and to her friends it has always been her boast, that, though a widow at the age of 18, the most malignant of her enemies had nothing to accuse her of in this respect.

            springs

springs that were to set it in motion, nor the means by which it was to be conducted : he was doubtful of its success; and, when Odart informed him that Catharine was desirous that the king of France would lend her 60,000 rubles, he hesitated to advance that trifling sum. Fearing however to mortify the self-love of the empress by a formal refusal, as well as to give too much credit to the assertions of Odart, whom he regarded in no other light than as a presumptuous adventurer, he told him that he might assure her majesty that the king his master would esteem it a pleasure to afford her, on that occasion, a proof of his attachment, and that he would without delay communicate to him what she desired. At the same time he drew up the form of a note which he put into the hands of Odart, that she might write it in her own hand, and return it to him. The note was conceived in these terms : " J'ai chargé le porteur du présent billet de " vous faire mes adieux, et de vous prier de me " faire quelque petite commission, que je vous " prie de m'envoyer le plutôt possible*."

* What a specimen of M. de Breteuil's style ! — " I have " commissioned the bearer of the present note to bid " you farewell in my name, and to request you to give me " some small commission, which I beg you to send me as " soon as possible."

R 2

The

The Piedmontefe, thinking that the emprefs would not have any fcruple to write this note, promifed it to M. de Breteuil.   But that princefs, enfibly hurt at the diftruft fhewn by the french minifter, the delays he put in practice, and the ftate of dependence in which he wanted to place her on a court fhe detefted, vouchfafed not even to give him an anfwer;- and M. de Breteuil, having waited fome days without any appearance of Odart, fet out from Ruffia and proceeded to Vienna, where he received, by Verfailles, the news of the fuccefs of the confpiracy, and the order to return to St. Peterfburg *.

On the preffure of the emergency, Catharine had confented to borrow of M. de Breteuil; but afterwards, willing to fhew him that fhe could difpenfe with his affiftance, fhe feized the inftant of his departure to fend him a note, which Odart privately delivered to Berenger, the chargé d'affaires, and contained the following words : " L'emplette que nous devions faire " fe fera fûrement bientôt, mais à beaucoup

---

* This is exactly the manner in which M. de Breteuil was of fervice to the confpiracy : and yet it is well known how fond he was of boafting in France how greatly he had forwarded it.

" meilleur

" meilleur marché : ainfi nous n'avons pas befoin
" d'autres fonds *."

However, Catharine was at this moment in
the moft tremendous fituation. The dread of
feeing her fchemes betrayed, the greater apprehenfion of being arrefted, dethroned, fhut up
for ever, all circumftances confidered, filled her
with the moft piercing difquietude.

Peter all this while feemed only intent upon
pleafure ; yet in reality he was not inattentive to
the condition of the unhappy Ivan, and to his
military preparations.

After having lodged this prince at Kexholm,
he caufed him to be fecretly conducted to Peterfburg, where he was put in a houfe of no
confpicuous figure ; in which he vifited him
during the night, accompanied by Gudovitch
and Volkoff.

The fleet he had deftined to act againft Denmark being completely equipped, one divifion
remained yet at Cronftadt, while the other lay
waiting for it at Revel. The regiments that
were to follow in this expedition were already in
Pomerania, and others were on their march to
join them. In a word, he was ready to put

* " The purchafe we intended to make will certainly
" be made foon, but at a much cheaper rate : therefore we
" have no need of other fupplies."

R 3   himfelf

himself at the head of his army for the invasion of Holstein. What seemed to flatter him most in this conquest was the being capacitated thereby to pay his respects to him whom he styled his friend, his brother, and his model, the king of Pruffia. In the expectation of this happiness, he treated the envoy of that monarch with such distinctions and even adulations as Frederic himself would never have endured: but this envoy* was young, and perhaps vaunted too much of the marks of deference shewn him by the emperor. Peter had at length fixed his departure for the day following the festival of Peter and Paul†, which he was, as usual, to celebrate

* It was baron Goltz, who was afterwards minister in France from Pruffia, and died at Bâle in 1794. It has been said, that while Goltz has been shut up for hours together with young women of the court, the tzar, with a firelock on his shoulder, stood sentry at the door, as a common soldier. But who does not see that this must be a story invented by the calumniators of that unfortunate prince?

† To make it believed that the tzar was completely stupid, the report has been studiously propagated, that when he was heated by wine and punch, he never failed to talk of schemes of conquest, and to give himself up to the transports of an extravagant ambition. Two days before the revolution that hurled him from the throne, he held, it is said, the following discourse: "Of what use are all those "petty sovereigns of Europe? What are they? I am re- "solved

celebrate at Peterhof, and at the end of which he purpofed to caufe the emprefs to be arrefted. But the emprefs was taking meafures effectually to prevent his defign.   Her party was waiting only for the moment of action*.   That moment was accelerated by chance.

They who plan a confpiracy have always more zeal, more vigilance and activity, than he againft whom it is directed.   Accordingly the friends of Catharine were carefully informed of all that paffed about the tzar, while he was ignorant of all their

---

" folved that, in future, there fhall be but three powers in
" this part of the world : Ruffia, Pruffia, and France.   I
" will have all the North, the king of Pruffia fhall have all
" Germany, and the king of France the reft." — " But,"
obferved one of his courtiers, " what does your majefty
" think of putting France into your divifion?" — " Oh!
" yes," replied the tzar; " France is likewife a great
" power!"   It is much to be doubted that, however intoxicated Peter might be, he ever intended to make fuch a
partition of Europe.

* Catharine's party confifted of the hetman Razumoffky,
the preceptor of the grand duke count Panin, the mafter of
artillery Villebois, general Volkonfkoi, the brothers Orloff,
the princefs Dafhkoff, (to whom the emprefs was as ftrongly
attached, as the emperor was to her fifter Elizabeth Vorontzoff,) &c.   With Peter was count Munich, who would
alone perhaps have outweighed all the others, if the emperor had but refolved to follow the counfels of this experienced veteran.

R 4   proceed-

proceedings.   Expecting, in indolent fecurity, the feftivities of Peterhof, his majefty was gone to pafs fome days at his country palace of Oranien-baum*, whither he had taken with him fome of the handfomeft women of the court.   On this occafion a report was fpread, that he wanted to demand divorces for thefe women, that he might marry them to fome of his courtiers.   It was

---

* The palace of Oranienbaum was built by prince Ment-chikoff, in 1727, as his country refidence: on whofe fall it reverted to the crown.   It ftands on the coaft of the gulf of Finnland in 59° 52', N. L. 40 verfts from St. Peterfburg, 8 from Peterhof, and 7 from the ifland of Cronftadt. The palace is fituated, like that of Peterhof, on a rife about 15 fathom above the level of the fea, formed into terraces; by means whereof it has a beautiful profpect of the gulf, of Cronftadt, and the fhips, galleots, &c. conti-nually paffing in the fummer feafon.   The palace is not large, confifts of a central building of two ftories, crowned with a turret, and two wings, each connected with it by a colonnade.   To walk on the top of thefe colonnades for en-joying the pure air and the fine profpect is extremely agree-able.   One of the wings is a chapel; and fome of the apart-ments are very richly fitted up; one with all kinds of coftly porcelaine, another lacquered in the chinefe tafte, black and gold, &c.   Within thefe few years the late emprefs Catha-rine II. gave it for the ufe of the noble fea-cadet corps.   It has fpacious gardens belonging to it. — That corps has fince been removed to the Vaffilly-oftrof, and the] palace of Oranienbaum has been granted to the grand duke Conftantine.

even

even added, that beds had been ordered for thefe
pretended nuptials ; and fhame, contempt, and
jealoufy created him new enemies, and procured
as many partifans to Catharine.

The confpirators, who at firft had agreed to
feize and carry off the tzar on 'his appearance
again at St. Peterfburg, thought, in confequence
of a new deliberation, that it would be too dangerous to wait fo long, and that it would be
better to execute their defign on his coming to
Peterhof.

The plan was well concerted : each of the
confpirators was reckoning on his own courage
and the fidelity of his friends, when all at once
their plot was difcovered.   This difcovery,
however, was not the effect of chance ; and, by
a ftrange caprice of fortune, the very accident
which, by its natural effect, ought to have dif-
concerted the traitors, emboldened them ; and
their precipitancy fecured their fuccefs.

By an excefs of diffidence or precaution,
princefs Dafhkoff and Odart had fet a trufty
perfon to watch the fteps of each of the chiefs
of the confpiracy, who regularly brought them
an exact account of whatever thefe chiefs might
be likely to do ; in fuch manner, that if there
had been the leaft tendency towards treachery
among them, they would have detected it in-
ftantaneoufly,

ſtantaneouſly, and have taken meaſures for their ſecurity or their vengeance.

Paſſick had gained the ſoldiers of the company of the guards in which he was lieutenant. One of theſe ſoldiers, imagining that Paſſick did nothing but in concurrence with his captain, aſked the captain on what day they were to take up arms againſt the emperor. The captain, ſurpriſed, had recourſe to diſſimulation; and anſwering the queſtions of the ſoldier in vague and indiſtinct terms, drew out of him the ſecret of the conſpiracy, and went, without delay, to make report of it to the chancery of the regiment.

It was nine o'clock at night. Paſſick was put under arreſt: but at firſt he was ſhoved into a room, where he had time to write with a pencil on a ſcrap of paper, " Proceed to execution this " inſtant, or we are undone." The man who watched his motions preſented himſelf at the door. Paſſick, not knowing him, but ſeeing that every thing was to be riſked, gave him the billet, telling him that if he ran with it in all ſpeed to the hetman Razumoffſky, he would be handſomely rewarded. The ſpy hurried to the princeſs Daſhkoff, and put the billet into her hand. Panin happened that moment to come in. She propoſed to haſten the execution of their project, obſerving that the only means of
saving

saving themselves from the vengeance of the tzar was to prevent it; and that, however weak he might be, if time were allowed him to put himself on his defence, it would be impossible to get the better of him. But whether or not Panin thought really that the enterprise could not succeed, whether his capacity was not sufficiently seconded by courage, for beginning to act, he refused to submit to the reasons of princess Dashkoff; and after having told her that it would be better to wait till the next day, to know what was fittest to be done, he withdrew.

In the mean time the emissaries of princess Dashkoff had already taken care to give intelligence to the other conspirators. On Panin's departure, she put on man's apparel, and went to join Orloff and his friends on the green bridge, where she was in the habit of seeing them, that she might avoid raising suspicion by getting to her too many subaltern officers and soldiers *.

* Besides the noble and beautiful river Neva, with its three bridges of boats ingeniously removed and replaced twice every year, and besides the canals with their elegant quays and magnificent stone bridges, there is yet another river, passing through the city, the Moika, the numerous drawbridges over which are still of wood, and these are denominated according to the colour with which they are painted, the red bridge, the blue bridge, the green bridge, &c.

These

These conspirators were neither less uneasy than princess Dashkoff, nor less impatient for hastening the execution of their plot. The delay till the morrow appeared to them to be big with consequences the most to be dreaded; and it certainly would have been fatal. The time of acting was the silence of the night, without allowing the tzar time to form an inclination to prevent them, nor the troops and the people time to arm for the defence of the tzar. The resolution was unanimous. While Gregory Orloff, one of his brothers, and his friend Bibikoff, repaired to the barracks for the purpose of preparing the soldiers of their party to act on the first signal, another brother of Orloff, Alexius, took upon him the perilous commission of going to find out the empress at Peterhof.

Under pretext of leaving the apartments free for the festival that was to be celebrated at the palace, and for enabling herself, in reality, to be more in readiness to escape, Catharine was lodged in a remote summer-house, at the foot whereof runs a canal that communicates with the Neva, and where she had caused to be fastened, as if without design, a small boat, that it might occasionally be of service in the secret visits of her favourites, and to facilitate her own escape
into

into Sweden, if the conspiracy should be discovered. Gregory Orloff having given his brother a key to this summer-house, instructed him in the methods he must employ for getting thither; and princess Dashkoff trusted him with a short note, to engage the empress to come to them without loss of time.

It was now two o'clock in the morning. The empress, not expecting any body, had retired to rest, and lay in a profound sleep, when she perceived herself suddenly roused, and saw standing at the side of her bed a soldier whom she knew nothing of. Without delivering her the note from princess Dashkoff, the soldier said to Catharine :—" Your majesty has not a moment " to lose ; get ready to follow me :" and immediately disappeared.

Catharine, astonished, terrified, called Ivanovna. They dressed themselves in haste, and disguised themselves in such manner that they could not be known by the sentinels about the palace. Scarcely were they ready, when the soldier returned, and told the empress that a carriage was waiting for them at the garden-gate. It was a coach which, under pretext of having change of horses for an excursion into the country, princess Dashkoff had kept for several days in readiness at a house inhabited by one of her

peasants

peafants a few miles from Peterhof, and which Alexèy Orloff had fent one of his comrades to fetch.

The emprefs reached the carriage without difficulty. She got into it. Alexèy Orloff took the reins, and fet off at full fpeed. Suddenly the horfes, being over-driven, ftopped fhort, and fell down. They were obliged to get out. Alexèy Orloff and his companion employed every effort to cheer the horfes, but in vain. The diftance from Peterfburg was ftill confiderable; it was in the midft of the night; they were in the greateft confufion, and the danger was every moment becoming more imminent: they refolved to proceed the reft of the way on foot. They had not gone far, when by good luck they met a light country cart. Alexèy Orloff feized hold of the horfes, the emprefs got in, and they fet off again as before. They prefently heard the found of another carriage coming after them with unufual rapidity. It was Gregory Orloff, who, calculating the moments, was alarmed at not yet feeing the emprefs. Immediately knowing her, he cried out, that they only waited for her; and without ftaying for her anfwer, drove on before to receive her at Peterfburg. At length Catharine, worn out with fatigue and anxiety, but fufficiently miftrefs of

herfelf

herself to assume a sedate and tranquil air, arrived in the city at seven in the morning *.

She proceeded directly to the quarter of the Ismaïloffky guards, of which three companies had been already won over; but the conspirators would not permit them to leave the barracks till Catharine appeared, for fear of failing in their aim by too great precipitancy. At the report of the arrival of her majesty, about thirty of the soldiers, half dressed, ran out to receive her with clamorous shouts of joy. Surprised and alarmed at seeing so small a number of soldiers she kept silence for a moment, and then told them, in a tremulous voice, " that her danger had " driven her to the necessity of coming to ask " their assistance; that the tzar had intended to " put her to death that very night, together with " her son; that she had no other means than by " flight of escaping death; and that she had so " much confidence in their dispositions as to put " herself entirely in their hands."

All who heard her shuddered with indignation, and swore to die in her defence. Their example, and the hetman Razumoffsky their colonel, who was not long ere he appeared, soon collected other soldiers, led by curiosity, in great numbers about the empress, who, with one

* The 9th of July N. S. 1762.

7

consent

confent declared her fovereign.   The chaplain
of the regiment of Ifmaïlof was immediately
called, who, fetching a crucifix from the altar,
received on it the oath of the troops.   Some
voices were heard in this tumultuous concourfe,
proclaiming Catharine regent ; but thefe founds
were prefently ftifled by the threats of Orloff
and the more numerous cries of " Long live the
" emprefs !"

The Simeonoffky and the Préobaginfky *
guards had already imitated thofe of Ifmaïlof.
The officers, with the utmoft docility, put
themfelves at the head of their companies, as
though they had been engaged in the plot.
Two alone, of the regiment of Préobaginfky,
had the boldnefs to counteract their foldiers ;
but they were fuddenly arrefted : and among
thofe who had been gained over, there were only
wanting the major Tfchapeloff and the lieutenant
Poufhkin, whom the emprefs had fent orders to
have put under arreft, obferving with coldnefs
that fhe had no further occafion for them.

While   the   hetman Razumoffky,   prince
Volkonfky, counts Bruce and Stroganoff, feve-

* Of the Afcenfion.   It was the regiment of Préobaginfky that placed Elizabeth on the throne.   Elizabeth, as
a grateful return, conferred nobility on all the grenadiers of
that corps.

ral

ral other general officers, and princefs Dafhkoff,
remained about Catharine, and fhe was completely fecuring the three regiments of guards,
Gregory Orloff ran to the regiment of artillery,
to draw it into the revolt, and march it to the
emprefs. But though he was treafurer of that
corps, and well enough beloved of the foldiers,
they unanimoufly refufed to follow him, and infifted on feeing the orders of their general Villebois. That officer for fome time feemed to be
favourably regarded by Catharine, and thought
that he was fo ftill; but as fhe difcerned in him
a probity too auftere to allow her to hope that
he would take part in the confpiracy, fhe had
never ventured to difclofe it to him; and when
one of the friends of Orloff appeared, and told
him that her majefty commanded him to come
and join her at the barracks of the guards at
the head of his regiment, he afked whether the
emperor was dead. The friend of Orloff, without anfwering his queftion, repeated the order;
and Villebois, in utter aftonifhment, went alone
to the emprefs.

Villebois, feeing Catharine furrounded by an
immenfe crowd of people, found no difficulty in
divining what it was fhe expected of him; but,
ftill withheld by the fidelity he had fworn to the
emperor, or by the danger to which he thought

VOL. I,   s   her

her majesty was exposing herself, he presumed to speak to her of the obstacles which yet remained for her to surmount; and added, that she ought to have foreseen them. She haughtily interrupted him; and replied, " that she had not sent " for him to ask him what she ought to have " foreseen, but to know how he intended to " act."

" To obey your majesty," returned Villebois in confusion; and went to put himself at the head of his regiment, and to deliver the arsenals to the friends of Catharine.

So many advantages cost the empress no more han two hours. She saw herself already surrounded by 2000 warriors, and a great part of the inhabitants of Petersburg, who mechanically followed the motions of the soldiers, and were eager to applaud them.

The hetman Razumofffky advised her then to repair to the church of Kasan, where every thing was prepared for her reception. She accordingly set out, attended by her numerous suite. The windows and doors of all the houses were filled with spectators, who mingled their acclamations with the shouts of the soldiers. The archbishop of Novgorod, who, appareled in his sacerdotal robes, and accompanied by a great number of priests, whose long beards and

s

hoary

hoary heads gave them a venerable appearance, stood at the altar to receive her, set the imperial crown on her head, proclaimed her in a loud voice sovereign of all the Ruffias, by the name of Catharine the Second; and declared, at the same time, the young grand duke Paul Petrovitch her fucceffor. A Te Deum was then chanted, accompanied with the fhouts of the multitude.

This ceremony being over, the emprefs repaired to the palace that had been occupied by Elizabeth. The gates were thrown open indifcriminately to all comers. During feveral hours the crowd flocked thither, falling on their knees before her, and taking the oath of allegiance.

In the mean time the confpirators were unwearied in their vifits to the feveral quarters of the town, to put them in a ftate of defence; every where ftationing a guard, and placing cannons with match lighted, without meeting any impediment or interruption. Prince George of Holftein, uncle to the emperor, dared to venture out, followed by a few faithful foldiers; but he was furrounded, forced to furrender, loaded with infults, roughly handled, and dragged to prifon, whence the emprefs delivered him after fome hours, in order to put him under arreft in his own houfe.

Not

Not only no refiftance was oppofed to the partifans of Catharine, but none of the friends of the tzar once thought of informing him of what was paffing at Peterfburg. One man alone, a foreigner, named Breffan*, who owed his fortune to that prince, had the refolution to inftance his gratitude and fidelity. He caufed a domeftic to put on the habit of a countryman, and gave him a written paper, with orders to deliver it only into the hands of the emperor. The fervant happened to pafs juft as the confpirators were placing a guard on the Kalinka bridge over the Fontanka, which muft be croffed for going out of the city on that fide, and made the beft of his way to Oranienbaum; but, on his reaching the palace, he found that the tzar was not there, and was obliged to go in queft of him to Peterhof.

All circumftances feemed to concur to favour the plot. On the Peterhof road, and at fome diftance from Peterfburg, a regiment of 1600 men was encamped, among whom no fort of intelligence had been practifed; and it was much to be apprehended that, on the very firft tidings of the revolt, the tzar would order them to break up the camp, and join his holftein troops. No

* He came into the country as a barber and perukemaker, being born in the ftate of Monaco, and was a naturalized Frenchman.

fooner

sooner were measures set on foot to prevent this
catastrophe, than colonel Olsufieff, who commanded that regiment, and had heard some con-
fused reports of what was going forward in town,
made his appearance for gaining further information.   The conspirators got about him, talked
to him with enthusiasm, persuaded him by arguments adapted to the purpose; and Olsufieff
presently returned to surrender his regiment to
Catharine.   At the very moment that he was
haranguing his men, an order from Peter arrived
for the regiment to march immediately to him.
The soldiers, perplexed and confounded, unanimously cried out, that they did not acknowledge him for emperor, and directly began their
march to go and augment the forces of the conspiracy.

Before the end of the day, Catharine had
already 15,000 men of picked troops.   The
city was in formidable state of defence.   Strict
order prevailed there; and by the greatest good
fortune, not one drop of blood was shed.

What principally tended to the service of that
princess, was the interest and concern that her
partisans inspired into all men for her, by pro-
pagating on every side, that the tzar had destined
that very day to put her to death with her son.
The atrocious falsehood was believed without

examina-

examination; and fuccefs was the reward of the calumny.

When the emprefs was at the palace, fhe fent without delay, for her fon Paul Petrovitch. A detachment, at the head of which marched a trufty officer, went to bring him; and that young prince, who had been often told of the defigns of the tzar againft him, on his waking in the midft of the foldiers, was feized with an alarming fright. Panin took him in his arms, and brought him to his mother. Catharine then led him into the balcony of the palace, holding him up to fhew him to the people, whofe acclamations redoubled at the fight of the child, thinking that in him they beheld the new emperor.

A report all at once got up, that Peter III. was no more, and that the proceffion with his corpfe was now going by. A profound filence then took place of the cries of the multitude. Several foldiers in long black cloaks, with torches in their hands, walked on each fide of a large coffin covered with a pall, and preceded by a number of priefts, chanting their litanies as the proceffion moved along; while the crowd refpectfully fell back on both fides, to make room for it to pafs. But afterwards it was not doubted that this was an additional ftratagem invented by the

the conspirators for deceiving the people, and for intimidating the partisans of the tzar.

The principal nobles, who, for the most part, had taken no share in this conspiracy, and who first learned the success of it at their rising in the morning, resorted immediately to the palace; where, forced to disguise their astonishment and vexation, they united their homages and their oaths of fidelity to those which the multitude had just been taking to Catharine.

The heads of the conspiracy, collected round that princess, now held a council, resolved to profit by the dispositions of the army, and to march in all haste directly to the emperor: but, in the mean time, for putting the empress in security from all attack by sea, or rather in order to quiet the soldiers, who imagined that she was liable every moment to be surprised and assassinated, they conducted her from the palace of Elizabeth, into an old palace built of timber, facing a large open place, and which they surrounded by troops.

Towards noon her majesty, entirely sure of St. Petersburg, caused a manifesto, which Odart had secretly caused to be printed a few days before, to be distributed throughout the city *.

* See the Appendix at the end of the volume.

s 4   This

This publication being made, the empress caused a notification to be delivered to the foreign ministers on the day when they were to be admitted to pay their court, and present their compliments of congratulation on the event.

While these things were transacting, the empress, decorated with the insignia of the order of St. Andrew, and habited in the uniform of the guards, which she had borrowed for the occasion of a very young officer, named Taliezin, mounted on horseback, and rode through the ranks with princess Dashkoff, who was also in uniform. It was then that the young Potemkin*, ensign of the regiment of horse-guards, perceiving that Catharine had no plume in her hat, rode up to offer her his. The horse on which Potemkin was mounted, being accustomed to form into the squadron, was some time before he could be brought to quit the side of that of her majesty, thereby affording her an opportunity of remarking for the first time the grace and agility of him who, in the sequel, gained such an ascendant over her.

The troops, being incessantly supplied with beer and brandy, incessantly likewise expressed their satisfaction by reiterated vociferations of

* He was then only sixteen.

bourra !

bourra! and by toffing up their hats and caps; but a regiment of cavalry, of which Peter III. had been colonel while yet only grand duke, and which he had incorporated with the guards on his acceffion to the throne, took no participation in this tumultuous joy. The officers, having all refufed obedience to Catharine, were under arreft, and replaced by the officers of other regiments; and the foldiers, by the fullen filence they obferved, formed a ftriking contraft with the furious noife and gefticulations of the reft.

But the party was too ftrong to have any thing to fear from this regiment; and they began now to march the troops from the city, to proceed againft the tzar. Her majefty fat down to dinner near an open window, in full view of the foldiers and the multitudes whom curiofity had affembled in the ample place before the palace.

Peter III. had yet no fufpicion of what was paffing. His fecurity was even fo great, that he had that morning caufed a faithful officer to be arrefted, who the evening before, having had fome intimations of the confpiracy, had haftened in the night to Oranienbaum, thinking it his duty to inform him of it. Peter afterwards fet out in a calafh, with his miftrefs, his favourites, and the women of his court, for Peterhof, to be prefent at the grand feftivities of the following day.

day.   The tzar's carriage was attended by feveral others ; and this numerous train proceeded
in a swift pace, the several companies within
gaily entertaining themselves with the pleasures
they expected, when Gudovitch, the general
aide-de-camp, who had galloped on before, was
perceived returning at full speed.   Gudovitch
had met on the road one of the chamberlains of
the empress *, coming on foot to his master to
inform him of Catharine's escape, and the uneasiness and perplexity that, in consequence of
it, filled the whole palace of Peterhof.   At this
unexpected news, Gudovitch turned back, and,
as he approached the tzar's carriage, called out
to the driver to stop.   Peter, surprised, and even
rather angry, not knowing what could cause
his aide-de-camp to ride back with so much
speed, asked him if he was mad.   Gudovitch
came close to the carriage, and whispered some
words in his ear.   Peter now turned pale, and,
strongly agitated, got out of the carriage, and
went aside with Gudovitch in order to inter-
rogate him more at his ease.   Then returning
to the carriage, and having desired the ladies to
come out, he shewed them a gate of the park,
through which he bade them join him at the
front of the palace, regained the carriage with

* His name was Ismailoff.

some

some of his courtiers, and departed with the greatest expedition.

On coming to Peterhof, the emperor ran to the pavilion that had been occupied by Catharine ; and in his confusion, in his extreme concern, he looked about for her as if she might have been concealed under the bed, or in one of the cupboards. He overwhelmed all he met with questions ; but nobody could give him any satisfaction. Those of greater penetration than the rest already foresaw the whole extent of his misfortune, but were silent, that they might not increase his affright. Countess Vorontzoff, his mistress, and the other women, who were now coming up the walks of the garden, were still entirely ignorant of what it could be that had forced the tzar to quit them in the midst of the road. As soon as Peter perceived the countess, he called to her : " Romanovna, will you be- " lieve me now ? Catharine has made her " escape. I told you that she was capable of " any thing !"

In the mean time some boors, who were returning from St. Petersburg, related to a group of valets whom they saw standing about the palace, what they knew of the insurrection that had happened, and these valets talked of it among themselves in whispers, but neither spoke

of

of it to their mafter nor to any of the courtiers.
A gloomy fufpicion already prevailed around the
unhappy emperor.   It feemed as if a fatal pre-
fentiment had taken poffeffion of every heart, as
the forerunner of his fall, and filled his own with
confufion and difmay.   He . prefently became
afraid to put any more queftions, and nobody
dared to give him any information.

At length a countryman fuddenly came up in
the midft of this affrighted concourfe, and with
the ufual falutation of a profound inclination
of body, without pronouncing a fingle word,
drew from the bofom of his caftan a fealed
note, which he prefented to the emperor.   This
countryman was Breffan's domeftic.   The emperor took the note, ran his eyes haftily over it,
and then reading it aloud, informed thofe who
were ftanding round him, that a rebellion had
broke out that morning at Peterfburg : that the
troops had taken arms in favour of Catharine ;
that fhe was going to be crowned in the church
of Kafan ; and that the whole of the populace
feemed to take part in the infurrection.

The tzar feemed greatly dejected at thefe
tidings.   The courtiers did their utmoft to communicate to him a courage which they did not
themfelves poffefs.   The chancellor Vorontzoff
obferved, that it was highly poffible that Catharine

rine might have ufed her endeavours to make
the foldiery and the people rife, but that this
flight fermentation could not be attended with
any dangerous confequences; and if the tzar
would give his confent, he would hafte immediately to Peterfburg, and be bound to bring the
emprefs back.

The tzar, without hefitation, accepted the
chancellor's propofal; and that minifter departed for town. On entering the palace, he
found the emprefs furrounded by a multitude of
people in the act of doing homage. He neverthelefs had the boldnefs to reprefent to her with
a becoming confidence the danger to which fhe
was expofing herfelf. " You may," faid he,
" madam, have fome fuccefs; but it will not be
" of long duration. Is it therefore acting wifely
" to truft to the blind zeal of your imprudent
" friends? Is it worth while, for the fake of
" fharing with them in a momentary reign,
" to make an irreconcileable enemy of your
" hufband? Why take up arms againft him,
" when it is fo eafy for you to obtain whatever
" you can defire by the gentlenefs of your per-
" fuafion, and the fuperiority of your mind?
" Confider, that the regiments of the guards do
" not compofe the whole army of the tzar, and
" that the inhabitants of St. Peterfburg are but a
" very

" very weak part of the ruffian nation." Catharine calmly replied, " You fee how it is : it
" is not I that am doing any thing ; I only yield
" to the ardent fenfibility of the nation."

The chancellor, who actually faw the crowd
every moment increafing, and read in the angry
looks of fome of the confpirators that thefe remonftrances might be attended with the worft of
confequences to him, forgot his duty, took the
oath with the reft, and added, " I will ferve you
" in the council, madam ; but I am ufelefs in the
" field. My prefence might even be difpleafing
" to thofe who have been hearing my addrefs to
" you ; and that I may avoid exciting their
" jealoufies, I befeech your majefty to let me
" remain in my houfe, under the guard of fome
" trufty officer." To this reafonable requeft
the emprefs confented. She fent him home,
with orders not to quit his houfe. By this prudent precaution, the chancellor was at once fafe
from the vindictive fpirit of the partifans of Catharine, and from the fufpicions of the tzar.

At fix in the evening, Catharine a fecond
time mounted her horfe ; and, with a drawn
fword in her hand, and an oaken wreath about
her temples, fhe haftened to put herfelf at the
head of her troops that were already on their
march. Princefs Dafhkoff and the hetman
Razumofffky

Razumofffky rode one on each fide of her. A
crowd of courtiers followed; all of them vying
with each other who fhould difplay the greateft
ardour in fharing her dangers, and partaking in
her triumph. Her army was augmented by a
new acceffion of 3000 kozaks well mounted,
whom the emperor had ordered to file off towards Pomerania, but who were ftopped on the
way by a meffenger from the hetman, with directions to join him.

In the mean time, after the departure of the
chancellor, the tzar had continued a prey to
the moft diftreffing anxieties. He was every inftant receiving fome news of the progrefs of the
revolution. It was impoffible for him any
longer to make it a matter of doubt. Surrounded by women in tears, and young courtiers
incapable of giving advice, he ftrolled with
great ftrides about the walks of the gardens,
forming twenty different plans, and adhering to
none : one while indulging in violent imprecations againft Catharine ; then dictating ufelefs
manifeftoes. When the hour of dinner was
come, he commanded it to be ferved up on the
margin of the fea, and feemed for fome time to
have a refpite from his forrowful reflections.

But this refpite was of fhort duration. His
affrighted imagination foon held up again the
danger

danger that menaced him, and he difpatched an
order to the 3000 Holfteiners whom he had left
at Oranienbaum, to come immediately with their
artillery. It was juft at this point of time that the
venerable marfhal Munich made his appearance.

Munich, whom the emperor refpected on account of his great military reputation, and whom
he had almoft affronted by requefting him to
adopt the new pruffian exercife; Munich was the
only man who was able to give him falutary
advice, and he gave it him. " Your majefty's
" troops are arriving," faid the veteran commander. " Let us put ourfelves at their head,
" and march ftraight to Peterfburg. You have
" ftill many friends there : immediately on your
" appearance they will arm in your defence.
" The principal part of the guards are only
" under a momentary alienation, into which
" they have been mifled, and will foon range
" themfelves under your ftandard. Befides, if
" we are forced to come to action, be affured
" that the rebels will not long difpute with you
" the palm of victory."

This refolution feemed feafible to the tzar,
but it was far from pleafing his timid courtiers;
and while they were preparing to begin their
march, news arrived of the emprefs's approach,
whofe army was faid to confift of 20,000 men.
            The

The women cried out, that it would be better to go back to Oranienbaum. Peter himſelf ſeemed determined not to expoſe his perſon. " Well!" returned Munich, " if you wiſh to decline a " battle with the rebels, it is not adviſable for " you, at any rate, to ſtay to be attacked by " them here, where you have no means of de- " fending yourſelf to advantage. Neither Ora- " nienbaumn or Peterhof are in a capacity to " hold out a ſiege. But Cronſtadt offers you " a ſafe retreat. Cronſtadt is ſtill under your " command. You have there a formidable " fleet, and a numerous garriſon. It is, in " ſhort, from Cronſtadt that you will find it an " eaſy matter to bring Peterſburg back to its " duty."

This advice was unanimouſly applauded. General Devier was immediately ſent off in a boat to take the command of Cronſtadt* ; and

ſcarcely

* The iſland of Cronſtadt lies oppoſite to Oranienbaum, at the diſtance of ſeven verſts. When in poſſeſſion of the Swedes it was called Retuſari, and by the Ruſſians Kotloi-oſtrof, kettle-iſland. In 1723 Peter the great named it Cronſtadt, or crown town, as being the crown to his new city : it is ſituate in the eaſtern extremity of the gulf of Finland, is 39 verſts W. N. W. diſtant from St. Pe- terſburg, and from Seſtrabek 12. The iſland is 8 verſts in length from E. to W. and about one verſt in breadth ; it is flat, about 8 fathom higher than the level of the ſea, with

scarcely were two yachts prepared for the departure of the tzar, than an officer came to affure

---

fome woody parts of birch and firs. Its ftrata, under the turf, as was feen in digging the canals, are clay and lime-ftone. Two fmaller iflands on its fouthern fide are ftrongly fortified, one of which has the name of Cronflot. The town and fort of Cronftadt were built by Peter I. in 1710. It has two fine, fecure, and fpacious harbours, one for the imperial navy, and the other for merchant-fhips, of which it is full during the fummer and autumn months. The town occupies the eaftern part of the ifland, is large, has many good houfes, feveral churches, a cuftom-houfe, and other public buildings. Here is alfo an englifh church with a minifter, for the benefit of the mafters and failors of the fhips that refort hither in the fervice of the ruffia trade. The harbour for the fhips of war is extremely remarkable, and frequently vifited by foreigners to their great fatisfaction. It is protected by piers and batteries, and belonging to it is the famous Peter's canal and the docks. The canal was begun by Peter I. and completed under Elizabeth, by general Lubras. It is faced with mafonry, 1050 fathoms in length, at bottom 60, and at top 100 fathoms broad, 24 fathoms deep, and in this ftate extends 358 fathoms into the fea. Adjacent to the canal are the docks, in which 10 and more fhips may be repaired at a time. They are provided with proper fluices, for admitting and for letting out the fhips. The evacuation of the bafon, after letting in a veffel, is performed by a fteam-engine. The other canals made by order of the late emprefs, the large mole furrounded by a pier of granite, conftructed under the direction of admiral Greig, with many other particulars, render Cronftadt richly worthy the obfervation of all travellers into thofe parts.

him

him that he might rely on the fidelity of that place. Peter, who thought he already faw Catharine at the gates of Peterhof, precipitately got on board, followed by his affrighted court and the intrepid Munich.

It feemed as if fome dreadful fatality hung over the head of the unfortunate monarch to fruftrate all the wifeft meafures he adopted. Every thing in Cronftadt had affumed a new face within the fpace of a few hours. The fleet and the regiments, which had juft received general Devier with cries of joy, and fwearing to continue their fealty to the tzar, had already broke out into open revolt: Devier was deprived of the command and put into prifon; and this rapid change was the effect of a ftratagem.

During the firft hours of the infurrection, and in the meafures that were primarily taken for enfuring its fuccefs, not one of the confpirators had beftowed a thought upon the fort of Cronftadt. It was not even till afternoon that fomebody, reflecting on the importance of that place, remarked the miftake they had committed in neglecting it fo long. Admiral Taliezin made the offer to go and take poffeffion of it. It was accepted. He embarked in his long-boat, exprefsly forbad his rowers to mention whence they came, and arrived at Cronftadt. General Devier, who

T 2   kept

kept on the look-out, as he expected every moment the emperor, ran forward to meet Taliezin, and artfully endeavoured to difcover whether he was of Catharine's party; but Taliezin, more artful than he, pretended ignorance of the effects of the revolt; faying, that being at his country-houfe, and hearing a confufed account of fome difturbance that had happened at Peterfburg, he was hurrying to get on board the fleet, whither his duty called him. Devier believed the ftory, and went his way. Taliezin immediately repaired to the quarter of the failors, harangued them, told them of the fuccefs of the emprefs, that they could not do better than to declare for her, diftributed among them brandy and money, and engaged them to follow him to arreft the commandant. Some foldiers joined themfelves to the failors. Devier was inftantly thrown into prifon, and Taliezin remained mafter, in the name of the emprefs, of a place, the poffeffion whereof might have been the falvation of the tzar, or at leaft have furnifhed him with the means of making a ftout refiftance.

Precifely while this fcene was transacting, Peter prefented himfelf before the mouth of the harbour. Taliezin had already made the difpofitions for preventing his coming on fhore. A part

A part of the garrifon, under arms, lined the coaſt. The cannons were levelled, the matches lighted, and at the moment when the foremoſt yacht caſt anchor, the centinel called out, " Who " comes there ?" — " The emperor," it was anſwered from the yacht. " There is no em- " peror," replied the centinel. Peter ſtarted forward; and, throwing back his cloak, to ſhew the badges of his order, exclaimed, " What ! " do you not know me ?" — " No," ejaculated a thouſand voices at once, " we know of no em- " peror. Long live the empreſs Catharine !" Then Taliezin threatened to ſink the yacht if it did not put off in an inſtant. Peter retired in great conſternation : but Gudovitch took him by the arm ; and, laying hold on one of the timbers at the entrance of the mole ; " Put your " hands by the ſide of mine," ſaid he, " and let " us leap on ſhore. None will dare to fire " upon you, and Cronſtadt will ſtill belong to " your majeſty *."

Munich ſeconded the advice of Gudovitch ; but in vain. In his diſmay, Peter III. would conſent to nothing but flight, and ran to hide himſelf in the cabin of the yacht, among the

* Counteſs Bruce and madam Zagreiſky, who were both preſent, have frequently related this tranſaction.

terrified

terrified women. They did not even give themselves time to raise the anchor; but cut the cable, and went off by the use of their oars.

When the yachts were at a considerable distance from the port, the rowers stopped. It was a fine night; and Munich and Gudovitch, sitting upon deck, contemplated in silent sorrow the starry sky and the calm surface of the sea. The steersman came down into the cabin, to ask the tzar whither he would please to be taken into the vessel. Peter ordered Munich to be called, and said to him, " Field-marshal, I perceive that I was too late in following your advice; but you see to what extremities I am reduced. You, who have escaped from so many dangers, tell me, I beseech you, what I ought to do." — " Proceed immediately to join the squadron at Reval," returned Munich; " there take a ship, go on to Pomerania, put yourself at the head of your army, return to Russia, and I promise you, that in six weeks Petersburg and all the rest of the empire will be in subjection to you."

The women and the courtiers, as if they had come to an agreement to ruin the unfortunate Peter, began directly to cry out, that the rowers would never have strength enough to reach Reval.

Reval *. " Well then," replied Munich, " we " will all row with them." But such generous counsel could not be agreeable to this timid or treacherous court. They shuddered at it. They seemed to try which should be most eager in assuring the emperor that his danger was not so great as he imagined; that Catharine only wanted to come to an accommodation with him, and that it was far better to negotiate than to fight. The imbecil prince, whose greatest misfortune it ever had been not to be able to resolve on the courageous side, yielded to these representations, and gave orders to the pilot to make for Oranienbaum.

It was four in the morning when they reached that place. Some of the emperor's domestics, in great alarm, came to receive him. He commanded them not to divulge the news of his return, shut himself up in his apartment, strictly forbidding any person to be admitted, and secretly wrote to the empress.

At ten o'clock he came out with a countenance tolerably calm and serene. Those of his holstein guards who were come back to Oranienbaum, ran and surrounded him, shedding tears of af-

* The ancient town of Reval, with its harbour and fort, is situate on the gulf of Finland, 59° 26′ 22″ N. L. and 42° 27′ 30″ long. distant 340 versts from St. Petersburg.

fection

fection and joy. They kiffed his hands, they embraced his knees, they preffed him to march them againft the army of the emprefs, and folemnly fwore that they were all to a man ready to facrifice their lives in defence of his. Old Munich once more tried what influence he might have upon Peter, and feized this occafion for exhorting him to make a courageous ftand in his own defence. " Come," faid he, " march " againft the rebels. I will go before you, " and their fwords fhall not reach you till they " have pierced my body." But the perfuafion of Munich had no more effect on the tzar than the noble devotednefs of his holftein troops.

While all this was transacting, the emprefs, at the head of her army, had come to a halt at Krafnoë kabac, a fmall public-houfe by the road-fide *, exactly eight verfts from Peterfburg,

* Krafnoë-kabac is rather a better fort of public houfe, frequented chiefly for little fundry excurfions, by the tradef-men of the town, particularly the Germans. A billiard-room is on one hand of the door, and on the other an ordinary parlour; into the latter the emprefs with princefs Dafhkoff entered: and here (the old landlady, who died about a dozen years ago, bas often related) they ordered a fmall fire to be lighted, and employed themfelves a con-fiderable time in burning a great ftore of letters and papers, Krafnoë fignifies *red*, and kabac, a public-houfe: the houfe is painted all over red.

and

and had turned into the firſt room, where ſhe repoſed for ſome hours, on the cloaks which the officers of her ſuite had made for her into a bed.   At break of day, Gregory Orloff, with a few determined volunteers, had been to recon- noitre the environs of Peterhof, and finding there only ſome peaſants armed with ſcythes, who had been collected the preceding evening, he dif- perſed them by blows with the flat of his ſabre, and made them join him in the cries of "Long live the empreſs!"   At five in the morning, Catharine got again on horſeback, and rode to the monaſtery of St. Sergius*, near Strelna, where ſhe made a ſecond halt.

The empreſs was ſtill there when ſhe received the letter from the tzar, in which he told her that he acknowledged his miſconduct, and pro- poſed to ſhare the ſovereign authority with her. But Catharine returned him no anſwer, detained the meſſenger, and preſently after ſet out again.

Peter now learning that the empreſs was approaching, ordered one of his horſes to be ſaddled, in the deſign of eſcaping, alone and dif-

* Svetotroïtſkaia Sergiyevſkaia puſtinæ, the holy-trinity hermitage of St. Sergius, is a ſmall monaſtery, ſubſtantially built of brick, ſurrounded by a quadrangular cloiſter, in- cloſing a church and three chapels, it is 16 verſts from St. Peterſburg, and has now but few monks.

guiſed,

guifed, towards the frontiers of Poland. But, always pufillanimous, always irrefolute, he fhortly after gave orders to difmantle his little fortrefs at Oranienbaum, in order to convince Catharine that he intended to make no refiftance; and wrote to her a fecond letter, imploring her mercy and afking her pardon in the moft humiliating expreffions. He affured her at the fame time that he would refign to her the crown of Ruffia, and petitioned her only to grant him a penfion, with liberty to retire into Holftein.

Catharine deigned no more to reply to this letter than fhe had done to the former; but after having converfed fome time with the chamberlain Ifmaïloff, who had brought it, and whom fhe eafily perfuaded to betray his mafter, fhe fent him back to the tzar to determine him to fubmit unconditionally to her will.

Ifmaïloff returned to Oranienbaum, attended by a fingle fervant. The tzar had then with him his holftein guard, confifting of 600 men. Thefe he ordered to keep at a diftance, and fhut himfelf up with the chamberlain, who exhorted him to abandon his troops and to repair to the emprefs, affuring him that he would be well received, and would obtain of her all that he wifhed. Peter hefitated for fome time: but Ifmaïloff telling him that he muft make no

delay,

delay, for that his life was in danger, he followed the advice of this traitor. Ifmaïloff then helped him into a carriage with Romanovna Voront- zoff and Gudovitch, and they took the road of Peterhof.

The unfortunate tzar thought that fo much refignation might move the heart of Catharine. He was prefently undeceived. When the car- riage in which he rode paffed through the army, the kozaks whom the emperor firft met, and who had never feen him, kept a mournful filence ; he himfelf felt a lively emotion : then the reiterated vociferations of " Long live Catharine!" com- pleted his defpondency.

On ftepping out of the carriage, his miftrefs was carried off by the foldiers, who tore off her riband *; with which princefs Dafhkoff, her fifter, was almoft inftantly decorated. His general aide-de-camp Gudovitch was likewife infulted ; but he preferved the utmoft tranquillity of mind, and in a dignified manner reproached the rebels with their infolence and treafon.

The tzar was led up the grand ftaircafe. There the attendants ftripped him of the marks of his order ; they took off his clothes ; and, on ranfacking the pockets, found feveral dia-

* It has been pretended by fome perfons, that it was princefs Dafhkoff herfelf that pulled it off.

monds

monds and pieces of jewellery. After having remained there some time in his shirt, and barefoot, a butt to the outrages of an insolent soldiery, they threw over him an old morning-gown, and shut him up alone in a room, with a guard at the door.

Count Panin, being sent by the empress, was admitted to the tzar, and had a long conference with him. He told him that her majesty would not long keep him in confinement, but send him into Holstein according to his own request. To this promise he added several others, probably without the design of keeping any. He concluded his visit by making him write and sign the following declaration :

" During the short space of my absolute reign over the
" empire of Russia, I became sensible that I was not able
" to support so great a burden, and that my abilities were
" not equal to the task of governing so great an empire,
" either as a sovereign, or in any other capacity whatever.
" I also foresaw the great troubles which must thence
" have arisen, and have been followed with the total ruin
" of the empire, and my own eternal disgrace. After
" having therefore seriously reflected thereon, I declare,
" without constraint, and in the most solemn manner, to
" the russian empire, and to the whole universe, that I for
" ever renounce the government of the said empire, never
" desiring hereafter to reign therein, either as an absolute
" sovereign, or under any other form of government ;
" never wishing to aspire thereto, to use any means, of any
" sort, for that purpose. As a pledge of which, I swear
" sincerely,

" fincerely, before God and all the world, to this prefent
" renunciation, written and figned this 29th of June O. S.
" 1762."

Thus, not fatisfied with depriving him of his
crown, it was thought fit to make him the mur-
derer of his own reputation ; and this unfortunate
prince, moved with the vain hope of life, figned
this paper declaring his conviction of his inability
to govern the empire, either as a fovereign, or in
any other capacity, and his fenfe of the diftrefs
in which his continuing at the head of affairs
would inevitably involve it.

Having obtained this fatal act, count Panin
left him ; and Peter feemed to enjoy a greater
compofure of mind.   In the evening, however,
an officer, with a ftrong efcort, came and conveyed him a prifoner to Ropfcha, a fmall imperial palace, at the diftance of about 20 verfts
from Peterhof.

Thus was a revolution of fuch immenfe importance effected in one day, and without fhed-
ding a fingle drop of blood.   The unfortunate
emperor enjoyed the power, of which he had
made fo imprudent and impolitic an ufe, no
longer than fix months.   His wife, without any
hereditary title, was fovereign miftrefs of the
ruffian empire; and the moft abfolute power on
earth was now held by an elective monarch.

Immediately

Immediately on this revolution a number of manifeftoes appeared, in which the conduct of the late tzar was feverely condemned, the weaknefs of his perfonal character expofed, and defigns of the blackeft kind, even that of murdering his confort, attributed to him. Thofe manifeftoes at the fame time were filled with the ftrongeft declarations of affection from the emprefs to the fubjects of Ruffia, of regard to their interefts, and of attachment to their religion ; and they are all filled with fuch unaffected and fervent ftrains of piety, as muft needs prove extremely edifying to thofe who are acquainted with the fentiments of pure religion, by which great princes are generally animated on occafions of this nature.

In the mean time Peterfburg had been, fince the preceding day, in a ftate of uncertainty and expectation. Nobody had yet come with intelligence of Catharine's fucceffes. Peter III. had ftill fome friends in that city ; and if he had had force enough to attack and repulfe the rebels, its inhabitants would have received him with eagernefs, as the means of appeafing his refentment. The foreign merchants, who live there in great numbers, dreaded above all things the fury of the ruffian foldiers, who perhaps, by plundering their houfes and abufing their perfons, would have thought they acted meritorioufly ritoriously in the opinion of the emperor.   Accordingly many of them haftily conveyed their moft valuable effects on board the veffels belonging to their nation, and at the fame time kept in readinefs to embark themfelves.   Towards evening the noife of cannon that was heard from a diftance, fpread a fudden alarm throughout the city; but it was foon remarked, that thefe firings, being heard at regular intervals, and the tzar fending no one to fecure Peterfburg, this noife could only announce the victory of the emprefs.   Tranquillity was thenceforward reftored, and hope took place of fear.

Catharine flept that night at Peterhof, no longer as a captive, but as abfolute fovereign. The day following, fhe received at her levée the homages of the principal nobility, who had joined her the foregoing evening, and thofe of the courtiers and young women who came from Oranienbaum. Among thefe were, the father, the brother, and feveral other relations of princefs Dafhkoff, who, on beholding them proftrate before the emprefs, faid, "Madam, pardon my family. You "know that I have facrificed it to you." Catharine commanded them to rife, and gave them her hand to kifs.

Marfhal Munich alfo prefented himfelf before her, to whom, as foon as her majefty perceived

3   him,

him, she called aloud :—" Feldt-mareshal, it was
" you then who wanted to fight me ?"—" Yes,
" madam," answered Munich, in a firm and
manly tone ; " could I do less for the prince
" who delivered me from captivity ? But it is
" henceforward my duty to fight for you ; and
" you will find in me a fidelity equal to that
" with which I had devoted my services to
" him."

In the afternoon, Catharine returned to Petersburg. Her entry was truly triumphant. She
was on horseback, preceded or followed by the
chiefs of the conspiracy. The whole army was
crowned with wreaths of oak ; the shouts of joy
and the applauses of the populace mingled with
those of the soldiers. The crowd formed into
lines for the empress, and she condescendingly
gave them her hand to kiss, as she passed along.
A great number of priests were assembled on the
occasion about the avenues of the palace : as she
rode through their ranks, she stooped down to
salute the cheeks of the principal clergy, while
they were kissing her hand ; a custom prevalent
in that country, and is significant of the highest
respect.

For some days after her return to the imperial residence, her majesty continued to shew
herself to the multitude with great condescension.

fcenfion. She knew how eafy it is to gain the applaufes of the public : fhe went to the fenate, and heard feveral caufes tried before her. She then held her court with a graceful and eafy dignity, that effaced the remembrance of the fudden revolution that had juft placed her on the throne. The foreign minifters had audiences of congratulation; and fhe received them with a particular addrefs to each in the moft flattering terms.

Her firft care was to have prince Ivan conveyed from the houfe where he was concealed, and to fend him back to Schluffelburg. She next proceeded to beftow magnificent rewards on the principal actors in the revolt. Nikita Ivanovitch Panin was made prime minifter; the Orloffs received the title of count; and the favourite Gregory Orloff was appointed lieutenant-general of the ruffian armies, and chevalier of St. Alexander Neffky, the fecond order of the empire. Several officers of the guards were promoted. Four-and-twenty of them obtained confiderable eftates, with fome thoufands of boors. The finances were infufficient to give any thing to the foldiers but brandy and beer: they were diftributed among them; and Catharine behaved to them with the greateft affability. At times fhe even put herfelf under

VOL. I.   u   conftraint

conftraint in order not to difoblige them. Three days fubfequent to the revolution a drunken foldier dreamed that the emprefs was carried off. He rofe up, ran about the barracks, every where fpreading alarm, crying out, that the Holfteiners and the Pruffians had got poffeffion of the emprefs. The regiment immediately took up arms, ran to the palace, and loudly infifted on feeing her majefty. The hetman Razumofffky, having learned the caufe of this tumult, appeared at a window, affured them that the emprefs was not carried off, and that after the difturbances and fatigues fhe had undergone for fome days, fhe was now repofing in peace and fecurity. But the foldiers refufed to believe him, and began to renew their clamours with redoubled violence. The hetman now went to the chamber of the fovereign, caufed her to be awaked; and praying her not to be frightened; " You know that " I am frightened at nothing," anfwered fhe boldly: " but what is the matter?" — " The " foldiers imagine that you are not here : they " infift upon feeing you," returned Razumoffky. " Well, they muft be fatisfied," replied fhe ; and immediately rofe up, dreffed herfelf, called for her carriage, with orders to drive to the kafanfkoi church. On her way the foldiers furrounded her carriage, interrogating each other:
" Is

" Is that indeed the emprefs? Is that indeed our
" mother?"   Being come to the church, Catharine fhewed herfelf to them, harangued them,
thanked them for their follicitude, and difmiffed
them highly fatisfied.

She made a point of fhewing clemency towards the officers and the friends of the emperor;
and if any of them were forbid the court, not
one was deprived of his property or his life.
Only Gudovitch, the aide-de-camp-general, Volkoff, and Milganoff, were imprifoned.   Countefs
Vorontzoff, who at firft had been treated rudely
by the foldiers, was fent to the houfe of the
fenator her father; and the emprefs exprefsly
forbad a repetition of the like affronts.   She was
afterwards exiled for fome time to a village
1000 verfts beyond Mofco.

All the courtiers now eagerly preffed about
the fovereign.   They endeavoured to difcover
on whom her favour would alight: every one
flattering himfelf that he fhould obtain the greater
fhare of it, while none fufpected that the heart
of that princefs had long been fixed on an officer
of humble birth.   The firft marks of diftinction
fhewn to Gregory Orloff appeared only as the
reward of his fervices, and not the pledges of
love.   It was princefs Dafhkoff who difcovered
it the firft.   Jealoufy is more watchful than am-

bition;

bition ; it is especially less discreet; and madame Dashkoff, not satisfied with reproaching Catharine with a choice that degraded her, spread the rumour of it among her friends, and thus brought on her own disgrace. The chiefs of the revolt now learned, with displeasure, that they had been working for a man whom they had always regarded as the instrument of their projects ; while the courtiers perceived that, in the art of intrigue, this man was more expert than themselves.

The most zealous partisans of Catharine were not, however, without uneasiness. Some regiments murmured, and began to repent the part they had acted against their lawful sovereign. The people, who easily pass from rage to compassion, now pitied the fate of this unfortunate prince. They forgot his defects, his caprices, his infirmities, in the recollection of his amiable qualities, and his sad reverse of fortune.* The sailors reproached the guards to their face, that they had sold their master for brandy and beer.

* The ingenious and judicious traveller Mr. Coxe very justly observes, in speaking of this revolution, " that Peter, " notwithstanding his violence and incapacity, possessed se- " veral qualifications of a popular nature, and was greatly " beloved by those who had access to his person." See Coxe's Travels, vol. iii. p. 43. 8vo. edit.

After

After the first tumult of the revolution was
over, they now waked as it were out of a profound intoxication: they contemplated what
had happened in solemn silence, and began to
consider whether all was right.   Without speaking of the peaceable burghers, who, during the
doubtful explosion, had kept close in their
houses, even a very great number of them who
had been exceedingly active in the business, and
loudest in their execrations of Peter, were now
seized with a deep and painful remorse, and
lamented the sufferings they had brought upon
their monarch.   But among the guards the same
sentiments displayed themselves in a still more
violent manner: numbers of the soldiers, re-
penting of their abominable treason, for in that
light they now beheld their late behaviour, expressed their resentment against their accomplices in the most intemperate language, and
the most abusive terms that resentment could
dictate to vulgar minds: imputing to their
seductions the crimes into which they had been
led, and loading them with reproaches for the
compunction they now suffered in consequence
of their guilt.   From words they proceeded to
blows, and even to murder.   Though throughout the revolution no blood had hitherto been
shed, now several were killed in these furious

squabbles,

squabbles.　The officers repeatedly interposed, at the hazard of their personal safety, to pacify the men, and make them hearken to reason: but in vain.　Such are the populace in all ages and nations: rash to perpetrate what their fury suggests; repentant at the sight of the mischief they have done; then prompt in their accusations against others, instead of confessing their own misconduct.　Nothing was wanting but some resolute leader, to have now replaced Peter III. on the throne, as suddenly as but three days ago he had been precipitated from it: the attachment of the common people to him was clearly evinced in the rebellion of Pugatsheff, eleven years after.　In short, apprehensions were entertained of a new insurrection.

While the public mind was agitated by these fears, the news that was brought from Mosco, served only to increase the panic. The governor of that capital, being informed of the revolution by the emissaries of Catharine, ordered the five regiments that composed the garrison to take to their arms; and after having drawn them up in the great place of the palace of the ancient tzars, he there convoked the people, who flocked together in crowds.　That officer then read aloud the ukase by which the empress announced her accession, and the abdication of her

her spouse * : at the conclusion of which he exclaimed, " Long live the empress Catharine " the Second !" But the people and the soldiers remained in silence. He repeated the same cry; the same silence ensued. No sound but that of sullen murmurs was heard. The troops complained that the regiments of the guards had insolently dared to dispose of the throne. The governor, startled at these unexpected expressions of discontent, called upon the other officers to join him. They cried out together, " Long live the empress !" This done, the multitude was dismissed, and the soldiers sent back to their barracks.

No one was more uneasy at this time than Catharine herself. Whether her situation be considered in a moral or a political light, it must have occasioned her emotions of no common force, especially as she had been so suddenly and unexpectedly brought into it ! She certainly never thought, on coming to Russia, nor, during the first years that ensued, ever busied herself in forming designs of ascending the throne as absolute sovereign. Generous and amiable by nature, she was true to these qualities from her infancy to the day of her death.

* See the appendix at the end of the volume.

Neither

Neither a felfifh contempt for all limitations, nor an inordinate thirft of power, formed any part of her natural character. But this generofity and amiablenefs of temper gave the young princefs undoubted pretenfions to happinefs and joy, which, as the confort of Peter, fhe faw were not anfwered, and of which fhe was likely to be deprived for the whole of her life. Now, after this firft ftep, her profpect, whichever way fhe turned, could certainly not be cheerful. If fhe looked backwards, no pleafing recollections enlivened the view; if forwards, the fcene was all darkened with impending clouds. It is well known that, haunted by the fpectres of the imagination, during this period, even in fleep fhe found no repofe; and that feveral times in a night fhe has quitted her bed, and even her palace.

And what muft have been the feelings of Peter in his lonefome captivity! It was eafy to forefee that his imprifonment, either mediately or immediately, would bring on his death, and fo it actually happened.

Undoubtedly no great efforts were neceffary to determine the confpirators to free themfelves from an object of difquietude. They who have taken one ftep in the road of guilt, make no he-fitation

sitation at taking a second, and the death of the
unhappy emperor was now decreed.

On his removal from Peterhof, the tzar was
still blind to the fate that awaited him.   Thinking he should be detained but a short time in
prison, previous to his being sent into Germany,
he sent a message to Catharine, asking her to
permit him to have the negro who was of service
to him by his attachment, and amused him with
his singularities, together with a dog he was fond
of, his violin, a bible, and a few romances; at
the same time telling her, that, disgusted at the
wickedness of mankind, he was resolved henceforward to devote himself to a philosophical life.
However reasonable these requests, not one of
them was granted, and his plans of wisdom were
turned into ridicule.   He was conducted to a
little imperial retreat at Ropscha.

Here he had been six days without the knowledge of any other persons than the chiefs of the
conspirators and the soldiers by whom he was
guarded, when Alexius Orloff, accompanied by
an officer named Teploff, came to him with the
news of his speedy deliverance, and asked permission to dine with him.   According to the
custom of that country, wine-glasses and brandy
were brought previous to dinner; and while the

officer

officer amused the tzar with some trifling dif-course, his chief filled the glasses, and poured a poisonous mixture into that he intended for the prince. The tzar, without any distrust, swallowed the potion: on which, he presently experienced the most cruel pains; and on his being offered a second glass, on pretence of its giving him relief, he refused it, with reproaches on him that offered it.

He called aloud for milk; but the two monsters offered him poison again, and pressed him to take it. A french valet-de-chambre, greatly attached to him, now ran in. Peter threw himself into his arms, saying, in a faint tone of voice, "It was not enough then to prevent me from "reigning in Sweden, and to deprive me of the "crown of Russia! I must also be put to "death!"

The valet-de-chambre presumed to intercede for his master; but the two miscreants forced this dangerous witness out of the room, and continued their ill-treatment of the tzar. In the midst of this tumult the younger of the princes Baratinsky came in, and joined the two former*.

Orloff,

* Her majesty, from the very first, thought it necessary to commit so important a charge as that of the dethroned emperor,

Orloff, who had already thrown down the emperor, was preffing upon his breaft with both his knees, and firmly griping his throat with his hand. The unhappy monarch, now ftruggling with that ftrength which arifes from defpair, the two other affaffins threw a napkin round his neck, and put an end to his life by fuffocation *.

Such is the account of the death of Peter III. as circulated in whifpers at Peterfburg, and which indeed has never been contradicted: whether it be the real manner in which the tzar came by his death is, after all, known only to that Being

---

emperor, to the cuftody of perfons in whom fhe could place the moft entire confidence, and who were not liable to corruption, rather than to mercenaries, who are never proof againft bribery. The three perfons whom fhe deemed worthy of her confidence on fo delicate an occafion, were count Alexius Orloff, brother of prince Gregory, and the two brothers Baratinfky, of whom one was marfhal of the court, and the other was fince envoy from Ruffia to the court of France. All the three were living in the year 1797.

* On the 17th of July, juft one week after the revolution. Thefe particulars are confirmed by the account of a gentleman who was in the confidence of prince Potemkin. It has been falfely pretended that Potemkin was with them. But perfons of great credibility, who were at that time in Ruffia, affert the contrary, and Potemkin always denied the fact with indignation.

to

to whom the heart is open, and from whom
no secrets are concealed. The partifans that
might have retained their attachment to him after
his fall; the murmurs of the populace, who quietly
permit revolutions to be effected, and afterwards
lament those who have fallen their victims; the
difficulties arising from keeping in custody a prifoner of such consequence; all these motives in
conjunction tend to give credit to the opinion
that some hand of uncontrollable authority
shortened his days. But the conduct of the emprefs before that event, and especially for four-
and-thirty years that she afterwards reigned, is
of itself alone a sufficient refutation of so atrocious a calumny, as would fix the guilt of it on
her.

Whatever were the failings and errors of
Peter III. it is not here intended to extenuate or
defend them; though certainly they were too
cruelly punished. Neither ought the good he
did to be paffed over in filence. His two ukafes
for abolishing the secret inquifition, and for
giving liberty to the nobles, muft for ever
fecure to this prince the grateful acknowledgment of Ruffia. The *clement* * Elizabeth had
left

* To what has been above related of that fovereign, the
following may be here fubjoined: She one day received at
her

left in subsistence a tribunal, before which the first persons of the empire, on the bare deposition of a villain on the way to execution, were delivered and put to the torture, for extorting the confession of imaginary crimes. Peter III. was dethroned; his name was never honoured with so flattering an epithet; and yet it was he who suppressed that tribunal. This prince was kind, humane, and beloved of all who composed his more intimate circle: this is asserted on the affirmation of many Russians who were attached to his person *. He recalled all the exiles that were

---

her toilet a lady of the court, who with great difficulty continued standing. Elizabeth at last perceived her uneasiness, and asked what was the matter with her. " My legs " are very much swelled." — " Well, well, lean against " that bureau; I will make as if I did not see you." This was truly characteristic. The same princess would not permit any lady to wear, not only the same stuffs that she had chosen, but the same patterns: a lady still living, in 1762, and very well known, ventured to infringe this prohibition. Her boldness had like to have cost her dear; and so much the more, as she had already incurred the indignation of the *clement* monarch by receiving the french fashions before her.

* In the just tribute of praise we have more than once taken occasion to pay to the memory of the unfortunate Peter, we are pleased with having the concurrence of the author

were lingering out their lives in Siberia (excepting Beftucheff); and it muſt have been a
ſpectacle curious enough to ſee Biren and Munich
together; the former embarraſſed, confounded,
not daring to lift up his eyes, dreading to meet
thoſe of the ſon or the brother of ſome unfortunate wretch who had been aſſaſſinated or ba-
niſhed by his command; Munich, on the other
hand, forming the moſt perfect contraſt with
him.   Fourſcore years of his life elapſed,
twenty of them paſſed in exile in the frightful
waſtes of Siberia, had not depreſſed that firm
and generous ſoul : — at the head of armies, —
condemned to death, — in frozen deſerts, — recalled to court, and reinſtated in all his employ-

___

author of a late publication, who, after expreſſing his indignation at ſome writers ſo contemptible as to traduce the
memory of this unfortunate ſovereign, adds, "that he was
" a victim to the undeſigning openneſs and integrity of his
" heart; a prince, whoſe anſwer to the precautions which
" were recommended to him by the king of Pruſſia was,
" *I do good to all the world, and with that what have I to
" fear?* a prince, who was the benefactor of his country;
" and whoſe laws (thoſe very laws which were brought in
" accuſation againſt him as crimes) have been religiouſly
" obſerved as models of wiſdom and humanity, and without
" which the reign of the empreſs would have been leſs
" glorious, and her people leſs happy."— Survey of the
Turkiſh Empire, p. 445.
    4   ments,

ments, Munich was every where the fame; he ever preferved that unalterable ferenity, that energy of character, which fall to the lot of fo very few*.

Had the emperor, during the fix months of his reign, done no more than iffue thofe two decrees juft mentioned, he would have been entitled to rank with thofe fovereigns who have a juft claim on the gratitude of their fubjects. The freedom of the nobility is undoubtedly the firft ftep to civilization. That indifpenfable preliminary had efcaped the attention of Peter the great: it was by this that he ought to have begun his work, and it is to be regretted that the ruffian legiflator failed of perceiving the abfolute neceffity of it. The feizure of the poffeffions of the church was one of the caufes of the public difcontent; but what fhews that the act was far from being bad in itfelf, is, that the emprefs never thought it expedient to reftore them: the odium did not fall upon her; the fault being committed, fhe had the addrefs to profit by it.

Alexey Orloff immediately mounted his horfe, and rode full fpeed to inform the emprefs that

* Field-marfhal Munich obtained the government of Efthonia and Livonia, and died three years afterwards at Riga, at the age of 85.

Peter

Peter III. had breathed his laft.   It was at the
inftant when her majefty was going to make her
appearance at court.   She appeared with a tranquil air ; and afterwards fhut herfelf up with
Orloff, Panin, Razumoffíky, Gleboff, and fome
other confidential perfons, to deliberate whether
the fenate and people fhould be immediately
made acquainted with the death of the emperor,
or whether it might not be more advifable to wait
for that purpofe till the enfuing day.   The latter
was determined.   Catharine dined in public as
ufual, and in the evening held a court.

.   The next day the news of the emperor's
death was communicated to the public at large,
while her majefty was at table.   At that inftant
fhe rofe from her feat with her eyes full of
tears.   She difmiffed the courtiers and the foreign
minifters, ran and fhut herfelf in her apartment,
and for feveral days together fhewed marks of
the profoundeft grief.   During this time the following declaration was publifhed on the part of
the emprefs :

" By the grace of God, Catharine II. emprefs and au-
       " tocratrix of all the Ruffias, to all our loving fub-
       " jeets, &c. greeting :
    " The feventh day after our acceffion to the throne of all
" the Ruffias, we received information that the late emperor
" Peter III. by the means of a bloody accident in his
" hinder parts, commonly called piles, to which he had
                                                   " been

" been formerly fubject, was attacked with a moft violent
" griping colic.   That therefore we might not be wanting
" in chriftian duty, nor difobedient to the divine command,
" by which we are enjoined to preferve the life of our
" neighbour, we immediately ordered that the faid Peter
" fhould be furnifhed with every thing that might be judged
" neceffary to prevent the dangerous confequences of that
" accident, and to reftore his health by the aids of me-
" dicine.   But, to our great regret and affliction, we were
" yefterday evening apprifed, that, by the permiffion of the
" Almighty, the late emperor departed this life.   We have
" therefore ordered his body to be conveyed to the monaftery
" of Nefsky, in order to its interment in that place.   At
" the fame time, with our imperial and maternal voice, we
" exhort our faithful fubjects to forgive and forget what is
" paft, to pay the laft duties to his body, and to pray to
" God fincerely for the repofe of his foul; willing them
" however to confider this unexpected and fudden death
" as an efpecial effect of the providence of God, whofe
" impenetrable decrees are working for us, for our throne,
" and for our country, things known only to his holy will.
    " Done at St. Peterfburg, July 7, 1762."

The body of the unfortunate Peter III. was
brought to Peterfburg, and expofed for three
days in the church of the monaftery of St. Alexander Nefsky.   The body lay in an open coffin,
dreffed in his holftein uniform, and perfons of
all ranks and conditions were admitted, as ufual
in that country, to kifs the hand of the deceafed * ;

* His face, it is faid, was become quite black; extra-
vafated blood was feen to ooze through the epidermis which
penetrated even the gloves which had been put on his hands;

and he was buried on the 21ft, exactly the very day which he had fixed for his departure on the expedition againft Denmark. His remains were depofited in a grave in the fpace before the rails of the altar, adjacent to that of the depofed regent Anne, the mother of the dethroned infant Ivan; and the place of his fepulture was diftinguifhed with neither tomb nor infcription. Peter had never been crowned, he had refigned the reins of empire. No court befide that of Sweden went into mourning for him.

The day of his interment was a day of trouble and defolation for Peterfburg. The populace that thronged to the funeral were very abufive to the foldiers of the guards, reproaching them with having bafely fhed the laft drop of the blood of Peter the great.

The holftein foldiers, who had hitherto remained at Oranienbaum, at liberty, but difarmed,

---

and the poifon which the tzar had been forced to fwallow muft have been exceedingly violent, as all thofe who had the lamentable courage to lay their mouth to his, returned with fwelled lips. The counfellors of Catharine knew well enough that fuch dreadful intimations might lead to a difcovery of the means that had been employed for fhortening the days of the unfortunate monarch, but they thought themfelves lefs interefted in faving appearances than in preventing the agitations which would have infallibly taken place if the people had imagined that the tzar was ftill alive.

reforted

reforted to thefe forrowful obfequies; and, weeping, furrounded the corpfe of their mafter. The Ruffians, no longer beholding them as preferred rivals, but as faithful fervants, took part in their grief.

The following day orders were fent down to embark thefe Holfteiners for their own country. They were put on board a veffel, which unhappily foundered foon after quitting the port of Cronftadt; numbers of them were feen clinging about the rocks above the water's level, where they were fuffered to perifh, while admiral Taliezin had difpatched a meffenger to Peterfburg to know whether he might be permitted to afford them relief.

Prince George, whom Peter III. had conftituted duke of Courland, was obliged to renounce that title: but the emprefs compenfated this lofs by committing to him the adminiftration of Holftein, whither he went with the reft of his family; and where he ever after ferved Catharine with fidelity and zeal.

The chancellor Beftucheff, who had been the moft inveterate enemy of Peter, was recalled from his exile*. Prince Vulkonfky and

* For the declaration publifhed by the emprefs fhortly after the recal of Beftucheff is too remarkable to be forgotten. Some portions of it are therefore inferted in the appendix at the end of the volume.

lieutenant

lieutenant Kalifhkin were fent off to him, who brought him to Peterfburg. Catharine reftored to him his rank of field-marfhal, and his place in the council, befides fettling upon him an annual penfion of 20,000 rubles, and difpenfing him from employment on account of his great age. Several other exiles and prifoners were on this occafion fet free, but neither Ivan nor any of his family. It was now a kind of refurrection at Peterfburg, when fo many perfons who had fo long been feparated from their acquaintance, forgotten by the world, and buried in the deferts of Siberia, again appeared about the town; and thefe apparitions had a farther fimilitude with the future life, as perfons who had reciprocally crufhed fuch as ftood in their way, and then, by a fingular retaliation of fortune, had afterwards fuffered the like treatment from others, now met here together in reconcilement and peace. Count Munich, in 1740, had occafioned duke Biren to be imprifoned and banifhed; nay, even fketched out the plan of the houfe for his confinement at Pelim: one year after this, the count came himfelf as an exile to the fame place, and was fhut up in that houfe, which he certainly never thought he was building for himfelf, and from which the duke was removed to a more comfortable

fortable abode. Their firft meeting afterwards
was in the prefence of Peter III. who recalled
them both; Munich being then 79, and Biren
72 years of age. Catharine completed the boon
to the latter, by reinftating him in his dukedom
of Courland, as has been before obferved *.
Beftucheff had overthrown Leftok, his patron
and promoter, and was afterwards himfelf fent
to fhare the fame fate: thefe likewife now found
themfelves here together, and likewife with
paffions much abated of their violence. Leftok
was 70 when Peter recalled him; but Catharine
firft gave him a yearly allowance: the former
chancellor of the empire fhe now prefented
with his freedom and dignities in his 69th year,
and raifed him to the poft of general field-marfhal. In that capacity he ftood on the right hand
of her throne at her coronation, during the public
dinner, where the emprefs fat alone at table †.

Biren,

* It may farther be remarked, that the independent
fovereignty of Wurtenberg in Silefia, which Biren poffeffed,
on his banifhment reverted to Munich. They now compromifed the affair, under the mediation of Catharine, in
fuch manner, that the latter, for a confiderable fum of money, fully made over the fovereignty to the former; to
whofe fon, the duke having been again depofed by Catharine, it belonged at the time of her death.

† Beftucheff, fome months after his return, publifhed a
book of devotion, which, during his exile, he had compiled

of

Biren, who, more exafperated that Peter III. had not reinftated him in his duchy, than grateful for the liberty to which he had juft reftored him, had joined himfelf to the triumphant party, and had occafionally enlightened it by his experience; Biren took the road to Courland, where he was without difficulty reinvefted with his former authority, and where he favoured, to the utmoft of his power, the views which Catharine had already formed on Poland.

To complete the picture of this man, who, after having devoted himfelf to the commiffion of the moft horrible cruelties, affumed a lenity which he carried even to weaknefs, and who united in his conduct the extremes of fervility and a ridiculous vanity, it will be neceffary to mention the manner in which he took leave of Catharine. Falling on his knees before her, in prefence of the whole court, he addreffed her in thefe terms:

---

of various paffages, from the Pfalms and other parts of the Bible. He afterwards caufed a medal to be ftruck, on one fide reprefenting his buft, with the legend: Alexius comes à Beftucheff Riumin, imp. Ruff. olim cancellar. nunc fenior, &c. On the other is a coffin, with his efcutcheon, orange trees, palm trees, fortitude, conftancy. Over the coffin: Tertio triumphat; and in the exergue: Poft duos in vita de inimicis triumphos, de morte triumphat. He died at St. Peterfburg, April 21, 1766.

" Moft

" Moft illuftrious and moft puiffant emprefs :
" moft gracious fovereign and great lady ! — Is
" it poffible to conceive of a magnanimity and
" clemency equal to thofe which your imperial
" majefty has difplayed towards me and my fa-
" mily ? A prince without liberty, without do-
" mains, without affiftance, without fupport, is
" all at once furrounded with thefe feveral ad-
" vantages of which he had been deprived by a
" fucceffion of misfortunes for a long feries of
" years. I am indebted for thefe advantages
" to that love of juftice which fills the throne in
" the perfon of your imperial majefty, and which
" has juft broke the plot which iniquity and vio-
" lence have been fo artfully labouring to com-
" plete.

" What can I do for properly acknowledging
" this grace and thefe bounties ? All my facul-
" ties in conjunction with thofe of my family are
" infufficient to that end ; and I fhould be in-
" confolable if I were not perfuaded that your
" benevolence acquits thofe who have nothing
" to offer but gratitude and fubmiffion. Thefe
" are the two fentiments which I fhall carry with
" me to the grave, and which I fhall inceffantly
" inculcate on all that belong to me.——With the
" moft humble proftrations then, at the feet of
" your imperial majefty, I promife you a grati-

X 4   " tude

" tude and fubmiffion without limitation, and I
" prefume to intreat you gracioufly to fhew to
" me and to mine your powerful protection *."

The news of the revolution was foon univerfally fpread; and this great change in the
government of Ruffia, it was univerfally feared,
would be followed by a total change of fyftem
with regard to foreign affairs. The peace and
alliance with the king of Pruffia were very un-
popular meafures in that empire. It was not
probable that the clofe and intimate connection
which had fubfifted between the king of Pruffia
and the late tzar, could greatly recommend him
to the fucceffor. And as it was imagined that
this revolution muft have been in a great degree
owing to the machinations of thofe courts, whom
the tzar had irritated by withdrawing from their
alliance, there was the greater reafon to apprehend that the power, which was now fet up,
would be exerted in their favour.

There were alfo great advantages on the fide
of Ruffia, if the emprefs fhould not hold the
peace concluded by her late hufband to be binding on her, as none of the conquefts were at this

* Although Biren well knew that he was the fon of a
courifh peafant, he had taken the name and the arms of the
Birons of France, defirous of paffing for a defcendant of
that houfe.

time

time evacuated. Every thing feemed to confpire towards plunging the king of Pruffia into the abyfs of his former diftreffes, after he had emerged from them, only for fuch a time, and in fuch a manner, as to make them more bitter and infupportable.

Fortunately, however, for this wonderful man the emprefs, who had come to the Ruffian throne in the extraordinary manner that we have feen, could not look upon herfelf as fufficiently fecure to undertake again a war of fo much importance as that which had been juft concluded. It was neceffary, for fome time at leaft, that fhe fhould confine her attention folely to her own fafety. Therefore it was expedient to collect, within it-felf, all the force of the empire, in order to op-pofe it to the defigns of the many malecontents, with which that empire always abounds, and who, though not attached to the intereft of the late tzar, and little inclined to revenge his fate, would find now both inducement and opportu-nity for raifing troubles and attempting new changes. Very plaufible pretences for fuch at-tempts exifted from the time of Peter the great ; who, whilft he improved and ftrengthened his kingdom, left in it, at the fame time, the feeds of civil wars and revolutions.

Thefe

Thefe confiderations, whatever her defires might be, induced the tzarina to continue fo much of the fyftem of her predeceffor, as coincided with her fituation. She therefore declared to the king of Pruffia's minifters, " that fhe was " refolved to obferve inviolably, in all points, " the perpetual peace concluded under the pre- " ceding reign; that neverthelefs fhe had thought " proper to bring back to Ruffia, by the neareft " roads, all her troops in Silefia, Pruffia, and " Pomerania."

It was not the critical fituation alone of the tzarina which produced this moderation; the prudent behaviour of his pruffian majefty, during the time of his connection with the late tzar, had a confiderable fhare in reconciling the mind of this emprefs to him, and of perpetuating fomething like the fame friendfhip, with interefts fo very different.

On the 21ft of July, the orders arrived at the allied camp from Peterfburg for the Ruffians to feparate themfelves from his army, and return without delay to their own country.

None of the fovereigns of Europe were ignorant of the fteps by which Catharine had mounted the throne; but they made no hefitation in acknowledging her title. Some of them even

13   teftified

teftified their joy on the occafion: their joy, however, was not of long duration.

Maria Therefa at firft thought, that the Ruffians, abandoning the pruffian ftandards, would unite their arms with hers, to enable her once more to give laws to Frederic. Maria Therefa was deceived; and fhortly after faw, with equal aftonifhment and difpleafure, Catharine not only ordering her troops to evacuate Pruffia, but confirming the peace concluded by the tzar.

Lewis XV. alfo flattered himfelf that the careffes with which Catharine had diftinguifhed his ambaffador, while fhe was no more than grand duchefs, were pledges of her attachment to France. But, no fooner was fhe feated on the throne, than, while indulging her tafte for french literature *, fhe manifefted her contempt and averfion for the court of Verfailles †. Her unfortunate

* She was a great admirer of the french writers, and efpecially the tragic poets. Catharine alfo manifefted a high efteem for the philofophers. She wrote to d'Alembert, offering him a falary of 50,000 rubles, if he would come to Peterfburg to finifh the Encyclopedie, and take upon him the charge of the education of the grand duke Paul Petrovitch. D'Alembert declined the offer. See the Appendix at the end of the volume.

† Catharine could never forgive the duc de Choifeul for patronizing the work of the abbé Chappe d'Auteroche, and fhe even complained of it not a long time before her death: againft

unfortunate hufband feemed in this refpect alfo to
have ferved her for a model.

The monarch who formed the beft judgment
of her character was the king of Pruffia *. That
prince,

---

against which work, in conjunction with Peter Ivanovitch
Schewaloff, fhe wrote " The Antidote," which was miferably tranflated into englifh by a lady.

* The king of Pruffia wrote thus to count Finkenftein,
one of his favourites : — " The emperor of Ruffia has been
" dethroned by his confort : it was to be expected. That
" princefs has much good fenfe and the fame inclinations as
" the defunct. She has no religion, but acts the devotee.
" It is the fecond volume of Zeno, the greek emperor, of
" his wife Adriana, and of Mary de Medicis. The late
" chancellor Beftucheff was her greateft favourite ; and as
" he has a ftrong propenfity to guineas, I flatter myfelf
" that the attachments of the prefent period will be the
" fame. The poor emperor wanted to imitate Peter I.
" but he had not the capacity for it." This letter was
certainly not intended to fee the light : and it is curious
enough to put it in parallel with what its author, that grand
comedian Frederic, wrote for the public in his " Hiftory of
" the Seven-years War." — " The king," fays he, " had
" cultivated the friendfhip of the grand duke, at the time
" when he was only duke of Holftein ; and from a fenfibility
" rarely found among mankind, more rarely ftill among
" kings, that prince, in return, preferved a grateful heart :
" he even gave marks of it in that war ; for it was he who
" moft contributed to the retreat of general Apraxin, in
" 1757 ; when, after having beaten general Lewald, he fell
" back into Poland. During all thefe troubles, that prince
" even

prince, having long foreseen the bold attempt
by which she obtained the crown, repeatedly
wrote to his minister Goltz, that, since Peter III.
was resolutely bent on his own destruction, it
was advisable for him to turn to the side of Catharine.   Accordingly baron Goltz, the assiduous companion and flatterer of the pleasures of
the tzar, was one of the first to abandon him the
moment his affairs were seen to take a disastrous
turn, and received from Catharine the most gracious reception.

The empress likewise received with distinction
the envoy of Copenhagen, and gave the king
of Denmark assurances that he might make himself easy on the subject of Holstein, it being her
intention always to keep up a good understanding
with him.

" even abstained from going to council, where he had a seat,
" in order not to participate in the measures which the em-
" press was taking against Prussia, and which he disap-
" proved.........The king acted with the emperor not
" as one sovereign with another, but with that cordiality
" which friendship demands, and which is the greatest
" blessing of it.   The virtues of Peter III. formed an ex-
" ception to the rules of policy ; it was but right to act the
" same by him."— *Histoire de la Guerre de sept Ans*, edit. de
Berlin, tom. ii.

Mr.

Mr. Keith, ambaſſador from England, had not exactly the ſame freedom of acceſs to this princeſs as his predeceſſor Williams had formerly had ; ſhe treated him however as the miniſter of a friendly power, and took the firſt opportunity to renew the treaty which had long procured the Engliſh almoſt the whole commerce of Ruſſia.

While ſhe was ſecuring peace with the kings of Europe, Catharine neglected nothing for the maintenance of it within the empire. She had more to fear from her own ſubjects than from foreign potentates ; ſhe therefore employed herſelf in theſe affairs alternately with art and ſeverity. The court preſently aſſumed a new face. Every thing there was ſubmiſſive to the ſecret will of Gregory Orloff, whoſe influence and haughtineſs were increaſing from day to day, humiliating and irritating the great, and making them ardently deſire his fall. Several of them ventured to ſpeak out, and a reſolution to remove them was the immediate conſequence. But Catharine thought it beſt to diſſemble a while longer, before ſhe openly avenged her favourite, and put the laſt ſeal to the patent of his power.

The ſecond accounts that arrived from Moſco were of a more favourable complexion than the former.

former. Brandy and money, diftributed judi-
cioufly by the governor, had worked a great
change in the minds of the garrifon. The
foldiers could not refufe to acknowledge the
fovereign who ordered them daily fuch marks
of her bounty. Sure of fuccefs in this quarter,
Catharine haftened her journey to Mofco, for
the purpofe of celebrating her coronation in that
ancient capital of the empire. But previous to
her departure from St. Peterfburg, fhe affembled
the regiments of the guards who had feated her
on the throne, and gave them further affurances
of her approbation. She left them under the
command of the hetman Razumofffky and
prince Volkonfky, beftowed the government of
the city on count Bruce, on whofe fidelity fhe
could rely, and charged Alexèy Orloff to watch
over all with his ufual activity.

The emprefs chofe for her attendants on the
journey Gregory Orloff, the old chancellor Beftucheff, count Stroganoff; in fhort, the greater
part of the nobles who had fhewn themfelves
the moft devoted to her, as well as thofe whofe
abfence fhe had reafon to dread. Above all,
fhe neglected not to take with her the young
grand duke Paul Petrovitch and the principal
ladies of the court.

This

This numerous calvalcade made its entrance with pomp into Mofco. But notwithftanding the money that had been previoufly diftributed, it was received without any tokens of public welcome, without acclamation. Catharine too eafily perceived, by this folitude and filence, that her prefence was difagreeable to the people. She neverthelefs repaired to the chapel of the tzars, where fhe lavifhed her flatteries on the archbifhop and the popes; and fhe was crowned in the prefence of the foldiery and the people of the court. The crowd, which retired at the approach of the emprefs, ran every where to meet the grand duke, and mingled with the emotions of tendernefs they felt for the child a vifible concern for the misfortunes of his father. Catharine, diffatisfied with Mofco, induftrioufly concealed her chagrin; and attending only to the neceffary delays, retook the road to Peterfburg.

The number of promotions, prefents, &c. that were made on occafion of the coronation, and which moftly fell to the fhare of her adherents in the late revolution, need not here be particularized. During her ftay at Mofco fhe honoured that ancient capital by iffuing feveral proclamations from it; and to flatter the military,

tary, which had been neglected by Peter, she published a manifesto, on the day of her coronation, in praise of the troops that had fought against Prussia, and caused a half-year's pay to be given to the subalterns and common soldiers who had been present at the victorious battles of Paltzig, or Kai or Zullichau, and at Frankfort or Kunersdorf. Of each of the four regiments of life-guards, the Préobajenskoy, Simeonoffky, Ismaïloffky, and the horse-guard, the empress appointed herself colonel. General-adjutant Gregory Orloff was made lieutenant-colonel of the last regiment; of the first, his brother Alexèy; of the third, Feodor, captain of the Simeonoffky; and the fourth, Vladimir, lieutenant of the Ismaïloffky guards.

Catharine now put off all constraint. The monks, who had long favoured her projects, and to whom she had often promised a restoration of the possessions they had been despoiled of by her husband, vainly recalled to her mind their services and her promises. She perceived that it would not be prudent to let them resume an ascendant which might prove as dangerous as it had been serviceable to her; and instead of revoking the edict of Peter III. she referred it to the examination of a synod, composed of persons

VOL. I.   Y   implicitly

implicitly fubfervient to her will.   The principal
members of the clergy were fecretly brought
over; the reft were facrificed; and, animated
with facred fury, vowed revenge againft their
former patron.

The rage of the priefts could not fail of having
fome effect.   They fanned the embers of fedition among the populace.   They communicated
the fparks of it to fome foldiers.   They called to
mind their prince Ivan.   They difcovered that
he was in St. Peterfburg on the very day of the
revolution; to which city Peter III. had myfte-
riously caufed him to be brought, in the defign
of declaring him his fucceffor; and whence
Catharine had fince, not lefs myfterioufly, had
him conveyed; and they openly faid, that it was
to that unhappy prince that the throne belonged.
They did more.   They detected and publifhed a
manifefto, all the copies whereof the care of the
friends of Catharine had not been able to fupprefs.
Peter III. had caufed it to be drawn up by the
ftate-counfellor Volkoff, and had figned it with
his hand.   In a melancholy mood he had here
put together all the weakneffes and faults of Catharine; and accufing her of adultery, declared
that he would not acknowledge the young grand
duke for his fon, fince he was the fruit of the
                              fcandalous

scandalous commerce of his wife with Soltikoff. This manifesto *, composed with great force and eloquence, was artfully dispersed among the people, and soon found its way among the soldiers, who, for the most part unable to conceive in what fit of distraction they had been drawn into the rebellion, already, as we have observed, repented their wickedness, or deplored the sad lot of a prince, mistaken but not malevolent, weak but not stupid; who had been barbarously put to death. He whom they lamented soon found them his avengers. Every thing seemed to portend a new revolution: but Gleboff, Passick, Teploff, and their emissaries, were not blind to all these proceedings. Suddenly an imperial proclamation came forth, forbidding the soldiers of the guards from assembling without orders received from their officers. Some of the most violent were imprisoned, and suffered the punishment of the knoot; others were banished into Siberia: terror for some time kept the rest in silence.

By thus chastising the regiments of the guards, the empress thought she should also shut the mouths of the priests. She refused even to temporize with the courtiers who displeased her,

* Perhaps a forgery of the exasperated clergy.

Y 2

and

and thought they had juft claims to her gratitude. Ivan Schuvaloff had not only taken part in the confpiracy; but he had promoted it before-hand by calumniating Peter III. and as foon as it broke out, he became its approver and fupport. By flattering the propenfities of Catharine, he hoped to find that eafy accefs with her which the emprefs Elizabeth had offered him. Schuvaloff was miftaken. He awakened the jealoufy of Orloff; Catharine fent him word that his pre-fence was not neceffary at court * ; then, adding derifion to harfhnefs, fhe made him a prefent, as the reward of his fervices, of an old negro, who played the part of a buffoon about the palace †.

The general of artillery, Villebois, who had yielded to a fentiment of tendernefs for her rather than follow the line of his duty, now paid the forfeit of his miftake. Orloff was afraid of his talents, and wanted his employments.

---

* Peter III. on his acceffion to the throne, acted with greater lenity towards Ivan Schuvaloff, of whom he had fo great a right to complain under the reign of Elizabeth. He not only did not forbid him the court, but he made him a prefent of 10,000 imperials in gold, which the chamberlain had juft received of the dying fovereign, and which, inftigated by fear, he fent to the new emperor.

† It was faid to be the fame negro whom the tzar was defirous of having with him in prifon.

Villebois

Villebois was difmiffed, and the favourite appointed grand mafter of the artillery.

The pretenfions of princefs Dafhkoff became odious to the emprefs. At the commencement of the revolution, princefs Dafhkoff had, like Catharine, put on the uniform of the guards, and marched at their head. She had facrificed her father, her fifter, her whole family, to the elevation of her friend *; in fome inftances fhe had facrificed herfelf. All the recompence fhe afked was the title of colonel of the regiment of Préobajenfky. But Catharine anfwered her, with an ironical fmile, that the academy would fuit her better than a military corps. Princefs Dafhkoff, cruelly mortified at this reply, gave fcope to her natural impetuofity, murmured among her friends of the ingratitude of Catharine, and fought opportunities for fhewing her refentment. The perfidious Odart, who obferved this alteration in the behaviour of the princefs, was the firft to carry an account of it to the emprefs. Princefs Dafhkoff immediately received orders to retire to Mofco †.

At

---

* This was the appellation mutually beftowed on each other by Catharine and princefs Dafhkoff.

† Here fhe was delivered of a daughter, afterwards married to M. de Tfcherbinin; a lady of remarkable accom-

X 3   plifhments

At the same time Catharine commissioned the
piedmontese Odart to engage the ambassador of
France to write to Voltaire, cautioning him to
be on his guard against the vanity of princess
Dashkoff, and to tell him, that if he should
transmit to posterity the event that had just happened in Russia, he need only make mention of
this young woman as having acted a very second-
ary part in a revolution, the success whereof
was owing solely to the wisdom and courage
of the empress *.   The same commission was
given to her ambassadors at London and at
Paris †.

The

---

plishments and the most agreeable manners.   It is no wonder
then if her society was frequented by all men of talents and
literature from every court in Europe.   After passing three
or four years in travelling through various parts of Germany
and the states of Italy, madame Tscherbinin afterwards
took up her residence at Warsaw; but since the commencement of the reign of Paul I. she is gone to reside with her
mother at her retirement in the vicinity of Mosco.

* M. de Breteuil rather went beyond his commission, by
adding in his letter : "C'est pousser bien loin la jalousie &
" la hardiesse d l'ingratitude."

† Upwards of five-and-twenty years after that event, Catharine held the same language to a minister from a foreign
power.   It was her earnest desire that the history of her life
and reign should have been undertaken by the historian of
Charles V.   Various suggestions were at several times given

The archbifhop of Novgorod, one of the principal inftruments in the revolution, and who had the moft affifted in diminifhing the privileges of the monks, having been gained over by money and promifes, found all at once that his towering hopes were fruftrated. When Catharine had no longer any need of his fervices, fhe prefently difmiffed him; and he was obliged to take back with him his rage and difgrace to a clergy who hated him, and a people who defpifed his ambition.

In the mean time Poniatoffky had learned, with inexpreffible joy, the triumph of Catharine. Since his departure from St. Peterfburg, he had kept up a regular correfpondence with her, through the means of fome obliging friends; and he placed the more dependence upon her, as, while fhe had a fecret partiality for others, fhe openly affected a romantic conftancy in her attachment to him. Perhaps Poniatoffky might flatter himfelf that he fhould foon be honoured with her hand whofe heart he imagined had long been his. He advanced to the frontiers of Po-

---

to that effect, and tranfmitted to Scotland; and for which all the neceffary papers and documents were to have been furnifhed by herfelf.

land, and sent to ask permission of her majesty
to pay a visit to her court.   But she returned
him for answer, that his presence was not necessary at Petersburg; and that she had different
views in his behalf.   Unwilling that he should
be farther informed of her new connections, she
continued to write to him in an affectionate style,
and sometimes shed tears before the confidants *
of the Pole, in speaking of her passion for him.
She complained that an inclination for Orloff was
attributed to her, and attempted to ridicule him
in their eyes.

But the period of fears was past.   Orloff had
done with mystery.   Haughty and coarse in his
manners, that favourite but aukwardly submitted
to dissimulation; and he now made it appear
that he had no longer occasion for an inconvenient
precaution.   Accustomed to live in the barracks
and cabaks †, Orloff at times would drink pretty
freely.   One evening, being at supper with the
empress, the hetman Razumofffky, and some
others of the court, and being flushed with
wine, he talked of the ascendant he had over
the guards; he boasted of having solely brought
about the revolution; and added, that his power

* M. de Mercy and M. de Breteuil.
† Tippling houses frequented by the lower orders of
people.

                                        was

was so great, that if he chose to abuse it, he could destroy in one month his own work, and dethrone the empress. " You might do so in " one month," returned the hetman, smiling at his insolence ; " but, my friend, within a fort- " night after we would have hanged you!" The other courtiers seemed offended ; but the favour of Orloff was not diminished.

The attachment of Catharine to her favourite arose more from policy than affection. She knew his activity, his vehemence, his boldness ; and she could neither arm herself against him by an empty pride, nor prefer to him courtiers doubtless more polite, but almost all without talents, and destitute of courage. Less gracious towards the other conspirators, who were only subaltern officers, and whom she had already sufficiently rewarded, she removed them by degrees from the court, leaving them to return to their soldier-like course of life, and their obscure libertinism. It may be that she would have done better to have kept on the mask a little longer *.

The

---

* Some persons made a handle of this behaviour to charge her with ingratitude and selfishness. The state counsellor Brodorf, private secretary to the tzar, and who had often prevented that prince from shewing his resentment against Catharine, spoke of it in these terms: " The empress thinks " it a sufficient happiness to be permitted to serve her, and " that it is recompence enough to have the honour which she " supposes

The chaftifement of the foldiers who were
the firft in the mutiny had not entirely quelled
the fpirit of revolt.   The removal of the archbifhop of Novgorod and princefs Dafhkoff, the
unfettled health of the young grand duke *, the
pity fhewn by all ranks of people for prince
Ivan; all furnifhed a handle to diftontents, which
the popes dexteroufly employed for inciting and
irritating the people.   There was a general
fermentation in the barracks.   The danger became even fo imminent, that her majefty was
thought, during a whole day†, to be in extreme
hazard of experiencing the fate of her hufband.
But her courage never forfook her.   Without
calling her council, fhe took private meafures
for calming the revolt; and when the hetman
Razumofflky, Beftucheff, Panin, Gleboff, with
feveral other members of the fenate, prefented
themfelves to her, to teftify their uneafinefs, fhe
faid to them, with that dignity which was peculiar to her: " Why are you alarmed?   Think

----

" fuppofes it fhould be reckoned; and when fhe has made
" what ufe fhe wanted of any one, or of which fhe thought
" him capable, fhe does with him as we do with an orange,
" after fucking out the juice we throw the peal out at
" window."

   * He was attacked with a fort of fcorbutic complaint.

   † It was fome time after her return from Mofco.

" ye

" ye that I am afraid to face the danger ? or
" rather, are you afraid that I know not how to
" overcome it ? Recollect that you have seen
" me, in moments more terrible than these, in
" full poffeffion of the whole vigour of my
" mind; and that I can fupport the moft cruel
" reverfes of Fortune with as much ferenity as
" I have fupported her favours. A few factious
" fpirits, a few mutinous foldiers, are to de-
" prive me of a crown that I accepted with re-
" luctance *, and only as the means of deliver-
" ing the ruffian nation from the miferies with
" which it was threatened! I know not with what
" pretence they colour their infolence ; I know
" not on what means they rely; but, I fay it
" again, they caufe me no alarm. That Pro-
" vidence which has called me to reign, will
" preferve me for the glory and the happinefs of
" the empire ; and that almighty arm which has
" hitherto been my defence, will now confound
" my foes."

The Orloffs, in the mean time, neglected
nothing for pacifying the guards; and prefents
foftened thofe whom fpeeches and promifes
could not appeafe. When their fidelity was

* It is certain that Catharine expreffed herfelf in thefe
very terms, and that even in the prefence of fome of her
accomplices.

again

again secured, four-and-twenty of their officers
were arrested and tried. The four principal
ringleaders * were declared guilty of high treason, and condemned to be quartered. But Catharine, thinking that less benefit was likely to
accrue from leaving them to their sentence,
commuted their punishment into a banishment
to Siberia; and wishing, at the same time, to
attempt at inspiring the Russians with some dread
of infamy, a dread which had so much influence
in other nations, she caused the four officers to
be degraded, and scourged by the hand of the
common executioner.

While Catharine was thus managing her subjects, she displayed to foreign courts all the
greatness of her character. The ambassador of
France sollicited her in vain for obtaining a
reversal similar to those granted by Elizabeth
and Peter III. at their accession to the throne,
the purport of which was to prove that the title
of empress changed absolutely nothing in the
ceremonial between the two courts; and per-
sisted in the refusal, notwithstanding the difficul-

---

* These were the three brothers Gourieff, officers in the
ismailoffsky regiment of guards, and Aroufcheff, an officer
of the regiment of Ingria or Ingermlandskoï. A brother
of the latter, serjeant in the same regiment, was also in the
plot, but was not subjected to the same punishment.

ties

ties it might occasion *.   In a word, she declared that the ceremonial should not be changed;
but that there should never more be any reversal
at the commencement of a new reign †.   Nevertheless she gave secret instructions to several of
her ambassadors to take precedence of that from
France, whenever occasion should offer ‡.

The empress, always combining policy with
firmness, found means to sooth the most dangerous of the priests, and to put a stop to the
cabals of the monks.   She recalled to court
princess Dashkoff, whose influence and enter-
prises at Mosco might disturb the tranquillity of

* These difficulties were not the only ones M. de Breteuil had with Catharine: and it may not be useless to
mention the grave minutiæ in which ambassadors are sometimes employed.   The custom is, that women as well as
men kiss the hand of the empress.   M. de Breteuil had the
vanity to insist that his lady, rather than conform to that
custom, should abstain from appearing at court.   He made
several remonstrances on this subject.   Catharine held out;
and that madame de Breteuil might not die of vexation in her
hôtel, the ambassador was obliged to submit.   However, by
a grand stroke of policy, he recommended to his lady not to
kiss her majesty's hand, but only to pretend to do so.

† See the declaration in the Appendix at the end of the
volume.

‡ The dispute that happened between the duc de Châ-
telet and count Chernicheff, ambassador from Russia to the
court of St. James's, is well known.

the

the empire. She sent away the piedmontese Odart, whose continual informations had rendered him odious to all the court. Her praise was resounded, by the trumpet of fame, from one end of Europe to the other, and reverberated to Petersburg. The health of the young grand duke was re-established. The promising expectations that were justly raised by the good conduct of that prince, drew off all eyes from the prison of the unfortunate Ivan; and the Russians accommodated themselves to a yoke which they had attempted in vain to shake off.

Ambition did not extinguish the love of pleasure in the breast of Catharine. It was even by the latter that she gained more and more the attachment of her courtiers; but she could quit her pleasures to engage in the most serious affairs, and apply to the most arduous concerns of government. She assisted at all the deliberations of the council, read the dispatches from her ambassadors, either dictated or minuted with her own hand the answers that were to be sent to them, and afterwards attended to all the particulars of their execution. Jealous of solid renown, she set before her the example of those illustrious monarchs who effaced their weaknesses by the grandeur of their exploits; and, with the infirmities of men, merited and obtained

tained the grateful acknowledgments of all succeeding times, as the friends and benefactors of
the human race. She followed those maxims
which she frequently quoted: " We should be
" constant in our plans," said she. " It is better
" to do amifs, than to alter our purpose. None
" but fools are irrefolute."

CHAP. III.

*Catharine is occupied in fchemes of aggrandifement.
— She fupports Biren in Courland. — Panin is
defirous of changing the form of the ruffian
government. — Beftucheff diffuades the emprefs
from it, and wifhes to induce her to marry
Gregory Orloff. — A plot concerted at Mofco
againft the life of Orloff. — A confpiracy againft
the emprefs. — Anfwer of princefs Dafhkoff. —
Poniatofsky defirous of coming to Ruffia, &c. —
Occurrences of 1762 and 1763.*

ALL fovereigns have their private hiftories:
but the anecdotes of their domeftic concerns are
in fome inftances not fo well authenticated, and
in others not of fuch a nature as to render them
proper objects of hiftory. The true life of a monarch

narch confifts in the actions which he performs in the capacity of monarch; efpecially if he rule with unlimited fway, and for the moft part govern in his own perfon: both circumftances met in Catharine. But though ordinances, laws, inftitutions at home, influence on foreign countries, wars, treaties of peace, properly form the fubject of the biography of a mighty potentate; yet accounts of occurrences that regard his own perfon alfo deferve to be interwoven, as often as they give rife to greater events, or are any otherwife infeparably connected with public hiftory.

The bloody war carried on againft Frederic, continued to rage in the reft of Europe. Ruffia had juft feparated from that formidable league, and Sweden was following her example. Peter had not merely put an end to hoftilities, and reftored to the king the territory of Eaft-Pruffia, which had been conquered by the ruffian arms; but he had even ordered his troops to join the army of that prince, to fight under him as allies, againft the remaining confederated powers. The latter relation thus immediately ceafed, and it was of the utmoft importance to know what refolutions would now be adopted by Catharine. For, though the ruffian army under Elizabeth had performed fo little in comparifon of what might have been reafonably expected from their numbers and force,

force, yet Ruffia was a very formidable enemy, to whom Frederic, in fpite of all the refources of his fertile genius, muft at length have fubmitted, efpecially if the bravery of the foldiers fhould have been properly enforced by a better command.

Frederic had been Peter's friend, was acquainted with all his fentiments and plans, had imparted to him counfel, and maintained a confidential correfpondence with him. Could it be expected that his fucceffor fhould have much inclination and confidence for the friend of him whom fhe had depofed from the throne? Was it not probable that he was informed, perhaps even approved of the meafures that the emperor had taken in regard to Catharine, and for the preventing of which fhe had undertaken that very ftep? Frederic had indeed been Peter's friend; but a worthy and paternal friend, an experienced and faithful monitor. He had the higheft reafon to be devoted to the emperor with the fincereft attachment; but Frederic was too generous to beftow his calm approbation on what he did not hold to be right. With tender concern he beheld Peter giving the rein to his paffions, and exerted all the influence of his friendfhip to reduce him to a better conduct. His letters abounded with admonitions to

the reftoration of domeftic concord, and the re-
eftablifhment of peace in the imperial family.
Catharine read them, and was convinced of the
perfevering good-will of the great prince, to
whom fhe was indebted for the firft poffibility
of obtaining the ruffian crown *.   Frederic had
even left nothing untried to diffuade the tzar
from his violent refolution of declaring war
againft Denmark: at length, however, a congrefs
was appointed at Berlin, in order to bring all
differences to an accommodation.

The negotiation went on with fuccefs, and
ended happily.   Catharine therefore ratified the
peace with Pruffia and with Denmark.

Ruffia then enjoyed a peace with foreign
powers, which had been begun by the unfortunate Peter III. and which Catharine had now

---

* On perufing thefe letters the emprefs burft into tears of
gratitude, and made in confequence the ftrongeft declarations in favour of this prince.   They were not without effect.   Orders had been given with relation to Pruffia, which
threatened a renewal of hoftilities.   They were foon fufpended.   The army of the Ruffians was indeed feparated
from that of Pruffia; but all the important places, which
the Ruffians had, with fo much bloodfhed, and through fo
many difficulties, acquired, and which gave them the command of every thing elfe that remained to the king, were
faithfully reftored.

confirmed ;

confirmed : but the interior *of the empire, in various parts, exhibited figns of fermentation. Neither the fevere fentence pronounced againft the four principal leaders of the tumult of the guards, nor the affumed clemency of the emprefs, were able to ftifle thofe fentiments of hatred and vengeance which the view of a great act of injuftice never fails to infpire.

Though Catharine perhaps had no great reafon to fufpect that her fubjects were not perfectly fatisfied with the methods by which the late revolution had been effected, yet fhe thought it expedient to call off their attention from a recent event of fuch magnitude and importance, by brilliant novelties and fuccefsful enterprifes. But fhe alfo knew that too many obftacles were oppofed to thefe enterprifes, and that the penury of her finances as well as the dictates of policy impelled her to peace.

With regard to any offenfive intentions againft Ruffia, they have long fince ceafed to compofe a part in the politics of any power whatever. Notwithftanding her permanent ftrength, and an occafional exertion of it, that are very menacing, it does not appear that there has, even once, been a plan ferioufly thought on for the reduction of the greatnefs of Ruffia, ever fince the time of Charles XII. which was the period of

z 2   her

her entering into the circle of our political fyftem : and this was rather an attempt to crufh
her in her infancy, than a plan to obftruct her
further growth, when once become formidable.

From that time fhe has been growing (not fo
much, perhaps, as might be expected in learning and the arts, but, certainly) to a very high
degree in fubftantial power, and in all the refources that fupport it; a ftrong military force,
an increafing commerce, prudent, becaufe, for
the moft part a lucrative fyftem of negotiation ;
and an unbounded influence over thofe nations
with whom fhe has the neareft connection.

Her friendfhip has been much fought, and
generally paid for. Her armies have been kept
up at very confiderable numbers; and if her
troops have not improved, the laft war evidently
demonftrated that they had not at all declined
from that difcipline to which they were formed
by Peter the great. That commerce, too, of
which he was the founder, had been far from
languifhing fince his death : and the balance of
trade was probably in her favour againft fome
of the nations with whom fhe has intercourfe.
The emulation which, for this century paft, has
fubfifted amongft all the maritime countries in
augmenting their marine, has, without the exertion of any deep policy on her fide, operated
powerfully

powerfully in her favour ; as nature has made her the great magazine of naval ftores to Europe.

Nothing fhews more clearly that Ruffia has the ftrongeft political ftamina, than that her condition is fuch as we have defcribed it, whilft her government has undergone very frequent fhocks and fudden revolutions, whilft the throne was feldom eftablifhed with great fecurity to the poffeffor, and never provided with any found and invariable rule of fucceffion.

At prefent it could not be faid that Ruffia was much improved in thefe particulars. On the contrary, nothing could be more critical than the fituation of that government.

The emprefs immediately applied with extreme affiduity and care to the adminiftration of her vaft eftates, the advancement of commerce, the augmentation of the marine, and efpecially to the means of recovering the finances, without being reduced to the neceffity of obferving a parfimonious œconomy. Her grand ideas of the fovereignty of Ruffia permitted her not to renounce that oriental magnificence, for which, from the beginning of the reign of Elizabeth, the court of St. Peterfburg had been famous throughout the world. This luxury might likewife feem the more neceffary as an object of attraction to the notice of the public both at home

and

and abroad, till she could excite its astonishment by the splendour of conquests.

After engaging in business with her ministers, her majesty would frequently converse and always in private, one while with Bestucheff and at another with Munich. With one she studied politics and the resources of the several courts of Europe; the other communicated to her the plan he had been meditating in his exile. in Siberia, for driving the Turks from Constantinople, a plan singularly gratifying to the aspiring mind of Catharine, and which, thirty years after, seemed to have been on the point of being carried into effect.

Her first cares were directed to domestic regulations. The style in all her ordinances has something uncommonly confidential and open : the subjects heard the voice of a careful mother, without feeling themselves treated like helpless children; on the contrary they all have a tendency to bring them to liberty. She frequently mentioned the duties of sovereigns, and particularly what the empress esteemed to be her own. For instance, in her first manifesto, dated July 6, 1762, immediately on her accession to the throne : " It is thus," said the empress, " without spilling one drop of blood, that we " have ascended the russian throne, by the assist-
" ance

" ance, of God, and the approving fuffrages
" of our beloved country.——Humbly adoring
" the decrees of Divine Providence, we affure
" our faithful fubjects, that we will not fail, by
" night and by day, to invoke the Moft High to
" blefs our fceptre, and enable us to wield it for
" the maintenance of our orthodox religion, the
" fecurity and defence of our dear country, and
" the equal adminiftration of juftice ; as well as
" to put an end to all miferies, iniquities, and
" violences, by ftrengthening and fortifying our
" heart for the public good.   And as we ar-
" dently wifh to prove effectually how far we
" merit the reciprocal love of our people, for
" whofe happinefs we acknowledge our throne
" to be eftablifhed, we folemnly promife on our
" imperial word, to make fuch arrangements in
" the empire as that the government may be
" endued with an intrinfic force to fupport itfelf
" within limited and proper bounds ; and each
" department of the ftate provided with whole-
" fome laws and regulations, fufficient to the
" prefervation of good order, at all times, and
" in all circ' mftances.

" By which means we hope henceforward
" to eftablifh the empire and our fovereign
" power, (however they may have been here-
" tofore weakened,) in fuch a manner as to

z 4   " comfort

" comfort the difcouraged hearts of all true
" patriots.   Not entertaining the leaft doubt,
" that all our loving fubjects will, as well for the
" falvation of their own fouls, as for the honour
" of religion, inviolably obferve the oath they
" have fworn in the prefence of Almighty God ;
" we thereupon affure them of our imperial
" favour."

Again in the ukafe of the 29th of July in the
fame year : " Not only all that we have or
" may have, but alfo our life itfelf, we have
" devoted to our dear country.   We value no-
" thing on our own account ; we ferve not
" ourfelf ; but we labour with all pains, with all
" diligence and care, for the glory and happinefs
" of our people."

In a manifefto of the 17th of July, the emprefs
publicly and folemnly promifed to employ her
principal care to the maintenance of juftice.
Under date of the 29th fhe informed the people
of her having received account that a certain
regiftrator of the government-chancery of Novgorod, named Jacob Rember, had taken money
for adminiftering the oath of allegiance ; for
which fhe had banifhed him for life to Siberia :
and on that occafion iffued a fevere decree againft
bribery and extortion.   The picture fhe here
drew of the ftate of things was truly alarming :
                                        " If

" If any one be defirous of an office, he muft
" pay for it ; if any one wifh to defend himfelf
" from flander, he muft do it with money ;
" if any one would flander another, he cor-
" roborates his malice by bribes.   In this man-
" ner do many judges convert the facred place
" where they are appointed to pronounce juftice
" in our name, into a market........Thefe ex-
" amples of perfons who, in the principal
" courts, have crept into office only for the
" purpofe of fcreening themfelves from punifh-
" ment, are imitated, particularly in remote
" parts of the empire, even by judges and offi-
" cers of the loweft orders, to the vexation
" and oppreffion of poor people ; practifing the
" arts of chicane, not only in cafes of little im-
" portance, but under the form of law, which
" they wrongly interpret, and bringing ruin on
" the perfons and families of even thofe who are
" rather deferving of our fovereign complacency
" and favour."

By an ukafe, dated Mofco, Oct. 13, the
emprefs confirmed the abolition of the fecret-
inquifition-chancery : " to the erection whereof
" the circumftances of the then times, and the
" yet uncivilized manners of the nation, had
" furnifhed occafion to the magnanimous and
" gracious monarch Peter the great ; but the
" necoffity

" neceffity whereof had ever fince been gradually
" diminifhing :" an honourable and genuine
teftimony to the high value fhe fet upon the in-
tellectual improvement of her people. For, if
the great reformer of the ruffian government had
to contend againft numerous infurrections and
confpiracies ; if even after his death, exclufively
of inferior or abortive plots, within forty years not
yet complete fix revolutions befel the perfons on
and next the throne : furely no man will afcribe
thefe convulfions to the high degree of mental
cultivation in the country. Improving the nation
upwards from the lower orders, and gentle treatment of it downwards from above, produced even
here at length, by a natural confequence, internal
peace and fecurity. Catharine was fenfible that fhe
could obtain the love and attachment of the people
by better means than by the encouragement of
fpies and informers ; no fooner was fhe placed on
the throne, but, fuperior to degrading fear, fhe
completely put an end to the political inquifition.

" Peter I. inftituted (as we learn by the
" ukafe) certain chanceries for fecret criminal
" caufes under various names." By thefe meafures he hoped to gain information of many
fchemes of mifchief before their execution : but
what a field was thus opened to the moft dangerous accufations ! How formidable to every family

mily muſt the regiſtries of this ſecret court of judicature have been, where the moſt innocent names might be inſcribed with a falſe accuſation annexed, and all refutation often rendered impoſſible to the profoundeſt concealment! Catharine now generouſly and nobly decreed, that " The " ſecret-inquiſition chancery is henceforth and for " ever aboliſhed. The acts of it ſhall be brought " into the ſenate, and there ſealed up in the " archives conſigned to everlaſting oblivion."— The capital crimes which were the matter of ſecret examination, were, high-treaſon, attempts againſt religion, treaſon againſt the ſtate. But its juriſdiction gradually increaſed ; criminal caſes, properly lying within the province of the ordinary courts, being frequently brought thither, which the officious induſtry of the inquiſitors very much encouraged ; particularly as it depended on the accuſer to mix ſomething in his accuſa[t]on that might make it touch upon ſome one or other of the points above ſpecified. Now, at the abolition of this inquiſition, Catharine ſettled the practice to be purſued in future in the ordinary tribunals in charges of real ſtate-crimes, and ſo plainly and diſtinctly determined the particular caſes of delinquency againſt the perſon of the ſovereign, and againſt the welfare of the ſtate, that there was no longer any room for

malicious

malicious or finister interpretation.   What went
under the name of religious crimes were entirely
fuppreffed.——The irregularity and feverity of the
proceedings had been truly fhocking.   The regular modes of evidence were held to be inade-
quate to the nature of a fecret denunciation and a
myfterious tribunal: imprifonment, nay even execution, was often the beginning of the procefs.
The manner of procefs was ufually this: when
the accufer failed in every kind of proof, he muft
undergo the dreadful punifhment of the knoot
three feveral times; after which his declaration
was admitted as legal.   The accufed might deliver his objections in the fame manner, unlefs
he rather chofe to be declared guilty.   We cannot relate it without horror that this mode of
proceeding was in ufe, without regard to ftation,
age, or fex, and even more than once repeated
when the judge wavered in his opinion between
the oppofite affertions thus proved by both parties.   But now, if the accufer had fome plaufible
ground in his behalf, then the accufed had a
more cruel coercion to undergo.   Catharine
therefore ordained that the truth fhould be in-
veftigated entirely without torture ; and, with
Frederic of Pruffia, was likewife in this refpect
a model for the reft of Europe.   Her criminal
laws throughout breathe a mild and gentle fpirit:
                             fhe

fhe had not, like Elizabeth, made a vow to punifh no one with death; for why fhould a philofo-phical character have recourfe to fo mechanical a compulfion to perfeverance in its principles? But during her long reign a fentence of death was extremely rare.

The fecret inquifition as a defirable inftrument for ill-difpofed perfons to employ in the gratification of the fordid paffions of envy and revenge againft their betters. But, to the honour of the nation be it faid, that in the latter years of Elizabeth's reign, fuch informations were be-coming lefs frequent from day to day: only among the lower claffes, among fervants, vaffals, nay, to the deftruction of all fubordination, even among failors and foldiers, while fuffering fome (frequently well-deferved) chaftifement, or with perfons who had cherifhed fome grudge againft their fuperiors, the cuftom ftill fubfifted to make themfelves formidable by the mifchief it enabled them to commit; on which account Peter III. in February publifhed his ukafe. The practice of the populace on fuch occafions, was, to *cry out the word*; which fignified, I have a fecret of importance to difcover of fomebody, and now mean to point out who it is. The moft horrible, and among them the moft ridiculous ftories are related of the application of this cuftom. A

patient

patient in the hofpital employed it to prevent
an operation the furgeon was about to perform.
The found was fo awful and tremendous, that if,
in the midft of a great crowd, any one called
out, " The word," all prefent turned pale, and
immediately feparated, running and croffing
themfelves as faft as they could. Perfons of
confequence, a mafter who had punifhed his
fervant, muft inftantly ftop fhort in the ftreet, and
go with him to the next guard-houfe, demanding
of the officers to be both fent to prifon together.——Catharine thus provided againft this
grievance: " The odious expreffion, *to cry the*
" *word* (flovo i delo) fhall henceforth have no
" fignification; every one is forbidden to ufe it.
" If any perfon, notwithftanding this prohibition,
" fhall, in drunkennefs, in quarrel, or to avoid
" lawful correction, prefume to employ it, fuch
" perfon fhall be fo punifhed on the fpot, as the
" police ufually punifhes vagabonds and difturb-
" ers of the public peace.

" If, neverthelefs, lazy, wicked, and worthlefs
" perfons, foldiers, failors, vaffals, boors, work-
" men in manufactories and fhops, fhould yet be
" found who fhall contravene this declaration
" of our will, fuch informer fhall be taken into
" cuftody [by a civil or military officer], and
" firft interrogated whether he underftands the
" two

" two points abovementioned [crimes againſt
" the ſovereign and the ſtate] in their true
" import.   If it be found that he underſtands
" them in their true import, and inſiſts that
" what he has to deliver really relates to theſe
" two points; he ſhall be directly aſked in what
" the matter itſelf conſiſts.   If he declare it,
" but can neither bring proofs nor produce evi-
" dence, nor point out any circumſtances to
" render his declaration credible, he ſhall be
" earneſtly admoniſhed, &c.   If after all theſe
" cautions and admonitions, he will not deſiſt
" from his aſſertion, then he ſhall be confined
" for two whole days without having any thing
" to eat or to drink, but left all that time alone,
" to collect himſelf, and to conſider; and after
" the expiration of that term he ſhall expreſsly
" be aſked whether, &c.   Does he now con-
" firm anew what he had before aſſerted; in
" ſuch caſe the informer ſhall be ſent, under
" cloſe cuſtody, according to the diſtance of the
" place, either to the ſenate in St. Peterſburg,
" or to Moſco, or to the neareſt government-
" chancery."

The wiſdom apparent in the whole (too long
for our purpoſe) of this mild and provident ordinance, and eſpecially as founded on the nature
of the human mind and the condition of the
country,

country, demands the higheſt admiration. To
ſhut up the informer of the lower claſs of people
two days long without the ſmalleſt nouriſhment,
is a precept always ſtrictly obſerved, and has very
often been attended with this conſequence, that
the raſh informer, having ſlept off his intoxication, or ſtifled his paſſion, or upon maturer con-
ſideration in ſolitude and ſilence, has retracted
his accuſation.

Catharine declared, by a manjfeſto, that coloniſts ſhall find welcome and ſupport in her country: ſeveral foreigners, therefore, preſently began
to migrate thither. Whereupon, in Auguſt 1763,
ſhe made more ſpecific regulations in relation to
them, particularly by inſtituting the tutelary
chancery (a chancery for the guardianſhip or
protection of foreigners). The next ſtep ſhe
took in this behalf was to point out by name
ſuch diſtricts as were proper for agriculture and
hitherto unoccupied, with particular notices of
what was foreſt, arable land, meadow land, &c.
what allotments bordered upon rivers, and what
the fiſheries might yield. Thus, in the government of Tobolſk, on the Barabinſkoï ſteppe, ſeveral hundred thouſand deſættines * of fertile
ſoil, and another large tract of land with ſeveral

* See before, p. 53, 54.

rivers

rivers running through it, were appropriated
to cultivation: in the government of Aftrakhan, from Saratof on the Volga upwards, above
34,000 defættines; on the Volga from Saratof downwards, above 36,000: in the government of Òrenburg, portions of land for
fome thoufand families: in the territory of
Bielgorod, free lands for fome hundred farms. ——
But not merely to the cultivation of fuch diſtricts
were foreigners encouraged, but to fettle for general purpofes in the ruffian empire, in whatever
town they would, as merchants, artificers, or
however elfe. The proclamation fets forth, that
" any one who is deftitute fhall receive money
" for the expences of the journey, and fhall be
" forwarded at the charge of the crown. On
" his arrival he fhall receive a competent affift-
" ance; and, if he want it, even an advance of
" a capital, free of intereft for 10 years. All
" that he brings for his own ufe is duty free;
" even for fale, a family may introduce to the
" value of 300 rubles. The ftranger is ex-
" empt from all fervice either military or civil;
" even from all taxes and impofts for a certain
" time: in Mofco, Peterfburg, and the livonian
" towns, he enjoys five free years; in the inland
" towns, ten; on the hitherto uncultivated dif-
" tricts, thirty. In thefe new tracts of land, the
" colonifts live according to their own good-

" will, under their own jurifdiction, without any
" participation or cognizance of the imperial
" officers.   All religions are tolerated." The
emprefs at once granted to the tutelary chancery
an annual revenue of 200,000 rubles.   Moreover, for colonifts in the government of Aftrakhan, a clergyman of every chriftian fect, a
parifh-clerk, a phyfician, a furgeon, an apothecary, &c. were appointed to be paid by the
crown.

Scarcely had this inviting voice refounded
over Germany through the organs of the feveral
minifters, than hundreds and thoufands flocked
to take poffeffion of the promifed land on the
fhores of the Volga and the Samara. For it muft
be confeffed that in Germany great numbers of
people are very reafonably diffatisfied with their
condition, fighing under the preffure of religion,
of juftice, or of finance, or of all the three at
once ; and there are certainly many fertile, beautiful, and highly improvable tracts of country in
the before-mentioned diftricts.   Individuals, and
whole families, numerous in women and children,
people of tolerable circumftances, beggars, pro-
jectors, vagabonds, literati, artificers, mechanics,
old and young, fet out in hafte to be ftowed on
board of fhip at Lubeck and other maritime
towns on the Baltic. Several of the petty princes
of Germany at firft iffued prohibitions againft
                                                    thefe

thefe emigrations, and their example was afterwards followed by others; and it is not to be denied, that many of the perfons employed in the colonial plan made ufe of fome indirect means for inticing inconfiderate perfons from their bufineffes. But it received the moft effectual check from the reports that foon ran about concerning the new fettlers themfelves. Letters came full of complainings that their expectations were deceived. The inconveniencies of the journey, the ignorance of the language, the want of their cuftomary accommodations, the harfhnefs of many perfons in office, might very well bring many of the colonifts to repent of the rafh ftep they had taken: others, who wanted only to live in idlenefs, wondered that they were to begin again to work, as it was exactly on that very account that they had left their home.——This whole method of fettling colonies, however, is very far from being the beft. A government moft furely improves the country by regulations and inftitutions of a humane and gentle nature, without oftentation and noife; wifdom and juftice give fpirit to the inhabitants, and increafe the population; thither the forcigner will go, that he may live and thrive under its foftering protection; and only he who comes on this inducement proves a ufeful and eftimable citizen.

A A 2

Catharine

Catharine underſtood and practiſed this better method of increaſing the inhabitants of her country. But Europe expects to ſee, eſpecially at the opening of a reign, ſplendid inſtitutions announced in brilliant deſcriptions. Beſides, in reſpect to thoſe of which we are now ſpeaking, very ſpacious diſtricts entirely void of people make a great difference : in this caſe a mere proclamation may doubtleſs produce ſome beneficial effect ; for the emigrants muſt come in large troops, that ſome may ſettle and multiply. — So it happened in Ruſſia. Beſides the Germans, ſettlers came from France, Poland, and Sweden. In the diſtrict of Saratof alone, theſe coloniſts amounted to upwards of 10,000 families. Indeed, in the year 1774, there were only about 6194, making 25,781 heads ; but in the firſt ten years the loſs is evidently the moſt conſiderable : thoſe who remained, with ſuch as have joined them ſince, give the moſt promiſing hopes of future progreſs. In the year 1760 the government had ſent as ſettlers in the territory of Nertſchinſk, adjacent to the borders of China, a ſtony and very cold province, but rich in gold and ſilver mines, perſons ordered for exile and other puniſhments, with diſorderly and lazy boors of the nobility, unſerviceable recruits, &c. But as agriculture would not flouriſh there, Catharine

15   aſſigned

affigned thefe people their abode in the government of Tobolfk * ; where there were, from 1769 to 1772, in general fettled 10,799 full-grown males, 9716 women and children ; confequently, all together, 20,515 perfons. It is true they came originally from other parts of the empire : but in the places they came from they were ufelefs and idle, whereas in their new refidence they were obliged to work : then in provinces longer and better peopled the chafm they left was foon filled up ; and all that was wanted was to bring a primitive race into defert regions. To this likewife contributed the event that happened in 1775, when the whole horde of zaporagian kozaks, on the cataracts of the Dniepr, was entirely abolifhed and difperfed ; and more recently, from the newly-conquered countries, Lithuania and Poland, a part of the inhabitants were conducted into the interior of the empire. A number of old greek families had formerly wandered from Ruffia into Podolia, and other polifh provinces : Catharine called them back, and allotted them habitations in Siberia on the banks of the Irtifh and the Selenga. Individuals and whole tribes were likewife voluntarily

* This government in Siberia deals chiefly in furs and tallow ; and there is ftill a great want of people.

coming

coming from the reſt of Europe and from middle Aſia, particularly ſuch as were diſſatisfied with the governments under which they had lived ; as was eſpecially the caſe with many Greeks and Armenians.

In order to increaſe the population, or more properly to eradicate a phyſical and moral cauſe of depopulation, the empreſs alſo, at the propoſal of lieutenant-general Betſkoy, laid the foundation of the foundling and lying-in hoſpital at Moſco, and afterwards of another at St. Peterſburg.   Whatever may be advanced againſt foundling hoſpitals, experience is incontrovertibly in their favour.

Catharine alſo now raiſed the means of providing for the health of the ſubjects into a national concern : ſhe founded in November, the medicinal college of the empire at St. Peterſburg ; which, in purſuance of a ſubſequent regulation, was placed immediately under the empreſs.

Catharine had ſeduloufly applied to the moſt excellent and uſeful of all ſciences, the ſtudy of mankind : and, as the true baſis of it, had acquired the knowledge of herſelf.   She underſtood ſo well her peculiar talents, her courage, and the whole extent of the benefits ſhe might derive from her influence, that, talking confidentially

fidentially with a foreign minister *, fitter to applaud her mistakes than to appreciate her genius, she asked him whether he thought that the peace just concluded at Hubertsburg † would be of long duration? The minister answered, that the exhaustion of the people, and the wisdom of the sovereigns by whom they were governed, seemed to promise a tranquillity of several years. But he added, that she was better able to judge than he, since by her sagacity she could appreciate the political system of the courts of Europe, and by her forces direct them at her will. Catharine then putting on an air of humility, said: " You think then that Europe " has at present its eyes fixed on me, and " that I have some weight in the principal " courts?" The answer could not fail of being in the affirmative. Catharine hearkened with condescension; then assuming the full display of imperial dignity: " I believe indeed," replied she, " that Russia merits attention. I have the " finest army in the world. I am rather short " of money, it is true; but I shall be abundantly " provided with it in a few years. If I gave the " reins to my inclination, I should have a " greater taste for war than for peace; but

* M. de Breteuil.   † Between Austria and Prussia.

A A 4   " I am

" I am reftrained by humanity, juftice, and
" reafon.   However, I fhall not be like the
" emprefs Elizabeth.   I fhall not allow myfelf
" to be preffed to make war: I fhall enter
" upon it when it will prove advantageous to
" me ; but never from complaifance to others."
Her majefty added, that the world could not
properly begin to form a judgment of her till
after five years ; that it required at leaft fo much
time to reduce her empire to order, and to
gather the fruit of her cares ; but that in the
mean time fhe fhould behave with all the princes
of Europe like a finifhed coquette.

The fe words were ftrictly true.   The minifter
imagined they were dictated by vanity.   Neverthelefs he did not venture otherwife to reply than
by a flattering compliment.

The firft trial that Catharine made of her influence, was in favour of Biren, who experienced
fome difficulties on the part of the fenate at
Mittau.   On recalling the troops that were
in Pomerania, her majefty fent orders to them to
pafs into Courland to fupport the pretenfions of
the duke, whom fhe patronized. She then caufed
another army to march into Poland, under the
command of count Romantzoff, an army that
was foon reinforced by 20,000 auxiliaries whom
general Chernicheff headed under pruffian colours.

During

During the long exile of Biren, the eſtates of Courland, conſidering him as lapſed from his title of duke, had elected in his place prince Charles of Saxony, ſon of Auguſtus III. king of Poland. This prince, ſupported by the authority of his father and by the wiſhes of the couriſh nation, ſeemed as if he ſhould neceſſarily carry it againſt a competitor, whoſe character for cruelty rendered him odious. But the preſence of the ruſſian armies eaſily put to ſilence the good-will that was entertained for duke Charles. Simolin*, the envoy of Catharine, was ſoon able to dictate to the ſenate of Mittau laws for its ſovereign; and a declaration promulgated at Moſco† in favour of Biren, by menacing the king of Poland with war, forced him to give the inveſtiture of Courland to the deſpoiler of his ſon.

Satisfied with ſo great docility, Catharine employed her mediation with Maria Thereſa and Frederic, to induce them to withdraw their troops from the hereditary dominions of the king of Poland: but ſhe could not ſucceed. The empreſs-queen laid the blame on the king of Pruſſia, who did not fail to throw it back

* The ſame who afterwards filled the character of ambaſſador at London and at Paris.

† The 31ſt of December.

upon

upon her.   Peace happily put an end to thefe acts of injuftice.

In the mean time, Frederic, who had long contemplated the friendfhip of Catharine as an object that might eventually be of the utmoft importance to him, and who therefore was defirous to gain it, was among the foremoft to try to procure her attachment by a profufion of complaifance.   He offered her the order of the black eagle, which fhe gracioufly accepted, and wore while fhe remained at Mofco.   It was not poffible that the emprefs could fo foon have forgotten that the wearing of a pruffian order had been imputed as a crime to her hufband: but fhe was defirous of fhewing to her fubjects that fhe was not without confideration in foreign courts; and what had been a fault in him became in her a mark of ability.

Some new differences now rofe between the court of Peterfburg and that of Copenhagen touching the adminiftration of Holftein.   By a treaty fecretly concluded twelve years before * between the king of Denmark and the king of Sweden, the latter had ceded to the former his rights to the regency of Holftein during the minority of the young grand duke; for the

* In 1750.

court

court of Denmark had for a long time coveted a principality fo commodioufly fituated, and which fhe has fince acquired. She beheld with concern the return of prince George, who had juft taken the command of it in behalf of Ruffia. She even at firft refufed to acknowledge his authority. But Catharine threatened : the Danes were afraid of fhortly feeing again the ruffian troops on their march to Holftein. The danifh commiffaries quitted Kiel, and an envoy extraordinary* from Copenhagen came to Mofco to apologife for the king his mafter.

The court of Peterfburg and that of Stockholm were at that time living in perfeét harmony. United by the ties of blood they were alike in want of peace, and Ruffia as yet gave no fymptoms of that enormous aggrandifement of power with which, fome years after, fhe ftruck terror into Sweden and the reft of its neighbours.

Sedately relying on the intentions of the princes of Europe, Catharine could not be fo tranquil in regard to her fubjeéts. She negleéted however nothing that ought to have attached them to her. Generous by nature, fhe was now ftill more fo from policy. The defire of augmenting the number of her dependents rendered

* M. Hachthaufen.

her

her even prodigal of her bounty, and her fears misguided her choice.

She shewed lenity to the friends of the deceased tzar. She not only granted liberty to Gudovitch, to Volkoff, and to Milganoff, but gave the latter a body of troops to command, and to the second the lieutenancy of the government of Orenburg. Gudovitch would accept of nothing.

In the first months that followed the sanguinary death of Peter III. the emprefs had but little time to bestow a thought upon the horror it must have excited in the public mind: but reflection on the circumstance of owing her elevation to so flagrant a crime must occasionally have harassed her own; and this, with the inceffant repetitions of petty conspiracies, kept her in continued disquiet. They were detected, they were defeated, but it was impoffible to annihilate their origin; and her majesty was so much the more uneafy as she affected to diffemble her vexation.

Another secret source of affliction to her was, that since Gregory Orloff had been acknowledged as her favourite, men the moft diftinguished by their birth, jealous at the fortune of this minion, or difgufted by his arrogance, kept aloof from the court. Catharine frequently faw none about her but rough foldiers, who ftrangely abufed the rights they imagined they had to her gratitude.

gratitude. It was not their paſt ſervices ſhe was recompenſing. Perhaps ſhe would have willingly diſpenſed with them: but ſhe was paying in advance for thoſe they might ſtill afford her; and her bounties, and the honours ſhe devolved upon them only augmented their inſolence, and ſharpened their greedineſs. She ſometimes, however, bluſhed at the deferences ſ. e thought herſelf obliged to ſhew them; and in order to excuſe their defects, ſhe aſcribed to them qualities which they did not poſſeſs. " The life I lead is far from agreeable " to me," ſhe one day obſerved. " I know " that I am ſurrounded by people of no educa- " tion; but I am indebted to them for being " what I am. They are men of courage and " probity; and I am ſure that they will never " betray me." One part of this confeſſion could not be ſincere. The accomplices of Catharine were not wanting in courage; but their probity was not very conſpicuous.

Among theſe proud and brutal courtiers, Panin was almoſt the only one who diſtinguiſhed himſelf by poliſhed manners and a tolerably cultivated mind. Yet he enjoyed but a ſecondary influence. His thoughts were always turned on the ariſtocratic ſenate he had wanted Peter III. to eſtabliſh; and he ſeized every opportunity for diſplaying this pretended advantage before thoſe

with

with whom he converfed.   Obferving, on fome
occafion, that Catharine feemed to be under an
extraordinary alarm, he thought it a favourable
moment for unfolding to her the whole of his
project, and for inducing her to adopt it.   After
exaggerating to her the dangers to which he
feared fhe was expofed, and the difficulty of
avoiding the troubles infeparable from a ufurpa-
tion, he added, that there was one way ftill of
efcaping them, and of immoveably fixing her
throne; but that he was much afraid left a falfe
delicacy might prevent her from recurring to it.
Catharine bid him explain.   He immediately
delivered to her the principles of a fyftem of government, which a long experience of its incon-
veniences did not prevent him from admiring.
" The fovereigns of this empire," proceeded he,
" have hitherto uniformly enjoyed an unlimited
" power; but it is the very extent of that power
" which renders it dangerous to him in whom it
" is lodged, fince it may at any time be ufurped
" by fome bold pretender, and the ufurper is
" thenceforth above the laws.   Truft me, ma-
" dam, make the facrifice of an abfolute au-
" thority.   Create a fixed and permanent council
" which will fecure to you the crown.   Solemnly
" declare that you renounce, for yourfelf and
" for your fucceffors, the power of depriving at
                                             " pleafure

" pleafure the members of that auguft body.
" Declare, that if they commit any crime or
" high mifdemeanor, their peers alone fhall
" have the right to judge and to condemn them,
" on accurate and fevere informations.   From
" the moment you fhall adopt this prudent
" meafure, it will be forgotten that you ob-
" tained the crown by violence, in the fenti-
" timent that you intend to preferve it only by
" juftice."

Catharine, who was delighted with whatever
was new or extraordinary, thought there was
fomething fublime in the propofal, conceiving,
that by renouncing the prerogative of abfolute
power, fhe fhould at once acquire immortal
glory, and for ever conciliate the love of her
fubjects.   She would doubtlefs have been in the
right if fhe had refolved to render them pro-
greffively and equally free, and have given them
a fenate, the members whereof fhould be taken
indifferently from all the feveral claffes, and
elected by the majority of fuffrages.   But to
leave a whole people in the moft degrading, the
moft cruel flavery, and to chufe by favour a
fenate from a privileged order, what was this but
to fet up twenty or thirty tyrants in the place of
one fovereign? And is not the defpotifm of
bodies

bodies always more terrible and more immoveable than that of individuals?

However, Catharine charged Panin to commit his plan to paper and present it to her, expressing herself in such a manner as to lead him to imagine that she meant to put it in execution. Panin lost no time in obeying her commands; and, in order more effectually to secure its success, he placed the name of Gregory Orloff at the head of those whom he destined to compose the new senate. The favourite seemed flattered with this distinction, but requested time to consider upon it; and before he gave answer to Panin, he consulted Bestucheff, who, that he might continue to play his part, consented to enlighten by his experience him whom his sovereign should vouchsafe to honour. Bestucheff was too sensible to the value of a power which he had a long time directed, not to be shocked at the idea of seeing it drop from the hands of Catharine. He presented himself immediately to her majesty, expatiated with energy on the perils that accompanied the measure to which Panin was endeavouring to persuade her, and conjured her not to expose herself to a long repentance, by dividing an authority which she had acquired with so much trouble, and which she

she would never recover if she suffered it to be ravished from her but for a single instant.

The empress easily perceived the wisdom of the old chancellor's advice, and promised to follow it. On appearing a second time before her, Panin found her already dissuaded. She did justice to his zeal, praised his sagacity, but owned to him that it was impossible for her to benefit by it. The minister was deeply mortified at so sudden a change. Forced to dissemble before Catharine, he gave vent to his ill-humour among his friends, and could not refrain from saying to one of them, on trusting him with these particulars: " If the empress is determined to " rule alone, you will see what a sad reign we " shall make of it." These words prove that Panin hearkened more to his resentment than to reason, or that he was very little capable of judging of Catharine.

1763. Panin, however, was not long in discovering that it was owing to Bestucheff alone that his enterprise had failed of success ; and he found an opportunity to retaliate upon him, by defeating in his turn a scheme that the ambitious old man had formed to render himself more necessary. As every thing concurred to evince the great influence of Orloff, and Catharine seemed no longer desirous to conceal it, the artful

courtier infinuated to the favourite how glad
he fhould be to fee him emperor.   He at once
roufed his   ambition and   exalted   his pride.
" Gregory Gregorevitch," faid he, " it is to
" no purpofe that Catharine has given you her
" heart, unlefs fhe prefents you with her hand.
" She knows with how much zeal and intrepidity
" you have acted in her fervice.   She knows
" from what dangers you freed her to inveft
" her with the fovereign power.   She cannot
" then worthily reward you but by giving you a
" fhare in that throne which fhe owes to your
" prowefs.   Indeed why fhould fhe refufe it ?
" Who is better able than you to fupport that
" throne againft all attempts of confpirators to
" overturn it ? Who would be more agreeable
" to the fovereign in the twofold capacity of
" her admirer and her defender ? Yes, I know
" her well enough to be convinced that fhe
" would confent to whatever you fhould dare to
" propofe.   You fhould therefore lofe no time
" in taking advantage of the inconftant favour
" of Fortune.   To-morrow, perhaps, the op-
" portunity may be paft.   Univerfal experience
" proves, that attachments are not eternal.
" Even death may remove her from your hopes ;
" and if you fhould not inherit her power,
" fuch a misfortune would expofe you to punifh-
                                              " ment

" ment for what you have undertaken in her
" behalf.

" I am sensible, however, that it might not
" be proper for you to make the proposal.
" Obstacles might probably be thrown in your
" way, with which your delicacy would forbid
" you to contend. A refusal might occasion
" you a mutual perplexity. Trust yourself to
" my long experience and my friendship. I
" shall contrive to determine the empress her-
" self to offer you her crown. I promise you
" that I shall hazard no proposal that I am not
" very certain of seeing accepted: but promise
" me, on your part, to leave me to pursue my
" own method, and that you will even feign an
" ignorance of my proceedings."

Orloff listened to the aged chancellor with
the most profound attention. Presumptuous and
volatile, he fancied himself for a moment on the
throne of the tzars; and, embracing Bestucheff,
promised a compliance with all he desired.

Bestucheff the same day, having an opportunity of discoursing with the empress, artfully
founded her on the subject. But Catharine,
after much hesitation, concluded by telling the
chancellor, that, however she might be inclined
to favour his proposal, she could never resolve
upon taking a step that might meet with so many

B B 2   difficulties;

difficulties; and confessed that, on considering it maturely, she saw no way of making the attempt without giving umbrage to the empire.

The chancellor engaged to find out the means. He ingeniously composed, in the name of the russian nation, a petition; in which, after making a just though pompous eulogium on all that the empress had done for the glory and the happiness of her people, he called to mind the weak constitution of the young Paul Petrovitch, and the disquietudes caused by the frequent alterations in his health; and conjured Catharine to give the empire an additional testimony of her love, by sacrificing her own liberty to its welfare in taking a spouse.

In order to conceal his real intentions from those whom he designed should promote them, Bestucheff began by proposing prince Ivan, very sure that all those who should sign the petition would reject that unfortunate captive. At the same time Catharine, who sometimes gave the old courtier room to believe she was under his guidance, putting on the air of approving this proposal, afraid too that Ivan might suddenly be taken from prison and crowned, caused him to be conveyed from the castle of Schluffelburg, and lodged in a monastery at Kolmogor, not far from Archangel; where, as though it
                                                          had

had been intended to make him more fenfible to the misfortune that awaited him, he was treated at firft with the honours that were due to his rank, but was foon carried back very fecretly to Schluffelburg-caftle.

What the old chancellor had forefeen failed not to happen. On his prefenting the petition to the clergy, twelve bifhops, previoufly gained over, eagerly put their fignatures to it, fpecifying that Catharine ought not to marry prince Ivan, becaufe he might punifh her for her benefactions, aud pretend to ftand indebted for the crown to his proper right alone. They at the fame time requefted that her majefty would condefcend to choofe, from among her fubjects, him whom fhe fhould think the moft worthy to participate in her throne.

A great number of general officers adhered to the fentiment of the bifhops. But for the dexterity of Panin and the courage of the hetman Razumoffíky, and the chancellor Vorontzoff, the ftratagem of Beftucheff would have fucceeded, and Gregory Orloff had been emperor of all the Ruffians *.

* Catharine, defirous of dignifying Orloff, that her marriage with him might appear lefs difproportionate, follicited the emprefs-queen to grant him a diploma of prince of the empire. This being done, it was her intention to decorate him with the title of duke of Ingria, and of Carelia.

Count

Count Panin engaged Razumofffky and Vorontzoff to reprefent to Catharine how humiliating the projected union would be, and how dangerous to her. The hetman fpoke to her with the roughnefs of his character and the authority that his fortune and his fervices gave him. Vorontzoff, cafting himfelf at her feet, intreated her not to engage in a marriage which would be attended with the greateft misfortunes. His remonftrances were very bold, and fhewed him to poffefs a firmnefs of which he was not thought capable. But Catharine, who was never embarraffed, affected extreme furprife; and, after having thanked Razumofffky for his friendfhip, and praifed the noble courage of Vorontzoff, fhe protefted that the idea of the marriage they fo much dreaded had never once entered her mind; that it was pofitively without her knowledge that fuch an odious intrigue had been carried on; and that, as Beftucheff was the author of it, fhe would refent it on him. Neverthelefs her majefty took care not to be fevere with the old man, who, in perfect harmony with her, only fought to footh her inclinations, and whom fhe thought it ftill neceffary to indulge in his humours.

Beftucheff thus faw his project fail without apparently receiving any fhock to his influence. He was, on the contrary, every day better received

ceived by the empress and the favourite, while Vorontzoff experienced from them nothing but coldness. Thoroughly now convinced that too much zeal for the glory of Catharine was not always the means of pleasing her, and that his disgrace was already determined, Vorontzoff was eager to prevent a forced retreat by a voluntary exile. He gave out that his health was impaired by the labours of the cabinet; and under pretext of recovering it, he asked permission to travel for two years in foreign countries. The empress, who found his presence rather irksome, granted him leave with secret satisfaction; notwithstanding that she feigned a regret at his departure. In public she shewed him great respect and good-will, and audibly intreated him to hasten his return to resume the functions of an administration which he filled, as she said, so successfully for the happiness of the empire.

In the mean time the apprehension of seeing Catharine bestow herself on the daring adventurer who had lent a hand to precipitate from the throne her unfortunate husband, occasioned violent murmurs. Several ineffectual plots were set on foot against her and her favourite. One of them for a moment was on the point of succeeding. A guard stood at Orloff's door, as

at

at that of the emprefs.   One of the centinels,
by means of a bribe, had promifed to deliver
him afleep to three of the confpirators.   But the
hour was wrongly marked; and when the confpirators appeared, the centinel who was to have
feconded them, had already been relieved by
another.   This latter, aftonifhed at feeing three
men applying for admiffion into Orloff's apartment, made fo much noife as to bring together
others of the guards.   The confpirators had but
juft time to efcape under favour of the uniform
they wore.

This movement fpread alarm over the palace.
Catharine was roufed.   Imagining that her life
was not in fafety at Mofco, fhe haftened to quit
that city, and return to St. Peterfburg.   The
day of her departure was fignalized by demon-
ftrations of infolent joy approaching to rage.
Her cypher had been placed on a triumphal arch
in the great place of Mofco: the populace tore
it down, and broke it to pieces after having
dragged it through the mire.

Catharine arrived at St. Peterfburg the day of
the anniverfary of her acceffion to the throne.
Well knowing that for overawing the minds of
the vulgar, it is neceffary often to dazzle their
eyes, fhe omitted nothing for rendering her
                                        entry

entry magnificent and folemn.   Her carriage
was preceded by all the regiments of guards,
and followed by thofe of the foreign minifters,
and the numerous train of courtiers whom ambition and vanity had drawn to her fuite.   This
pompous fpectacle, however, had not the effect
that Catharine had expected from it.   It raifed
more aftonifhment than joy, and tended only to
increafe the irritation of the public mind.   The
number of malcontents augmented.   Confpiracies were multiplied, and became more dangerous by the names of confequence that were
affociated to them.   The public report counted
among the enemies of Catharine the moft powerful perfonages of the empire, and even thofe
who had ferved her with the utmoft affiduity and
zeal.   The hetman Razumoffſky, count Panin,
and his brother *, were of this number ; and it
feemed certain that if thefe different confpirators
could have turned their eyes on a prince worthy
of being the central object of their wifhes, Catharine would have loft the crown.   But fome
wanted to raife Paul Petrovitch to the throne,
while others were defirous of recalling the unhappy Ivan ; and all embarraffed, all irrefolute,

* General Panin, brother of the minifter, gained confiderable reputation in the firft turkifh war.

5 ＇

they

they alike formed the plan of dethroning the emprefs, without agreeing on the fucceffor to be given her.

Catharine, fecretly advertifed, of the defign of Panin and of Razumoffiky, was for a moment ready to have them arrefted: but having only fuch evidence as was but little to be relied on, and fufpicions in which fhe might be deceived, fhe felt, after all, that by an ill-timed feverity againft men of fuch high confideration, fhe ran the rifk of occafioning a general infurrection. She thought it might be expedient to employ a little artifice: a means which had frequently been of ufe to her.

Although, fhortly after the revolution which had placed her on the throne, fhe had repaid with feeming ingratitude the devotednefs and fortitude of princefs Dafhkoff, and even fince fhe had been forced to recal her to court, fhe behaved to her with fufficient coolnefs, fhe now feigned all at once to wifh to reftore her to her confidence. She made no doubt that princefs Dafhkoff had a fhare in the plots that were hatching by her old friends. She knew her to poffefs a refolute foul; but fhe alfo knew that fhe was precipitate and imprudent. She was therefore in hopes of being able to draw out of her fome confeffions that might clear up her doubts.

doubts. She wrote her a very long letter, wherein, after lavishing upon her the most tender epithets, the most advantageous promises, and the most seducive flatteries, she conjured her, in the name of their long-standing friendship, to reveal to her what she knew of the recent conspiracies; assuring her, at the same time, that she would grant a full pardon to all that were concerned. Princess Dashkoff, nettled that Catharine should think to make of her an instrument of her vengeance, as she had made her that of her elevation, replied, in no more than four lines to the four pages she had received from the empress. This was her answer: "Madam, I have heard nothing: but if I had "heard any thing, I should take good care how "I spoke of it. What is it you require of me? "That I should expire on a scaffold? I am "ready to mount it."

Astonished at so much haughtiness, and not hoping to conquer it, Catharine attempted to attach to her those whom she dared not to punish. Some of the subaltern conspirators, who had been arrested, and yet kept an obstinate silence on their accomplices, were banished to Siberia: but Panin and Razumofffky received several additional marks of favour.

However,

However, as plots were inceſſantly renewing, and as the clemency exhibited towards the guilty ſeemed to harden them in guilt, Catharine declared that, for the future, ſhe would not conform to the edict by which the empreſs Elizabeth had promiſed never to ſuffer a criminal to be ſentenced to death. She thought it unhappily impoſſible to keep the Ruſſians in order by any other means than by the dread of puniſhment. She afterwards ſaw that this dread was not a ſufficient check to their exceſſes. In fact, the only means of diminiſhing the number of criminals is to diſſeminate inſtruction, ſolemnly to eſtabliſh the principles of ſound morality, and to honour thoſe who put them in practice. While legiſlators have been for ever multiplying laws againſt vice, they have always been too negligent of making inſtitutions in favour of virtue.

Catharine was invariably ſenſible of the benefits ariſing from ſuch inſtitutions, and neglected nothing of all that ſeemed likely to promiſe a tendency to the proſperity of her empire. At the very time when ſhe had the ſtrongeſt reaſons to apprehend for the ſafety of her perſon, ſhe was buſied in all the particulars of government with as much aſſiduity and calmneſs as if her reign was to be everlaſting. She founded colleges

leges and hofpitals in every part of her empire.
She encouraged commerce and induftry; fhe
ordered new fhips of war to be put upon the
ftocks.

In regard to commerce, Peter III. on the
7th of April 1762, had iffued an important and
exprefs decree: Catharine took it into confideration on the 11th of Auguft, on the propofal of
the fenate, where fhe was prefent, found much
of it to confirm, but likewife many things to
omit and to improve; and executed on the fame
day, with her own hand, the imperial edict: in
which it is faid:—" On the whole furface of the
" earth there is no country better adapted for
" commerce than our empire. Ruffia has fpa-
" cious harbours in Europe; and over land the
" way is open through Poland to every region.
" Siberia extends, on one fide, over all Afia;
" and India is not very remote from Oren-
" burg; but on the other fide it feems to touch
" upon America. Acrofs the Euxine is a paf-
" fage, though as yet unexplored, to Ægypt
" and Africa: and bountiful Providence has
" bleffed the extenfive provinces of our empire
" with fuch gifts of nature, as can as rarely be
" found as they are wanted in all the four
" quarters of the world."

During

During Catharine's reign thefe fplendid advantages have been improved to an eminent
degree.   Courland on the Baltic, with its havens,
was fubjected by her to the ruffian fceptre; and
on the oppofite fide of Europe the Euxine laves
her extenfive conquefts: Otchakof, Kherfon,
the Krim, and the Kuban, bear witnefs to the
force of her arms.   The fails of her fhips of
commerce and of war are fpread in the Mediterranean.   On the greek iflands the ruffian
banners are difplayed.   Her troops opened a
road into Ægypt, and there in 1772 fought in
fupport of Ali-bey againft the Turks.   The
free inhabitants of the extreme north-eaftern
point of Afia, the Tfchuktfches, were at length
obliged to fubmit; and a channel of no great
width (the ftreights of Behring) there only divides
the empire from America.   A multitude of ruffian
iflands, of various dimenfions, in the northern
part of the fouthern ocean, the Kurilli and feveral
additional acquifitions, connect it with other
iflands, and even with the continent of the fourth
quarter of the world: nay, even upon that the
Ruffians have got firm footing.   The increafe of
navigation by thefe acquifitions, and the extremely lucrative commerce in the furs here procured,
the coftly fkins of the fea-otter and other ani-

2*   mals,

mals, is of the utmost confequence. The differences that arofe with China in 1778 are at length
compromifed; and if no more caravans go from
Mofco to Pekin, yet the merchants of thefe two
great empires profecute their trade together, and
perhaps better, in the frontier town of Kiachta
and Maimatfhin. Orenburg in afiatic Ruffia is
excellently fituated for commercial intercourfe
with the Eaft Indies: the caravans require only
three months for the whole journey: accordingly, at the half-way thither, at Balk, a town in
Bactriana or Khorafan, ruffian and eaft-indian
caravans already meet together.

Well-founded as all this evidently is, yet we
have feen that it is poffible for unfavourable occurrences completely to annihilate the advantages
of this whole fituation at leaft on a very important fide. When, in the year 1788, Sweden,
Poland, Pruffia, the Turks, and an englifh fleet,
had clofely combined in a war againft Ruffia, this
great empire was in a manner cut off from all
trade and commerce with the reft of Europe.
So true it is, that the bare " gifts of nature,
" wherewith Providence has bleffed the exten-
" five provinces of Ruffia," are not able to procure her the balance; fo greatly do the articles
of finer manufacture and of luxury outweigh in
commerce the indifpenfable neceffaries of life.
This

This Catharine knew very well towards the latter end of her reign ; and therefore by a policy, the foundnefs of which is not fo apparent, fhe prohibited, with unexampled feverity, the importation of almoft all wrought goods from abroad, which ferve only to conveniency and pleafure.

Commercial regulations are naturally fubject to alteration. Accordingly nothing more circumftantial can here be adduced on the fubject. It will fuffice to give a farther fketch, to fhew the fpirit of the laws. The corn trade is, in confideration of a moderate duty, entirely free ; only all exportation immediately ceafes, when the market price in the country exceeds fuch a fum, which for the various provinces is differently fettled :——a regulation which, whether beneficial or not, it is well known, is the fame in England. This limitation of the exportation does not attach to corn of the growth of Poland, which may at all times be fhipped for the foreigner, in order not to opprefs this branch of commerce. Siberia may never fend corn out of the country. The condition of a ftated market price in the country does not affect the exportation of linfeed ; but of horned cattle it does. The port of Archangel was favoured equally with that of St. Peterfburg. The export of fine and coarfe linens, againft the ufual prohibition, was permitted ; that of linen
                                                    yarn

yarn remained prohibited. Several monopolies belonging to private individuals and whole trading companies were abolished; indeed by an arbitrary step, but certainly with beneficial effect to the country : neither did the government exempt itself. The trade in rhubarb, in pot-ashes and wood-ashes, belonging exclusively to the crown, was now declared open to every one. An end was thenceforth put to the caravan trade of the crown to China : and also the contracting for the sea-dog fishery, other fisheries, and the tobacco trade ; the monopoly of sugar-works, and of chintz manufactories ; the exclusive right of one man to import foreign silk : the trading companies to Persia, China, and the Bukharèy ; the company to the Euxine and the Mediterranean, from Temernikof, a town on the Don. Every person may freely trade in all these commodities and to all these countries. Only a limitation took place in the asiatic commerce, but to the security and the greater profit of the russian merchants themselves. To them only two ports were assigned on the Caspian, Baku and Sinsili, there to keep market, and wait the arrival of the persian merchants. It is farther regulated, that they must there tax the several commodities intended for Persia, the Bukharèy, &c. in the presence of the resident imperial consul : the like muſt be done by the merchants of Aſtrakhan and Orenburg, and enter into a bond with one another not to ſell any thing below the fixed price, under penalty of confiſcation; that the foreigners may not profit by the ſpoiling of the market by the ruſſians themſelves.

The tobacco trade was next declared free; proper meaſures were likewiſe taken in February 1763, conducive to the better culture of it in the Ukraine*, where it may be made to flouriſh ſo well from the excellent quality of the ſoil.

The coinage was afterwards frequently altered. In December 1763 Catharine decreed, that the proportion of the gold to the ſilver coin ſhould be as 1 to 15. An error almoſt general throughout Europe is, in the having of a twofold ſtandard, as if they imagined it poſſible to fix by legiſlation a proportion that, from commerce and in its own nature, is always fluctuating. The gold ſhall be of a fineneſs of 88 ſolotniks; the ſilver of 72. Out of a pound of ſuch gold ſhall be ſtruck 31 imperials and 2 rubles 88$\frac{2}{5}$ copeeks; out of a pound of ſilver ſo alloyed 17 rubles 6$\frac{2}{5}$ copeeks. Siberia had a coinage (with the arms

* The ſclavonian parent-word is Krai, *the border*; and u, *on* or *near*. The primary import, therefore, of Ukrainer is *borderer*, from ukraine, *on the borders*. Hence the Ukern (in the mark Brandenburg), the Krainer and the Ukrainer.

of

of that kingdom, two wolves, which was not to be current beyond the confines of the government) affigned it, of the copper peculiar to the mines of Kolyvan, which is impregnated with gold and filver, obtained by the fmelting away of the filver ore, the tranfport whereof would be too difficult, and its farther feparation from the noble metals too expenfive. The pood of this copper contains $1\frac{3}{6}\frac{1}{6}$ folotniks of fine gold, and $31\frac{2}{6}\frac{1}{6}$ folotniks of filver *.

About this time Poniatoffky renewed his follicitations for permiffion to vifit Peterfburg. The emprefs would not liften to them, but affured him of her conftant friendfhip, of which fhe promifed to give him convincing proofs on all occafions. Nor was it long before fhe realized her promife.

Towards the end of this year Catharine gave a proper form to the fupreme college of the empire, the directing fenate, which had been inftituted by Peter I. In order to give an eafier, plainer, and more rapid courfe to the bufinefs of it, fhe divided the fenate into fix departments, whereof the four former fhould have their feat in St. Peterfburg, and the two latter in Mofco. In fome particulars fhe removed incumbrances, in others fhe made new regulations, and diffufed

* For the relative proportions of thefe weights, monies, &c. fee before, p. 56. 58.

through

through the whole a spirit of simplicity and order.

Undoubtedly many of these new institutions were rather preparatory than finished works; undoubtedly several plans were sketched out by her, and even put in execution under her eyes, of which, in the far distant parts of her vast empire, no trace is any longer to be seen; undoubtedly some things had more of show and a shining outside than of an exactly calculated utility.   But only as preparatives, even only as reform in the more proximate sphere of action, even only as the display of a truly imperial magnificence, they could not be unattended by important consequences. All men saw that the comprehensive mind of Catharine embraced all objects; they were convinced of her activity and of her benevolence, (and what higher qualities can the ruler of a people possess?) of her treasures and her magnanimity.   They were the capital towns, they were the colleges of the empire that gained another form, and which must naturally, though slowly, operate upon the provinces.   A new vital spirit was infused into the nation, a more elevated impetus into all minds. To this greatly contributed even the personal reverence paid to the beautiful, the spirited woman, the glow of enthusiasm for the monarch whom foreigners praised, praifed, whom the univerfe admired. The court was brilliant and agreeable ; in the expenditure of large fums, magnificence, tafte, and lafting enjoyment were ftudied. Foundations for the cultivation of arts and literature, fuperb embellifhments of the refidence and other towns, regulations for ufe and convenience were manifeft to every beholder. Milder and more amicable difpofitions began to appear ; induftry and diligence were quickened, and by their means the comforts of life were more widely diffufed ; the nation was no longer dependent on the foreigner; and ruffian fhips were feen riding at anchor in the ports of Cadiz and Leghorn.

CHAP. IV.

*State of Poland from the time of the kings of the
first race to the death of Augustus III. — Election of prince Poniatofsky. — Fresh conspiracy at
St. Petersburg. — Journey of the empress into
Livonia. — Assassination of prince Ivan in the
castle of Schlusselburg. — Punishment of Mirovitch, and other events of 1763, 1764, &c.*

POLAND, which had sometimes acted so
conspicuous a part in the politics of Europe, and
which, from the extent of its territory, the fertility of its foil, the high spirit and courage of its
inhabitants, seemed formed for acquiring a still
greater preponderance, has loft, by the defects
of its government, a part of the advantages it
had received from nature.

This kingdom had long been under the influence of Ruffia ; and that influence had become
the more powerful under Catharine, as, independently of the army of Romantzoff, encamped
on the banks of the Vistula, 50,000 men had
taken up their quarters in Livonia, Esthonia,
and Courland. Augustus III. declining in his
health, as well from the irregularities of his life

7   as

as from the vexation occafioned him by the in-
vafion of Saxony, was now verging faft to the
grave. All fuch as had formed pretenfions to
the fucceffion, accordingly began to examine
their ftrength ; and the court of Peterfburg was
the centre of their intrigues. The afpiring mind
of Catharine was flattered at feeing herfelf the
arbiter of thefe ambitious rivals. But, while 'fhe
thought proper to foment their divifions and to
encourage · their hopes, fhe was fecretly decided
in her choice. She was in want of a king,
whofe weaknefs and fervility fhe knew : fhe
made choice of Poniatoffky.

It will not be ufelefs here to caft an eye upon
the ftate of that rich and unhappy country,
which we fhall fee more than once exciting the
ambition of Catharine, and which fhe long continued to harafs, the better to prepare it for
being ufurped.

The hiftory of Poland, like that of almoft
all the other countries of Europe, reaches back
to an æra extremely remote, and filled with uncertainty. All that we know with tolerable
precifion is, that Poland at firft was governed
by a race of kings *, whofe power was nearly
abfolute. To this race fucceeded the Piafts,

---

* The race of Lefko.

(for fo they ufually call their native fovereigns,)
who are thought to have been elective, but who,
for feveral generations, preferved the crown in
their family.   The kingdom was frequently difturbed by the pretenfions of the magnats, who
combined againft the monarch, and oppofed to
him a power which balanced that of the crown.

One of the laft kings of the race of the Piafts,
Cafimir III. furnamed the great, or the father of
the peafantry, repreffed the dangerous and always
turbulent authority of the grandees, by conferring
a variety of privileges on the inferior nobleffe,
and by that means alarming them with a dangerous rivalfhip.   But that prince, however, generally guided by the dictates of juftice, and how
great foever his concern in behalf of the unhappy
peafants, was never able to mitigate the barbarous lot to which they are doomed in Poland.

Lewis of Hungary, nephew and fucceffor of
Cafimir, was not in a capacity to benefit by the
advantages that monarch had acquired, becaufe
on beftowing on him the crown, the nobility
obliged him to fubfcribe to burdenfome conditions.   On the death of Lewis, without leaving
a male heir, that turbulent nobility made an offer
of the throne to Ladiflaus Yagellon, duke of
Lithuania, and impofed on him the fame conditions as had been accepted by Lewis.   One of
thefe

thefe conditions was, not to raife fubfidies without the confent of the diets. His fucceffors
were, equally with him, forced to be continually
making new facrifices for obtaining the impofts
that were neceffary to their government; and
Sigifmond Auguftus was at length induced to
confent*, that at his death the crown fhould become abfolutely elective. This prince, who had
no fon, was without difficulty brought to agree
to make a declaration, by which he purchafed
his repofe. In a fhort time afterwards a charter
was framed †, which became the bafis and guarantee of that privilege. The four principal
articles of the charter were:

1. That the crown fhould be elective; and
that the king fhould never appoint a fucceffor
during his lifetime.

2. That general diets fhould be affembled
every two years.

3. That every nobleman of Poland fhould
have the right of voting at the election of a
king.

4. That if the king fhall prefume to infringe
the laws, and to difavow the privileges of the

* In the year 1550.
† Known under the name of *Pacta conventa.*

nation,

nation*, the subjects shall be absolved from their oath of allegiance.

The privileges secured by this charter were still farther extended; and all the successors of Sigismond Augustus down to Stanislaus Poniatofsky inclusively, were only elected upon their swearing to maintain them. Could less then be expected from princes who received the crown as a matter of favour, and who, if they had not accepted it on these conditions, would have been obliged to forego it in favour of a less scrupulous competitor? The nobles, the more they increased their power, abused it the more. Not contented with freely granting their suffrages, they sold them. Henry de Valois was the first who purchased, by means of promises and gold, the throne of the Yagellons; means which have since only yielded to the terror of arms.

On every accession to the throne the nobility usurped some additional privilege. During the reign of John Casimir, the *liberum veto* was created. This was a right given to each nobleman singly to put a stop to the deliberation of a whole diet, and to dissolve it by the sole act of his will; a right which has been one of the prin-

---

* That is to say, of the nobles; for the rest is counted for nothing.

cipal

cipal fources of the troubles, the anarchy, and
the total deftruction of Poland.

But by fuch an extent of power as every nobleman had, we may form a judgment of that
enjoyed by the palatines*, the great officers,
and, in general, all the wealthy Poles. Sometimes they raifed regiments independent on the
authority of the king; at other times they
formed confederacies, which, under pretence of
defending the laws, fowed fedition and revolt,
and in the facred name of liberty exercifed the
abfurdeft tyranny.

It is the blind ambition of the polifh nobles
that has been for three hundred years gradually
confummating the ruin of their country. That

* In Poland are 32 palatines, who are properly governors
of provinces, 3 caftellans, and 1 ftaroft. Though the quality of the two latter be inferior to that of a palatine, yet
there are four of them who poffefs the firft ranks amongft
the temporal nobles, the caftellan of Cracow being the firft
of all. The office of a palatine is to lead the troops of his
palatinate to the army; to prefide in the affemblies of the
nobility in his province; to fet a price upon merchandizes
and commodities; to take care that the weights and meafures be not altered; and to judge and defend the jews.
He has a vice-palatine under him, who muft take an oath to
him, and who ought to have an eftate in land, which they
call *poffeffionatus*. To thefe follow the order of nobility, who
are alone capable of poffeffing all the offices and lands in the
duchy and kingdom.

nation,

nation, naturally brave, which has often conquered the Ottomans, and which has given **law**
to Pruffia and to Ruffia, has not been able,
fince thefe diffenfions, to refift any of the armies
by which it has been attacked.　The forces of
the kings of Sweden, Charles Guftavus and
Charles XII. alternately found it an eafy prey;
and from the moment that the Ruffians were able
to oppofe difciplined troops to its brilliant and
licentious pofpolite *, they have found themfelves
in a capacity to dictate laws to the nation.

Under fuch circumftances the Poles called
themfelves free.　But what fort of a freedom
was that they enjoyed, even while they were
exercifing the boafted right of electing their
kings?　The age in which we live has produced
examples to the contrary; and one † of the men

---

* The military force of the Poles confifts chiefly in the
pofpolite, that is, the whole body of the gentry, which, upon
extraordinary occafions, the king and the national general
can order into the field to ferve for a limited time.　The in-
convenience and inutility of this military inftitution, in the
prefent ftate of the art of war, need not be infifted on.
They have alfo a ftanding army which ought to amount to
about 40,000 men, but, from being undifciplined, irregular,
and incomplete, it is a body altogether contemptible, efpecially the foot, as they confift almoft wholly of their wretched
peafants.

† Sarnifky.

who

who beft underftood their hiftory, has defied
them to fhew but two inftances of a free election.

There is fcarcely a great potentate in Europe
that has not had more or lefs influence in thefe
elections: but for upwards of fifty years Ruffia
has been the only power by which they have been
actually directed.

Such was the fituation of Poland when the
death of Auguftus III.* revived the cabals of
the pretenders to the throne, and furnifhed Catharine the means of difplaying her political
talents with the utmoft effect. That fovereign,
whom the courts of Vienna and Verfailles were
in hopes of detaching from Pruffia, began her
operations by artfully obtaining from thofe courts
an affurance that they would not interfere in
the affairs of Poland. In 1764, the marquis de
Paulmy, ambaffador from France at Warfaw,
declared† at the diet, that Lewis XV. would
have nothing to do in the election of the new
king; and fhortly after the count de Mercy
held the fame language on the part of Maria
Therefa.

The promife of thefe two courts, however,
was not fufficient for Catharine. She was de-

* The 5th of October.   † The 16th of March.

firous

firous of fome affurance that fhe fhould not be thwarted by that of Berlin: in this fhe fucceeded. Frederic had long been folliciting her to fign a treaty of defenfive alliance; and fhe coveted it the more as fhe had employed fo much art in inducing him to defire it. Imagining that the delays which fhe made to the conclufion of this bufnefs arofe only from the repugnance fhe had to a minifter * who had been the friend of her hufband, the pruffian monarch made choice of a plenipotentiary who fhould neceffarily be more agreeable to that princefs: he fent to St. Peterfburg the count of Solms, who had married a princefs of Anhalt-Bernburg, coufin-german to Catharine. The count de Solms was extremely well received by the emprefs, with whom he fhortly after, in the name of the king of Pruffia, concluded a treaty, fubjoined to which was the fecret article as follows:

" It being for the interest of his majefty the king of
" Pruffia and of her majefty the emprefs of all the Ruffias,
" to exert their utmoft care and all their efforts for main-
" taining the republic of Poland in its ftate of free election,
" and that it fhould not be permitted to any one to render
" the faid kingdom hereditary in his family, or to make
" himfelf abfolute therein; his majefty the king of Pruffia
" and her imperial majefty have promifed and mutually en-
" gage themfelves, in the moft folemn manner, by this

* The baron de Goltz.

" fecret

" fecret article, not only not to permit any one, whoever
" he be, to attempt to diveft the republic of its right of
" free election, to render the kingdom hereditary, or to
" make himfelf abfolute therein, in all cafes whenever fuch
" attempt fhould be made; but alfo to prevent and to fruf-
" trate, by all poffible means, and in common confent, the
" views and defigns that have a tendency to that end, as
" foon as they fhall be difcovered, and even, in cafe of ne-
" ceffity, to recur to the force of arms, to defend the re-
" public from the overthrow of its conftitution and its
" fundamental laws.

" The prefent fecret article fhall have the fame force and
" vigour as if it had been inferted word for word in the
" principal treaty of defenfive alliance figned this day, and
" fhall be ratified at the fame time.

" In virtue whereof two fimilar copies of it have been
" made, which we, the minifters plenipotentiary of his ma-
" jefty the king of Pruffia, and of her majefty the emprefs
" of all the Ruffias, authorized to that purpofe, have figned
" and fealed with the feal of our arms.

" Done at St. Peterfburg, the 11th of April (the
" 31ft of March O. S.) 1764.
" C. DE SOLMS. PANIN. GALLITZIN."

The new fovereign of Saxony, who flattered
himfelf with the profpect of inheriting the throne
of Auguftus III. as he had inherited his electorate, addreffed himfelf to the emprefs, to prevail
upon her to approve his pretenfions: but fhe
made no hefitation to deprive him of all hope.
She wrote to him, " That fhe advifed him, as
" a true friend, not to expofe his interefts in an
" affair

" affair which in the issue could not answer his
" expectations."

Conscious of her power in Poland, Catharine
dismissed, one after another, the candidates who
were not agreeable to her, without, however,
giving any intimation as yet concerning the
person whom she intended to favour.   The
greater number of the Poles were for electing
a Piast, a descendant of their ancient kings.
Catharine also for some time appeared to be of
the same sentiment.   But all at once it was heard
with amazement at Warsaw, that it was count
Poniatofsky whom that monarch had destined to
the throne.   This choice excited an almost universal discontent and violent murmurs.   The polish magnats, incensed at the prospect of being
governed by a young man* of a birth not very
illustrious, and whose elevation was neither justi-
fied by shining actions nor extraordinary virtues,
reciprocally interrogated one another, what services count Poniatofsky had rendered the republic, to entitle him to so glorious a reward?

Count Poniatofsky was endowed with those
qualities which are more adapted to conciliate
the friendship of particular persons, than to fit
him for swaying a sceptre. Tall, well-made, of
a figure at once commanding and agreeable, he

* He was at that time 32 years of age.

spoke

fpoke and wrote with fluency the feven principal languages of Europe, and in a graceful diction : but he poffeffed only a flight knowledge of affairs.   His eloquence was vague and defultory, his prefumption too apparent.   Rather weak than gentle, rather prodigal than generous, he might eafily miflead women, and dazzle a thought-lefs multitude, but not perfuade men of cultivated minds.   He was doubtlefs fitter to fubmit to be governed than to govern himfelf.   Never-thelefs, fupported by the influence and arms of Ruffia, and having no obftacle to fear on the part of other powers, his triumph was not long in fufpenfe.   The confequence of Catharine was involved in this triumph.   That princefs fet fo great a value on feeing the crown of the Sarmates on the brow of her former favourite, that fhe wrote without delay to count Kayferling, her ambaffador at Warfaw, to employ every means in behalf of Poniatoffky.   One of her letters was intercepted, and contained the fol-lowing words :—" Mon cher comte, fouvenez-" vous de mon candidat.   Je vous écris ceci " deux heures après minuit : jugez fi la chofe " m'eft indifférente * !"

* " My dear count, remember my candidate.   I write " this to you at two o'clock in the morning ; judge whether " I am indifferent about the affair !"

Count Kayferling was careful not to difobey. Neither he nor the ruffian generals neglected any thing for fecuring the choice which their fovereign defired. The dyetines were already convoked. That of Warfaw elected Poniatoffky by an unanimous fuffrage ; but whatever pains had been taken for bringing thofe of the provinces to the fame favourable difpofition, his fuccefs was not the fame. His competitors obtained a majority of voices in fome, and at leaft an equal number with his in the others.

At the affembling of the diet of convocation, the ruffian troops entered Warfaw, under pretence of preferving liberty and order.

Crowds of foreigners at the fame time poured into that city, all ready to unite at the very firft fignal. Count Branichky, grand general of the crown, and prince Radzivil, took arms in order to prevent the Ruffians from extorting the fuffrages : but what could they do againft foreign armies who were mafters of the country ; and againft a part of their countrymen difpofed to join thofe armies ? It is a difficult matter to form an adequate idea of the tumult that began to prevail in the diet of Warfaw. Count Malakoffky, venerable for his great age and his virtues, had been appointed its marfhal. He endeavoured in vain to reduce it to order, and

to

to clear it of ſtrangers. He was anſwered by furious vociferations, and ſabres were drawn. The eloquent Mokranoſſky, nuncio of Cracow, ran the riſk of his life under the ſwords of the ruſſian officers, who endeavoured to pierce him from the galleries of the ſpeakers. He at firſt thought of ſtanding on his defence; but, preſently returning his ſabre into the ſheath, and expoſing his breaſt :——" If you muſt needs have " a victim," ſaid he to the Ruſſians, " I ſtand " here before you. But at leaſt I ſhall die " free, as I have hitherto lived."——It is not improbable that he would have fallen a prey to their fury, had not prince Adam Chartorinſky had the generous courage to throw himſelf in the way, and to ſhield him with his body. Thus, in the firſt ſittings of the diet nothing paſſed but injurious ſpeeches and tumultuous quarrels.

Some one at Peterſburg, who knew what diſpleaſure the election of Poniatoffſky would occaſion to the Poles, and wanting to vilify him in the eyes of Catharine, had the boldneſs to tell that monarch, that he whoſe intereſt ſhe eſpouſed ſeemed the leſs proper to fill the throne of Poland, as his grandfather had been intendant of a little eſtate belonging to the princes Lubomirſky.——" Though he had been ſo himſelf,"

returned she, somewhat nettled, " I will have
" him to be king, and king he shall be."

Holding this language, Catharine was under
no apprehensions of being deceived. Independently of the troops which she had already in
Poland, she caused a body of 12,000 men to
enter Lithuania, and fresh reinforcements were
advancing towards Kief. Her ambassador ruled
at Warsaw, and her armies, if the expression
may be allowed, compressed the republic.

Several of the provinces now heavily accused
their nuncios of having badly corresponded with
their desires in submitting to the influence of the
court of Petersburg. They did not confine themselves to murmurs. They had recourse to arms;
they formed into different confederacies; but
these movements were attended by no consequences. The Russians threatened: the malcontents were presently silenced.

At length the diet of election was opened;
held, according to custom, in the plain of Vola,
at the distance of about three miles from Warsaw. This diet began by a solemn mass, and a
sermon *. Count Kayserling, ambassador from
Russia, being at that time indisposed, could not

* The preacher took his text from these words : Eligite
ex vobis meliorem, qui vobis placuerit, et posuite eum super
folium. 2 Kings, x. 3.

repair

repair to Vola, but fent to the diet a letter, addreffed to him by the emprefs, recommending count Poniatoffky in the moft preffing terms.

The other party, however, had not been idle, either during the election of the nuncios or reprefentatives, who, in the name of the body of the nobility, were to chufe a king, nor at the firft affembling of the ftates *. In the former cafe great tumults were raifed, but they fubfifted not long. In the latter twenty-two fenators entered a proteft againft the proceedings of the diet, the principal reafons of which were grounded on the prefence and interference of the foreign troops. Forty-five nuncios figned an act of adhefion to this proteft.

Count Branichky, who was at the head of thefe protefters, retired from the diet. But that affembly, foon after its opening, took its revenge. An order was made for divefting him of the poft of crown general. Branichky denied their power; drew together into one body a great part of that army of which they had attempted to deprive him, but which ftill faithfully adhered to him; augmented it by levies; and prepared to maintain himfelf by force; poffeffed, as it

* May 7, 1764.

fhould

fhould feem, by a fpirit of defpair and fury, having no power in the leaft adequate to the height of his attempt. Prince Radzivil, on his part, was alfo up in arms, and with the fame obftinacy, and no greater ftrength, ftruggled againft the election.

The ambaffadors of France, Spain, and the empire, finding their political intrigues of no more avail towards obftructing the election, than the hoftile attempts of prince Radzivil and count Branichky were likely to be, retired from the diet and left Poland, declaring that they had not been fent to a party, but to the entire republic *.

An action at length happened † between prince Radzivil and the ruffian troops, wherein the Poles, having fought a long time with their ufual irregular bravery, were as ufual defeated by the Ruffians.

The fpirit of Poland appeared ftrongly in all the circumftances of this action. The princefs Radzivil, but newly married, and a fifter of that prince, both of them young and beautiful, fought on horfeback with fabres, and encouraged the foldiery both by their words and their example.

* June the 7th, 1764.   † On the 3d of July.

Branichky

Branichky was alfo defeated by a body of Ruffians; and thefe two nobles, the only very confiderable perfons who oppofed the ruffian nomination, were obliged to fly out of their country, and to take fhelter in the turkifh dominions, where they particularly value themfelves on protecting the unfortunate; and thefe noble fugitives found refuge where Charles XII. had found it.

During all this time Poniatoffky, accompanied by a great number of his friends, was vifiting each nuncio in particular, and endeavouring to gain them by teftimonies of benevolence and flattering promifes. The palatines being all affembled and ranged in order round the fhopa *,

* The general diet for the election of a king is always held in the open field, about two miles from Warfaw, near the village of Vola, where a fort of booth is erected, covered with boards, at the public charge, which in the polifh language is called *fhopa*, or a fhelter from bad weather. This place is built and prepared by the treafurer of the crown: it is furrounded with a ditch, and has three doors. The day appointed for the diet being come, the fenate and the nobility proceed to St. John's church at Warfaw to hear the mafs of the holy ghoft, to implore its influence in the election of a new king, who may have all the qualities neceffary to defend the interefts of the church and of the republic: after which they go to the fhopa and proceed to bufinefs.

a large

a large building open on all sides, occupied by the senate and the equestrian order, the primate asked with a loud voice, at three distinct periods, whom they would have for king? All answered unanimously :——" Count Poniatofsky!"——The next day * he was proclaimed king of Poland, and grand duke of Lithuania, under the name of Stanislaus Augustus. Thus the diet and the kingdom being freed, in the manner we have seen, from all those who were the declared opposers of Poniatofsky, the election was soon concluded in favour of that prince with an unanimity unknown in the annals of Poland.

The new monarch, on his return to Warsaw, passed along the streets of that capital amidst the acclamations of all the people, and from that very day took possession of the palace of the republic. Some nuncios had abstained from appearing at the diet; the greater part of the prime nobility took umbrage at the appointment of Poniatofsky: but no sooner was he on the throne than they came almost all to do him homage; and he began to reign in as much tranquillity as if his election had not been effected by violence †.

Some

* The 7th of September.
† Stanislaus Poniatofsky behaved at first with great judgment and circumspection. He received with kindness those
who

Some time previous to this election, Catharine had declared her intention of visiting the scene
                                                    of

---

who had acted seemingly in the most direct opposition to his interest. The son of count Bruhl exerted himself to his prejudice, and yet that prince left him in possession of the post of grand master of the artillery which he had promised to count Branichky, palatin of Belsh, and of which indeed the latter had the generosity not to wish to deprive him. —— Soon after his election he received letters of congratulation from many of the courts of Europe. The most remarkable is that from the king of Prussia, written with his majesty's own hand. From the matter and the occasion, as well as the character of the writer, it is extremely worthy of being inserted at length. Nothing can be more glorious than a communication of such sentiments in the intercourse between sovereigns. " Your majesty must reflect, that, as
" you enjoy a crown by election and not by descent, the
" world will be more observant of your majesty's actions than
" of any other potentate in Europe : and it is but reasonable.
" The latter being the mere effect of consanguinity, no more
" is looked for (though much more is to be wished) from
" him, than what men are endowed with in common : but,
" from a man exalted by the voice of his equals, from
" a subject to a king, from a man voluntarily elected to
" reign over those by whom he was chosen, every thing is
" expected that can possibly deserve and adorn a crown.
" Gratitude to his people is the first great duty of such a
" monarch : for to them alone (under Providence) he is
" indebted that he is one. A king who is so by birth, if he
" act in a manner derogatory to his station, is a satire only
" on himself ; but an elected one, who behaves inconsistently
                                                    " with

of her fucceffes, and to make the tour of Livonia. But whilft this monarch was employed abroad in difpofing of crowns, at home her throne feemed to be tottering under her; and that vaft power, which extended to the remoteft part of Afia, which awed all Europe, and abfolutely governed fo many of its neighbours, was not fecure of its own duration for a moment. Every breath of a confpiracy feemed to fhake it: and fuch was the critical ftate of that empire, that the defigns of the obfcureft perfon in it were not unattended by danger.

In the courfe of this fummer an event of that nature happened in Ruffia which is highly deferving of a place in hiftory, from the extraordinary circumftances by which it was accompanied, though fo extremely myfterious and unaccountable in many particulars, that we defpair of affording any clear fatisfaction to the reader concerning them.

The emprefs, in purfuance of her intentions already mentioned, fet out on her journey through Efthonia, Livonia, and Courland. On

<hr>

" with his dignity, reflects difhonour alfo on his fubjects.
" Your majefty, I am fure, will pardon this warmth. It is
" the effufion of the fincereft regard. The amiable part of
" the picture is not fo much a leffon of what you ought to
" be, as a prophecy of what your majefty will be."

her

her way, she passed over from Oranienbaum to Cronstadt; and thinking to give the foreign ministers an advantageous idea of her marine, she invited them to follow her to that port. They did so: but the opinion they formed of her naval forces fell far short of that which she entertained of them herself. There was but a small number of ships, which they judged but little adapted to keep the sea; and the english ambassador, with that frankness peculiar to his nation, did not dissemble that her navy was far from appearing to him to be very formidable. She afterwards proved that it was possible for it to become so.

On quitting Cronstadt her majesty, having left the government of Petersburg to count Panin, took the road of Livonia, accompanied by count Gregory Orloff and a small retinue of nobility of both sexes. During her absence on this expedition, in the prison of the dethroned Ivan an insurrection broke out under the conduct of a certain Mirovitch, which cost that unfortunate prince his life.

Ivan Antonovitch, styled Ivan the third in the manifestos that were published in his name while emperor, was born in 1740; great grandson of tzar Ivan Alexèyevitch, the elder half-

brother

brother of Peter the great*.   On running over
the feries of ruffian monarchs from Alexèy Michailovitch downwards, our feelings are at every
moment hurt by the inteſtine diſturbances that
have happened from different pretenders, of
which ſo many within ſo ſhort ſpace of time,
and in general attended with ſuch ſhocks, as no
princely houſe in Europe has experienced, eſpecially in modern times.   But a cruel fatality

* See the genealogical tables in the former part of this
volume, tab. iii.
    Ivan III. if we reckon by the line of the tzars, or VI.
if from the firſt ſovereign of Ruſſia, was proclaimed emperor
on the death of empreſs Anne, and Biren regent; but this
high elevation was ſoon to be followed by a dreadful fall.
The father and the mother of the young emperor were difcontented at ſeeing themſelves excluded from the regency;
and the inſolence with which they were treated by Biren increaſed their diſpleaſure.   Munich, on his part, not having
obtained from the regent what he thought due to his ſervices, joined himſelf to thoſe princes, and, in the night between the 20th and 21ſt of November, Manſtein, aid-de-
camp to Munich, arreſted the regent.   The princeſs Anne
cauſed herſelf to be proclaimed regent during the minority of
her ſon.   The whole nation rejoiced at being freed from an
abominable tyrant: he was conducted to Schluſſelburg, tried,
and condemned to death: but his puniſhment was mitigated to
an exile for life in Siberia.   This exile was again moderated,
by transferring him to Yaroſlaf, where he remained till
1762, when Peter III. as we have already ſeen, recalled him
to court; and he was ſhortly after reſtored to his dukedom
by Catharine.

                                        ſeems,

feems, in a particular manner, to have propagated the feeds of difcord between the families of the two imperial brothers.

We have feen him feized and confined with his parents and relations; at firft conveyed to the citadel of Riga, then in the fortrefs of Dunamund; thence removed to Oranienburg, at the fouth-eaftern extremity of european Ruffia. At all thefe places the being together alleviated the miferies of imprifonment, and efpecially the humane behaviour of captain Korf, which firft awakened the gratitude of the infant emperor, and was all his life after recollected with emotion; folely on account of this lenity, the fufpicion of the court fell upon Korf*, and he was removed from his office. About the latter end of 1745, or the beginning of the year 1746, the family was feparated; all the reft being brought more northward to Kolmogory, Ivan was left behind in Oranienburg. To his great misfortune it came into the mind of a monk to carry him off; in their flight they had reached Smolenfk, where the affair was difcovered, and they were detained. From this place the wretched captive, lately the envied emperor of a quarter of the globe, was now brought, for greater fecu-

* Afterwards promoted to the rank of general by Peter III.

rity,

rity, to Schluffelburg, and there lodged in a
cafematt of the fortrefs, the very loop-hole of
which was immediately bricked up. He was
never brought out into the open air, and no ray
of heaven ever vifited his eyes. In this fubter-
ranean vault it was neceffary to keep a lamp
always burning; and as no clock was either to
be feen or heard, Ivan knew no difference between day and night. His interior guard, a
captain and a lieutenant, were fhut up with him;
and there was a time when they did not dare to
fpeak to him, not fo much as to anfwer him the
fimpleft queftion. What wonder if his ignorance fhould at length border on ftupidity?
This dreadful abode was however afterwards
changed for that prefently to be defcribed, in the
corridor under the covered way, in the caftle.
Elizabeth caufed him once to be brought in a
covered cart to Peterfburg, and faw and converfed with him. Peter III. alfo vifited him
incognito; and what paffed on this occafion has
been already related. Catharine too had a converfation with him foon after the commencement
of her reign, as fhe relates in her manifefto of
the 28th of Auguft 1764*, in order, as is
there faid, to form a judgment of his under-

* See the Appendix at the end of the volume.

6   ftanding

standing and talents. To her great surprise she found him to the last degree deficient in both. She observed in him a total privation of sense and reason, with a defect in his utterance, that even had he any thing rational to utter, would have rendered him entirely unintelligible.

All persons, however, were not so thoroughly convinced of the incapacity of this prince. He was now arrived at the age of twenty-four years, and he might evidently be made an instrument, or at least a pretence, for exciting dangerous commotions. His just title to the crown, of which he had been formerly in possession, his long sufferings, without any other guilt than that possession and that title, his youth, and even the obscurity which attended his life, and which therefore gave latitude for conjecture and invention, formed very proper materials for working on the minds of the populace. At the moment when Catharine was taking her departure from the residence, she had intelligence of fresh conspiracies among the guards. Several of them were taken up: but experience having shewn that the detection of one conspiracy always encouraged the hatching of some other; and, willing to avoid irritating the multitude by the frequency of punishments, the conspirators were

proceeded

proceeded againſt in private, and many of them were ſuffered to pine out their lives in priſon.

From the depth of this dungeon prince *Ivan* afforded hopes to thoſe who held in abhorrence the preſent uſurpation. It was for reſtoring the throne to this unfortunate captive that almoſt all theſe plots were formed. It was for his ſake that men, who had never ſeen him, and whoſe very exiſtence was utterly unknown to him, were continually braving the ſcaffold. Faithful to the ſyſtem of calumny that had been of ſuch ſervice to the deſtruction of Peter III. the court of Ruſſia inceſſantly employed it againſt Ivan. One while it was given out that he was ſtupid, and incapable of uttering articulate ſounds; at another, that he was a drunkard, and as ferocious as a ſavage. Sometimes it was even pretended, that he was ſubject to fits of madneſs, and believed himſelf a prophet. But many there were to whom theſe reports ſeemed no better than tales invented by the blackeſt malignity, and afterwards innocently propagated by perſons who did not reflect on the numberleſs intereſts that might concur in their invention. Doubtleſs, Ivan, to whom all kinds of inſtruction were refuſed*, and who was kept ſhut up in a loath-

---

* It however has been affirmed, that a german officer who for ſome time had the cuſtody of him, clandeſtinely taught him to read.

fome prifon, denied the converfe of any human being from whom he could derive information, muft neceffarily have been of a very confined underftanding; but there is ftill a great diftance betwéen ignorance and imbecility or madnefs. What evidently proves that Ivan was neither mad nor ftupid is, in the firft place, the converfation he had * at count Schuvaloff's with the emprefs Elizabeth. Not only the graces of his figure and the accents of his voice, but the moving complaints he uttered, awakened the fenfibility of all that were prefent, and even drew from the emprefs abundance of tears. If that young prince had committed fome act of lunacy, would it have failed of publication? Again, afterwards we find a frefh proof of his good fenfe and his fenfibility in the difcourfe which he held to Peter III. when he faw him, for the firft time at Schluffelburg. Baron Korf has faithfully tranfmitted it to us, as we have related it in a former part of this volume †. Peter III. talked with him feveral times afterwards, and perfifted in his intention of declaring him his heir. Now it may well be imagined, that Volkoff, Gudovitch, and his other confidants, would have diffuaded him from it, if they

* In 1756.   † See p. 211, 212.

could

could have brought themfelves to imagine Ivan likely to be for ever unfit to wear the crown. But, to conclude, whatever might be the character of that prince, the daring attempts that were repeatedly made in his favour did not render him lefs formidable to Catharine and to the tranquillity of the empire.

Chance foon furnifhed an inftrument to put him out of the way of being any difturbance to either. The regiment of Smolenfk was in garrifon in the town of Schluffelburg; and a company of about 100 men guarded the fortrefs in which prince Ivan was confined. In this regiment, as fecond lieutenant, was an officer named Vaffily Mirovitch, whofe grandfather had been implicated in the rebellion of the kozak Mazeppa, and had fought under Charles XII. againft Peter the great. The eftates of the family of Mirovitch had accordingly been forfeited to the crown. This young man, who had a good fhare of ambition, preferred with warmth his pretenfions to have them reftored; and this it was that made him known at court. The family-eftates were not given back; but he was continually flattered with the hopes of their recovery, if he would fhew himfelf active in fecuring the tranquillity of the empire.

The

The inner guard placed over the imperial prisoner consisted of two officers, captain Vlassieff and lieutenant Tschekin, who slept with him in his cell. These had a discretionary order, signed by the empress, by which they were enjoined to put the unhappy prince to death, on any insurrection that might be made in his favour, on the presumption that it could not otherwise be quelled.

The door of Ivan's prison opened under a sort of low arcades, which, together with it, form the thickness of the castle-wall within the ramparts; in this arcade or corridor eight soldiers usually kept guard, as well on his account, as because the several vaults on a line with his contain stores of various kinds for the use of the fortress. The other soldiers were in the guard-house, at the gate of the castle, and at their proper stations. The detachment had for its commander an officer, who himself was under the orders of the governor.

It has been affirmed, that some time before the execution of his project, Mirovitch had opened himself to a lieutenant of the regiment of Veliki Luki, named Uschakoff; and that Uschakoff bound himself by an oath, which he took at the altar of the church of St. Mary of

Kazan

Kazan * in St. Petersburg, to aid him in the enterprife to the beft of his power. But as this latter was drowned, a few days after this is faid to have happened, as he was affifting in the launch of a veffel ; it is impoffible to afcertain the fact.

It is more apparent that he talked in vague terms of the confpiracy with one of the valets of the court, and that he mentioned it afterwards to Simeon Tfchevarideff, lieutenant of artillery, and fpoke of the advantages that would accrue from the refcue of Ivan, and the delivering of him to the regiments of the guards. While he thought to raife his confequence by putting on the air of a confpirator without accomplices, he however faid nothing to Tfchevarideff pofitively either of the time or the manner of executing his plot.

He had already performed his week's duty in the fortrefs, without venturing an attempt. But, tormented by the anxieties arifing from fufpenfe, and condemning his own irrefolution, he afked permiffion to be continued on guard for one week longer. This extraordinary ftep feems not to have excited any fufpicions in a governor who was entrufted with fo very important and critical a charge ; and the requeft of Mirovitch was granted him without hefitation.

* Vulgarly called the Kazanfkoi church.

After

After having admitted into his confidence a
man of the name of Jacob Pifhkoff, he began
at about ten o'clock on a fine fummer's night *,
to fall into converfation with three corporals
and two common foldiers ; and after tampering
with them fome time, and obviating fuch difficulties as were fuggefted by their fears, they were
foon gained over to his plan, and they promifed
to follow his orders. Neverthelefs, whether from
timidity or from precaution, they refolved with
one confent to wait till the night was farther advanced. Between the hours of one and two in the
morning, they came together again. Mirovitch
and the corporals then procured about fifty †
of the foldiers who were on guard to put themfelves under arms, and thus marched towards
the prifon of Ivan. On the way they met Berednikoff, the governor of the fortrefs, whom
they thought faft locked in the arms of fleep ;
but who, roufed by fome noife, whether made
by them, or accidentally occafioned, had come
out to fee what was the matter. The governor,
authoritavely demanded of Mirovitch the reafon of his appearance in arms at the head of the
foldiers ? Without returning any anfwer, Mi-

* The ₁₃⁴th of July.
† It is probable that 38 was the exact number.

rovitch

rovitch knocked him down with the butt end of his firelock, and, ordering some of his people to secure him, continued his march.

Having wounded and secured the governor, Mirovitch lost no time to improve his advantage. Being arrived at the corridor into which the door of Ivan's chamber opened, he advanced furiously at the head of his troop, and attacked the handful of soldiers who guarded prince Ivan. He was received with spirit by the guard, who quickly repulsed him. He immediately ordered his men to fire upon them, which they did. The centinels returned their fire; when these conspirators, at the same time the most desperate and the most timid of mankind, were obliged to retire, though neither on one side nor the other was there a single man killed, or even wounded in the slightest degree.

The soldiers of Mirovitch, surprised at the resistance they met, shewed signs of an inclination to retreat. Their chief withheld them; but they insisted on his shewing them the order which he said he had received from Petersburg. He directly drew from his pocket and read to them a forged decree of the senate, recalling prince Ivan to the throne, and excluding Catharine from it, because she was gone into Livonia to marry count Poniatoffky. The ignorant and
credulous

credulous foldiers implicitly gave credit to the
dectee, and again put themfelves in order to
obey him.   A piece of artillery was now brought
from the ramparts to Mirovitch, who himfelf
pointed it at the door of the dungeon, and was
preparing to batter the place ; but at that inftant
the door opened, and he entered, unmolefted,
with all his fuite.

The officers Vlaffieff and Tfchekin, commanders of the guard which was fet on the
prince, were fhut up with him, and had called
out to the centinels to fire.   But, on feeing this
formidable preparative, and hearing Mirovitch
give orders to beat in the door, they thought it
expedient to take counfel together.   And, firft,
they held it impoffible to refift fuch a fuperior
force as that which they had lately beaten off.
Then they took into confideration the dreadful
confequences which muft inevitably enfue, to
the public peace and the fafety of the empire, if
their prifoner fhould be enlarged ; and, laftly,
they fet before their eyes the punifhment that
would be inflicted on them by the government
in cafe their charge fhould be taken from them,
though againft their will, and after all poffible
refiftance.

On this confultation, they came to the dreadful refolution of affaffinating the unfortunate captive,

tive, over whose life they were to watch, unter-
rified with the dangers which manifeftly waited
this horrid act, directly hanging over them from
a defperate force, which (to give any colour to
their proceeding) they muft have concluded irrefiftible.

At the noife of the firing Ivan had awoke ;
and, hearing the cries and the threats of his
guards, he conjured them to fpare his miferable
life. But, on feeing that thefe barbarians had no
regard to his prayers, he found new force in his
defpair ; and, though naked, defended himfelf
for a confiderable time. Having his right hand
pierced through and his body covered with
wounds, he feized the fword from one of the
monfters, and broke it ; but while he was ftruggling to get the piece out of his hand, the other
ftabbed him from behind, and threw him down.
He who had his fword broke now plunged his
bayonet into his body, and feveral times repeating his blow, under thefe ftrokes the unhappy
prince expired.

They then opened the door, and fhewed
Mirovitch at once the bleeding body of the
murdered prince, and the order by which they
were authorifed to put him to death, if
any attempt fhould be made to convey him
away.

Mirovitch,

Mirovitch, ftruck with horror, at firft ftarted back fome paces; then threw himfelf on the body of Ivan, and cried out : — " I have miffed " my aim ; I have now nothing to do but to " die." — But he prefently rofe up. So far from attempting to flee from the punifhment which he muft now forefee, or to take his revenge on the two affaffins by fhooting them on the fpot, he returned to the place where he had left the governor in the hands of his foldiers ; and, fur-rendering to him his fword, coldly faid : — " It " is I that am now your prifoner."

The next day the body of the poor unfortunate Ivan was expofed before the church * in the caftle of Schluffelburg, clothed in the habit of a failor. As foon as it was known, immenfe crowds of people flocked thither from the neigh-bouring towns and from St. Peterfburg ; and it is impoffible to defcribe the grief and indigna-

---

* An old lutheran church built of timber for the ufe of the garrifon while Nœteburg was in poffeffion of the Swedes, long before it was taken from them by Peter the great. The church is in a very decayed ftate, full of rubbifh, and not employed in any religious purpofes. The painted altar is removed from its proper place at the eaft end, and ftands againft the north fide wall, and in its place filling the en-clofure where the altar rails have been, is a large pile of deal planks, in a ftate of rottennefs : under this ftack of wood the body of Ivan was thrown, where it lay for fome time.

15   tion

tion that were excited at the view of an unfortunate being, who, after having been cruelly precipitated from the throne while yet in his cradle,
paſſed his days in a dark and doleful dungeon,
where he was inhumanly put to death by
aſſaſſins.   Ivan was full ſix feet high, with a
fine blond head of hair, a red beard, regular
features, and of a complexion extremely fair:
accordingly, the beauty of his perſon and his
youth* heightened the ſenſibility that was uni-
verſally diſcovered at the unhappineſs of his lot,
and the cruelty of his murderers.   His body was
wrapt up in a ſheep-ſkin, put into a coffin, and
inhumed without ceremony.

The concourſe and the murmurs increaſed
to ſuch a degree that a tumult was now apprehended.   To avoid any fatal conſequences to
themſelves the two aſſaſſins Vlaſſieff and Tſche-
kin, as ſoon as they had perpetrated their crime,
put themſelves on board of a veſſel which they
found on the point of ſailing for Denmark, where,
on their arrival, the ruſſian miniſter took them
under his protection†.

The governor of Schluſſelburg diſpatched to
Peterſburg a full relation of the horrid outrage

* He had not yet completed his 24th year.

† They ſhortly after returned to Ruſſia, and were advanced
in the ſervice.

of

of Mirovitch, and of the tragical end of Ivan. He accompanied this account with a manifesto that had been found in the pocket of Mirovitch, and which, it was said, had been long fabricated in concert with lieutenant Ushakoff. This manifesto, which contained many scurrilous invectives and imprecations against Catharine, and represented prince Ivan as the sole legitimate emperor, it was observed, was to have been published at the moment the prince was set at liberty and was making his entry into St. Petersburg. Panin immediately sent off a courier to the empress with an exact account of these particulars.

Her majesty was then at Riga; and, under a visible impatience of mind, was frequently inquiring after news from the residence: a circumstance by no means unaccountable, if we consider the frequent causes of alarm from plots and cabals with which she had been incessantly harassed since the beginning of her reign. Her inquietude increased from day to day, and she would often rise in the night to ask whether no courier was arrived*. Some persons after-

---

* These facts have often been confirmed by general Brown; who, being a good roman catholic, honestly attributed these perturbations of Catharine to supernatural presentiments.

wards

wards recollected thefe circumftances to her difadvantage, as if fhe was anxioufly counting the days fince the period when Mirovitch was ftationed on guard *. At length, after three days had elapfed, the difpatches of Panin were brought to hand.

The trial of the confpirators was remitted to the fenate; they condemned Mirovitch to death; and he was publicly executed † in purfuance of his fentence. The inferior actors in this defign did not fuffer death, but were fubjected to other punifhments perhaps not lefs fevere. The officers, who put the prince to death, were, in confideration of their good intentions to the quiet of the ftate, amply rewarded for their fidelity. A manifefto appeared by authority ‡, giving an account of the whole procedure. It was filled with expreffions of humanity and piety, which fort of language feemed now to be the office ftyle of the court of Peterfburg.

The public was much divided in opinion concerning the whole of this tranfaction. It

* The circumftance that Mirovitch had fuffered his week's duty on guard to expire before he could fummon up courage enough to attempt the execution of his project, was not, on this occafion, forgotten.

† September the 26th.

‡ See the Appendix at the end of the volume.

                                        was

was thought inconceivable that an insignificant private individual should hazard an enterprise, that, if even at first all things should go well, yet could never be prosecuted to final success by him. That in the attack no one should be hurt; that upon Ivan's death all should be immediately as quiet as if nothing had happened; that no inquiry was set on foot about any accomplices in Petersburg, of which there had been some talk at first; seemed to give room to surmise that simply this death was the object in view, and to this sole end the whole machinery was directed. None of the court party could have done this service to the absent empress, without her knowledge and consent. But, on the other hand, the slanderous manifesto found upon Mirovitch was produced, which he intended to have published immediately upon his having Ivan in his possession, and which count Panin, it was said, had actually read and sent to the sovereign; but particularly the execution of the rebel: if indeed it were he, and not some unknown malefactor, who underwent that punishment, was urged in support of their sentiments by those who espoused the opposite side of the question. — Let it suffice, the public emotions of pity and displeasure at the sad catastrophe of the imperial progeny, and himself once emperor, were plainly manifested by every kind of expression. The

The multitudes of people who, notwithstanding all that could be done to check their impetuosity, still flocked to the castle, insisting on seeing the body, were so great, that the government was obliged to give orders to remove it from the castle-church, and convey it in the silence of the night with the utmost secrecy, to the monastery of Tichfina, 200 versts from Petersburg. Among the regiments of guards in that city, who thought they had the exclusive right to depose and to murder emperors, violent commotions arose; that especially in the night of the 24th of July, caused the greatest alarm: it was only by the prudent measure of prince Gallitzin, who caused powder and ball to be publicly distributed among the marching regiments that were encamped in the vicinity of Petersburg, that tranquillity was restored. When the two officers by whom the prince was assassinated appeared at court, every one beheld them with looks of undissembled contempt and abhorrence.

Catharine's throne was now firmly established. Even the angry spirit that persecuted the family of Ivan seemed at length appeased. As her majesty afterwards set at liberty the other members of it, it may be necessary to make some brief mention of them here. The parents and relations of the unfortunate young emperor had been brought to Kolmogory, a village-like town in the government

of

of Archangel, on an ifland of the Dvina. Here they dwelt poor and melancholy, in clofe confinement. The mother, Anna Carlovna, died in child-bed, while Elizabeth was yet reigning, in March 1746, and was taken hence, and buried in the fame monaftery where afterwards Peter III. at laft found reft. The father, Anthony Ulric, died in 1776. He left behind him two princes, Peter and Alexey, two princeffes, Catharine and Elizabeth, and feveral natural children: all, except the elder of the princeffes, born in prifon. For a feries of feventeen years they were very feverely treated by Golovtzin, the laft viceroy of Archangel. After his death, which happened in 1779, Catharine appointed in his place a man of more generous fentiments, the general-governor Melgunef, who vifited the unfortunate captives, adminiftered to them every confolation in his power, took with him a letter from the princefs Elizabeth to the emprefs; and, on delivering it, defcribed their fituation in fuch affecting terms, that her majefty immediately refolved to open a negotiation with the court of Denmark. The dowager-queen of that kingdom, Juliana Maria, was a fifter of duke Anthony Ulric. In the following year, 1780, the bufinefs was brought to a conclufion: the accommodation was eafy, as Catharine acted with her
wonted

wonted magnanimity. If, as is probable, a deed
of renunciation of all pretenfions to the ruffian
throne was required of the ftate-prifoners in behalf of themfelves and their pofterity, it could
not be a matter to occafion any difficulty. The
emprefs directly fent them 200,000 rubles, to
provide the family with clothes, plate, porcelaine, &c. befitting their rank. This fhe accompanied with a prefent of rich furs and jewels from
the imperial cabinet; and appointed perfons of
quality to attend the princes and princeffes on
their voyage. At Archangel Melgunef firft
difcovered to them their liberation, and the intended voyage to Denmark. They heard the
news with forrow, and earneftly intreated to be
fent back to their old prifon; till the perfuafions
of the generous Melgunef raifed their fpirits,
and infpired them with courage*. In July a
frigate brought the whole family to Bergen in

* The Dowager-queen of Denmark, in the letter of thanks
which fhe wrote to the emprefs in terms of the tendereft fenfibility, highly extolled, as fhe had reafon to do, the behaviour of this worthy man in the whole of his conduct. This
teftimony faved him, on occafion of an unmerited accufation
that was brought againft him concerning his behaviour in this
bufinefs, and which threatened him with imminent danger:
and, on his having juftified himfelf, to the fatisfaction of all
impartial judges, Catharine rewarded him with the order of
St. Andrew, and made him many prefents befides.

Norway,

Norway, where the princes and princeffes were taken on board a danifh fhip, leaving the illegitimate children to return with the imperial frigate. The parting with thefe half-relatives excited the moft painful emotions in the breafts of the family. The moft fenfible of them, Elizabeth, furvived not long her grief and the fhock her frame had received at this fudden change of fortune. The four brothers and fifters of Ivan were, at the time when they obtained their liberty, between 30 and 40 years of age. The danifh court affigned them the city of Horfens in Yutland, as the place of their refidence. Towards their eftablifhment there Catharine prefented them with 20,000 rubles, and paid annually to the maintenance of their dignity 30,000 rubles. In October 1782, the princefs Elizabeth died at Horfens ; and her death was followed by that of her brother Alexéy in October 1787. The natural children of the duke of Brunfwic received in Ruffia an annual penfion : one of them, a daughter named Amelia, after her return, married lieutenant Karikin, who, for twelve years, had the guard of the family at Kolmogory, and with whom fhe had long been intimately acquainted.

To return to our hiftory. Catharine foon after the fhocking event that had happened at

Schluffelburg, arrived from off her journey through the conquered provinces. On her entry into Peterfburg, fhe was furrounded by an immenfe concourfe of people, who endeavoured to find out by her countenance what was paffing in her heart ; but, always miftrefs of herfelf, the face of that princefs was ever covered with fmiles. Her ftep was as firm, her front as ferene, as thofe who feel no inward reproaches ufually are.

Lieutenant-general Veymar had already been charged to repair to Schluffelburg. After having privately examined Mirovitch and his accomplices, they were brought to Peterfburg, where their trial was opened before a commiffion compofed of five prelates, of an equal number of fenators, and feveral general officers. Mirovitch appeared before the judges with all that tranquillity which only the hope of pardon can communicate to a criminal like him. He replied with a frivolous and often infolent air to the interrogatories that were put to him. It is true that the judges themfelves feemed not to make it a matter of great importance, and rather appeared as if they dreaded to fathom this execrable myftery. One alone * had fo much fenfe of propriety as to declare againft fuch an extraordi-

---

* He was a fenator.

nary

nary mode of procedure. But he was blamed
for his indifcreet zeal, and advifed to keep
filence, if he would not lofe his office, and be
degraded from his rank of nobleffe. In fine,
after fome days fpent in the trial, Mirovitch
was condemned to lofe his head *, not as guilty
of high treafon, but only as a difturber of the
public peace. Unmoved at this fentence, he
walked to the fcaffold like a man who had
nothing to fear, and who thought himfelf fure of
obtaining a pardon, as indeed, according to a
report, it had been promifed him. But if he
really reckoned on a pardon, he was cruelly
deceived. The time for his execution was
accelerated, and the unhappy wretch, if he had
before been the inftrument, was now the victim
of a barbarous policy. Thofe who confidered
him in the former point of view were aftonifhed
that the emprefs fhould fuffer him to fall under
the axe. But how could fhe have fcreened him
from punifhment without manifeftly drawing
upon herfelf the charge of having prompted his
crime ? and if fhe were really concerned in it,
can it be thought that fhe would hefitate a moment in getting rid of a witnefs who would have
expofed her to everlafting vexation ?

* On the 26th of September.

F F 2   Mirovitch

Mirovitch was the only person condemned to death. The soldiers whom he had engaged to join him in the intended rescue were punished with various degrees of severity. Pishkoff, who was considered as the most guilty, was sentenced to run the gantlet twelve times through a line of a thousand men. The three corporals and the two fuzileers, seduced after Pishkoff, were flogged ten times along the same line; after which they were put to the public works, with a log chained to their leg. The other soldiers who acted under the orders of Mirovitch were likewise whipped through the ranks; and after being incorporated in other regiments, were sent into distant garrisons. Tschevarideff was degraded from his rank of officer, for having heard without revealing the vague confidential communications of Mirovitch. Fifty-eight persons were punished. A great appearance of severity was exercised against them; and this, among other circumstances, was calculated to obviate any suspicions that might arise concerning any more eminent instigators of their crime.

CHAP. V.

Difcontents at Peterfburg. — Mifunderftanding between the counts Gregory Orloff and Panin. — Viffenfky becomes favourite of the emprefs. — Refignation of the chancellor Vorontzoff. — Prince Radzivil at the head of the confederates. — The bifhop of Cracow carried off. — The duke de Choifeul incites the Turks to declare war againft Ruffia. — Treaty entered into by the emprefs with England. — Tournament at Peterfburg. — Reform of the courts of juftice. — Convocation of deputies from all the provinces of the empire. — Wife reply of the Samoyèdes. — Wicked attempt of Tfchoglokoff. — Travels of feveral learned men in the interior of Ruffia. — Academical inftitutions. — Inoculation of the emprefs and the grand duke; with other events from 1764 to 1768.

THE beneficial effects of Catharine's regulations and eftablifhments for the internal adminiftration of government were every day becoming more apparent in all parts of Ruffia. That vaft empire, rendered more compact,

better

better regulated, more fimply organifed, animated with a new fpirit, muft naturally have a
powerful influence on the commerce, on the
finances, the politics, nay even on the exiftence
of the other nations of the earth : and it certainly had.   The time was paft when foreign
cabinets, with a fort of affurance of effect, could
direct affairs, give birth to refolutions, and put
a ftop to proceedings at Peterfburg; the government difplayed that fpirit of independence
which became fo great a monarchy : on the
contrary, the queftion was now, how Catharine
was acting, and what fhe was purpofing in regard
to all that the princes and republics, from the
Memel to the Tagus, were meditating and
tranfacting.   A fagacious hiftorian, who is certainly no flatterer of defpots, fays of the late
emprefs of Ruffia, to which every one muft
readily fubfcribe, " The volumes of modern
" hiftory can produce no reign like this : for no
" monarch has ever yet fucceeded in the attain-
" ment of fuch a dictature in the grand republic
" of Europe, as Catharine II. now holds ; and
" none of all the kings who have heretofore
" given caufe to dread the erection of an uni-
" verfal monarchy, feem to have had any
" knowledge of her art ; to prefent herfelf
                                        " with

" with the pride of a conqueror in the moft
" perilous fituation, and with an unufual, a
" totally new dignity in the moft common
" tranfactions.   And it is manifeftly not alone
" the fupreme authority which here gives law,
" but the judgment which knows when to
" fhew that authority, and when to employ
" it *."

Theoretical politicians, indeed, and ftatiftical
calculators, have pretended to affirm, that this
complaifance of the reft of Europe has been
fhewn without reafon; and that the affumption
that the power of Ruffia is fo formidable is one
of thofe that are only admitted upon truft.   But
the confequence feems here demonftrable, if any
where in a cafe like this : whoever undertakes
many things, and performs all that he undertakes, is probably ftill able to undertake and to
perform more.   Whoever, juft at the time when
the politician has calculated that he is reduced to
his laft foldier and his laft ruble, appears with a
formidable army, and difpofes of millions with
magnanimous prodigality, cannot be yet at the
extremity of his forces or his wealth.   And
(what is completely decifive) whoever, in the

* M. Spittler, in his " Sketch of the Hiftory of the
" Governments of Europe," part ii. p. 420.

grand european republic, at the time when a
Frederic and a Joseph, when the intriguing
French and the enterprifing Britons compofe the
fenate of that republic, can hold the dictature,
is furely born to be dictator, is endowed with
all the qualities requifite to that end : the power,
the art, and the judgment.   This will apply to
Catharine.   In her were united what the world
has feldom feen together.   From merely phyfical
power many things may afford fecurity ; but the
fuperiority of mind, the refinement of policy, is
capable of reaching lengths, of which the former
will fall fhort.—Whoever was favoured with her
efteem and friendfhip, never advanced farther to
intimacy, but remained in a refpectful, almoft
dependent fituation.   Whoever incurred her
wrath, was fo placed by her before all Europe,
that the effects of it were no longer beheld as a
hoftile contention between two equal potentates,
but as the chaftifement of a felon. — When fhe
iffued her commands, it was in the fweet accents
of righteoufnefs and peace. However her paffions
were excited, fhe yet remained tranquil, till the
proper maturity enfured the event ; and thus her
actions acquired the diftinctive marks of irrefiftible majefty.   But never yet has a monarch
underftood, like her, how to be bountiful exactly
at the fitteft time, and to make prefents with
                                              fuch

such significance as to fix the gratitude of the re-
ceiver, and to acquire the veneration that is
due to a beneficent deity *.

While Catharine was giving law to Poland,
amusing Austria, conciliating the friendship of
Prussia, and treating with England, she was also
tampering with the other courts of Europe, and
labouring efficaciously towards very soon making
herself dreaded by them. She exerted herself
to the utmost in giving new spirit to the
commerce of her country, in augmenting her
navy, and above all in softening the manners of
her people, as yet not far advanced in civilization. But, badly seconded by the great personages of the empire, and even by such as were
about her, the progress of her institutions was at

* We will take the liberty of making here one other extract
from Spittler's work, concerning the interference of Russia in
the affairs of Poland: — " It was an ingenious contrivance,
" formed in a truly roman style, and completed accordingly.
" Not only a numerous and free nation was to be deprived of
" its liberty and national subsistence, but all Europe was to
" be lulled asleep. The annexations of Lewis XIV. were
" a trifling business in comparison of what Catharine II. per-
" formed in Poland and against that country. But what
" loud and violent cries were raised against the former ; and
" in what soft murmurs did the voice of truth repeat the
" ancient law of nations, when there seemed to be no longer
" any law between Russia and Poland ? &c." See Spittler's
work on the governments of Europe, p. 423.

                                                    first

firſt but flow. The ſpirit of diviſion continued to reign in Peterſburg. The outrages that were to be prevented or puniſhed, always made it neceſſary for Catharine to keep well with the conſpirators to whom ſhe was indebted for the throne: but the favours ſhe was inceſſantly heaping on that greedy and inſolent crew, were ſo many additional ſources of hatred and diſcontent. Some new plot or conſpiracy was forming every day; and every day the good fortune of the empreſs, or rather her prudence, delivered her from danger. Puniſhments were ſecret and terrible. The authors of one plot could but rarely undertake a ſecond.

What moſt afflicted the empreſs was the miſunderſtanding that prevailed between her favourite and her chief miniſter, becauſe the devotedneſs and audacity of the one were not leſs uſeful to her than the name and abilities of the other. Panin had certainly conſiderable imperfections; but he was the only one who had a true notion of buſineſs. His cold imagination, his melancholy, his pride, his obſtinacy, and above all his indolence, were highly diſpleaſing to Catharine: but ſhe did ample juſtice to his talents, and continued to give him her confidence. Beſides, though the empreſs was not ſatisfied with him, he had the art of reviſing his

opinions,

opinions, when he found them difagreeable to her.

The influence of Orloff was founded on a different bafis: but he ufed it without difcretion, and was continually leffening its ftability.   No longer employing thofe affiduities which were the only means in his power of fecuring the favour he enjoyed, and even negligent of his ufual attendance at court, abfenting himfelf for feveral weeks together in purfuing the chace of the bear, and indifferent to the amufements of the palace, if ever any warmth of attachment fubfifted, it muft naturally now fubfide, and decline into perfect indifference.

Panin, remarking this conduct, thought he might improve it to bring on the difmiffion of the arrogant favourite.   Perceiving that the emprefs frequently beheld with complacency a young officer, named Viffenfky, thenceforward he put in practice every thing he could devife to encourage the inclination.   Viffenfky was foon admitted into favour; and, directed by the artful minifter, behaved in fuch a manner as to give reafon to believe that Orloff would foon be difcarded.   But the latter, who was not willing to lofe his confequence, made a fudden alter-ation in his conduct, and by that means preferved

ferved his ftation. The new favourite was difmiffed with brilliant prefents, and an employment that fixed him in one of the remoter
provinces.

Though Panin enjoyed great intereft and a
high refpect, with the advantages accruing from
his poft of governor to the grand duke and his
title of minifter, the return of the chancellor
Vorontzoff, whofe functions he performed *ad
interim*, gave him uneafinefs. Jealous to preferve his authority entire, and the fplendor of a
reprefentation which was of great value to him,
he humbled himfelf fo far as to flatter the favourite, whofe downfall he had been endeavouring to
procure. Orloff was not of an impracticable
temper. Always recollecting with bitternefs
the fteps which the chancellor had taken to
prevent him from fharing in the throne, he
requefted the emprefs to keep him away fiom
the management of affairs; and he became the
apologift for an enemy lefs bold, but more artful. Catharine accofted the chancellor with
extreme coldnefs. Inftead of replacing him in
the functions of minifter, as at his departure fhe
had given him reafon to hope, fhe caufed it to
be fuggefted to him that it would not be taken
amifs if he were to refign a place which he

                                                could

could no longer fill to the fatisfaction of his fovereign. The chancellor hefitated for fome time: but at length the advice of his friends prevailed. He feemed voluntarily to refign what was actually taken from him. His refignation was accepted with expreffions of regret, which were not more fincere than his wifhes for retirement; and, in order to convince him of the fecret joy his compliance gave, he was prefented with a gratuity of 50,000 rubles and a penfion of 7000.

Among the numberlefs means employed by Catharine for detecting the authors of the plots that were perpetually difturbing her repofe, fhe did not neglect the interception of the correfpondence of the foreign minifters. That of the agent* of France was fold to her. She even fucceeded in procuring a duplicate of his cypher; and fhe thought fhe perceived in his letters, if not the adherence to the machinations of the confpirators, at leaft the knowledge of all the myfterious affairs that were carrying on among the people about her. Her pride was hurt at this difcovery; her refentment againft the court of Verfailles increafed; and the cold reception fhe gave to the agent of that court

---

* Berenger, who had the title of chargé d'affaires.

reduced

reduced him to the neceffity of making his
retreat *.

Lewis XV. then fent to Peterfburg the marquis
de Beauffet †, a man of great vanity and but
fmall capacity, to whom the minifters of Catharine complained heavily of the chargé d'affaires
his predeceffor. But, as Beauffet was unacquainted with the true caufe of thefe complaints,

---

* That princefs, furmifing afterwards that Voltaire
might have learnt fome of the facts contained in the correfpondence of the agents of his nation, wrote to that celebrated genius in fuch a manner as to diffuade him from
giving credit to them, if he were acquainted with the bufinefs, and to inform him of nothing if he were not. " All
" your countrymen," fhe writes to him, " do not entertain
" the fame fentiments of me as you do. I know fome who
" wifh to perfuade themfelves that it is impoffible for me
" to do any thing that is good; who put their invention to
" the rack to perfuade others to think fo likewife; and
" woe to their emiffaries if they dare to think otherwife
" than as they are taught. I have candour enough to be-
" lieve it an advantage which they give me over them,
" becaufe whoever only knows facts from the mouth of his
" flatterers, knows them but badly, fees them in a falfe
" light, and acts in confequence. Since, however, my
" fame does not depend on them, but entirely on my
" principles, on my actions, I comfort myfelf, as well as I
" can, in not obtaining their approbation. As a good
" chriftian, I forgive them; and I pity thofe who envy
" me,"

† He was prefented to the emprefs the 1ft of May.

13   he

he paid them but little attention, and took no precautions to prevent their being renewed againſt him.   He even thought they were only to be aſcribed to the blind jealouſy which the glory of the french nation excited in the empreſs ; ſo far from it, that her ambition was ſtriving to uſurp the eſteem and draw upon her the praiſes of that nation.   She correſponded with Voltaire and d'Alembert.   She made an offer to the latter of the place of governor to the grand duke, with a ſalary of 24,000 livres, and all conveniencies for finiſhing the Encyclopédie at Peterſburg ; advantages which the philoſopher thought proper to refuſe *.   Being informed that Diderot was not in good circumſtances, and was deſirous of ſelling his library to enable him to portion out his daughter ; ſhe bought that library, left it in his own poſſeſſion, and ſettled on him a handſome appointment as the librarian of it.   Some time previous to this, ſhe had ſent to Morand, the famous ſurgeon, a collection of gold and ſilver medals which had been ſtruck in Ruſſia, as a teſtimony of her ſatisfaction with the anatomical ſubjects and chirurgical inſtruments which he had procured for he.   Almoſt

* See the Appendix at the end of the volume.

all

all the men of letters and the moſt diſtinguiſhed
artiſts of Paris received ſome proofs of her munificence, and admiring her bounties, forgetting
or unacquainted with her frailties,

    They ſwelled with lies the hundred trumps of Fame.

In the mean time the ſecret deſign propoſed
by that princeſs in crowning count Ciolek Poniatoffky began to unfold. Thinking herſelf ſecure
of the entire ſubmiſſion of that monarch, ſhe
put off all conſtraint, and openly avowed the
deſigns which even policy had made it a crime in
the Poles to have imputed to her. Her preten-
ſions were, doubtleſs, extravagant : but, as ſhe
was deſirous that they ſhould not be uſeleſs, ſhe
only declared them when on the point of marching the troops that were deſtined to ſupport
them, and propoſed nothing but in an imperious
tone. After having traced out on the map the
lines of demarcation, by which Ruſſia pur-
loined a great part of the territory of Poland,
Catharine inſiſted on the recognition of the
validity of theſe lines, and that the limits of the
two countries ſhould thus be fixed. She exacted,
farther, that the king and the republic ſhould
contract with her a treaty of alliance offenſive
and defenſive, and that they ſhould allow the
diſſidents to enjoy all the ſame rights with
                    the

the catholics, not excepting that of a capacity for being members of the senate. The laſt of theſe demands, the only one that was equitable, raiſed the indignation of an intolerant and deſpotic nobility. Murmurs were now heard on all ſides: mention was made of having recourſe to arms. Whether he was really aſhamed of the ſacrifices that were preſcribed to his recognition, or rather afraid of putting the nation in a ferment, the king himſelf declared that he could not conſent to theſe ſacrifices. But in order to be the better able to form a judgment of the pretexts with which Catharine covered her ambition, it will be neceſſary to underſtand what the poliſh diſſidents were.

Poland was originally circumſcribed within very narrow bounds. The inhabitants, between the 9th and 10th centuries, adopted the chriſtian religion as it was then profeſſed by the church of Rome. About the ſame time many of the neighbouring provinces, which were then independent ſtates, at different periods embraced that worſhip according to the ritual of the Greeks. In proceſs of time, many of theſe neighbouring ſtates, either by conqueſt, by right of ſucceſſion, by marriage, or by compact, became united to the kingdom of Poland; upon all which acceſſions the new provinces were upon

VOL. I.   G G   an

an exact equality with the old in every respect, and each observed their own peculiar modes of worship.

Of all these accessions, that which fell to it by the marriage of Yagellon, grand duke of Lithuania, with the daughter and heiress of Lewis king of Poland, in 1386, was the largest and most considerable. By this event the grand duchy of Lithuania, together with the provinces of White-Russia, Podlakhia, Volhinia, Podolia, and shortly afterwards Red-Russia, became annexed to the kingdom of Poland; with this distinction, that the union between the kingdom and the grand duchy depended only on the continuance of the line of the Yagellons, that family being the natural sovereigns of Lithuania. The inhabitants of all these provinces were of the greek religion, as well as those of Moldavia, Valakhia, and the Ukraine, which were added to the kingdom by the successors of Yagellon: so that by these great accessions, the members of the greek church became at that time far superior, both in numbers and power, to those of the roman catholic persuasion. It was thought a happiness peculiar to Poland, that, while other countries have at different times been a prey to intestine feuds and rancour on the score of the religion of Christ, the great variety of opinions

on

on that subject never produced any strife or animosity among the people of this nation.

The reformation made very early progress in Poland, and the majority of the senators and nobility became members either of the lutheran or calvinistic communions. To prevent therefore any mischiefs that might arise from these differences of religion, Sigismund Augustus passed a law at the diet of Vilna, on the 16th of June 1563, declaring that all those of the equestrian and noble orders, whether of lithuanian or russian extraction, should enjoy equal rights, provided they profess the christian religion. This he afterwards confirmed at the diet of Grodno, in 1568, adding, to prevent all misconstructions in favour of any party, that it was to be understood of every such person, of whatever christian communion or confession he be.

It would not be easy to produce instances of equal moderation, in matters of religion, amongst a people who differed so widely in their opinions on that head, as these we have shewn; especially if it be considered that these constitutions were passed by a fierce and warlike nobility, each of whom was not only a member of the general sovereignty, which they had just taken into their own hands; but also looked upon himself, in his own particular right, as in some degree

a sove-

a fovereign, as far as his eftate and power extended.   We fhall pay the greater regard to the
memory of thofe illuftrious Poles, if we reflect
that the age they lived in was far from being a
temperate one, and that moderation was but
little cultivated in the moft civilized and beft
regulated governments in Europe: at the fame
time it cannot be fufficiently lamented, that their
pofterity fhould fo fatally lofe fight of the poli-
tic, humane, and noble precedent, that was fet
them by their fathers.

Under favour of this toleration proteftantifm
made rapid advances in Poland.   By this wife
act of Sigifmund Auguftus, all fects, whether
proteftant, greek, or arian, enjoyed the full liberty
of exercifing their worfhip, and the right of
voting in the diets, and of holding the fame offices
as the catholics.   None were at the time offended
by this act of juftice : on the contrary, all were
glad to fee that the difference of religion produced none in the political and civil rights
of the feveral members of the community.   As
a diftinction among themfelves, the followers of
the different modes of worfhip were called diffidents : but that name, which has fince been
made a fignal for profcription, had nothing then
injurious in it; and the fucceffors of Sigifmund
Auguftus, when they fwore to obferve the
pacta

pacta conventa, fwore alfo to preferve peace
among the diffidents *. When Henry de
Valois † was elected king of Poland, he wanted
to difpenfe himfelf from an oath that wounded
his intolerant fuperftition: but his attempts
were in vain. He muft relinquifh the crown

* It appears, from the very beginning of the republic,
that the term *diffidents* equally comprehended the greeks,
catholics, reformed and lutherans. The words of that
famous conftitution which was paffed by the diet, which
formed the republic in the year 1573, are, *Nos qui fumus
diffidentes in religione*, i. e. We who differ in religious matters.
In the fame conftitution it is declared, that they will
acknowledge no man for king or fovereign, " who fhall not
" confirm by oath all the rights, privileges, and liberties,
" which they now enjoy, and which are to be laid before
" him after the election. Particularly, he fhall be bound
" to fwear, that he will maintain the peace among the diffi-
" dents in points of religion." In the conftitutions of the
fame diet are the following remarkable ftipulations: " We
" will engage in our own names, and in the names of our
" fucceffors for ever, by the obligations of our oath, of our
" faith, of our honour, and of our confciences, to preferve
" peace among us who are diffidents in religion; to fhed
" no blood, nor to inflict on any one the penalties of con-
" fifcation of goods, defamation, imprifonment or exile, on
" account of the difference of our faith, and rites in our
" churches. More than that, if any one fhould undertake,
" for the above reafon, to fhed the blood of his fellow-
" citizens, we fhould be all obliged to oppofe him, even
" though he fhould fhelter himfelf under the pretext of a
" decree, or any other judicial act."

† The bigoted and vicious Henry III. of France.

or

or fwear to protect the diffidents: he took the oath.

Thofe who have not confidered that perverfe dipofition, by which almoft every denomination of mankind would endeavour to plunder, enflave, and perfecute every other part of their own fpecies; and who have not obferved that words can always be found, when attended with power, to explain away the moft explicit fenfe, and the moft indubitable rights; may well be furprifed how a law, fo folemnly paffed, and fo ufeful to the whole community, could be rendered fruitlefs. A law fanctified by the moft folemn acts, which the framers bound themfelves and their pofterity, by the moft facred oaths, to preferve inviolate to all futurity, which formed a principal part of the conftitution of the ftate, and which every king at his acceffion was fworn to obferve. Yet this law, without any material change, much lefs a fubverfion of the conftitution of the country, has been manifeftly broken through, while three of the religions, which formed the original compact, have been fpoiled of their rights, liberties, and immunities, by the fourth; and all this outrage and wrong committed under colour and fanction of the very laws they were tearing to pieces at the inftant.

However,

However, when the roman catholics, after the death of Sigifmund III. had gained an evident fuperiority, they gave full fcope to that fiery zeal by which they are made to believe that their religion is the only one that is good, and will not permit them to endure any other. They began by perfecuting the arians, whofe opinions had already made great progrefs; they proceeded to diveft them of all their rights, and even to drive them out of Poland. The greek and proteftant chriftians, who had affifted in perfecuting the arians, were very foon punifhed for their imprudence. The catholics attacked them in their turn, and fucceeded in 1733, in entirely excluding them from the diets*.

The

* Upon the death of Sigifmund Auguftus, in 1574, the polifh conftitution was entirely changed, and the nation affumed the form of a republic. His grandfather Cafimir III. was the firft who convened the nobility, in order to oblige them to accept the new impofitions. Sigifmund and his father ufed the fame method; but after his death the whole legiflative authority fell into the hands of the nobility. At this period, we are told by their hiftorians, the roman catholics in the kingdom did not bear a proportion in number to the Greeks and reformed, of more than one to feven. The grand marfhal Firley, who convened the firft diet of the republic, that diet which formed its prefent model, and made the crown elective, was a proteftant. A perpetual peace betwixt the Greeks, the roman catholics, and the proteftants, was therein eftablifhed as a fundamental

law

The humiliation they felt on being deprived of the right of fuffrage, converted many of the Poles to catholicifm.   But if the diffidents dimi-nifhed in numbers, thofe who remained were only fo much the more attached to their fects. Againft thefe proceedings they urged the treaty of Oliva, concluded in 1660, by which their privileges were fecured, and of which fo many potentates were the guarantees.   The catholics, who ruled alone in the diets, and confequently

---

law of the republic. The wars in Germany under Charles V. and in France under Catharine de Medicis, made them fen-fible of the neceffity they were under of tolerating each other.   They therefore entered into an engagement of mu-tual defence and affection, and that a difference of religion fhould never prove the caufe of civil diffenfion, unanimoufly refolving to make an example of that perfon who, under fuch a pretext, fhould excite difturbance.   As this law has been repeated in all the public acts, conftitutions, and pacta conventa, from that time to the prefent, it cannot but be allowed to be a fundamental law: nor can any other law be produced, whofe fanction has been more folemnly, more conftantly, and more frequently repeated.   However, when the roman catholics, after the death of Sigifmund III. had acquired a manifeft fuperiority, though they did not think proper openly to controvert it, yet they fhewed a difpofition, when opportunity was favourable, to infringe it, by placing under their fignatures, *falvis juribus ecclefiæ romanæ catholicæ*, with a faving to the rights of the roman catholic church. Whereupon the diffidents, by way of reprifal, wrote under their fignatures, *falva pace inter diffidentes*, with a faving to the peace amongft the diffidents.

might

might give ample range to their intolerance, without molestation or obstacle, procured a decree attaching the guilt of high treason to such diffidents as should have recourse to foreign powers for obtaining the execution of the treaty thus atrociously infringed, and the re-establishment of the laws so despotically repealed. This decree was the finishing stroke to the patience of the diffidents. Russia observed their indignation, and fanned it in secret. The greek diffidents then addressed themselves to the court of Petersburg. The protestants implored the interceffion of those of London, Copenhagen, and Berlin. These courts promised to support them ; and this was the most specious pretext for the military interference of Russia. This was the state of affairs at the close of the year 1765.

On the assembling of the diet on the 1st of September 1766, the ministers of the protecting courts presented their memorials in behalf of the diffidents, which excited a violent murmur. Soltyk, bishop of Cracow, a haughty and fanatical prelate, maintained that the diffidents had no right of appeal to privileges that were abolished, and that they had violated the constitution of the republic, in having recourse to the intervention of foreign powers. Not satisfied with the iniquitous

laws

laws that had been paſſed againſt the diffidents, he moved for the enacting of new ones ſtill more ſevere. His opinion was adopted by Maſſalſky, biſhop of Milna, and a great majority of the nobles, who blindly confounded religious pre-judices with political rights; and the oppoſition of ſome perſons more enlightened or more equitable, occaſioned violent debates. The diſorder roſe to its height. The king attempted to deliver himſelf in favour of more moderate ſentiments: he was abruptly reproached with being an abettor of the enemies of the ſtate. He took the reſolution to retire *. Several other ſittings followed, not leſs ſcandalous than the former; and the terrible laws enacted againſt the diffidents were imprudently confirmed. The ruſſian troops now advanced to the gates of Warſaw. Prince Repnin demanded in the name of the empreſs, not only a toleration ſecured by law in behalf of the diffidents, but a

* The biſhop of Kief had already taken the liberty to ſay in an aſſembly, "that if they would take his advice, they would have the king hanged; as there were ſtill ſurely ſome men to be found among the Poles charitable enough to do the ſtate that ſervice." The ſame prelate afterwards proceeded from inſolence to fury, ſo far as to tell the king to his face, in preſence of all the court:—" I formerly uſed to pray to God for your proſperity; my prayer to him at preſent is, that he would ſend you to the devil."

complete

complete political equality with the catholic
party. This was rejected with a furious triumph.
Nothing was now left for the diffidents, but,
what the conftitution allowed, to confederate :
this courfe they immediately adopted under the
ruffian protection. Fear feemed for a moment
to open the eyes of the diet. It thought to
fatisfy the emprefs by granting the diffidents
fomewhat more liberty in the exercife of their
religion. But this palliative was not fufficient
for Catharine. The diffidents, continuing to
infift on an entire equality of rights, formed into
divers confederations, which were prefently joined
by numbers of catholics, won over by Ruffia.

This was a lamentable time for Poland ;
parties and counter-parties, uniting and fplitting
again into others in the moft unexampled manner.
From grievances in religion political feuds arofe;
feveral of the difcontented went over to the
diffidents, without otherwife agreeing with them
in opinion. A civil war raged now with all
its horrors, and ruffian troops were every day
entering the territories of the republic in greater
numbers. A general confederation fprung up,
compofed of the moft heterogeneous parts,
united neither by a common underftanding nor
by the cement of affection ; prince Charles
Radzivil, who had been abfent from the country,

3   was

was their marſhal.   This prince had been one of the foremoſt of the opponents to the election of Poniatoffky ; for which he had been obliged to quit the country, and ſuffer the confiſcation of his property.   He even affected more contempt than hatred towards him.   He no ſooner ſaw him abandoned by the Ruſſians, than he united his confederation with thoſe of the diſſidents, and convened the principal leaders of them in his palace in Warſaw, under the very eyes of the monarch.

1767.   In this extremity Staniſlaus Auguſtus, who felt the neceſſity of regaining the protection of Ruſſia, aſſembled a diet extraordinary.   This diet, however, but ill correſponded with his views.   Notwithſtanding the preſence of the ruſſian army, and the haughty behaviour of prince Repnin, who lorded it in Warſaw far more than the king himſelf, the biſhop of Cracow and his adherents, as raſh and fanatical as ever, had the preſumption to make ſpeeches againſt the diſſidents, which common prudence, if not ſound reaſon, ſhould have adviſed them againſt.   It was not long before they ſuffered for their folly. The ruſſian troops, who had for ſome months nearly ſurrounded as well as interſected the kingdom of Poland, had now cloſely inveſted
the

the city of Warfaw, and were in poffeffion, and kept ftrict guard upon all the avenues leading to it.   That very evening *, while the bifhop was at table at count Minifheck's, the ruffian colonel Igelftrom, followed by a detachment of foldiers, entered the room, in the name of the emprefs, and feized on the prelate without meeting the fmalleft refiftance from any that were prefent.   Prince Repnin dictated to the diet the act of confirmation of the rights of the diffidents; and, to the utter aftonifhment of the Poles, who always boafted of their freedom, caufed the furious oppofers of that act in the diet, the bifhop of Kief, the voivode of Cracow, count Rjeurfky, voivode of Dolin, his eldeft fon †, and fome other nobles, to be feparately arrefted in Warfaw, and, together with the bi-fhip of Cracow, carried off to Siberia.

The day following this outrage, prince Repnin addreffed to the confederates a note, in which he pretended that he had only violated the liberty of the Poles for the benefit of Poland‡.
                                               The

* The 13th of October.

† The fecond fon of count Rjeurfky requefted permiffion to accompany his father in bondage.   He was anfwered, that they had no orders to arreft him.

‡ The declaration of prince Repnin delivered to the con-federated eftates was as follows : " The troops of her impe-" rial majefty, my fovereign, friends and allies of the confe-
                                               " derated

The members of the diet sent up an address to the king, requesting him to demand the prisoners. The king immediately prayed prince Repnin to release them : but Repnin rejected it with disdain ; and they did not return from the deserts of Siberia till after an exile of six years *.

" derated republic, have arrested the bishop of Cracow, the
" bishop of Kief, the voivode of Dolin, &c. for having
" failed, by their conduct, in the respect that is due
" to the dignity of her imperial majesty, by attacking
" the purity of her salutary, disinterested, and amicable
" intentions in favour of the republic. The illustrious ge-
" neral confederation of the republic, of the crown, and of
" Lithuania, being under the protection of her imperial
" majesty, the undersigned notifies this to it, with positive
" and solemn assurances of the continuation of that high
" protection and of the assistance and support of her impe-
" rial majesty to the general confederation united for the
" preservation of the polish laws and liberties, with redress
" of all the abuses that have crept into the government
" contrary to the fundamental laws of the country. Her
" majesty is only desirous of the welfare of the republic, and
" will not discontinue to grant it her assistance to the attain-
" ment of that end, without any interest or pecuniary
" consideration ; wishing for no other than the safety, the
" happiness, and the liberty of the polish nation, as that has
" been already clearly expressed in the declarations of her
" imperial majesty, which guarantee to the republic its
" actual possessions, as well as its laws, its form of govern-
" ment, and the prerogatives of each individual. Done at
" Warsaw, the 14th of October 1767.
             (Signed)   " NICHOLAS Prince REPNIN."
    * In the beginning of the year 1773.

In

In the mean time the deliberations of the diet were carried on under the impulfes of fear; and after feveral ufelefs fittings, a committee was nominated for fettling the rights of the diffidents, in concert with the minifters of the patronifing courts. They regularly applied for orders to prince Repnin, whofe anti-chamber was the refort of the plenipotentiaries from Pruffia, England, Denmark, and Sweden; and when the committee had received thefe orders, it made a report of them to the diet, who were careful not to contradict them. The diffidents therefore obtained whatever the ruffian ambaffador was pleafed to demand in their behalf. The ancient laws to which they appealed were once more put in force; and others were enacted which were ftill more favourable to them. It was, however, no more than an act of juftice, which had nothing againft it but the manner in which it was performed. They had been arbitrarily abolifhed: it was therefore but right to reftore them. The fole caufe of affliction to the true friends of the liberty of Poland was a heap of regulations admitted by the orders of Catharine, tending to prolong the troubles, and anarchy of that unhappy country, and to leave it for ever without defence againft the ufurpations which fhe had in contemplation.

A fer-

A fervile obedience had fuddenly fucceeded in Warfaw to the exceffes of a proud independence. But this forced fituation could not long continue. Murmurs were on all lips, and vengeance was in every heart. No fooner had the diet broke up, but the catholic nobles were clamorous in their complaints on account of the laws promulgated in favour of the diffidents, and formed new confederations for the defence of the romifh religion. The confederates had ftandards, on which were painted the virgin Mary and the infant Jefus: they, like the crufaders of the fifteenth century, wore croffes embroidered on their clothes; and, what was more ridiculous ftill, they put themfelves under the protection of the Turks; and the difciples of Mohammed were preparing to fight in the caufe that bore the name of Chrift.

Staniflaus Auguftus, unable either to infpire confidence into his fubjects, or to recover the friendfhip of the Ruffians, was the fubject of accufation to all parties, and lived in his capital more like a prifoner than a king. Catharine might perhaps have pardoned him fome moments of defection, but the influence of Orloff oppofed it. Prince Repnin commanded like a defpot in Warfaw; and, to flatter the favourite of his fovereign, he let no opportunity efcape of humi-

humiliating a feeble and unfortunate king. We shall just cite one single fact to prove what little respect the ruffian ambassador had for the polish monarch. One evening that the king was at the theatre, the ambassador made it late before he came. As he did not appear, the curtain drew up, and the piece began. The performers were in the second act, when a fort of buftle being made in the ambassador's box, the king sent a page to know what was the matter. Answer was brought that prince Repnin was come, and was surprised to find that they had not waited for his arrival before the curtain was drawn up. The king ordered the curtain to be dropped, and the piece to begin again.

All Europe beheld with astonishment the conduct of the court of Ruffia. It was thought scarcely conceivable that Catharine should become, all at once, the enemy of a king whom she herself had put upon the throne. But what could the faint remembrance of an extinguished attachment avail in the heart of a princess, who was aiming, by imposing shackles on Poland, to domineer over the powers of the north, and to make herself formidable to those of the south?

She was sure that the king of Pruffia defired nothing better than to share the polish provinces

VOL. I.   H H   with

with her. She managed at her pleasure both Sweden and Denmark, the one by her intrigues, and the other by the hope she held out to it of the cession of Holstein. She flattered England by a treaty of alliance and commerce. All seemed to concur to favour her ambition.

The duke de Choiseul, who, under the appearance of levity, concealed a deep and penetrating genius, and who perhaps was deficient in nothing, for being a great minister, but more constancy in his designs, and less propensity to dissipate the treasures of France, was the first who discovered the secret views of Catharine. He saw that the augmentation of power which she was about to acquire must have a natural tendency to diminish the consideration and influence of the court of Versailles. He resolved to attack the evil in its source, and, in order to defeat the projects of Russia by dissipating its means, he fell upon the design of involving it in a war with the ottoman porte.

That minister then made application to count de Vergennes, ambassador from France to Constantinople; and, after having stated to him the particulars of his apprehensions, exhorted him to second his projects. The duke de Choiseul was not ignorant either of the weakness and decline of the ottoman empire, nor of the vices of a govern-a government which were the fole caufe of that weaknefs: but he ftill thought it capable of giving Ruffia employment for a good while to come; and whatever might be the fuccefs of the war, he wifhed them to undertake it.

Vergennes adminiftered with no lefs ability than zeal to the views of his court. A long refidence in Turkey had fupplied him with an intimate knowledge of the principal members of the divan, and the means of fucceeding with it. He employed thofe means. He reprefented to the ottoman minifters how unjuft and dangerous it was that Ruffia fhould dare to violate the rights of the Poles, and invade their territory. He convinced them that the demarcation of the limits exacted by the court of Peterfburg would be attended with confequences fatal to the fecurity of the Euxine; and he advifed them refolutely to oppofe that demarcation *.

The porte, whom the polifh confederates had already petitioned for fuccour, immediately

---

* The duke de Choifeul had authorifed M. de Vergennes to employ the moft efficacious meafures for inducing the Turks to declare war againft Ruffia. "If you have any "expectation of fuccefs, if you think it poffible," he writes to him, "every neceffary fupply of money fhall be "tranfmitted to you." M. de Vergennes had the merit of wifhing to employ no other means than thofe of perfuafion. They were fufficient with him.

H H 2   complied

complied with the advice of Vergennes. The turkish minister fent a note to the king of Poland, requesting that the regulation of the limits might be fufpended till fome explanations fhould be given the fultan of a nature to remove his alarms concerning the danger with which the ceffion of the polifh territory threatened the ottoman empire. But Staniflaus Auguftus, who was for ever afraid of giving umbrage to Catharine, and who was defirous, whatever it might coft him, of regaining her friendfhip, anfwered the grand fignor, that there was not the leaft propofal of altering the limits between Ruffia and Poland; and having received this affurance, the divan returned for fome time into its accuftomed apathy. Notwithftanding which, however, the great empires of Ruffia and Turkey, the moft powerful in Afia as well as in Europe, were foon to be engaged in a bloody conflict. Religion had entered into the quarrel, and added to its bitternefs. The miferable country of Poland was the theatre of a contention, not more deftructive in its confequences, than fingular in its caufes and pretexts. The defpotic power of Ruffia becomes the guardian of polifh freedom; and the catholic religion flies for protection to the ftandard of Mohammed.

                                        The

The court of Petersburg then* concluded a treaty of alliance and commerce with that of London; a treaty which extended the privileges of the English, lowered the duties of importation on their merchandize, and granted them great advantages.   Her natural goodwill towards England, as well as her defire of fecuring additional fuccours in the war which she was meditating againft the Turks, determined Catharine to feek the alliance of the court of London.

Juft at this time, when Catharine was difplaying her partiality in the moft fignal manner to the britifh nation, an affair of gallantry between the minifter of the latter and one of the maids of honour became fo public, that the emprefs could no longer pretend to be ignorant of it; she therefore difmiffed the guilty lady from her poft, and forbad, for fome time, the minifter to appear at court.

The feverity fhewn on this occafion by Catharine formed doubtlefs a ftriking contraft with fome parts of her own behaviour.   It feems impoffible that she could fo ftrangely deceive herfelf as to imagine that the world was not aware of the indulgencies she permitted herfelf; but it is neverthelefs certain, that she fometimes

* In the month of December.

put

put on, in the prefence of thofe who knew her beft, as great an appearance of aufterity of manners as of attachment to religion.   Two ladies* of her court, one of whom had formerly been her confidante, being at a mafquerade, were talking pretty loud concerning one of their admirers : the emprefs went up to them, and, with a ftern countenance ordered them to leave the ball-room, fince they knew no better than to pay fo little regard to decorum.

The diftance Catharine often found it neceffary to affume could neither be fuppofed to gain her the affection of her courtiers, nor to contribute to reftore tranquillity to the empire. Princefs Dafhkoff had been, for the fecond time, banifhed to Mofco.   That young lady, who feemed to find her greateft pleafure in braving dangers, revenged herfelf for the ingratitude fhe thought fhe experienced, by revealing the crimes of the confpiracy in which fhe had acted a principal part, and in fomenting the difcontents againft the emprefs.   Without efteeming princefs Dafhkoff, many perfons partook in her refentments; and the poifon of fedition, artfully mingled by her, was making new progrefs from day to day.

* Madame Narifhkin and Madame Goloffkin.

Being

Being informed of the murmurs at Mofco, Catharine feigned to defpife them, and refolved to fupprefs them by her prefence. But as the feverity of the winter would fcarcely permit her to take a long journey, fhe endeavoured, in the mean time, to divert the difaffected by the tumult of the pleafures fhe contrived for the court. The inhabitants at St. Peterfburg now faw two or three tournaments, at which the ruffian courtiers, arrayed in the habits and the armour of the ancient knights in the days of chivalry, difplayed more magnificence than gallantry, and greater ftrength than dexterity. Thefe fhows, which were continued for feveral days, were beheld with general difapprobation, as frivolous and expenfive.

In the amphitheatre erected on purpofe for the occafion were two fuperb boxes, for the emprefs and the grand duke. In the centre of the arena was raifed a throne, whereon fat the grand judge of the exercifes, furrounded by forty officers, four heralds at arms, and two trumpets for the purpofe of giving fignals. Befides thefe, at four feveral places, all equally diftant from the circus, were kettle-drums and trumpets, making warlike mufic during the whole time of the carouzel. In fhort, nothing was neglected that could con-

H H 4   tribute

tribute to the magnificence and effect of the exhibition.

The dames and knights of the tournaments were divided into four quadrilles or troops of horfe, reprefenting combatants of four different nations: Sclavonians, Turks, Indians, and Romans; all perfectly obferving the cuftoms of thofe nations, in their drefs and ornaments, in their chariots, in their mufic, and attendants; and were all, ladies and knights, adorned with fuch a profufion of gold and filver, pearls, and precious ftones, on their gorgeous dreffes of velvet, filks, feathers, and ermine, that they might truly be faid * to

" Shine with the wealth of Ormus and of Ind,
" Or what the gorgeous eaft, with richeft hand,
" Showers on her kings, barbaric pearl and gold."

But that of the Romans, led on by count Gregory Orloff, was brilliant beyond defcription. The drefs of his brother count Alexèy Orloff, chief of the turkifh cohort, was likewife particularly fplendid.

The four quadrilles róde in great pomp through the principal ftreets of the city, previous to their affembling in the circus.

* With a flight alteration from Milton.

The

The ladies of the court joufted at thefe tournaments, as well as the chevaliers. Tilting at the ring, cutting off the heads of ferocious animals and Saracens, artificially reprefented, then toffing up the head and catching it on the point of the fabre, letting off a piftol at a fhield, with a variety of atchievements of a fimilar nature, all performed at full gallop, and exactly in time with the mufic, formed the other parts of this magnificent entertainment.

When the carouzel, which had been repeated with confiderable variations for feveral days, was ended, and the company were drawn up in their refpective troops, the famous marfhal count Munich, who had been appointed grand judge of the field, previous to decreeing the prizes, delivered the following fpeech, which fhews that the veteran foldier was not unacquainted with the art of flattery.

" Illuftrious ladies and chevaliers,

" None of you is ignorant that not a fingle " day paffes, not a fingle moment, in which we " do not behold the attention of our moft " gracious fovereign, towards augmenting the " fplendour of her empire, towards enlarging the " fphere of the happinefs of her fubjects in " general, and towards adding in particular to " the luftre of her nobility.

" That

" That incomparable fovereign has made
" choice of this grand day, for giving the prime
" nobility of her empire an opportunity for
" fignalizing their addrefs and agility in the
" martial exercifes of a brilliant carouzel, and
" fuch as has never yet been feen in Ruffia.
" Who does not fhare with me the fentiments
" of admiration and gratitude fo juftly due to
" her majefty for this act of goodnefs and ma-
" ternal care ?

" Illuftrious ladies and chevaliers, you have
" acquitted yourfelves, in thefe noble exercifes,
" in a manner worthy of your birth, and adapted
" to give you the affurance of having merited
" the gracious regard of her majefty, the favour
" of monfeigneur the grand duke, and univerfal
" applaufe."

Then, turning towards countefs Boutturlin *,
who had gained the principal prize, and which
was valued at 5000 rubles, he faid,

" It is to you, madam, to whom her imperial
" majefty authorifes me to prefent the principal
" prize, the acquifition of an uncommon dexte-
" rity and grace which have won the fuffrages
" of all beholders. Permit me, madam, to be

* Countefs Boutturlin was fifter to princefs Dafhkoff
and countefs Elizabeth Romanovna Vorontzoff, the favourite of Peter III.

" the

" the firft to congratulate you on that honourable
" diftinction, which confers on you the right of
" diftributing with your victorious hands, the
" reft of the prizes to the ladies and the
" chevaliers.

" As for me, become hoary under arms during
" a fpace of fixty-five years of fervice*; I, the
" oldeft in rank as well as in years of any of the
" generals in Europe ; after having had the glory
" of leading the ruffian armies more than once
" to victory ; I regard, as the recompence and
" the crown of all my toils, the honour to have
" been this day, not only the witnefs, but the
" firft umpire of your refplendent exploits."

After this the company, to the amount of
fome hundred perfons, fat down to a fplendid
fupper, the deffert at the conclufion of which
admirably reprefented the circus wherein the
carouzel had been performed. The imperial
fummer-gardens were illuminated throughout,
the walks lighted with numerous arches of lamps
burning with naptha, temples of one general
radiance, illuminated fountains, and magnificent
fireworks ; the whole feftival terminating with a
mafquerade in thefe gardens, which continued
till day-light the following morning.

* He was at that time 84 years of age.

But

But Catharine knew also how beft to employ
more worthy means for eftablifhing her authority.
She ftill bufied herfelf in making reforms and in
the erection of ufeful inftitutions.   She corrected
the tribunals, fhe founded fchools, fhe built
hofpitals, and planted colonies. She endeavoured
to infufe into her people a love for the laws, and
to foften their manners by inftruction.   Jealous
of a power that knew no bounds, greedy of
every fpecies of glory, fhe was determined to
be at once both conqueror and legiflatrix.
Amidft confpiracies formed for overturning her
throne, occupied with preparations for war,
which feemed fufficient to arreft her whole attention, and yet finding time for attachments of
gallantry, fhe was unmindful of nothing that
could attract the reverence of mankind, and
captivate their admiration.

There was at that time no country where the
jurifprudence was more perplexed and uncertain
than in Ruffia.   The intricate code of Alexey
Michailovitch, compiled that it might ferve
as the bafis of legiflation, was, if not abrogated,
at leaft contradicted by the numerous edicts of
his fucceffors, which were always dictated by
the intereft or the caprice of the moment.   The
laws of this vaft empire were voluminous to a
degree of the greateft abfurdity, were perplexed,

4   infufficient,

infufficient, in many cafes contradictory, and fo
loaded with precedents, reports, cafes, and opinions, that they afforded an eternal fcene of
altercation, and were fcarcely to be reconciled
or underftood by the very profeffors of them.
This augean ftable the emprefs was determined
to cleanfe ; and though the fuccefs of her pa-
triotic attempt has not as yet been complete,
yet, in confequence of it, a great fimplification
has taken place in the laws, and a milder and
more impartial adminiftration of juftice. The particular laws of the different provinces were alfo
continually interfering and clafhing, and caufed
fuch confufion, that the whole prefented an
endlefs chaos, and effaced almoft every trace
of original fyftem or defign. The fenate, the
colleges, all the tribunals of the empire, embarraffed by fo many authorities and fuch oppofite laws, protracted caufes without end, or
terminated them without juftice. To thefe evils
a greater yet was added, the venality of the
judges, and their unlimited power *.

Catharine refolved to apply a remedy to
all thefe diforders. She profecuted what fhe

* The loweft judge, who frequently had never learnt
to read, ufed arbitrarily to put culprits to the torture
to extort confeffion, and condemn a man to the knoot, or to
be banifhed into Siberia.

had

had begun in the fenate and in the colleges, by forming them into feparate departments, which, having each but one line of bufinefs, could neceffarily proceed in a more regular courfe, execute their bufinefs with much greater difpatch, and give fewer openings to artifice and chicane. In order then to deprive the judges of all pretext or excufe for either negligence or prevarication, fhe augmented the emoluments of their offices, a means unhappily infufficient, but which proves that Catharine was well acquainted with the fpirit of the nation which fhe governed. Indeed, if the magiftrates had been poffeffed of any virtue, would it not be rather from the fentiment of reputation, than by pecuniary recompences, that they would have been ftimulated to juftice? The emprefs therefore put in motion that fpring which fhe thought would act with the greateft force upon them. She tells them, in the ukafe fhe publifhed on the occafion : — " Indigence may perhaps
" hitherto have given you a propenfity to felf-
" intereft ; but now the country itfelf rewards
" your labours ; and therefore what might here-
" tofore have been pardonable, will hence-
" forward be criminal." —

Catharine did more than augment the falaries of the judges; fhe fecured to them an appointment of half-pay for that feafon of life when

when age and infirmities fhould oblige them to retire.

Thefe primary matters being arranged, the emprefs fet herfelf to work on a new code.

All the provinces of Ruffia, not excepting the barbarous nations who dwell in the remoteft parts of that vaft empire, had orders to fend deputies to Mofco, to prefent their ideas on the laws that were the fitteft for their peculiar exigencies. Catharine herfelf repaired to that antient capital. The opening of the ftates was held with extraordinary pomp. It was furely an interefting and novel tranfaction, to fee deputies of numerous people, different in their manners, their drefs, their languages; and they themfelves muft have been aftonifhed at being here thus affembled for the purpofe of difcuffing their laws, people who had never thought about law any farther than to obey the arbitrary will of a mafter, whom it often happened that they did not know.

The emprefs, defirous to leave to this affembly the appearances of the completeft liberty, had a fort of gallery conftructed in the hall in fuch manner, that, without being perceived, fhe could fee and hear all that paffed. The bufinefs was begun by reading the inftructions tranflated into the ruffian language, the original whereof in french, almoft entirely in the hand-writing of
Catharine,

Catharine, has fince been depofited, enclofed in a magnificent cafe of filver gilt, in an apartment of the imperial academy of fciences at St. Peterfburg.

" The fovereigns of Ruffia poffeffed the moft " extenfive dominions in the world, and every " thing was yet to be done : at laft," fays M. de Voltaire *, " Peter was born and Ruffia was " formed ;" that is, doubtlefs, to fay, that at this period it arofe out of chaos. The bare idea of forming it was grand, and its execution might juftly excite aftonifhment. Tzar Alexèy Michailovitch, his father, had already fketched out the work, and it muft be confeffed that Peter advanced it to a furprifing degree. To leave his country, that he might return to govern it with greater glory ; to go and feek light in all parts where it enlightened mankind ; to fubmit for feveral years to be the difciple of other nations, in order to become the mafter and the reformer of his own; to work as a fimple carpenter at Saardam, to prepare himfelf for creating a navy that fhould be formidable to his enemies; to lower himfelf to a common foldier, in order to become a great commander ; to form on all hands eftablifhments of great utility, till then

* Hiftory of the ruffian empire, vol. i. p. 74.

unknown

unknown to his fubjects; to attack at once all the
abufes both in church and ftate, in the manners
and cuftoms that had been moft fanctioned by
inveterate habit; to extend reformation, and
care to every particular that was deferving of
them; to temper the feverity of his difcipline by
the total abolition of the word flave: to mix
pomp with toil, and annex profperity to tri-
umphs; all together characterifed him as the
great genius, the great man, and the great monarch.

But if that prince, fo juftly renowned to all
pofterity, polifhed his country in fo many refpects; if he made regulations worthy of admiration and praife, with all this he framed no
permanent laws, and much lefs a fyftem of legiflation that fhould embrace all objects. That
great work * was left for Catharine II. She
alone conceived the grand idea of undertaking it,
and fhe alone had the courage to put it in
execution. A code of laws, and efpecially laws
founded on wifdom, is the nobleft prefent that
can be made to a people: no woman had yet been

* This work may be chiefly taken from the writings
of Montefquieu, and feveral others of the french philofophers; but it muft always redound to the glory of Catharine that fhe had the liberality of mind to draw from
fuch fources.

a legiflatrix; and that part the emprefs of Ruffia refoved to act.

The reading of the inftructions was frequently interrupted by burfts of applaufe. All prefent extolled the fagacity, the wifdom, the humanity of the fovereign. But fear and flattery had a greater fhare in thefe exclamations than an admiration proceeding from a juft knowledge of the matter. It was hoped, perhaps, by that means to attract the favour of the emprefs, or at leaft to efcape Siberia. The deputies of the Samoyedes alone had the courage to fpeak freely. One of them ftood up in the name of his brethren, and faid : —— " We are a fimple and honeft people. " We quietly tend our rein-deer. We are in " no want of a new code : but make laws for the " Ruffians, our neighbours, that may put a ftop " to their depredations."

The following fittings did not pafs fo quietly. Much had been faid about giving liberty to the boors. Some thoufands of this opprefled clafs of beings were preparing to fupport by force what they expected from equity. The nobility dreaded an infurrection; they dreaded, above all, a defalcation of their revenues; and fome nobles were rafh enough to affert, that they would poignard the firft man who fhould move

for

for the affranchifement of the vaffals *.   Notwithftanding this, however, count Scheremetoff,
the richeft individual of all Ruffia †, got up, and
declared that he would willingly agree to this
affranchifement.   The debate was carried on
with great warmth, which grew to fuch a height,
that fatal confequences were to be apprehended ;
and the deputies were difmiffed to their refpective
provinces.

However, previous to the diffolution of this
affembly, the members were required to fignal-
ize the meeting by fome confpicuous act of
gratitude.   It was thought right that, though
the benefit that was intended for the fubjects
fhould be loft to them, it ought not to be fo to
the fovereign who had conceived the noble
idea of it.   Accordingly, by a general acclamation, the titles of Great, Wife, Prudent, and
Mother of the Country, were decreed to that
princefs ; but when fhe was petitioned to accept
of thofe titles, fhe anfwered, with an affumed
modefty, " That if fhe had rendered herfelf

* This fact has been feveral times attefted by Andrew
Schuvaloff, known in France by his pretty epiftle to Ninon.
† Potemkin was not as yet favourite. Count Schereme-
toff poffeffed an annual income of 170,000 pounds fterling.
He had belonging to him 150,000 peafants.

" worthy

" worthy of the firft, it belonged to pofterity
" to confer it upon her; that wifdom and pru-
" dence were the gifts of heaven, for which fhe
" daily gave thanks, without prefuming to
" derive any merit from them herfelf; that
" laftly, the title of mother of the country was
" the moft dear of all in her eyes, the only one
" that fhe could accept, and which fhe regarded
" as the moft benign and glorious recompence
" for her labours and follicitudes in behalf of a
" people whom fhe loved."

Proud of the work which had obtained her
fuch flattering marks of homage, Catharine
eagerly difpatched copies of her inftructions to
the fovereigns whofe approbation fhe moft coveted. They complimented her on her laborious enterprife, and made no hefitation to pronounce that it would be an eternal monument to
her glory. The king of Pruffia, who knew
how fenfible fhe was to praife, and who was
always lavifh of it with lefs delicacy than
eafe, wrote to her a long letter, which,
among other things, contained this flattering obfervation : " No woman has hitherto
" been a legiflatrix. That glory was re-
" ferved for the emprefs of Ruffia, who well
" deferves it."

The

The emprefs received this letter *,at Kazan, having had a defire to vifit her provinces in Afia, and the famous fhores of the Volga.

Count Solms, minifter of the king of Pruffia, on fending this letter to count Panin, wrote him a note to the following purport : " I haften to tranfmit to your excellency the letter which the king my mafter has had the honour to compofe, in anfwer to that with which her imperial ma- jefty was gracioufly pleafed to accompany the prefent of her inftruction for the formation of the new code in Ruffia, ordering me to caufe it to be prefented to her imperial majefty.   He fub- joins, with his own hand, in the difpatch which he has addreffed to me , " I have read with " admiration the work of the emprefs.   I was " not willing to tell her all that I think of it, " becaufe fhe might have fufpected me of flat- " tery ; but I may fay to you, with due defer- " ence to modefty, that it is a mafculine per- " formance, nervous, and worthy of a great " man.   We are told by hiftory, that Semi- " ramis commanded armies.   Queen Elizabeth " has been accounted a good politician.   The " emprefs-queen has fhewn great intrepidity on " her acceffion to the throne ; but no woman " has ever been a legiflatrix.   That glory was

* Which fee in the Appendix at the end of the volume.

I I 3   " referved

" reserved for the empress of Russia, who de-
" serves it."

It certainly redounds much to the praise of
Catharine, that these instructions are founded
on the principles of an enlightened humanity;
and that, though autocratrix and of unlimited
power, she recognizes no legitimate authority
but that which is founded on justice; every particular in her laws has a tendency to enervate
despotism, and to render a just authority respectable. Her purpose is to form a solid, and not
an arbitrary legislation. Her whole plan is directed to prevent all those who govern under her
from exercising a capricious and cruel authority,
by subjecting them to invariable laws, which no
authority should be able to infringe.

The accomplishment of this grand design,
however, did not proceed so smoothly as the first
steps gave room to expect. Either it was found
that the plan of a convocation of the nation by
its deputies was beginning at too high a pitch,
and that in an assembly composed of such a
diversity of tribes, manners, and tongues, it
would be impossible to come to any common
conclusions; or the whole apparatus was used
only as a machine, and suffered to fall when
it had answered the end for which it was contrived.

A few

A few articles in these instructions will suffice to shew the principles on which they are drawn up.

" The spirit of the nation, the nation itself,
" ought to be consulted in the framing of laws.

" These laws should be considered no other-
" wise than as a means of conducting mankind
" to the greatest happiness.

" It is our duty to mitigate the lot of those
" who live in a state of dependence.

" The liberty and the security of the citizens
" ought to be the grand and precious objects
" of all laws ; they should all tend to render
" life, honour, and property, as stable and se-
" cure as the constitution of the government
" itself.

" The liberty of the subjects ought only to be
" restricted concerning what it would be disad-
" vantageous to them to do.

" In causes purely civil, the laws should be
" so clear and precise, that the judgments re-
" sulting from them be always in perfect unison
" in the same cases, in order to remove that ju-
" risprudence of decisions which is so often a
" source of uncertainties, of errors, or acts of in-
" justice, according as a cause has been well or ill
" defended at one time or at another, gained or
" lost according to influence or circumstances."

We

We read with equal pleasure the instructions she prescribes to be followed in the criminal constitution:

" It is incomparably better to prevent crimes " than to punish them.

" The life of the meanest citizen is of conse- " quence ; and no one should be deprived of it, " except when it is attacked or required by the " country.

" In like manner his liberty should be re- " spected, by being difficult about imprison- " ment, by carefully distinguishing the cases " where the laws will dispense with it, as also " those in which the public safety requires arrest- " ation, detention, or formal imprisonment, and " in this case even concerning different prisons.

" In the methods of trial, the use of torture " is contrary to sound reason. Humanity cries " out against this practice, and insists on its being " abolished.

" A prisoner is not to be sacrificed to the " torrent of opinions. Judgment must be no- " thing but the precise text of the law ; and the " office of the judge is only to pronounce whether " the action is conformable or contrary to it."

Concerning punishments :

" The aim of punishment is not to torment " sensible beings.

" All

" All punifhment is unjuft when it is not
" neceffary to the maintenance of the public
" fafety.

" The atrocity of punifhments is reprobated
" by the compaffion that is due to human na-
" ture ; whenever it is ufelefs, it is a fufficient-
" reafon to regard it as unjuft, and, as fuch, to
" reject it.

" In the ordinary ftate of fociety, the death
" of a citizen is neither ufeful nor neceffary."

All that follows under this head, touching the
proportion that fhould be obferved between
crimes and punifhments ; on the rarity of the
cafes where the crime deferves death ; on the
rule to be obferved in confifcations, which
the emprefs would not extend beyond acquired
property, and a number of other ideas are fuch
as could only proceed from goodnefs of heart
and profound meditation. The whole amount
of the articles of her inftructions is in number
525 ; and the very publication and difperfion of
the book throughout the empire has been attended with falutary effects. It was doubtlefs a
great and arduous undertaking, and worthy of an
exalted mind.

The inftruction of the emprefs is not a law-
book itfelf. She only fays, " Such regulations
" fhould

" should be made. — In the first place it should
" be examined, whether," &c.   But it must be
confessed, that excellent suggestions are thus delivered, which certainly have produced, and must
continue to produce, great effects.   Thus we
find it said, chap. xi. " Peter I. promulgated a
" law in 1722, that persons who were not of sound
" mind, and who oppress their serfs, should be
" put under guardians.   The former point of
" this law has been kept up; why the latter is not
" enforced is not known." — Again, chap. xii.
" It seems too, that the new manner in which
" noblemen exact their dues from the peasantry
" is hurtful to population.   There is scarcely a
" village which does not pay certain tributes to its
" lord in money.   The lord, who never, or but
" very rarely, sees his village, imposes on every
" head a tax of one, two, and even to five rubles,
" without concerning himself how the peasant is
" to pay that sum.   It will be absolutely indif-
" pensable to prescribe laws to the nobility,
" obliging them to act more circumspectly in
" the manner of levying their dues, and to
" require of the peasant tributes of such a nature
" as shall remove him as little as possible from
" his house and family.   By this means agricul-
" ture will be better followed, and the popula-
                                                " tion

" tion of the empire be increased. At present,
" a labourer leaves his home at the age of fifteen
" to go and seek his subsistence in distant towns;
" roams about the empire, and pays his dues
" annually from what he earns."

" If, for some political reason, it be not prac-
" ticable to free the boors throughout the empire
" from their vassalage, yet means should be
" thought of to enable them to acquire property.
" In pursuance of this idea, should not a method
" be devised for gradually bettering the condi-
" tion of this lower class of people ?" Is not
such language, which evinces so much sagacity and
benevolence, the fittest for the mouth of a
monarch who is desirous of making improvements, without undertaking the boisterous and
intemperate part of an austere reformer ? It is a
great matter, if a prince shews that he under-
stands the vices of the country, and knows how
they may be remedied. Suppose even that
nothing farther is done, must not every con-
siderate spectator feel himself inclined to believe
that this sagacity and this benevolence have met
with difficulties which were absolutely not to be
overcome ? But such words are never lost :
under Catharine much was effected by what she
planned with prudent moderation. In some

3   places,

places, however, fhe expreffes herfelf decifively, and with command; and wherever this is the cafe, the inftruction retains the virtual force of a law.

The whole performance is an excellent com-. pendium of choice obfervations, of juft maxims, and of generous fentiments; and at the fame time a beautiful collection of ftriking paffages from the celebrated philofophers of Greece and Rome, of apt examples from ancient and modern hiftory, from the manners of cultivated and favage nations, and even from fuch nations as are not very much known to the reft of Europe, the Chinefe and other Afiatics. Whoever would make himfelf acquainted with the philofophy of legiflation, might reap confiderable advantage by taking it as his manual.

In addition to the paffages above cited from this work, as a fpecimen of the fentiments of Catharine, it will not be amifs to extract a few others, if it be only to fhew, that upwards of thirty years ago a monarch delivered the beft of thofe which, in the opinion of fome, were firft difcovered by the republicans of the prefent day. A lofty philofophical ftation is taken in the 6th chapter: " Several things influence " mankind, religion, climate, laws, maxims " of government, examples of things paft,
" manners,

" manners, cuftoms, from which, as the re-
" fult, a public mind is formed." Elucidations
of this maxim from the characteriftics of various nations fucceed to this.   Then, " It is
" the bufinefs of the legiflator to follow the tem-
" per of the nation; for we do nothing better than
" what we do voluntarily, and in purfuance of our
" natural difpofition.   For eftablifhing a more
" perfect legiflation, it is neceffary that the
" minds of men fhould be previoufly prepared
" for it.   But in order to defeat the pretext
" ufually alleged, that it is not poffible to do
" good, becaufe the minds are not yet difpofed
" to admit it, take the pains to prepare them for
" it : this will be already a great ftep advanced."
" When it is intended to make great changes in a
" nation, that may turn to its benefit, that which
" has been eftablifhed by laws fhould be reform-
" ed by laws; and what cuftom has brought into
" practice fhould be changed by cuftom ; and it
" is very bad policy to change by laws what ought
" to be changed by cuftom."
Chap. viii. of punifhments. .. " Examine with
" attention into the caufe of all relaxations, and
" it will be feen that they arife from the impunity
" of crimes, and not from the moderation of
" punifhments."—" It often happens that a
" legiflator, who intends to correct an evil, con-
.   " fines

" fines his thoughts to that correction : his eyes
" are open to that object, and shut to the incon-
" veniences attending it." — Chap. ix. " If you
" confider the forms of law in regard to the
" trouble a citizen has to obtain his right, or
" to get fatisfaction for fome injury, you will
" doubtlefs find them too many; if you regard
" them in the relation they bear to the liberty
" and fecurity of the citizens, you will often find
" them too few, and you will fee that the punifh-
" ments, the expences, the delays, even the
" danger of the decifion are the price that
" every citizen pays for his liberty." Not to
be farther tedious, we will conclude with the
following : " Would you prevent crimes ; con-
" trive that the laws favour lefs the different
" orders of citizens, than each citizen in parti-
" cular. Let men fear the laws and nothing
" but the laws. Would you prevent crimes;
" provide that reafon and knowledge be more
" and more diffufed among mankind. To con-
" clude; the moft fure, but the moft difficult
" method of making men better is by rendering
" education more complete." Nothing that
relates to government is left untouched in this
little book. The maxims of politics, of toleration, and of juftice, are thus loudly and powerfully delivered from the throne, and have
                                        thereby

thereby received, as it were, one sanction more.

Still proceeding on the same enlarged and enlightened plan which we have before had occasion to commend, the emprefs continued to cultivate and encourage the arts and fciences; to make her empire an afylum to the learned and ingenious; and to reform the manners and inftruct the minds of the people, through the extent of its moft diftant provinces.

The tranfit of the planet Venus over the fun, which was to happen in the fummer of 1769, added a new opportunity of fhewing as well the munificence of Catharine as the attention fhe paid to aftronomy. This great princefs wrote a letter from Mofco with her own hand, to count Vladimir Orloff, director of the academy of fciences at Peterfburg*; wherein fhe defires the academy to inform her of the moft proper places in her dominions for the making of thofe obfervations; with an offer to fend workmen and artifts, and to conftruct buildings in all thofe places which the academy might think proper for the purpofe, and to grant every other affiftance requifite to the undertaking. She alfo de-

* For which the reader is referred to the Appendix at the end of the volume.

fired,

fired, that if there were not sufficient aftronomers in the academy to make obfervations
in all the places required, to give her notice,
that fhe might fend a proper number of the
officers of her marine, to qualify themfelves
under the eye of the profeffors in the academy,
for that undertaking. Such is the extent of
that vaft empire, that the obfervations which
were made, both on the tranfit and exit of this
planet, the one in the frozen regions towards the
pole, and the other on the borders of the
Cafpian, were made within its own limits; to
fome part of which aftronomers from every corner
of Europe went to behold that remarkable oc-
currence.

The academy at Peterfburg applied to a
member of the royal fociety of London, to
procure the neceffary inftruments for the purpofe of proceeding fuccefsfully in that important obfervation *. Mr. Ramoffky, who
was the writer upon this occafion, candidly
acknowledged the great joy of the academy,
and their obligations to Mr. Short, for procuring them thofe inftruments; and confeffed
their doubts of being able to anfwer the views
of the emprefs, till they had received his
letter.

* See the Appendix at the end of the volume.

What

What appears fomewhat furprifing is, that while Catharine was ftriving to build her fame upon a folid bafis, fhe made it a matter of much importance to obtain from all the powers of Europe, the title of Imperial majefty, which fome of them had refufed her. The king of Sweden had long fince given it to Catharine; but the Swedifh diet could not be brought to grant it till the commencement of this year*.

1768. Lewis XV. pertinacioufly delayed to mention her by that ftyle. Knowing that the fovereigns of Ruffia only began to affume the title of emperor in the time of Peter the great, he regarded them in fome fort as a new no-bility : never confidering that it is the power of princes, and not the antiquity of their race, on which their rights are built. This refufal of the king of France mortified Catharine; but it was not the only reafon fhe had to be irritated againft him. She had no doubt that this monarch was informed of all the fecrets of the confpiracy that had placed her on the throne ; and fhe knew, befides, that the am-baffador of France at the Porte, had been labouring long to make the Turks declare againft Ruffia.

* The 6th of February.

What then would she have thought if she had read a letter concerning this, written by the duke de Choiseul ? — " We know," said he, " the ill- " judged animosity of the court of Russia against " France. The king so heartily despises at " once the princess who reigns in that country, " and her sentiments and her conduct, that it is " our intention not to take a single step towards " inducing her to change them. The king " thinks that the hatred of Catharine II. is " far more honourable than her friendship. At " the same time he is desirous of avoiding an " open rupture."

But the shuffling tricks of a foreign court and the dangers of war could cause no great disturbance to Catharine; perhaps they were even as necessary to her as the cares she bestowed on the administration of the empire, for eluding the bitterness of such reflections as might occasionally arise in her mind. She often imagined that in one adverse moment she might be despoiled of the fruit of her labours and ingenuity, and that some of her subjects might be ardently wishing for its arrival. The name of Peter III. was become dear to the Russians. They recollected with pleasure the good he had done, and the desire he had of doing more: they forgot his failings and infirmities, expiated

by

by a series of misfortunes. They lamented
the deplorable end of that prince; and the
multitude of malcontents dispersed throughout
the empire might secretly contain more than
one avenger.

Sensibly touched with the deplorable death of
the tzar, and incensed at seeing his murderers
sharing his power, a young officer, named
Tschoglokoff, resolved to avenge it, and even
thought himself inspired with the design by
the suggestions of heaven. After having long
reflected on the means of executing his sanguinary project, he resorted to the palace for
several days in succession, always lurking in
some of the dark passages leading to the inner
apartments, to which the empress retired when
she wished to be alone. The preservation of
her majesty was on this occasion owing to an
accidental circumstance, which prevented her
from going, according to custom, along the passage where Tschoglokoff was waiting her coming.
Disconcerted by a delay which he had not foreseen, and impatient to strike the blow which he
thought beneficial to his country, and glorious
to himself, this young man had the imprudence
to trust his secret to another officer whom he
thought his friend. This officer ran in haste to
betray him. Orloff, thus informed of the mea-

sures

fures that were taken by Tfchoglokoff, and the inftant when he was again to expect the emprefs, caufed him to be arrefted in his ambufcade. He was found armed with a long poignard, and confeffed, without hefitation, the ufe for which he defigned it. Catharine, always fufficiently miftrefs of herfelf for concealing her indignation and her fears, pretended to forgive the rafh attempt of the youth, whom political fanaticifm had deluded from his duty. She even had him brought into her prefence, and fpoke to him with mildnefs. This generofity was only apparent. Catharine wifhed to conceal from the public a wicked defign, which, if it had been known, might foon have been imitated. But, as fhe did not flatter herfelf with the hopes of entirely converting a man who, from an excefs of humanity, was about to become an affaffin, fhe quickly caufed Tfchoglokoff to be put into prifon, and afterwards banifhed to the heart of Siberia.

Some time before the period of which we are treating, the deputies of the two ruffian trading companies, one eftablifhed at Kamtfhatka, and the other at the mouth of the river Kovima, gave the court of Peterfburg an account of their difcoveries. Thofe of Kovima, fetting out from that river, doubled the cape called Tfchut-fkoi-nofs, in 74 deg. north lat. and falling down to

to the fouth, through the ftrait which feparates
Europe from America, they difcovered fome
inhabited iflands in the 64th degree of latitude,
where they went afhore, and fettled a trade with
the inhabitants, for their fineft furs, fome of
which they brought to the emprefs, particularly
a parcel of the moft beautiful black foxes fkins
that ever were feen.   They named thefe iflands
the iflands of Aleyut; fome of them are very
near the continent of America *.   Thofe of
Kamtfhatka went to the northward, and met
their companions at the above iflands; fo that,
for the convenience of trade, they fixed a factory
at the ifle of Behring.   When this report was
made, the court came to a refolution of pufhing
thefe difcoveries; and lieutenant-colonel Blenmer
was fent, accompanied by feveral able geogra-
phers, with orders to fail from the river Anadyr
to the fame coafts, and even beyond them.

About the middle of the year 1767, the
emprefs conceived the ufeful project of fending
feveral learned men to travel into the interior
of her vaft territories, for the purpofe of determining the geographical pofition of the principal places, of marking their temperature, and of

* For a farther account of fome of thefe difcoveries the
reader is referred to " Varieties of Literature," vol. ii. p. 1.
printed for Debrett, Piccadilly.

K K 3   examining

examining into the nature of their foil, their productions, their wealth, as well as the manners and
characters of the feveral people by whom they
are inhabited.

A country of fuch a prodigious extent as the
ruffian empire muft naturally attract the notice
of every man who wifhes to increafe his knowledge, whether it be confidered in regard to the
aftonifhing number of tribes and nations by
which it is inhabited, the great diverfity of
climates under which they live, or the almoft in-
finite quantity of natural curiofities with which
it abounds.   But the greater part of this country
is ftill immerfed in the profoundeft barbarifm,
and almoft inacceffible to the inveftigations of
the ordinary traveller.   Here, vagrant hordes of
people, who, entirely addicted to the paftoral
life, roam from place to place, fhunning the
focial manners of towns and villages, negligent of
agriculture, and leaving uncultivated and almoft
in a defert ftate vaft tracts of land bleffed with the
moft favourable foil and the moft happy temperature of feafons: there, peafants, and even
in many places inhabitants of towns, flaves to a
thoufand prejudices, languifhing in bondage to
the moft ftupid fuperftitions; brought up, befides, in the fevereft fervitude, and being
accuftomed to obey by no other means than
blows,

blows, are forced to fubmit to the harfheft treatment: none of thofe affectionate admonitions, thofe prudent and impelling motives, which ufually urge mankind to action, make any impreffion on their degraded minds; they reluctantly labour the fields of a hard mafter, and ftudioufly conceal from his knowledge thofe riches which fome accident, fo defirable in other countries, fhould have led them to difcover; as they would only augment the number of their toils and the heavinefs of their yoke. Hence that carelefs contempt for the treafures prefented them by nature, and the neglect of thofe bounties fhe lavifhes on them. Hence thofe immenfe deferts almoft totally deftitute of cultivation, and fo many towns that are falling to decay.

Peter the great, of too penetrating a view not to perceive both the evil and its caufes, took all imaginable pains, and adopted the wifeft meafures to ameliorate the condition of an empire, fo powerful from numberlefs other circumftances, to free his fubjects by gentle degrees from the fhackles of barbarifm, to diffufe on all fides the benign light of arts and fciences, to difcover the treafures concealed in his dominions, and to furnifh agriculture with the remedies and affiftances adapted to its improvement. His travels into feveral countries of Europe for

the

the acquifition of fuch kinds of knowledge as were moft applicable to the ufe of his dominions, are fufficiently known; as well as that in 1717 he honoured the royal academy of fciences at Paris with his prefence, and expreffed his defire the following year to be admitted a member; that he kept up a regular correfpondence with that illuftrious body, and that he fent to it, as the firft effay of his ingenious and magnificent enterprifes, an accurate chart of the Cafpian, which he caufed to be fcrupuloufly taken on the fpot.   At the fame time he fitted out and difpatched feveral men of letters to various parts of his empire; one of them to make the tour of Ruffia, and two others to proceed to Kazan and Aftrakhan, to gain information of every thing of confequence to be known in thofe countries.   In the year 1719, Daniel Amadeus Mefferfchmidt, a phyfician of Dantzic, was fent into Siberia, for the purpofe of making inquiries into the natural hiftory of that immenfe province, from which expedition he only returned at the beginning of 1727.   This learned man did honour to the choice that had been made of him, by an indefatigable activity, and by the proofs he gave of his profound knowledge, not only in every department of natural hiftory, but likewife in antiquities, as

well

well as in aftronomy, having carefully determined the elevation of the pole in all the places where he ftopped.

The northern regions, particularly thofe of Siberia, being as yet but little known, and it being very uncertain whether the extremity of thefe latter might not touch upon America, Peter I. fent from Archangel two fhips, with orders to proceed, by the White-fea and the Northern-ocean into the Frozen-ocean, where they experienced the fame difafters as had befallen the other veffels that had gone before them in this attempt; for one of the two was caught among the fields of ice, and difabled from proceeding any farther; and as no tidings were ever heard of the other, it in all probability perifhed.

Peter I. was not difcouraged by the failure of this undertaking; but he was carried off by death as he was preparing a new expedition; he had given the charge of it to two danifh captains, Behring and Spangberg, and a Ruffian named Tfchirikoff, with orders to go to Kamtfhatka, whence they were to fail for exploring the northernmoft coafts of Siberia. The forrowful event of the emperor's death made no alteration in thefe difpofitions; and the plan was carried into execution, the fame winter, by the emprefs

Catha-

Catharine the firſt, who ſent a ſmall company of literati, provided with a paper of inſtructions, which Peter had framed with his own hand. They returned in 1730, after having penetrated very far towards the north.

The empreſs Anne was deſirous of proſecuting theſe important reſearches ſtill farther, and ordered the erection of a new company, in which Behring was to be employed as captain of the ſhip. Kamtſhatka was again the point of departure for making the principal diſcoveries, and the travellers had orders to neglect nothing that might ſhed any light on the knowledge of the globe. One part of this ſociety was to navigate the northern ſeas, while the others were to repair by land to Kamtſhatka over Siberia. Theſe latter were to act conformably with the inſtructions of the imperial academy of Peterſburg, and to employ themſelves particularly in aſtronomical obſervations, geometrical operations, and deſcriptions relative to the political and natural hiſtory of the countries through which they were to paſs.

In 1760, M. l'abbé Chappe d'Auteroche was ſent into Ruſſia, by order and at the expence of the king of France, for obſerving at Tobolſk the tranſit of Venus over the ſun : his obſervations, publiſhed with great oſtentation, contain

not

not near fo much as was expected from that aca-
demician; and many of thofe which he relates
had been already long fince known.

The emprefs Catharine II. determined to
profecute thefe ufeful inveftigations, and accordingly gave orders to the academy of fciences to
make choice of a company of able and learned
men to travel over different diftricts of the
empire with attention and obfervation. The
felection of the learned travellers, the helps that
were granted them, the excellent inftructions and
advice that were given them will be a lafting
honour to that academy. The very names of a
Pallas, a Gmelin, and a Guldenftædt, already
promifed much. M. Lepekhin had likewife
acquired a reputation by different papers inferted
in the academical collections: and the refult of
the labours of thefe enlightened men has been
feen in the extenfive utility which they have fince
produced. Very few of the accounts that have
been given by travellers contain fo great a variety of new and important matters. The jour-
nals of thefe celebrated fcholars even furnifh
fuch a great quantity of materials, entirely new,
for the hiftory of the three kingdoms of nature,
for the theory of the earth, for rural œconomy,
in fhort, for fo many different objects relative to
the arts and fciences, that it would require, according

cording to the judicious remark of M. Bekmann of Gœttingen, whole years and the labour of several literary men only to put thefe materials in order, and properly to clafs them.

The difcoveries made by the Ruffians at fea at various epochas, and particularly during the reign of Catharine II. have been faithfully laid before the public by Mr. Coxe in his well-known work profeffedly written on that fubject. It is impoffible to confider thefe expenfive and important miffions without teftifying our acknowledgment of the benefits that have accrued to fcience from thefe learned and laborious-inveftigations.

The court of Catharine became now the afylum of the fciences, to which fhe invited learned men from every part of Europe. Among the reft the celebrated profeffor Euler from Berlin, on whom her majefty fettled a large annual ftipend, made him a prefent of a houfe, befides fhewing him many other marks of her imperial favour and protection. Well knowing, that it is not fo much by the power of arms as by precedence in the fciences and the arts that nations obtain a confpicuous place in the annals of the world, Catharine with a laudable zeal encouraged artifts and fcholars of all denominations. She granted new privileges to the academy of fciences, and exhorted its members

to

to add the names of several celebrated foreigners to those which already conferred a lustre on their society.

Nor was she less attentive to the academy of arts, by increasing the number of its pupils, and adding such regulations as tended more than ever to the attainment of the end of its endowment. Scholars were now not to be taken in after the age of six years, that the defects of a bad education might not yet have had time to spoil their temper or corrupt their manners. Delivered for three years to the care of women, they are then put into the hands of tutors, and are devoted to the art to which they shew the most inclination. They may become painters, sculptors, architects, watchmakers, engravers, or learn the art of casting in metals, and of making mathematical and optical instruments. During the whole of the time they are in the academy they are not permitted to receive any thing from their parents. They are clothed, fed, and lodged at the public expence. At the end of fifteen years they leave the institution; and, if their behaviour correspond with the pains that have been bestowed on their education, they are presented with patents of nobility.

Independently of these advantages, such of the pupils as have carried the highest prizes, receive

receive the before-mentioned penfion for travelling three years over Europe.

It is frequently obferved, that though this inftitution has now fubfifted upwards of half a century, yet it has produced no great artift ; and that it has ferved no other purpofe than to furnifh Voltaire with a fubject of pompous declamation, and to make annually a paragraph in the newfpapers of Germany, oftentatioufly defcribing the ceremony of diftributing the prizes in the prefence of the emprefs and the grand duke, with their pathetic fpeeches on the occafion ; and that, anfwering that purpofe, nothing farther was intended. Yet even admitting the love of fame to be the only motive at the time, the inftitution may hereafter find motives of its own, arifing from intereft, or a defire of excelling, as a civilized public fhall increafe, and the approbation of their performances no longer be confidered as a matter of form and confined to the court.

Still farther to encourage the fine arts in her dominions, the emprefs affigned an annual fum of 5000 rubles for the tranflation of foreign literary works into the ruffian language.

At this time the fmall-pox was very rife in St. Peterfburg, which occafioned the emprefs and the grand duke her fon to remain at Tzar-fko-felo, ſko-ſelo, inſtead of coming to town as uſual. The counteſs Scheremetoff was carried off by that diſtemper a few days before ſhe was to have been married to count Panin, for which event great preparations had been made. It was neither poſſible, nor was it material, to aſcertain how the infection penetrated the receſſes of the court; but perſons of rank and fortune were alarmed that neither one nor the other afforded any ſecurity againſt the ravages of this dreadful diſeaſe. The danger to which her majeſty and the grand duke were expoſed, together with her majeſty's zeal for the welfare of her ſubjects, gave riſe to a propoſal for introducing the practice of inoculation.

The firſt perſonages in the empire determined to ſet the example, by ſubmitting to the operation; and a reſolution was accordingly taken by the empreſs, to invite a phyſician from England, where inoculation had been moſt practiſed, and was generally allowed to have received ſome modern and very conſiderable improvements *.

Accordingly Dr. Thomas Dimſdale, about the beginning of July 1768, received a letter at

* See tracts on inoculation, written and publiſhed at St. Peterſburg in the year 1768, by command of the empreſs of Ruſſia, by the hon. baron T. Dimſdale, 1781.

Hertford

Hertford from M. Poufchin, the ruffian minifter at the court of London, reprefenting that the emprefs, having a defire to engage an able phyfician to go to St. Peterfburg, in order to introduce inoculation, he wifhed to fee him as foon as poffible. At the interview that enfued, great encouragements were held out ; but the doctor, from domeftic confiderations, at firft fhewed fome hefitation ; when a fecond courier arriving, and fome circumftances rendering it apparent that the emprefs and grand duke were immediately interefted in the application, he prepared for his journey with all expedition, and accordingly fet out on the 28th of July.

Two days after his arrival, the doctor, in confequence of a previous notice, waited on count Panin, who, after the ufual falutations, faid to him, " You are now called, fir, to the moft " important employment that perhaps any gen- " tleman was ever entrufted with. To your " fkill and integrity will probably be fubmitted " no lefs than the precious lives of two of the " greateft perfonages in the world, with whofe " fafety the tranquillity and happinefs of this " great empire are fo intimately connected, that " fhould an accident deprive us of either, the " bleffings we now enjoy might be turned to " the utmoft ftate of mifery and confufion. " May

" May God avert fuch unfpeakable calamities!
" But the hazard of the infection of the fmall-
" pox, in the natural way, is fo threatening,
" that we are compelled to have recourfe to the
" expedient of inoculation; which, though fo
" little known in this country, has been adopted
" and practifed in England with the greateft
" fuccefs.   We have phyficians of great learn-
" ing and abilities in their profeffion; but not
" being experienced in this new branch of
" practice, her imperial majefty was pleafed to
" lay her commands upon her minifters, to
" inquire after and engage a perfon of the beft
" abilities in it, and whofe fuccefs had been
" confirmed by long practice.   You come to
" us well recommended in thefe effential points;
" I fhall therefore repofe the utmoft confidence
" in you, and have only to requeft that you
" will act without the leaft referve.
    " As to the refolution of the emprefs in this
" particular, with regard to herfelf, I muft
" leave to her majefty to explain her own fen-
" timents; but with refpect to the grand duke,
" he is already determined on the operation,
" provided you encourage it: it has been fub-
" mitted to his own confideration; he approves,
" and even wifhes it.   I have therefore to
" requeft, that before an affair of fo great con-

" fequence is finally fettled, you would make
" yourfelf well acquainted with his conftitution
" and ftate of health.

" His imperial highnefs knows you are ar-
" rived, expects to fee you, and invites you to
" wait on him to-morrow. I can venture to
" affure you, that he will be eafy of accefs,
" and willing to be acquainted with you. Be
" with him as much as poffible ; fee him at his
" table, and at his amufements ; make your
" obfervations, and, in fhort, ftudy his confti-
" tution. Let us not be too precipitate ; but
" when every circumftance has been duly
" attended to, report your opinion freely, and
" depend on this, that if you fhould deem the
" operation hazardous, and advife againft it,
" we fhall think ourfelves equally obliged to
" you ; nor will the acknowledgments on ac-
" count of this expedition be inferior to what
" it will be upon the utmoft fuccefs."

In anfwer to this, the doctor affured the count
that he would in every refpect attend to his intimations, and that he might depend on his making
a juft report.

The emprefs came to town that evening, and
the next day, the two Dimfdales were prefented.
On this occafion there were only prefent with her
majefty, count Panin and baron Cherkaffoff,
                                        prefident

president of the college of medicine, who having been educated at the univerfity of Cambridge, fpoke very good Englifh. Catharine fhewed great perfpicacity in the queftions fhe put concerning the practice and fuccefs of inoculation. On his retiring, Dr. Dimfdale was invited to dine with her majefty the fame day; and as the account of the manners obferved at the emprefs's table will neither be foreign to our purpofe, nor unentertaining to the reader, we fhall give it in the doctor's own words:

"The emprefs fat fingly at the upper end of a long table, at which about twelve of the nobility were guefts. The entertainment confifted of a variety of excellent difhes, ferved up after the french manner, and was concluded by a deffert of the fineft fruits and fweetmeats, fuch as I little expected to find in that northern climate. Moft of thefe luxuries were, however, the produce of the emprefs's own dominions. Pine-apples indeed are chiefly imported from England, though thofe of the growth of Ruffia, of which we had one that day, are of good flavour, but generally fmall. Water-melons and grapes are brought from Aftrakhan; great plenty of melons from Mofco, and apples and pears from the Ukraine.

L L 2   "But

"But what enlivened the whole entertainment was the moſt unaffected eaſe and affability of the empreſs herſelf. Each of her gueſts had a ſhare of her attention and politeneſs; the converſation was kept up with a freedom and cheerfulneſs to be expected rather from perſons of the ſame rank, than from ſubjects admitted to the honour of their ſovereign's company."

On the following day another converſation with the empreſs enſued, in which Dr. Dimſdale requeſted the aſſiſtance of the court phyſicians, to whom he deſired to communicate every propoſed regulation and medicine; but the empreſs would by no means conſent to any ſuch conſultation, and gave her reaſons as follows:

"You are come well recommended to me;
"the converſation I have had with you on this
"ſubject has been very ſatisfactory; and my
"confidence in you is increaſed. I have not
"the leaſt doubt of your abilities and knowledge
"in this practice; it is impoſſible that my
"phyſicians can have much ſkill in this opera-
"tion; they want experience; their interpoſi-
"tion may tend to embarraſs you, without the
"leaſt probability of giving any uſeful aſſiſtance.
"My life is my own; and I ſhall with the
"utmoſt cheerfulneſs and confidence rely on

15   "your

" your care alone.   With regard to my confti-
" tution you could receive no information from
" them.   I have had, I thank God, fo good a
" fhare of health, that their advice has never
" been required; and you fhall, from myfelf,
" receive every information that can be necef-
" fary.   I have alfo to acquaint you, that it is
" my determination to be inoculated before the
" grand duke, and as foon as you judge it conve-
" nient.   At the fame time I defire that this
" may remain a fecret bufinefs; and I enjoin
" you to let it be fuppofed that, for the prefent,
" all thoughts of my own inoculation are laid
" afide.   The preparation of this great experi-
" ment on the grand duke will countenance
" your vifits to the palace; and I defire to fee
" you as often as it may feem neceffary, that
" you may become ftill better acquainted with
" what relates to my conftitution, and alfo for
" adjufting the time and other circumftances of
" my own inoculation."

He promifed obedience to her majefty's commands; and only propofed that fome experi-
ments might firft be made by inoculating fome
of her own fex and age, and as near as could be
of fimilar habit.   The emprefs replied, " that
" if the practice had been novel, or the leaft
" doubt of the general fuccefs had remained,

" that

" that precaution might be neceſſary; but, as
" ſhe was well ſatisfied in both particulars, there
" would be no occaſion for delay on any
" account."

The empreſs, on being inoculated privately,
went * the next morning to Tzarſko-ſelo.
At firſt no other perſons were there but the
neceſſary attendants, it being given out that
her majeſty's journey was only to give directions
about ſome alterations, and that her ſtay would
be ſhort. But ſeveral of the nobility ſoon
followed, and the empreſs obſerving among them
ſome whom ſhe ſuſpected not to have had
the ſmall-pox, ſaid to Dr. Dimſdale: " I muſt
" rely on you to give me notice when it is
" poſſible for me to communicate the diſeaſe:
" for, though I could wiſh to keep my inocula-
" tion a ſecret, yet far be it from me to conceal
" it a moment, when it may become hazardous
" to others." The empreſs, during this interval, took part in every amuſement with her
uſual affability, without ſhewing the leaſt token
of uneaſineſs or concern; conſtantly dined at the
ſame table with the nobility, and enlivened
the whole court with thoſe peculiar graces of

* On the 12th of October.

con-

converfation, for which fhe was ever diftinguifhed *.

The grand duke fhortly after † fubmitted to
the operation ; and, on his recovery, Catharine
rewarded the fervices of Dr. Dimfdale by creating
him a baron of the ruffian empire, and appointing
him actual counfellor of ftate, and phyfician to
her imperial majefty, with a penfion of 500l.
a-year, to be paid him in England ; befides
10,000l. fterling which he immediately received ;
and alfo prefented him with a miniature picture
of herfelf, and another of the grand duke, as
a memorial of his fervices.   Her majefty was

---

* Shortly after being inoculated Catharine wrote to
Voltaire : — "I have not kept my bed a fingle inftant, and I
" have received company every day.   I am about to have
" my only fon inoculated.   The grand mafter of artillery,
" count Orloff, that hero who refembles the antient
" Romans in the beft times of the republic (1), both in
" courage and in generofity, doubting whether he had ever
" had the fmall-pox, has put himfelf under the hands of our
" Englifhman ; and the next day after the operation, went
" to the hunt, in a very deep fall of fnow.   A great num-
" ber of courtiers have followed his example, and many
" others are preparing to do fo.   Befides this, inoculation
" is now carried on at Peterfburg, in three feminaries of
" education, and in an hofpital, eftablifhed under the infpec-
" tion of M. Dimfdale."

† On the 1ft of November.

(1) Romans !—the Orloffs !

L L 4   like-

likewise pleased to express her approbation of
the conduct of his son, by conferring on him the
same title, and ordering him to be presented
with a superb gold snuff-box, richly set with
diamonds.

The examples of these illustrious personages
had such immediate influence, that most of
the nobility both of St. Petersburg and Mosco
were impatient to have their families inoculated.
This business being happily accomplished, baron
Dimsdale was preparing to return to England,
and indeed was just setting out, when a nobleman
came to inform him that the empress was
desirous of seeing him. The baron was much
concerned to find her with every symptom of a
pleuretic fever, and therefore at her desire again
took up his residence in the palace. The
symptoms increased; but, upon being bled, her
majesty received immediate relief, and in a short
time the most alarming symptoms abated. So
soon as the empress was recovered, which was in
about three weeks, the baron again prepared for
his journey to England. Having taken his
leave, and received farther proofs of the munificence of her imperial majesty, the baron was
attended to Riga by an officer commissioned to
see that every necessary accommodation should
be

be provided, in the fame manner as at his firft arrival in the country *.

On the 3d of December 1768, a thankfgiving fervice was performed in the chapel of the palace, on accountof her majefty's recovery and that of the grand duke, from the fmall-pox. The ceremony was very folemn and magnificent.   On each fide of the imperial chapel, which is a lofty and fpacious room in the winter palace, is a row of gilt ionic columns. The walls are covered with taudry and ill-executed pictures of ruffian faints.   On the roof, over the catapetafma and holy doors, is a reprefentation of the Supreme Being, under the figure of an old man in white raiment. Within a railing that extends acrofs the room, and contiguous to the pillar neareft to the holy doors, on the fouth fide, ftood the emprefs and her fon ; for, by the greek ritual, no perfon is allowed to fit in church : accordingly there are no feats, not even for the fovereign, who always ftands during the whole fervice under a canopy, when not making the ufual proftrations. In the fame area, and on both fides of the fanc-

* Before baron Dimfdale took his departure from St. Pe-terfburg, the emprefs purchafed the houfe that had been built by baron Wolff, formerly britifh conful in that city, for the purpofe of converting it into an inoculation hofpital, which fhe accordingly did, and the inftitution is ftill fup-ported.

tuary,

tuary, were chorifters, gaudily appareled. All the reft of the congregation ftood on the outfide of the baluftrade.

The ceremony opened with folemn vocal mufic, no other being admiffible in the greek church ; to this fucceeded the prayers and ejaculations, which conftituted the firft part of the office. Prefently the folding doors of the holieft were opened from within, and difplayed to view the penetralia of the temple. Directly oppofite appeared a large picture of the defcent from the crofs ; on each fide a gilt colonnade of the ionic order : in the middle of an altar covered with golden tiffue ; and on the altar a crucifix, a three-armed candleftick, with lighted tapers, emblem of the trinity, and chalices, flagons, patens, and other holy veffels. A number of venerable priefts with hoary heads and flowing beards, wearing mitres, ftudded with precious ftones of every colour, and coftly robes of filk and damafk, ftood in folemn attitudes, among the columns of this gorgeous fanctuary.

From the adytum, or inmoft recefs, with flow and folemn fteps, advanced a prieft, bearing in his hand a two-branched candleftick with lighted tapers, fignificant of the hypoftatic union of the two natures of the Son of God. He was followed in like manner by another, reciting
                                        prayers

prayers as he moved along, and swinging a censer smoking with fragrant odours. Advancing towards her majesty, he waved the censer thrice before her, during which she several times gracefully bowed, and as often made the sign of the cross upon her breast. A third priest succeeded him, bearing on his arms the volume of the gospel; out of which having read some passages adapted to the occasion, he presented it to the empress, who kissed it with great devotion.

The priests then retired: the folding doors of the sanctuary were closed: the choristers sung an anthem, and were answered by musical voices from within. The intonations were deep and sublime. In a few minutes the folding doors again flew open; the ceremonies of the tapers and incense were repeated. Two priests advanced, bearing the sacred symbols, the bread and wine of the holy eucharist, veiled with cloth of gold. Having administered this *, they retired. The doors were closed, and the choral harmony began afresh.

The doors were opened, and the same ceremonies a third time repeated. After this the metropolitan ascended the pulpit against a column opposite to the empress, and delivered a dif-

* In the greek church the bread and wine are mixed up together, and administered with a spoon.

course:

courfe; in which he celebrated her refolution and magnanimity; and in the courfe of his fermon remarked, " that the Ruffians had bor-" rowed affiftance from Britain, that ifland " famed for wifdom, bravery, and virtue." The fermon ended, feveral priefts came from the recefs, and concluded the fervice with prayers and benedictions.

The fenate decreed that the event of the reco-very after inoculation of the fovereign and his imperial highnefs fhould be folemnized by an anniverfary feftival, which has been regularly obferved ever fince.

END OF THE FIRST VOLUME.

APPENDIX

TO THE

FIRST VOLUME.

No. I.

Succeſſion of the SOVEREIGNS *of* RUSSIA, GRAND PRINCES *or* GRAND DUKES, TZARS, *and afterwards* EMPERORS; PATRIARCHS, ARCHBISHOPS, BISHOPS, *&c.*

	A. M.	A. C.
Rurik - - - - -	6369	861
Igor, his fon, at firſt under the regency of his uncle Oleg - - -	6386	878
Svetoſlaf, fon, firſt under the regency of his mother Olga, who embraced chriſtianity. Kief was at this time the reſidence or capital - - - -	6453	945
Tarepolk, fon of the grand duke -	6480	972
Vladimir, brother, firſt chriſtian prince, and apoſtle of his nation - -	6488	980
Tareſlaf, fon of the grand duke at Kief: his brothers have appanages: thence the different dukedoms - -	6523	1015
Iſiaſlaf, fon - - -	6562	1054
Vſevolod, brother - - -	6586	1078
	Sviatopolk,	

	A. M.	A. C.
Sviatopolk, fon of the grand duke Ifiaflaf	6601	1093
Vladimir II. brother of Vfevolod	6622	1114
Mftiflaf, fon - - -	6633	1125
Yaropolk, brother - - -	6640	1132
Viatcheflaf, brother, abdicates -	6646	1138
Vfevolod II. great grandfon of the grand duke Yaroflaf - - -		
Ifaflaf II. fon of Mftiflaf -	6654	1146
Roftiflaf, brother of Vfevolod II.	6662	1154
Ifaflaf III. fon of David, and great grandfon of Yaroflaf - -		
Youri, or *Igor*, or *George*, fourth fon of the grand duke Vladimir II. He built Mofco: his fucceffors leave Kief, and refide at Vladimir - - -	6663	1155
Michael, fon, governs with his brother Andrew, and after his death alone -	6665	1157
Vfevolod III. brother - -	6685	1177
Igor, or *George* II. fon. Conftantine his brother during two years - -	6721	1213
Yaroflaf II. brother, in fubjection to the Tartars, as the following - -	6746	1238
St. *Alexander Nefsky*, fon - *	6753	1245
Yaroflaf III. brother - - -	6771	1263
Vaffili, or *Bafil*, brother - -	6778	1270
Dmitri, or *Demetrius*, brother. His brother Andrew fet up by the Tartars -	6785	1277
Daniel, fourth brother: fince whom the grand dukes refide at Mofco - -	6802	1294
Igor, or *George*, fon, depofed -	6810	1302
Michael, fon of Yaroflaf III. -	6813	1305
Vaffili, or *Bafil* II. brother - -	6828	1320
Igor, re-eftablifhed - - -	6833	1325
Ivan, or *John*, brother - -	6836	1328
Simeon, fon - - -	6848	1340
Ivan II. brother - - -	6861	1353

Demetrius

	A. M.	A. C.
Demetrius II. fon. Demetrius, his relation, fet up by the Tartars, two years	6867	1359
Vaffili, or *Bafil* III. fon - -	6897	1389
Vaffili IV. fon. Igor, his uncle, ufurps	6933	1425
Ivan III. fon. The famous Ivan Vaffillievitch who threw off the yoke of the Tartars - - -	6970	1462
Vaffili V. fon ' - - -	7014	1506
Ivan IV. fon, furnamed the tyrant, affumes the title of tzar - - -	7042	1534
Feodor, or *Theodore*, fon ; the laft of the race of Rurik - - -	7092	1584
The following are of different families :		
Borice Godunof - - -	7106	1598
Feodor II. fon - - -	7113	1605
Gregory Atrepief, falfely calling himfelf Demetrius, brother of Feodor I. - -		
Vaffili Zuifki (or *Bafil* VI.) elected	7114	1606
Vladiflaus of Poland, elected, afterwards rejected - - - -	7118	1610
Michael, of the family Romanof (ftill reigning) elected - - -	7121	1613
Alexey, or *Alexius*, fon - -	7153	1645
Feodor, or *Theodore* III. fon '-	7184	1676
Ivan V. and *Peter*, brothers, together	7190	1682
Peter alone, afterwards ftyled, the great, emperor - - -	7204	1696
Ruffians ceafe to reckon by the year of the world.		
Catharine, widow of Peter - -		1725
Peter II. grandfon of Peter the great -		1727
Anne, daughter of Ivan - - -		1730
Ivan VI. grandfon of Ivan - -		1740
Elizabeth Petrovna, or daughter of Peter the great - - - -		1741
Peter III. nephew, depofed - -		1762
Catharine II. his widow - -		1762
Paul, fon - - - --		1796

Before

Before the great reformation made by Peter I. both in church and state, the ruffian ecclefiaftics lived in the moft confummate indolence and licentioufnefs, maintaining, at the fame time, an unlimited authority over the people. All matters of controverfy were prohibited them under pain of death. Public inftruction was given but twice in the year to the people; and that confifted only of a portion of fome homily tranflated from one of the greek fathers.

The hierarchy confifted of the patriarch, who was the next in dignity and authority to the tzar, and always refided in the city of Mofco; of four metropolitans, feven arch-bifhops, and but one bifhop: the other clergy were arch-deacons, proto-popes, and popes or priefts.

The patriarchs of Ruffia were:

Job, eftablifhed by Jeremiah of Conftantinople, in 1588.
Ignatius, placed by the falfe Demetrius - 1605.
Hermogenes, after the expulfion of Ignatius 1606.
Philaretes, father of the tzar Michael - - 1615.
Joafaph - - - - - - 1634.
Jofeph - - - - - - 1642.
Nicon, depofed afterwards, in a full fynod, for
    ambition and turbulency - - - 1660.
Joafaph - - - - - - 1667.
Pityroum, or *Pefterim* - - - - 1675.
Joachim - - - - - - 1680.
Adrian - - - - - - 1684.

Since whofe death, in 1702, there has been no patriarch.

The patriarch was abfolute judge in all ecclefiaftical affairs: he had the power of taking what fteps he pleafed towards the reformation of manners, and to condemn capitally fuch as he judged guilty of profligacy, or of violating the moral order. His fentences were executed with the quickeft difpatch; and fuch as appealed to his tribunal could not be cited to that of the fovereign. They had fometimes even ftruggled with the authority of the throne.

throne. Nicon openly oppofed its power * ; and Joachim endeavoured to undermine it by artifice and fraud.

On Palm Sunday, which is a great day in Ruffia, the patriarch, mounted on a horfe, reprefented our Saviour riding into Jerufalem. The tzar ufed to go from the caftle, with the patriarch, to the church which is called Jerufalem. After a number of people, whofe bufinefs it was to clean the way, followed a very large chariot drawn by fix horfes, in the manner of a pageant ; in this chariot was placed a tree, with apples, grapes, and figs tied upon its branches, and a number of boys about it, with green twigs and boughs in their hands. All the boyars and nobility of the court attended this magnificent ceremony, and joined in the exclamation of " *Hofannah to the Son of David! Bleffed is he that comes in the name of the Lord! Hofannah in the higheft !*" as the patriarch moved along, clothed all in white. The tzar, fupported by two boyars, and with the imperial diadem on his head, led the horfe by the bridle, which was three or four yards in length. The patriarch wore on his head the great patriarchal infula or mitre, richly fet with jewels. In his right hand he held a crofs of gold, embellifhed with a profufion of diamonds, and other precious ftones, with which he made the fign of the crofs over the multitude that thronged about him with great reverence and devotion, expreffed by genuflections and proftrations. The

---

* The patriarch Nicon, whom the monks regard as a faint, and who filled the patriarchate in the time of Alexey Michailovitch, the father of Peter the great, wanted to raife his chair above the imperial throne ; he not only claimed the right of fitting in the fenate by the fide of the tzar, but he pretended that neither war nor peace could be made without his confent. His authority, fupported by his riches and his intrigues, by the clergy and by the people, held his mafter in a kind of fubjection. He dared to excommunicate certain fenators who oppofed his exceffes. In fhort, Alexius, being fenfible that he was not powerful enough to depofe the patriarch by his fole authority, was obliged to convoke a fynod of all the bifhops. He was accufed to them of having received money of the Po es ; he was depofed ; he was confined for the reft of his days in a cloifter, and the prelates chofe another patriarch.

horfe on which he fat was adorned with fplendid trappings, and the richeft caparifons; but difguifed, fo as to bear fomewhat of the refemblance of an afs. On each fide of the patriarch went feveral bifhops on foot, clothed all in white, and holding thuribles in their hands. The pictures of faints, the chalice, books, bells, tapers, and other things ufed at mafs, as well as the reft of the church ornaments, were borne by the fuperior clergy, fome of whom alfo carried the confecrated banners of the faints. The way from the palace to the Crefent was all laid with fcarlet cloth. At this place it was that the patriarch ufed firft to take horfe. He found it tied to a pale, and fent two of the bifhops to untie it, and bring it to him. As the proceffion paffed along, fome of the people pulled off their upper garments, and fpread them in the road; others, who had more piety, purchafed cloths and filks, of feveral yards in length, on purpofe; and the reft, who had but little covering, and no money, contented themfelves with cutting branches and boughs from the birch-trees, and ftrewed them in the way.

Thus they proceeded to the beforementioned church: where having ftayed above half an hour, they returned in the fame order, till they came to a fort of ftage or platform, where the patriarch prefented the tzar and the principal boyars with palm twigs; after which he took off the tzar's crown, and laid it in a filver difh, and then gave him the diamond crofs to kifs. This being done by the tzar with a very profound reverence, the patriarch lifted up the crofs, and waved it aloft on different fides, firft towards thofe upon the platform, and then towards the people in general, who at that inftant proftrated themfelves flat upon the ground. The whole ceremony was concluded by finging a number of hymns; and the patriarch, as an acknowledgment to the fovereign for leading his horfe, prefented him with a purfe of 200 rubles.

We have been thus explicit on this ceremony, that the reader may be the better able to judge of the magnificence

7

and authority of the patriarchs during their exiltence. The above account was had from a gentleman whofe anceftor related it to his father, as one that he was prefent at in the patriarchate of Joafaph.

Peter the great abolifhed this dignity, and eftablifhed a perpetual fynod for all decifion in matters of religion. This fynod is compofed of a prefident, which the tzar feems to have intended to fill himfelf, as he never appointed any one to that dignity ; a vice-prefident, who muft be an arch-bifhop (at prefent the archbifhop of Mofco) ; fix counfel-lors, who are bifhops ; and of fix archimandrites *, who have the quality of affeffors.

Upon the prefent eftablifhment, there are in Ruffia, three metropolitans, feven archbifhops, and eighteen independent bifhops :

Mofco and Kaluga, metropolitan.
Novgorod and St. Peterfburg, metropolitan.
Kief, metropolitan †.
Pfcove and Riga, archbifhop.
Tver and Kafhin, archbifhop.
Roftof and Yaroflavl, archbifhop.
Mohilef, Mftiflavl, and Orfha, archbifhop.
Kazan and Sviafhfk, archbifhop.
Aftrakhan and Stavropol, archbifhop.
Ekatarinoflaf, Kherfon, and Taurida, archbifhop ‡.
Archangel and Olonetz, bifhop.
Vologda and Velikoy Uftiug, bifhop
Koftroma and Galitch, bifhop.
Viatka and Velikaya Perme, bifhop
Tobolfk and Siberia, bifhop.

* Archimandrite, in the greek church, is much the fame thing as bifhop in other chriftian churches.

† This metropolitan has a coadjutor, who lives in the town of Sloutfk, beyond the frontier, and has the direction of the greek clergy refiding in Poland.

‡ He is alfo vicar of the exarchy of Moldavia and Valakh'a.

Smolenſk and Dorogobuiſh, biſhop.
Tchernigof and Niejin, biſhop.
Novgorod-Sieverſkoy, and Glukhof, biſhop.
Bielgorod and Kurſk, biſhop.
Orel and Sievſk, biſhop.
Krutitzi, biſhop.
Kolomna and Tula, biſhop.
Riazane and Shatſk, biſhop.
Sufdal and Vladimir, biſhop.
Niſhney-Novgorod and Alatyr, biſhop.
Tambof and Penza, biſhop.
Voronetch, biſhop.
Irkutſk and Nertchinſk, biſhop.

The biſhops enjoy in their dioceſes the ſame rights and privileges as the archbiſhops. Theſe dioceſes, which are called eparchies, have each its peculiar conſiſtory, and for the moſt part a ſeminary for the inſtruction of ecclefiaftics. The number of religious houſes may amount to 960, whereof thoſe for nuns compoſe a fourth part. The greek churches are reckoned at about 18,350, and the whole number of eccleſiaſtics is calculated at 67,900.

Several of the biſhops had formerly the honorary title of archbiſhops.

Before the erection of the patriarchate, the chief of the clergy was called metropolitan, and had his reſidence firſt at Kief, afterwards at Vladimir, and finally at Mofco. As the liſt of them all is not very long, we ſhall inſert it from the chronicle :

AT KIEF.			
Michael Syrus, ſent by		Theopentus - - - - 1048
the patriarch of Con-		Hilarion - - - - 1051
ſtantinople to be head		Igor II. - - - - 1071
of the clergy, in -	988	Ivan II. - - - - 1076
Leontei, or Leon - -	992	The three laſt were Ruſſians,
Ivan I. - - - -	1008	and were choſen by the
Igor Nikephor - - -	1038	clergy.
		Ivan III. - - - - 1077
		Ephraim

Ephraim - - - - 1078
He received the bull from
   pope Urban II. for the
   feaſt of the tranſlation of
   St. Nicholas.

Nikephor II. - - - 1103
Niketa - - - - - 1132
Michael - - - - 1142
Cyril - - - - - 1161
Clement - - - - - 1165
He was ordained in Ruſſia,
   on account of the revival of
   the ſchiſm of the Greeks.

Conſtantine - - - - 1176
Theodore - - - - 1182
Ivan IV. - - - - 1191
Nikephor III. - - - 1195
Matthias - - - - 1226
Cyril II. - - - - 1238
Joſeph of Nicæa - - 1248
Cyril III. - - - - 1252
Maxime - - - - 1283

    AT VLADIMIR.
Peter, the wonder-
   worker - - - - 1308

    AT MOSCO.
Theognoſtus - - - 1328
Alexius, the wonder-
   worker - - - - 1353
Zoſimus, or *Timen* - 1373
Cyril IV. - - - - 1376
Cyprian - - - - 1378

Phocius - - - - - 1409
He was depoſed by a
   party of Ruſſians, on
   account of his zeal
   for the ſchiſm, in - 1415
Iſidore - - - - - 1438
Rejoins the latin church
   at the council of
   Florence, and is de-
   poſed in Ruſſia, on
   his return, in - - 1442
The ſchiſm is thenceforward
   fixed and total.

Jonas, or *Jonathan* - 1448
Theodoſion - - - - 1460
Philip I. - - - - 1468
Hieronti - - - - 1473
Zoſimus II. - - - 1489
Simon - - - - - 1492
Varlaam - - - - 1511
Daniel - - - - 1522
Joſeph - - - - 1539
Macarion - - - - 1542
Athanaſius - - - 1564
Philip II. - - - - 1866
Cyril V. - - - - 1568
Anthony - - - - 1570
At his death, *Job* was ap-
   pointed patriarch, in 1588:
   the ſucceſſion under which
   title has been given in the
   former part of this article.

No. II.

The ORDINANCE, *or* UKASE, *which rendered* PETER *so dear at first to the* RUSSIAN *Nobility, ran as follows :*

We Peter III. &c.

THE troubles and inconveniencies experienced by the wife fo ereign our late dear grandfire, Peter the great, of immortal memory, in his endeavours for the good of his country, and for procuring his fubjeds a competent knowledge as well in military difcipline, at in civil and political affairs, are known to all Europe, and the greater part of the globe.

In the attainment of this end, he found it neceffary to begin by convincing the ruffian nobility, which is the firft body of the ftate, of the immenfe advantages poffeffed by the nations well verfed in the fciences and the arts, over thofe people who continue benighted in ignorance and floth. The ſtate of things at that time imperioufly demanded that he fhould oblige his nobility to enter the military fervice and engage in civil functions ; that he fhould fend them to travel into foreign countries, that they might get a tincture of the ufeful arts and fciences, and therefore he eftablifhed in his own country fchools and academies, that the feeds of thefe his falutary regulations might be cherifhed in their growth, and more fpeedily matured. The nobility had the lefs reafon to complain of the conftraint thus laid upon them, as, independently of the utility both public and private that naturally refulted from it, it was their duty to concur with the wifhes of an emperor to whom they were under fo many obligations.

The execution of thefe projects feemed at firft to be attended with the utmoft difficulty. They were intolerable to the nobility, who faw themfelves obliged to abandon a foft and indolent life, to quit their dwellings, to ferve in war and in peace, and to enrol their children for future fervices. Several members of their body withdrew from the fervice,

and

and were therefore deprived of their estates, which were confiscated, and that for the best of reasons. They rendered themselves criminal towards their country, which they basely deserted.

These excellent ordinances, though at the beginning inseparable from certain methods of constraint, have served as a model to all the successors of Peter the great, and especially to our dear aunt the empress Elizabeth Petrovna, of glorious memory ; who, determined to follow the example of her father, encouraged, by a special protection, the advancement of the arts and sciences. Of this we are now reaping the fruits ; and every impartial man will agree that they are considerable. Manners have been improved ; minds indifferent to the happiness of the country have been roused from their fatal lethargy, and have habituated themselves to reflect on the public welfare ; zeal in the service is augmented ; generals, already valiant, are become experienced ; intelligent ministers ; enlightened magistrates ; in a word, patriotism, love and attachment to our person, activity in all offices and posts, and every generous sentiment, are now the happy lot of the russian nation. —— For all these reasons, we have judged it to be no longer necessary to compel into the service, as hitherto has been the practice, the nobility of our empire.

In consideration whereof, in virtue of the full power to us granted by God, and of our imperial especial grace, we grant to the russian nobility, from this moment and for ever, in the name of all our successors, permission to take service in our empire, as well as in all those of the european powers in alliance with us ; and to this end we have given the following ordinance as a fundamental law, &c.

[Then follow nine articles concerning the terms on which liberty of resignation, of travelling abroad, of entering the service, &c. may be asked for and granted : concluding thus :]

Granting

Granting as we do, gracioufly and to perpetuity, to our nobility this franchife, making it a fundamental and unalterable law, we promife them equally on our imperial word, and in the moft folemn manner, to obferve the prefent ordinance facredly and irrevocably, in all its tenor, and to maintain the prerogatives therein expreffed.——Our fucceffors on the throne ought not to alter it in any manner.   The execution of our faid ordinance being the principal fupport of the imperial throne, we hope that, from gratitude for this benefit, the ruffian nobility will ferve us faithfully and zealoufly ; and that, inftead of withdrawing from our fervice, will enter it with eagernefs, and that they will carefully educate their children. ——We therefore command all our faithful fubjects and true fons of the country, to defpife and avoid thofe who have wafted their time in idlenefs, and who have not educated their children in the ufeful fciences, as people who have never had the public good at heart, who fhall have no accefs to our court, nor be admitted to the public affemblies and the national feftivities.

Given at St. Peterfburg, Feb. 18, 1762.

No.-III.

PAPERS *relating to the re-eftablifhment of* PEACE.

- DECLARATION *delivered by order of* PETER III. EMPEROR *of* RUSSIA, *to the* IMPERIAL, FRENCH, *and* SWEDISH *Minifters refiding at St.* PETERSBURG.

HIS imperial majefty, who, upon his happy acceffion to the throne of his anceftors, looks upon it to be his principal duty to extend and augment the welfare of his fubjects, fees with extreme regret, that the flames of the prefent war, which has already continued for fix years, and has
                                                        been

been for a long time burthensome to all the powers engaged in it, far from tending now to a conclusion, are, on the contrary, gathering fresh strength, to the great misfortune of the several nations; and that mankind has so much the more to suffer from this scourge, as the fortune of arms, which has hitherto been subject to so many vicissitudes, is equally exposed to them for the future.

Wherefore his imperial majesty, compassionating, through his humane disposition, the effusion of innocent blood, and being desirous, on his part, of putting a stop to so great an evil, has judged it necessary to declare to the courts in alliance with Russia, that, preferring to every other consideration the first law which God prescribes to sovereigns, which is the preservation of the people intrusted to them, he wishes to procure peace to his empire, to which it is so necessary, and of so great value; and, at the same time, to contribute, as much as may be in his power, to the re-establishment of it throughout all Europe.

It is in order to this, that his imperial majesty is ready to make a sacrifice of the conquests made by the arms of Russia in this war, in hopes that the allied courts will, on their part, equally prefer the restoration of peace and tranquillity to the advantages which they might expect from the war, and which they cannot obtain but by the continuance of the effusion of human blood. And to this end his imperial majesty, with the best intention, advises them to employ, on their side, all their power towards the accomplishment of so great and so salutary a work.

St. Petersburg, Feb. $\frac{11}{4}$, 1762.

The Answer of the Empress-Queen to the foregoing Declaration.

THAT animated with the same zeal, and being of the same opinion, as his imperial majesty, with regard to the salutary work of peace, and to the putting an end to the troubles and ravages that desolate Germany, she was ready to

to concur with him therein; but that, for that end, she
desired his imperial majesty to furnish her with the means of
beginning the negotiation, by imparting to her the proposed
terms of peace, which she would, without loss of time,
communicate to her high allies, who, as well as herself,
would be always ready to co-operate in a matter so much
desired, provided the terms were not inadmissible, and contained nothing injurious either to their honour, or her own.

The ANSWER *given by the* FRENCH COURT *to the aforesaid*
DECLARATION.

THE king maintaining with regret, these six years past,
a twofold war for his own defence and that of his allies, has
sufficiently manifested, on every occasion, how much he
abhors the effusion of human blood, and his constant desire
to put an end to so cruel a scourge. His personal disin-
terestedness, the steps which he thought could be taken
consistent with his dignity, and the sacrifices which he did
offer, in order to procure to Europe the desirable blessing of
peace, are sure pledges of the humane sentiments with
which his heart abounds. But, at the same time, his paternal tenderness, which makes the happiness and preservation of his subjects a duty to him, cannot make him forget
the first law that God prescribes to sovereigns, even that
which constitutes the public safety, and fixes the condition
of nations and empires, fidelity in executing treaties, and
punctuality in performing engagements to their full extent,
preferably to every other consideration.

It is with this view, that after having given so great
examples of constancy and generosity, his majesty declares
that he is ready to listen favourably to propositions for a
solid and honourable peace, but will always act in the most
perfect concert with his allies; that he will receive no counsels but such as shall be dictated to him by honour and probity; that he should think himself guilty of a defection, in
lending a hand to secret negotiations; that he will not tar-
nish

with his glory, and that of his kingdom, by abandoning his allies; and that he rests assured each of them will, on their part, faithfully adhere to the same principle.

ANSWER *given by the* KING *of* POLAND, ELECTOR *of* SAXONY, *to the same* DECLARATION.

ALL my allies wish as much as myself, that the public tranquillity may be restored upon solid foundations. It is well known to all Europe, that I did not seek the war; but, on the contrary, employed every means to keep the calamities of it at a distance from my dominions. My love to mankind in general, and to my own subjects in particular, ought to engage me to facilitate, as much as in me lies, the restoration of peace, and to exercise all moderation as to my equitable pretensions. I am of opinion, that a just and solid peace cannot be agreed on but by the congress proposed and accepted by all the powers at war.

I place a full confidence in the friendship of your imperial majesty, to whom the house of Saxony is bound by sacred ties. It is not unknown to your majesty, that Saxony hath been attacked merely on account of its connections with the russian empire; and that the king of Prussia has taken occasion to charge us with entering into defensive treaties with that empire against him. We therefore flatter ourselves with the hope, that so ancient and so equitable an ally of Saxony will not suffer our dominions, which are already reduced to the utmost distress, as well by exorbitant contributions, as by the alienation of our revenues, and of the funds which were allotted for the payment of debts, to be completely ruined.

The whole world agrees, that we are entitled to an equitable restitution and reparation of the damage sustained. But notwithstanding all these considerations, and though all the powers at war shew themselves inclined to contribute to the general pacification, yet Saxony remains threatened with irretrievable ruin.

We therefore hope that your majesty's philanthropy and magnanimity will prevail with your majesty to take care that,
                                                                            before

before all things, the electorate of Saxony be speedily evacuated, in order thereby to put an end to the calamities
which overwhelm it; this being the means of facilitating
and accelerating the conclusion of a general peace.

No. IV.

MANIFESTO *of the* EMPRESS CATHARINE II. *which was
caused to be printed and distributed about the city.*

By the grace of God, Catharine II. empress and autocratrix of all the Russias, &c.

ALL true sons of Russia have clearly seen the great danger
to which the whole russian empire has actually been exposed.
First, the foundations of our orthodox greek religion have
been shaken, and its traditions exposed to total destruction;
so that there was absolutely reason to fear, that the faith
which has been established in Russia from the earliest times,
would be entirely changed, and a foreign religion introduced. In the second place, the glory which Russia has
acquired at the expence of so much blood, and which was
carried to the highest pitch by her victorious arms, has
been trampled under foot by the peace lately concluded with
its most dangerous enemy. And lastly, the domestic regulations, which are the basis of the country's welfare, have
been entirely overturned.

For these causes, overcome by the imminent perils with
which our faithful subjects were threatened, and seeing how
sincere and express their desires on this matter were; we,
putting our trust in the Almighty and his divine justice,
have ascended the sovereign imperial throne of all the Russias,
and have received a solemn oath of fidelity from all our loving
subjects.

St. Petersburg, June 28, 1762.

No. V.

MANIFESTO *of the* EMPRESS CATHARINE II. *giving an account of her motives for taking the reins of government into her hands.*

By the grace of God, we Catharine II. emprefs and fovereign of all the Ruffias, make known thefe pre- , fents to all our loving fubjeƈts, ecclefiaftical, military, and civil.

OUR acceffion to the imperial throne of all the Ruffias, is a manifeft proof of this truth, that when fincere hearts endeavour for good, the hand of God direƈts them. We never had either defign or defire to arrive at empire, through the means by which it hath pleafed the Almighty, accord- ing to the infcrutable views of his providence, to place us upon the throne of Ruffia, our dear country.

On the death of our moft auguft and dear aunt, the em- prefs Elizabeth Petrovna, of glorious memory, all true patriots (now our moft faithful fubjeƈts) groaning for the lofs of fo tender a mother, placed their only confolation in obeying her nephew, whom fhe had named for her fucceffor, that they might fhew thereby, in fome degree, their ac- knowledgments to their deceafed fovereign. And although they foon found out the weaknefs of his mind, unfit to rule fo vaft an empire, they imagined he would have known his own infufficiency. Whereupon they fought our maternal affiftance in the affairs of government.

But when abfolute power falls to the lot of a monarch, who has not fufficient virtue and humanity to place juft bounds to it, it degenerates into a fruitful fource of the moft pernicious evils. This is the fum, in fhort, of what our native country has fuffered. She ftruggled to be deli- vered from a fovereign who, being blindly given up to the moft dangerous paffions, thought of nothing but indulging them, without employing himfelf in the welfare of the empire committed to his care.

During

During the time of his being grand duke, and heir to the throne of Rullia, he often caufed the molt bitter griefs to his molt augult aunt and fovereign, (the truth of which is known to all our court,) however he might behave himfelf outwardly; being kept under her eye by her tendernefs, he looked upon this mark of affection as an infupportable yoke. He could not, however, difguife himfelf fo well, but it was perceived by all our faithful fubjects, that he was poffeffed of the molt audacious ingratitude, which he fometimes fhewed by perfonal contempt, fometimes by an avowed hatred to the nation. At length, throwing afide his cloak of hypocrify, he thought it more fit to let loofe the bridle of his paffions, than conduct himfelf as the heir of fo great an empire. In a word, the leaft traces of honour were not to be perceived in him. What were the confequences of all this?

He was fcarcely affured that the death of his aunt and benefactrefs approached, but he banifhed her memory entirely from his mind; nay, even before fhe had fent forth her laft groan. He only caft an eye of contempt on the corpfe expofed on the bier; and as the ceremony at that time required obliged him to approach it, he did it with his eyes manifeftly replete with joy; even intimating his ingratitude by his words. We might add, that the obfequies would have been nothing equal to the dignity of fo great and magnanimous a fovereign, if our tender refpect to her, cemented by the ties of blood, and the extreme affection between us, had not made us take that duty upon us.

He imagined that it was not to the Supreme Being, but only to chance, that he was indebted for abfolute power; and that he had it in his hands, not for the good of his fubjects, but folely for his own fatisfaction. Adding, therefore, licence to abfolute power, he made all the changes in the ftate which the weaknefs of his mind could fuggeft, to the oppreffion of the people.

Having effaced from his heart even the leaft traces of the holy orthodox religion, (though he had been fufficiently
taught

taught the principles thereof,) he began firſt by rooting
out this true religion, eſtabliſhed ſo long in Ruſſia, by ab-,
ſenting himſelf from the houſe of God, and of prayers, in
ſo open a manner, that ſome of his ſubjects, excited by
conſcience and honeſty, ſeeing his irreverence and contempt
of the rites of the church, or rather the railleries he made
of them, and ſcandalizing them by his behaviour, dared to
make remonſtrances to him concerning it; who, for ſo
doing, ſcarcely eſcaped the reſentment which they might
have expected from ſo capricious a ſovereign, whoſe power
was not limited by any human laws.   He even intended to
deſtroy the churches, and ordered ſome to be pulled down.
He prohibited thoſe to have chapels in their own houſes,
whoſe infirmities hindered them from viſiting the houſe of
God.   Thus he would have domineered over the faithful, in
endeavouring to ſtiſle in them the fear of God, which the
holy ſcripture teaches us to be the beginning of wiſdom.

From this want of zeal towards God, and contempt of
his laws, reſulted that ſcorn to the civil and natural laws of
his kingdom; for having but an only ſon, which God had
given us, the grand duke Paul Petrovitch, he would not,
when he aſcended the throne of Ruſſia, declare him for his
ſucceſſor; that being reſerved for his caprice, which tended
to the detriment of us and of our ſon, having an inclination
to overthrow the right that his aunt had veſted in him, and
to make the government of our native country paſs into the
hands of ſtrangers; in oppoſition to that maxim of natural
right, according to which nobody can tranſmit to another
more than he has received himſelf.

Although with great grief we ſaw this intention, we did
not believe that we ourſelves, and our moſt dear ſon, ſhould
have been expoſed to a perſecution ſo ſevere: but all
perſons of probity having obſerved that the meaſures that he
purſued, by their effects, manifeſted that they had a natural
tendency to our ruin, and that of our dear ſucceſſor, their
generous and pious hearts were juſtly alarmed: animated
with zeal for the intereſt of their native country, and aſto-
niſhed

nished at our patience under these heavy persecutions, they secretly informed us, that our life was in danger, in order to engage us to undertake the burthen of governing so large an empire.

While the whole nation were on the point of testifying their disapprobation of his measures, he nevertheless continued to grieve them the more, by subverting all those excellent arrangements established by Peter the great, our most dear predecessor, of glorious memory, which that true father of his country accomplished by indefatigable pains and labour through the whole course of a reign of thirty years. The late Peter the third despised the laws of the empire, and her most respectable tribunals, to such a degree that he could not even bear to hear them mentioned.

After one bloody war, he rashly entered upon another, in which the interests of Russia were no way concerned. He entertained an insuperable aversion to the regiments of guards, which had faithfully served his illustrious ancestors, and made innovations in the army, which, far from exciting in their breasts noble sentiments of valour, only served to discourage troops always ready to spill their best blood in the cause of their country. He changed entirely the face of the army; nay, it even seemed that, by dividing their habits into so many uniforms, and giving them so many different embellishments, for the most part fantastical to the greatest degree, he intended to infuse into them a suspicion that they did not, in effect, belong to one master, and thereby provoke the soldiers, in the heat of battle, to slay one another; although experience demonstrated that uniformity in dress had not a little contributed towards unanimity.

Inconsiderately and incessantly bent on pernicious regulations, he so alienated the hearts of his subjects, that there was scarcely a single person to be found in the nation who did not openly express his disapprobation, and was even desirous to take away his life; but the laws of God, which command
mand

mand sovereign princes to be respected, being deeply engraved on the hearts of our faithful subjects, restrained them, and engaged them to wait with patience, till the hand of God struck the important blow, and by his fall delivered an oppressed people. Under those cicumstances, now laid before the impartial eyes of the public, it was, in fact, impossible but our soul should be troubled with those impending woes which threatened our country, and with that persecution which we, and our most dear son, the heir of the russian throne, unjustly suffered ; being almost entirely excluded from the imperial palace ; in such sort, that all who had regard for us, or rather those who had courage enough to speak it (for we have not been able to find that there is one person who is not devoted to our interest) by expressing their sentiments of respect due to us, as their empress, endangered their life, or at least their fortune. In fine, the endeavours he made to ruin us, rose to such a pitch, that they broke out in public ; and then charging us with being the cause of the murmurs, which his own imprudent measures occasioned, his resolution to take away our life openly appeared. But being informed of his purpose by some of our trusty subjects, who were determined to deliver their country, or perish in the attempt, relying on the aid of the Almighty, we cheerfully exposed our person to danger, with all that magnanimity which our native country had a right to expect in return for her affection to us. After having invoked the Most High, and reposed our hope in the divine favour, we resolved also either to sacrifice our life for our country, or save it from bloodshed and calamity. Scarcely had we taken this resolution, by the direction of favouring Heaven, and declared our assent to the deputies of the empire, than the orders of the state crowded to give us assurances of their fidelity and submission.

It now remained for us, in pursuance of the love we bore our faithful subjects, to prevent the consequences which we apprehended, in case of the late emperor's inconsiderately placing his confidence in the imaginary power of the holstein troops, (for whose sake he stayed at Oranienbaum, living in indolence, and abandoning the most pressing exigencies of the state,) and there occasioning a carnage, to which our guards and other regiments were ready to expose themselves, for the sake of their native country, for ours, and that of our successor.   For these reasons we looked upon it as a necessary duty towards our subjects (to which we were immediately called by the voice of God) to prevent so great a misfortune, by prompt and proper measures.   Therefore, placing ourselves at the head of the body-guards, regiments of artillery, and other troops in and about the imperial residence, we undertook to disconcert an iniquitous design, of which we were as yet only informed in part.

But scarcely were we got out of the city, before we received two letters from the late emperor, one quick on the heels of the other.   The first by our vice-chancellor the prince Gallitzin, entreating us to allow him to return to Holstein, his native dominions ; the other by major-general Michael Ismaïloff, by which he declared, that of his own proper motion he renounced the crown and throne of Russia. In this last he begged of us to allow him to withdraw to Holstein with Elizabeth Vorontzoff and Gudovitch.   These two last letters, stuffed with flattering expressions, came to our hands a few hours after he had given orders for putting us to death, as we have been since informed from the very persons who were appointed to execute those unnatural orders.

In the mean time, he had still resources left him, which were to arm against us his holstein troops, and some small detachments then about his person ; he had also in his power several personages of distinction belonging to our court ; as he might therefore have compelled us to agree to terms of accommodation still more hurtful to our country, (for after having learned what great commotions there were among the people, he had detained them as hostages at his palace of Oranienbaum, and our humanity would never have consented to their destruction, but, to save

15

their

their lives, we would have rifked feeing a part of thofe dangers revived by an accommodation,) feveral perfons of high rank about our perfon requefted us to fend him a billet in return, propofing to him, if his intentions were fuch as he declared them to be, that he fhould inftantly fend us a voluntary and formal renunciation of the throne, wrote by his own hand, for the public fatisfaction. Major-general Ifmailoff carried this propofal, and the writing he now fent back was as follows:

During the fhort fpace of my abfolute reign over the empire of Ruffia, I became fenfible that I was not able to fupport fo great a burden, and that my abilities were not equal to the tafk of governing fo great an empire, either as a fovereign, or in any other capacity whatever. I alfo forefaw the great troubles which muft have thence arifen, and have been followed with the total ruin of the empire, and covered me with eternal difgrace. After having therefore ferioufly reflected thereon, I declare, without conftraint, and in the moft folemn manner, to the ruffian empire, and to the whole univerfe, that I for ever renounce the government of the faid empire, never defiring hereafter to reign therein, either as an abfolute fovereign, or under any other form of government; never wifhing to afpire thereto, or to ufe any means, of any fort, for that purpofe. As a pledge of which, I fwear fincerely, before God and all the world, to this prefent renunciation, written and figned this 29th of June 1762. O. S.

PETER.

It is thus, without fpilling one drop of blood, that we have afcended the ruffian throne, by the affiftance of God, and the approving fuffrages of our dear country.—Humbly adoring the decrees of Divine Providence, we affure our faithful fubjects, that we will not fail, by night and by day, to invoke the Moft High to blefs our fceptre, and enable us to wield it for the maintenance of our orthodox religion, the fecurity and defence of our dear native country, and the fupport of juftice; as well as to put an end to all miferies, iniquities, and violences, by ftrengthening and fortifying our heart for the public good. And as we ardently wifh

N N 3   to

to prove effectually how far we merit the reciprocal love of our people, for whose happiness we acknowledge our throne to be appointed, we solemnly promise, on our imperial word, to make such arrangements in the empire, that the government may be endued with an intrinsic force to support itself within limited and proper bounds; and each department of the state provided with wholesome laws and regulations, sufficient to maintain good order therein, at all times, and under all circumstances.

By which means we hope to establish hereafter the empire and our sovereign power, (however they may have been formerly weakened,) in such a manner as to comfort the discouraged hearts of all true patriots. We do not in the least doubt but that our loving subjects will, as well for the salvation of their own souls, as for the good of religion, inviolably observe the oath which they have sworn to us in the presence of the Almighty God; we thereupon assure them of our imperial favour.

Done at Petersburg, July 6, 1762.

No. VI.

DECLARATION *published by the* EMPRESS CATHARINE II. *upon recalling Count* BESTUCHEFF RIUMIN *from his banishment in* SIBERIA.

THE most ordinary understanding cannot be ignorant of the intimate obligation which all mankind contract towards God and towards each other, to transgress on no occasion whatever the demands of justice, and especially not to heap misfortunes and oppression on the head of the innocent.

Ere we mounted our imperial throne of Russia, we were well acquainted with the long and signal services rendered to this empire by the unfortunate but irreproachable count Bestucheff Riumin. Her public decrees of the 27th of
February

February 1758, induced us to prefume that the crime which had drawn upon him fo fevere an animadverfion on the part of our dear aunt the emprefs Elizabeth, muft have been very heinous; but the fecond manifefto, of the 6th of April 1759, which contained a vague detail of the crimes attributed to him, and whereof none were fpecified, obliged us to fufpend our judgment, and led us to fufpect that the indignation of that humane fovereign, and the vengeance to which fhe had been brought, were no more than the effects of calumny and intrigue; for the contents of this fecond manifefto related not to a malefactor, but to an oppreffed man condemned beforehand.

From our natural humanity we have thought fit to foften the feverity of the fentence, to pardon the guilty rather than to leave in oblivion the fervices which the faid count Beftucheff rendered during fo many years to our empire, and to let him (which would have been ftill more blamable) terminate his days in an ignominious exile.

As foon therefore as Providence placed the fceptre in our hand, fubmiffive to the emotions of our fenfibility, and to the voice of juftice, we have recalled from his exile that old and faithful fervant of our empire; but, not ignorant of our readinefs to hearken to the dictates of juftice, he, prefenting himfelf before us, has humbly implored the permiffion to make his innocence appear to our eyes, a permiffion which we granted him with all our heart; and, after having fpecified the intrigues and the calumnies, which appeared to us authenticated and clearer than light, he excited in our heart the moft lively compaffion. We experienced at the fame time a tender fatisfaction, on perceiving that the liberty to which we reftored him was in perfect agreement with that love of order and juftice by which we commenced our reign.

His example has convinced us, that the more weighty the accufation, the more fevere ought the examination to be, as without this precaution fentence of condemnation may fall upon an innocent perfon. Granting that our very dear aunt

the

the empress Elizabeth had, to our knowledge and to that of the whole world, great intelligence and sagacity; nevertheless, as no one is infallible . . . . the affair of count Bestuscheff took a turn highly disadvantageous to the honour of our dear aunt. . . . . .

For these reasons, desirous of restoring the lustre of her name, and the virtues which guided her reign, and to prove how much we cherish her memory, and to fulfil with exactitude the duty of every christian, as becomes a mother of the country, we have thought ourselves obliged to declare solemnly that the said count Bestucheff Riumin was deserving, in the highest degree, of the confidence of our deceased aunt, &c. . . . .

Given at St. Petersburg, this 13th of August 1762.

No. VII.

TRANSLATION *of a* LETTER *from the* EMPRESS *of* RUSSIA, *to* M. D'ALEMBERT, *at* PARIS, *whom she had invited into* RUSSIA *to educate her* SON.

M. D'ALEMBERT,

I HAVE just received the answer you wrote to Mr. Odart, in which you refuse to transplant yourself to assist in the education of my son. I easily conceive that it costs a philosopher, like you, nothing to despise what the world calls grandeur and honour: these, in your eyes, are very little; and I can readily agree with you that they are so. Considering things in this light, there would be nothing great in the behaviour of queen Christina [of Sweden] which has been so highly extolled; and often censured with more justice. But to be born and called to contribute to the happiness and even the instruction of a whole nation, and yet decline it, *is*, in my opinion, refusing to do that good which you wish to do.

Your

Your philosophy is founded in a love to mankind : permit me then to tell you, that to refuse to serve mankind, whilft it is in your power, is to mifs your aim.　I know you too well to be a good man, to afcribe your refufal to vanity.　I know that the fole motive of it is the love of eafe, and leifure to cultivate letters and the friendfhip of thofe you efteem. But what is there in this objection ?　Come, with all your friends ;　I promife both them and you, every conveniency and advantage that depends upon me ；　and perhaps you will find more liberty and eafe here, than in your native country. You refufed the invitation of the king of Pruffia, notwith-ftanding your obligations to him ；　but that prince has no fon. I own to you, that I have the education of my fon fo much at heart, and I think you fo neceffary to it, that perhaps I prefs you with too much earneftnefs.　Excufe my indifcretion for the fake of the occafion of it ；　and be affured that it is my efteem for you that makes me fo urgent.

Mofco,　　　　　　　　　　　　CATHARINE.
Nov. 13, 1762.

In this whole letter I have argued only from what I have found in your writings ;　you would not contradict yourfelf.

No. VIII.

The Declaration *which the* Empress *caufed to be delivered to the Foreign Minifters.*

THE ftyle of imperial, which Peter the great, of glo-rious memory, affumed, or rather revived for himfelf and his fucceffors, has long appertained as well to the fovereigns as to the crown and to the monarchy of all the Ruffias.

Her imperial majefty regards as contrary to the fubftance of that principle, all renewal of the reverfals which have been given fucceffively to every potentate on its acknowledg-ment of that title.　In confequence whereof, her majefty has juft given orders to her minifter to make a general declaration, that the ftyle of IMPERIAL being by its very nature once attached to the crown and to the monarchy of Ruffia, and perpetuated for a long courfe of years and fucceffions, neither herfelf, nor her fucceffors for ever, can any more renew the faid reverfals, and ftill lefs preferve any correfpondence with the powers who fhall refufe to acknowledge the imperial title in the perfons of the fovereigns of all the Ruffias, as well as in their crown and their monarchy: and to the end that this declaration may terminate for ever all difficulties in a matter which ought not to admit of any, her majefty, in conformity to the declaration of Peter the great, declares that the ftyle of IMPERIAL fhall communicate no alteration to the ceremonial in ufe among courts, which fhall remain always on the fame footing.

(Signed)   VORONTZOFF.

Mofco, Nov. 21, 1762.   B. A. GALLITZIN.

[The ambaffador Breteuil having tranfmitted this declaration to Verfailles, Lewis XV. wrote the following anfwer, which was delivered to the minifters of Catharine:]

Titles are of themfelves nothing.   They poffefs no other reality than inafmuch as they are acknowledged, and their value depends on the idea attached to them, and the extent given to them by thofe who have the right to admit them, to reject them, or to limit them.—Sovereigns themfelves cannot attribute to themfelves titles at their own choice ;   the confent of their fubjects is not fufficient ; that of the other powers is neceffary ; and every crown, at liberty to acknowledge or to refufe a new title, may alfo adopt it with fuch modifications and conditions as are agreeable to it.

Agreeably to this principle, Peter I. and his fucceffors to the emprefs Elizabeth, have never been known in France but under the denomination of TZAR.—That princefs is the firft of all the fovereigns of Ruffia to whom the king granted the ftyle IMPERIAL ; but it was under the exprefs condition that this title fhould communicate no prejudice to the ceremonial in ufe between the two courts.

The

The emprefs Elizabeth fubfcribed, without fcruple, this condition, and explained herfelf on that head moft circumftantially in the reverfal framed by her order, and figned in the month of March 1745, by the counts Beftucheff and Vorontzoff.——The daughter of Peter I. therein teftifies her entire fatisfaction. She therein acknowledges, that it is *from friendfhip, and from a truly peculiar attention of the king to her, that his majefty had condefcended to the acknowledgment of the ftyle of* imperial, *which other powers had already conceded;* and fhe confeffes that *this complaifance of the king of France is highly agreeable to her.*

The king, actuated by the fame fentiments for the emprefs Catharine II. makes no hefitation in granting to her at prefent the ftyle of IMPERIAL, and to acknowledge it in her, as attached to the throne of Ruffia: but his majefty means that this acknowledgment fhould be made under the fame conditions as under the two foregoing reigns; and he declares, that, if hereafter any one of the fucceffors of the emprefs Catharine, unmindful of this folemn and reciprocal engagement, fhall think proper to form any pretenfion contrary to the ufage uniformly followed between the two courts, concerning rank and precedence; from that moment, the crown of France, by an equitable reciprocity, fhall refume its antient ftyle, and ceafe to give the ftyle of IMPERIAL to that of Ruffia.

This declaration, tending to prevent all fubject of difficulty for the future, is a proof of the friendfhip of the king for the emprefs, and of the fincere defire he has to eftablifh between the two courts a folid and unalterable union.

(Signed)   PRASLIN.

Done at Verfailles, Jan. 18, 1763.

No. IX.

Substance of a Memorial *delivered on the 16th of July by the* Chancellor *of* Russia *to the* Polish Resident *at* Petersburg.

IN this memorial her imperial majesty first sets forth her great love of peace, and how careful she has been to preserve it ; and then proceeds thus : " Filled with these sentiments, " it is with regret, that the empress sees his Polish majesty " follow different maxims with regard to her, and make no " return to her friendly proceedings but by proceedings " directly opposite.

" In the first place, in the affair of Courland, her imperial " majesty, attentive to every thing that concerned the dignity " of the king of Poland, has not ceased to claim his justice, " in which she always placed the greatest confidence.

" Secondly, she has not only paid all possible regard to the " representations made to her, touching the damage which " the Poles might have suffered by the passage of the russian " troops ; but even at this moment she waits only for the " naming of commissaries by the republic, to settle and give " orders for indemnification.

" Her imperial majesty is not content with convincing his " Polish majesty of her friendship in those two general " objects which regard the respective estates ; she has no less " at heart the giving proofs of her personal regard for his " majesty and his family. She has already interested herself, " and will still interest herself at every favourable opportu- " nity, to procure a proper establishment for his royal high- " ness the king's son, prince Charles : nevertheless, his " majesty the king of Poland has hitherto refused to listen " to any overtures for an accommodation, or for making " satisfaction for the many complaints of the empress : not " to mention the treaty of perpetual peace established " between Russia and the republic of Poland, and which has

" been

" been infringed by Poland, in many points ; her imperial
" majesty complains, first, that, notwithstanding the requi-
" sition made by her ambassador, the king has not given her
" satisfaction with regard to the irregular conduct of the
" four ministers, who signed a memorial highly offensive
" to the court of Russia and its sovereign. Secondly, that
" the king has not yet acknowledged the lawful duke
" of Courland. Thirdly, that the laws and liberties of
" Poland are oppressed, as well as the friends of Russia, who
" are kept from all employments, and from all favours,
" because they support liberty and the laws ; and who, on
" that very account, merit the protection of Russia ; who,
" being the guarantee of the rights of the republic, must not
" suffer any change in its constitution, but must be its firmest
" support," &c.

No. X.

MANIFESTO *published by the Court of* PETERSBURG, *on
occasion of the Death of Prince* IVAN.

By the grace of God, we Catharine the Second, empress and sovereign of all the Russias, &c. to all
whom these presents may concern.

WHEN, by the divine will, and in compliance with the
ardent and unanimous desires of our faithful subjects, we
ascended the throne of Russia, we were not ignorant that
Ivan, son of Anthony, prince of Brunswic-Wolfenbuttle,
and the princess Anne of Mecklenburgh, was still alive.
This prince, as is well known, was, immediately after his
birth, unlawfully declared heir to the imperial crown of
Russia ; but, by the decrees of Providence, he was soon
after irrevocably excluded from that high dignity, and the
sceptre placed in the hands of the lawful heiress, Elizabeth,
daughter

daughter of Peter the great, our beloved aunt of glorious
memory. After we had afcended the throne, and offered
up to heaven our juſt thankſgivings, the firſt objeƈt that
employed our thoughts, in confequence of that humanity
that is natural to us, was the unhappy fituation of that
prince, who was dethroned by the Divine Providence, and
had been unfortunate ever fince his birth ; and we formed
the refolution of alleviating his misfortunes, as far as was
poſſible. We immediately made a vifit to him, in order to
judge of his underſtanding and talents, and, in confequence
thereof, to procure him an agreeable and quiet fituation,
fuitable to his charaƈter and the education he had received.
But how great was our furprife, when, befides a defeƈt in
his utterance, that was uneafy to himfelf, and rendered his
difcourfe almoſt unintelligible to others, we obferved in him
a total privation of fenfe and reafon ! Thofe who accompanied us during this interview faw how much our heart
fuffered at the view of an objeƈt fo fitted to excite compaffion ; they were alfo convinced that the only meafure we
could take to fuccour the unfortunate prince, was to leave
him where we found him, and to procure him all the comforts and conveniences that his fituation would admit of.
We accordingly gave our orders for this purpofe, though
the ſtate he was in prevented his perceiving the marks of our
humanity, or being fenfible of our attention and care ; for
he knew nobody, could not diſtinguifh between good and
evil, nor did he know the ufe that might be made of reading, to pafs the time with lefs wearinefs and difguſt : on the
contrary, he fought after pleafure in objeƈts that difcovered,
with fufficient evidence, the diforder of his imagination.

To prevent, therefore, ill-intentioned perfons from giving
him any trouble, or from making ufe of his name or orders
to diſturb the public tranquillity, we gave him a guard, and
placed about his perfon two officers of the garrifon, in whofe
fidelity and integrity we could confide. Thefe officers were
captain Vlaffieff and lieutenant Tfchekin, who, by their
long military fervices, which had confiderably impaired
                                                    their

their health, deferved a fuitable recompence, and a ftation in which they might pafs quietly the reft of their days; they were accordingly charged with the care of the prince, and were ftrictly enjoined to let none approach him.   Yet all thefe precautions were not fufficient to prevent an abandoned profligate from committing at Schluffelburg, with unparalleled wickednefs, and at the rifk of his own life, an outrage, whofe enormity infpires horror.   A fecond lieutenant of the regiment of Smolenfko, a native of the Ukraine, named Bafil Mirovitch, grandfon of the firft rebel that followed Mazeppa, and a man in whom the perjury of his anceftors feems to have been infufed with their blood; this profligate, having paffed his days in debauchery and diffipation, and being thus deprived of all honourable means of advancing his fortune; having alfo loft fight of what he owed to the law of God, and of the oath of allegiance he had taken to us; and knowing prince Ivan only by name, without any knowledge either of his bodily or mental qualities; took it into his head to make ufe of this prince to advance his fortune at all events, without being reftrained by the confideration of the bloody fcene that fuch an attempt was adapted to occafion.   In order to execute this deteftable, dangerous, and defperate project, he defired, during our abfence in Livonia, to be upon guard, out of his turn, in the fortrefs of Schluffelburg, where the guard is relieved every eight days; and the 15th of laft month, about two o'clock in the morning, he all of a fudden called up the main guard, formed it into a line, and ordered the foldiers to load with ball. Berednikoff, governor of the fortrefs, having heard a noife, came out of his apartment, and afked Mirovitch the reafon of this difturbance, but received no other anfwer from this rebel than a blow on the head with the butt-end of his mufket.   Mirovitch, having wounded and arrefted the governor, led on his troops with fury, and attacked with fire-arms the handful of foldiers that guarded prince Ivan.   But he was fo warmly received
by

by those soldiers under the command of the two officers mentioned above, that he was obliged to retire. By a particular direction of that providence that watches over the life of man, there was that night a thick mist, which, together with the inward form and situation of the fortress, had this happy effect, that not one individual was either killed or wounded. The bad success of this first attempt could not engage this enemy of the public peace to desist from his rebellious purpose. Driven on by rage and despair, he ordered a piece of cannon to be brought from one of the bastions, which order was immediately executed. Captain Vlassieff and his lieutenant Tschekin, seeing that it was impossible to resist such a superior force, and considering the unhappy consequences that must ensue from the deliverance of a person that was committed to their care, and the effusion of innocent blood that must follow from the tumults it was adapted to excite, took, after deliberating together, the only step that they thought proper to maintain the public tranquillity, which was to cut short the days of the unfortunate prince. Considering also, that if they set at liberty a prisoner, whom this desperate party endeavoured to force with such violence out of their hands, they ran the risk of being punished according to the rigour of the laws, they assassinated the prince, without being restrained by the apprehension of being put to death by a villain reduced to despair. The monster (Mirovitch), seeing the dead body of the prince, was so confounded and struck at a sight he so little expected, that he acknowledged, that very instant, his temerity and his guilt, and discovered his repentance to the troop which about an hour before he had seduced from their duty, and rendered the accomplices of his crime.

Then it was, that the two officers, who had nipped this rebellion in the bud, joined with the governor of the fortress, in securing the person of this rebel, and in bringing back the soldiers to their duty. They also sent to our privy-counsellor Panin, under whose orders they acted, a relation

of

of this event, which, though unhappy, has nevertheless, under the protection of Heaven, been the occasion of preventing still greater calamities. This senator dispatched immediately lieutenant-colonel Kafchkin, with sufficient instructions to maintain the public tranquillity, to prevent disorder on the spot, (*i. e.* where the assassination was committed,) and sent us, at the same time, a courier with a circumstantial account of the whole affair. In consequence of this, we ordered lieutenant-general Veymarn, of the division of St. Petersburg, to take the necessary informations upon the spot; this he has done, and has sent us accordingly the interrogatories, depositions, and the confession of the villain himself, who has acknowledged his guilt.

Sensible of the enormity of his crime, and of its consequences with regard to the peace of our country, we have referred the whole affair to the consideration of our senate, which we have ordered, jointly with the synod, to invite the three first classes, and the presidents of all the colleges, to hear the verbal relation of general Veymarn, who has taken the proper informations; to pronounce sentence in consequence thereof; and, after that sentence has been signed, to present it to us for our confirmation of the same.

The original is signed by her imperial majesty's own hand. CATHARINE.

No. XI.

ALPHABETICAL LIST *of the* TOWNS *of the* RUSSIAN EMPIRE, *shewing in what Government they lie, and how many Verfts diftant from the Refidence, from the Métropolis, and from their refpective Government Towns, as far as could be collected from the Accounts delivered to* CATHARINE II.

The names of the government towns are diftinguifhed by *italics*.

Towns.	In what government.	Verfts from St. Peterfb.	Verfts from Mofco.	Verfts from government town.
Aktyrka	Kharkof	1453	723	106
Aklanfk	Irkutfk	10497	9767	4674
Alapayefsk	Perme			510
Alatyr	Simbirfk	1358	618	133
Alexandriya	Ekatarinoflavl			184
Alexandrof	Vladimir	824	101	117
Alexandrofak	Caucafus			150
Alexin	Tula	860	130	60
Alexopol	Ekatarinoflavl			115
Archangel		1145	1136	
Ardatof	Nifhnè-Novgorod			150
Ardatof on Alatyr	Simbirfk	1337	597	148
Arenfberg	Riga	626	1356	319
Arfamas	Nifhnè-Novgorod	1120	380	109
Arfk	Kafan	1463	735	55
Afof	Ekatarinoflavl	1998	1268	625
Aftrakhan	Caucafus	2142	1412	630
Atkarfk	Saratof	1630	902	79
Atfchinfk	Tobolfk	4694	3964	1809
Babinovitfchy	Mohilef			111
Bachmut	Ekatarinoflavl	1490	760	368
Balachna	Nifhnè-Novgorod	1145	415	32
Balafchof	Saratof			244
Baltic port	Reval	394	1122	44
Bargufinfk	Irkutfk	6345	5617	524
Belebey	Ufa			139
Berefin	Tfchernigof			36

Berefof

Towns.	In what government.	Versts from St. Peterfb.	Versts from Mosco.	Versts from government towns.
Berefof	Tobolfk	3814	3084	929
Blelef	Tula	973	239	120
Bielgorod	Kurfk	1356	626	132
Bielitza	Mohilef			194
Bieloy	Smolenfk	709	410	143
Bielopolye	Kharkof	1585	857	217
Bieloferfk	Novgorod	569	540	532
Bielovodfk	Voronetfh	1545	803	307
Biezvefk	Tver	625	287	121
Biifk	Kolhyvan			260
Biryutfch	Voronetfch	1357	617	150
Birfk	Ufa	1927	1197	105
Bobrof	Voronetfch	1265	535	87
Bogatye	Kurfk	1330	600	106
Bogodukhof	Kharkof	1471	741	60
Bogoroditzk	Tula	957	227	45
Bogorodfk	Mofco			50
Bogutfchar	Voronetfch	1475	735	238
Bolkhof	Orel	1020	290	54
Borifoglyebfk	Yaroflavl	*	†	32
Borifoglyebfk on the Vorona	Tambof	1359	629	152
Borovitfchi	Novgorod	360	454	183
Borofsk	Kaluga	893	163	78
Borfna	Tchernigof	1396	666	90
Brianfk	Orel	1077	347	138
Bronnitzy	Mofco	781	51	
Bugulma	Ufa	1687	957	220
Boguruflan	Ufa			279
Bui	Koftroma	932	396	130
Buinfk	Simbirfk	1462	722	70
Bufuluk	Ufa			375
Cronftadt	St. Peterfburg	47	777	
Dalmatof	Perme			510
Danilof	Yaroflavl	810	316	63
Dankof	Riazane	950	220	158
Defchkin	Orel	1060	330	58
St. Dmitri fort	Ekatarinoflavl	1968	1238	595
Dmitriyef	Kurfk	1241	511	99

* By the way of Uglitfch 814, by the way of Pofchek 797.
† By the way of Yaroflavl and Koft. 273, by the way of Pofchek 265.

Dmitrof

Towns.	In what government.	Verfts from St. Petersb.	Verfts from Mofco.	Verfts from government-town.
Dmitrof	Mofco	702	62	
Dmitrofsk	Orel	1181	451	84
Dnieprofsk	Tavrida			300
Donetzk	Ekatarinoflavl			443
Dorogobufh	Smolenfk	793	298	86
Doroninfk	Irkutfk	6644	5964	871
Dorpat	Riga	319	1049	230
Driezin	Polotfk	691	697	68
Dukhofshina	Smolenfk	727	363	51
Dynaburg	Polotfk	794	800	173
Ekatarinenburg	Perme	2308	1578	358
Ekatarinoflaf		1596	868	
Elizabethgrad	Ekatarinoflavl	1759	1411	211
Epiphan	Tula	962	232	50
Eupatoria	Tavrida			60
Fatefch	Kurfk	1193	463	46
Fellin	Riga			241
Frederikfham	Vyburg	326	1056	186
Gadyatch	Tchernigof	*	†	254
Galitch	Koftroma	919	396	117
Gdoff	St. Petersburg	216	871	
Georgiefsk	Caucafus	2528	1800	60
Glafof	Viatka			214
Glinfk	Tchernigof			210
Glukhof	Novgorod Sieverfkoi	1280	550	
Goltva	Kief			283
Gordatof	Nifhnè-Novgorod			70
Gorodetz	Polotzk	698	553	144
Gorodifchtfche	Penfa			42
Gorodnia	Tchernigof			50
Gorokovetch	Vladimir	1039	332	157
Gradifchtfche	Ekatarinoflavl			186
Griafovetch	Vologda	709	384	42
Giafk	Smolenfk	581	160	242
Habfal	Reval	456	1126	95
Infara	Penfa	1290	560	89
Irbit	Perme	2683	1953	578
Irkutfk		5823	5093	
Ifchim	Tobolfk	2935	2205	844

* *Via* Mtrenfk and Kurfk	— —	1450	720
† *Via* Smolenfk and Baturin	— —	1712	982

Ifchiginfk

Towns.	In what government.	Verſts from St. Peterſb.	Verſts from Moſco.	Verſts from government town.
Iſchiginſk	Irkutſk	10307	9577	4484
Iſium	Kharkof	1550	820	111
Kadnikof	Vologda	695	468	42
Kadyi	Koſtroma	950	427	147
Kaigorod	Viatka	1972	1242	246
Kainſk	Tobolſk	3788	3058	903
Kaliaſin	Tver	734	294	168
Kalitva	Voronetch	1421	681	193
Kaluga		890	160	
Kamyſchin	Saratof	1806	1076	174
Kamyſchlof	Perme			483
Kanadyei	Simbirſk	1537	797	131
Karatſchef	Orel	1102	372	84
Kargopol	Olonetz	618	1078	342
Karſun	Simbirſk	1423	683	91
Kaſan		1465	735	
Kaſchin	Tver	716	312	150
Kaſimof	Riazane	1010	280	140
Kem	Olonetz	885	1479	455
Kerenſk	Penſa	1199	460	135
Kexholm	Viborg	146	876	130
Kharkof		1421	680	
Kherſon	Ekatarinoſlavl	*	†	290
Kholm	Pleſkof	336	592	268
Khoperſk	Saratof	1419	689	
Khorol	Kief			223
Khotmyſhſk	Kharkof	1455	725	71
Khvalynſk	Saratof			197
Kief		1582	852	
Kinburn fort	Tavrida	2091	1361	
Kineſchma	Koſtroma	885	347	83
Kirenſk	Irkutſk	6768	6038	945
Kirilof	Novgorod	590	495	580
Kirſanof	Tambof	1295	565	88
Kirſhatſh	Vladimir	850	123	115
Kiſliar	Caucaſus	2642	1912	
Klimovitſchy	Mohilef			128
Klin	Moſco	648	82	
Kniaginin	Niſhnè-Novgorod			96

* *Via* Mtzenſk, Kurſk, and Krementſhuk — 1903 1174

† *Via* Smolenſk, Baturin, Polt. and Krementſhuk 2141 1411

Towns.	In what government.	Verfts from St. Peterfb.	Verfts from Mofco.	Verfts from government town.
Kola	Archangel	1379	2109	1021
Kolmogory	Archangel			
Kologrif	Koftroma	968	534	254
Kolomna	Mofco	830	100	
Kolyvan		5154	4424	
Konotop	Novgorod Sieverfkoi	1345	615	115
Konftantinograd	Ekatarinoflavl	973	864	104
Kopyfs	Mohilef			49
Korop	Novgorod Sieverfkoi			70
Korotoyak	Voronetch	1313	573	80
Korotfcha	Kurfk	1359	629	135
Kortfcheva	Tver			82
Kofchira	Tula	900	170	80
Kofeletz	Kief	1510	780	72
Kofelfk	Kaluga	940	210	57
Koflof	Tambof	1155	425	72
Koftroma		802	280	
Kotelnitfch	Viatka	1811	1081	95
Kotiakof	Simbirfk	1404	664	110
Kovrof	Vladimir	964	237	62
Krafnoborfk	Vologda	1100	1006	580
Krafnoy	Smolenfk	823	430	46
Krafnoy-Kholm	Tver	586	326	161
Krafnoy-Yar	Aftrakhan	2112	1382	30
Krafnoyarfk	Kolyvan	4839	4109	1981
Krafnokutfk	Kharkof	1508	767	86
Krafnoflobodfk	Penfa	1564	834	173
Krafnoufimfk	Perme	2077	1347	188
Kreftzy	Novgorod	279	451	93
Krolevetch	Novgorod Sieverfkoi	1319	589	64
Kromy	Orel	1133	403	36
Kropivna	Tula	952	222	40
Kungur	Perme	2051	1323	91
Kupenfk	Voronetch	1663	923	283
Kurgan	Tobolfk	2875	2145	414
Kurmyfch	Simbirfk	1237	500	257
Kurfk		1224	494	
Kufmodemyanfk	Kazan	1294	564	181
Kufnetzk	Kolyvan	4737	4007	
Kufnetzk	Saratof			197
Ladoga	St. Peterfburg	150	744	
Laifchef	Kazan			51

Lalfk

Towns.	In what government.	Verſts from St. Peterſb.	Verſts from Moſco.	Verſts from government town.
Lalſk	Vologda	1110	981	555
Lebedyan	Tambof	1104	374	177
Lebedin	Kharkof	1540	810	147
Levkopol	Tavrida			80
Lgof	Kurſk	1295	565	71
Lichvin	Kaluga	940	210	45
Lipetzk	Tambof	1162	432	149
Linbim	Yaroſlavl	826	354	101
Liutzin	Polotzk	593	758	164
Livenſk	Voronetch	1403	654	175
Livny	Orel	1090	360	128
Lochvitza	Tſchernigof	1462	732	210
Lodeinoë Pole	Olonetz	276	809	215
Lubney	Kief	1505	775	190
Luch	Koſtroma	913	347	129
Luga	St. Peterſburg	135	614	
Lukoyanof	Niſhnè-Novgorod			158
Makarief	Niſhnè-Novgorod			80
Makarief	Koſtroma	98	474	195
Malmyſh	Viatka			249
Maloarchangel	Orel	1143	413	70
Maloyaroſlavl	Kaluga	847	113	52
Mamadyſh	Kazan			146
Mariupol	Ekaterinoſlavl			321
Medynſk	Kaluga	869	135	57
Melenki	Vladimir	1040	313	138
Melitopol	Tavrida			220
Menſelinſk	Ufa	1769	1035	236
Meſchtſchofsk	Kaluga	980	250	69
Meſen	Archangel	1445	1575	511
Mglinſk	Novgorod Sieverſkoi			141
Michailof	Riazane	910	180	50
Mirgorod	Kief	1784	1054	233
Miropolie	Kharkof	1515	785	133
Mobilef		751	534	
Mokſchan	Penſa	1368	638	37
Mologa	Yaroſlavl	740	260	110
Morſchanſk	Tambof	1156	426	88
Moſalſk	Kaluga	940	210	77
Moſdok	Caucaſus		243	34
Moſhaiſk	Moſco	816	99	
MOSCO	*Metropolis*	728		

Mſtiſlavl

Towns.	In what government.	Versts from St. Petersb.	Versts from Moscoa.	Versts from government town.
Mſtiſlavl	Mohilef	914	501	94
Murom	Vladimir	1022	295	120
Myſchkin	Yaroſlavl	763	209	92
Mzenſk	Orel	1044	314	53
Nakhitſche.an	Ekatarinoſlavl			
Nagaibak	Orenburg	1733	1003	540
Naroftſchat	Penſa	1356	626	125
Narva	St. Peterſburg	145	875	
Narym	Tobolſk	4644	3934	1759
Nedrigailof	Kharkof	1574	844	195
Nerechta	Koſtroma	846	236	43
Nerſchinſk	Irkutſk	6784	6054	961
Neyſhlott	Viburg	390	1120	250
Nevel	Polotzk	1338	618	99
Nieſhin	Tſchernigof	1444	714	74
Nikitſk	Mosco		31	
Nikolſk	Vologda	1164	1061	637
Niſhnaia Dievitza	Voronetch	1284	544	57
Niſhnè Kamtſhatka	Irkutſk	11699	10969	5876
Niſhnè Lomof	Penſa	1339	609	96
Niſhnè Novgorod		1120	390	
Niſhneudinſk	Irkutſk	5348	4618	475
Nolin	Viatka			112
Novgorod		186	544	
Novgorod Sieverſkoi		*	†	
Novomieſto	Novgorod Sieverſkoi			144
Novomirgorod	Ekatarinoſlavl			288
Novomoſkofak	Ekatarinoſlavl	.		18
Novorſhef	Pleſkof	478	853	132
Novoſil	Tula	1292	458	176
Oboian	Kurſk	1283	553	59
Obvinſk	Perme			50
Odoyef	Tula	940	210	70
Okhanſk	Perme			67
Okhotſk	Irkutſk	9259	8529	3436
Olekminſk	Irkutſk	7754	7024	1931
Olenſk	Irkutſk	9309	8579	3496
Olonetz	Olonetz	280	874	150
Omſk	Tobolſk	3286	2556	693

* By Star, and Smolenſk	—		1150	540
† By Tula and Moſco	—	—	1328	598

Onega

Towns.	In what government.	Verfts from St. Peterfb.	Verfts from Mofco.	Verfts from government-town.
Onega	Archangel	900	1560	232
Opotfcha	Plefkof	491	727	137
Oranienbaum	St. Peterfburg	40	768	
Oranienburg	Riazane	1093	363	170
Orel		1097	367	
Orenburg	Ufa	1984	1254	319
Orlof	Viatka	1663	933	51
Orfcha	Mohilef	685	466	66
Ofa	Perme	2020	1290	113
Ofkol, old	Kurfk	1309	579	130
Ofkol, new	Kurfk	1379	639	191
Oftafchkof	Tver	426	347	183
Ofter	Kief	1532	802	89
Oftrogofk	Voronetch	1326	588	95
Oftrof	Plefkof	425	800	56
Pavlograd	Ekatarinoflavl			202
Pavlofsk	Voronetch	1380	640	150
Penfa		1394	660	
Pereyaflavl	Kief	1533	823	78
Perekop	Tavrida			140
Peremyfchl	Kaluga	925	195	28
Pereflavl Riaz.		910	180	
Pereflavl Saliefk	Vladimir	750	125	120
Perevolotfchna	Novgorod	2002	1272	50
Perevos	Nifhnè Novgorod			90
Perme		1949	1219	
Pernau	Riga	479	1190	72
Petropavlofskoi	Irkutfk	10648	9918	4620
Petrozavodfk	Olonetz	430	1024	
Petrofsk	Yaroflavl	819	167	76
Petrofsk	Saratof	1490	760	105
Petfchory	Plefkof		807	54
Phanagoria	Tavrida			240
Pinega	Archangel	1245	1288	210
Piriatin	Kief	1480	750	161
Ples	Koftroma	856	295	54
Plefkof		*	717	
Podol	Mofco	765	35	
Pogar	NovgorodSieverfkoi	1400	670	64
Pokrof	Vladimir	824	97	78

* By way of Narva   —   —   346
      By way of Luga   —   —   326

Polotzk

Towns.	In what government.	Versts from St. Petersb.	Versts from Mosco.	Versts from government town.
Polotzk		643	1373	
Poltava	Ekatarinoflavl	1535	805	171
Porkhof	Pleßkof	336	694	85
Porietfchy	Smolenſk	752	430	73
Pofchekonia	Yaroflavl	718	314	112
Potfchinky	Nifhnè Novgorod			212
Povienetz	Olonetz	595	1189	765
Priluky	Tfchernigof	1453	723	
Pronſk	Riazane	950	220	50
Pudaſh	Olonetz	516	996	240
Putevl	Kurſk	1404	674	100
Refitza	Polotzk	619	784	190
Reval		340	1070	
Riaſhſk	Riazane	1000	270	
Riga		552	1053	
Rogatſheff	Mohilef	1396	636	102
Romanof	Yaroflavl	796	266	34
Romen	Tfchernigof	1412	682	194
Roſheſtvenſk	St. Peterſburg	79		
Roſlavl	Smolenſk	880	443	116
Roſtof	Yaroflavl	806	189	54
Rſhef	Tver	631	300	127
Rufa	Mofco	759	88	
Rybnoy	Yaroflavl	806	252	78
Rylſk	Kurſk	1340	610	116
Sadonſk	Voronetch	1130	400	85
Samara	Simbirſk	1633	893	177
ST. PETERSBURG	*Refidence*	728		
Sapoſhok	Riazane	1030	300	120
Saraiſk	Riazane	860	130	56
Saranſk	Penfa	1276	546	123
Sarapul	Viatka	1812	1082	380
Saratof		1632	902	
Safchiverſk	Irkutſk	9192	8462	3369
Schadrinſk	Perme	2488	1758	556
Schatzk	Tambof	1090	360	157
Schenkurſk	Archangel	800	848	388
Schefchkeyef	Penfa	1306	576	144
Schluſſelburg	St. Peterſburg	60	790	
Schtfchigry	Kurſk	1290	478	50
Schuya	Vladimir	969	239	90
Sebeſh	Polotzk	533	718	104
				Selenginſk

Towns.	In what government.	Verfts from St. Peterfb.	Verfts from Mofco.	Verfts from governament-towns.
Selenginfk	Irkutfk	6226	5496	403
Semeonoff	Nifhnè Novgorod			60
Semipalatfk	Kolyvan	2992	2262	
Semlianfk	Voronetch	1204	464	40
Serdob	Saratof			175
Serdobol	Viburg			238
Sergatfch	Nifhnè Novgorod			138
Sergiefsk	Ufa			350
Serpeifk	Kaluga	980	250	82
Serpukhof	Mofco	818	88	
Sevaftopol	Tavrida			
Shiganfk	Irkutfk	9125	8395	3302
Shifdra	Kaluga	1054	320	156
Sienkof	Tfchernigof			286
Siennoi	Mohilef			151
Sievfk	Orel	1242	512	145
Simbirfk		1485	745	
Simpheropol	Tavrida	2187	1459	
Singileyef	Simbirfk	1519	779	49
Skopin	Riazane	1026	296	88
Slavianfk	Ekatarinoflavl	1440	710	200
Slobodfkoy	Viatka	1740	1010	28
Smolenfk		716	384	
Solgalitzkaia	Koftroma	799	502	223
Solikamfk	Perme	2227	1497	263
Solotonofcha	Kief			130
Solotfchef	Kharkof	1459	718	36
Solvytfchegodfk	Vologda	1086	988	560
Sophia	St. Peterfburg	22	796	
Sofnitza	Novgorod Sieverfkoi			
Spafk	Kazan			134
Spafk	Riazane	966	232	52
Spafk	Tambof	1300	570	207
Staraia Ruffa	Novgorod	306	664	120
Staritza	Tver	595	237	73
Staro Bykhof	Mohilef	984	569	38
Starodub	Novgorod Sieverfkoi	1083	480	81
Stavropol	Caucafus			
Stavropol	Simbirfk	1589	849	133
Sterlitamazk	Ufa			115
Strietenfk	Irkutfk	6866	6136	1043
Subtzof	Tver	628	280	116

Towns.	In what government.	Versts from St. Petersb.	Versts from Mosco.	Versts from government.
Sudogda	Vladimir			
Sudscha	Kursk	939	212	37
Sumy	Kharkof	1315	585	91
Surash	Polotzk	1383	653	175
Surashsk	Novgorod Sieverskoi	769	558	149
Surgut	Tobolsk			141
Susdal	Vladimir	3610	2875	725
Svenigorod	Mosco	936	209	32
Sviyabsk	Kazan	718	48	
Syfran	Simbirsk	1445	715	30
Sytschofka	Smolensk	1565	825	123
Tagay	Simbirsk		219	227
Taganrok	Ekatarinoflavl	1436	696	49
Tambof		2036	1306	460
Tara	Tobolsk	1207	477	
Tarufa	Kaluga	3445	2715	560
Temnikof	Tambof	848	118	62
Tetyufchy	Kazan	1279	549	291
Theodofia	Tavrida	1585	855	85
Tichvin	Novgorod			
Tim	Kurfk	243	744	210
Tiumin	Tobolfk	1243	513	64
Tobolfk		2631	1901	254
Tomfk	Tobolfk	2885	2155	
Toropetz	Pscove	4309	3579	1424
Torfhok	Tver	610	497	347
Totma	Vologda	503	227	63
Troïtzk	Penfa	889	626	209
Troïtzk	Ufa	1386	656	134
Trubtfchevfk	Orel			462
Tfchaufy	Mohilef	1166	436	169
Tfchebokfar	Kazan			43
Tfchelyabinfk	Ufa	1350	620	124
Tfchembar	Penfa	2488	1758	400
Tfcherdyn	Perme			129
Tfcherekof	Mohilef	2321	1591	364
Tfcherepovetch	Novgorod			82
Tfcherkafk	Ekatarinoflavl			476
Tfchernigof		1936	1208	
Tfchern	Tula	1124	676	
Tfchernoi Yar	Saratof	970	240	
Tfchiftopoliye	Kazan	1972	1242	499
Tfchuchloma				125

Towns.	In what government.	Verfts from St. Peterfb.	Verfts from Mofco.	Verfts from government town.
Tfchuchloma	Koftroma	920	473	167
Tfchuguyef	Kharkof	1414	684	34
Tula		912	182	
Turinfk	Tobolfk	2480	1750	405
Turuchanfk	Tobolfk	6190	5460	3305
Tver		568	162	
Tzarevo Kokfhaifk	Kazan	1354	624	126
Tzarevo Santfchurfk	Viatka	1414	684	253
Tzaritzin	Saratof	1772	1042	355
Tzyvilfk	Kazan	1390	660	102
Ufa		1913	1183	
Uglitfch	Yaroflavl	734	180	101
Urfhum	Viatka	1631	901	163
Ufman	Tambof	1226	496	158
Uftiugvelikoy	Vologda	1000	899	473
Ultiofhna	Novgorod	450	368	357
Uftfyfolfk	Vologda	1400	1300	876
Valday	Novgorod	338	392	152
Valk	Riga			149
Valky	Kharkof	1466	725	53
Valniky	Voronetch	1376	630	208
Varnavin	Koftroma	1132	666	387
Vafil	Nifhnè Novgorod	1255	525	144
Veiffenftein	Reval			34
Velikiye Luky	Pfcove	528	601	259
Velifk	Polotzk	809	598	189
Velfk	Vologda	870	706	280
Vende	Riga			100
Venef	Tula	860	130	40
Verchney Lomof	Penfa	1339	609	106
Verkhoturiye	Perme	2503	1773	540
Verkhoudinfk	Irkutfk	6116	5388	295
Verkhouralfk	Ufa			309
Vereya	Mofco	831	98	
Verro	Riga			236
Vefenberg	Reval			80
Vefyegonfk	Tver	502	406	241
Vetluga	Koftroma	1084	619	339
Viafma	Smolenfk	587	221	163
Viafniky	Vladimir	1022	295	120
Viatka		1815	1085	
Vilmanftrand	Vyburg	190	920	50
				Vitebfk

Towns.	In what government.	Versts from St. Petersb.	Versts from Mosco.	Versts from government town.
Vitebsk	Polotzk	729	518	109
Vladimir		902	175	
Volmar	Riga		1171	103
Vologda		689	426	
Voloko Lamsk	Mosco	712	101	
Volsk	Saratof			110
Voltschansk	Kharkof			60
Voronetch		1220	490	
Voskresensk	Mosco		42	
Vyburg		140	870	
Vyschney Volotschok	Tver	432	298	134
Vytegra	Olonetz	426	876	
Yadrin	Kazan	1250	520	186
Yakutsk	Irkutsk	8309	7579	2486
Yalutorofsk	Tobolsk	2715	1985	254
Yamburg	St. Petersburg	121	854	
Yaransk	Viatka	1706	972	202
Yarensk	Vologda	1721	1147	721
Yaroslavl		830	243	
Yegoriefsk	Riazane	814	80	95
Yelabuga	Viatka			373
Yelatma	Tambof	1055	325	264
Yeletz	Orel	1094	364	183
Yelna	Smolensk		326	90
Yeneseisk	Tobolsk	5032	4300	2147
Yenotaiyefsk	Astrakhan	2084	1354	
Yephremof	Tula	1024	294	112
Yuknof	Smolensk		251	194
Yurief Polskoy	Vladimir	820	90	50
Yuryevetz Povolskoy	Kostroma	974	347	172

END OF THE APPENDIX.

P. 83. laft line, note, *for* April 25 *read* May 2d

J. Watts de Peyster:
LL. D.

MASTER OF ARTS, COLUMBIA COLLEGE, OF NEW YORK. 1872.
ROSE HILL, in the TOWNSHIP of RED HOOK, near TIVOLI P. O., DUCHESS CO., N. Y.

May, 1883.

JUDGE ADVOCATE. with the rank of MAJOR, 1845,
COLONEL N. Y. B. I., 1846; assigned for *"Meritorious Conduct,"* 1849;
BRIGADIER-GENERAL for *"Important Service"* [first appointment—in N. Y. State—to that rank, hitherto
elective] 18 , M. F. S. N. Y.
ADJUTANT-GENERAL. S. N. Y., 1855.
BREVET MAJOR-GENERAL. S. N. Y., for *"Meritorious Services,"*
[first and only General officer receiving such an honor (the highest) from S. N. Y., and the only officer thus
brevetted (Major-General) in the United States.]
by *"Special Act,"* or *"Concurrent Resolution,"* New York State Legislature, April, 1866.

LAWS OF NEW YORK. Vol. 1.—89th Session, 1866. Page 2142.
Concurrent Resolution requesting the Governor to Confer upon Brigadier-General J. WATTS DE PUYSTER
[de Peyster] the brevet rank of Major" (General) in the National Guard of New York.
Resolved, (if the State concur,) That it being a grateful duty to acknowledge in a suitable manner the services
of a distinguished citizen of this State, rendered to the National Guard and to the United States prior to and dur
ing the Rebellion, the Governor be and he is hereby authorized and requested to confer upon Brigadier-General
J. WATTS DE PUYSTER [de Peyster] the brevet rank of Major-General in the National Guard of New York, for
meritorious services, which mark of honor shall be stated in the Commission conferred.
STATE OF NEW YORK. in Assembly. April 9th, 1866.
By order of the Assembly.

The foregoing Resolution was duly passed.
J. B. CUSHMAN. Clerk.
STATE OF NEW YORK, in Senate. April 20th, 1866.
By order of the Senate.
The foregoing Resolution was duly passed.
JAS. TERWILLIGER. Clerk.
* So in original.

MILITARY AGENT, S. N. Y., (in Europe,) 1861-'3.
HONORARY MEMBER, THIRD CLASS, of the MILITARY ORDER of the LOYAL LEGION of the U. S.
FIRST HONORARY MEMBER Third (Army of the Potomac) Corps Union.
HONORARY MEMBER of the CLARENDON HISTORICAL SOCIETY of Edinburgh, Scotland, and of the
NEW BRUNSWICK (Canada) HISTORICAL SOCIETY (of St. John).
MEMBER—10th June, 1873, DIRECTOR—of the GETTYSBURG BATTLEFIELD MEMORIAL ASSOCIATION.
and VICE PRESIDENT of the SARATOGA (Battlefield) MONUMENT ASSOCIATION.
MEMBER of the NETHERLANDISH LITERARY ASSOCIATION
[Maatschappij der Nederlandsche Letterkunde] at Leyden, Holland.
RECIPIENT, 1856, of Three Silver Medals from H. R. M. OSCAR, King of Sweden and Norway, &c., for a Military
Biography of LEONARD TORSTENSON, Field Marshal, Generalissimo; of a Gold Medal in
1851, from WASHINGTON HUNT, [Governor S. N. Y.,] for "Efforts to Improve
the Military System of New York," &c., &c., and Suggestions for a
Paid Fire Department with Steam Fire Engines, &c., &c.:
of a Gold Medal, only similar distinction ever ordered and directed, and conferred by the supreme military authority of the State of New York, by a Special Order, dated 9th September, 851, of WASHINGTON
HUNT, Governor and Commander in Chief of the Military Forces (S. N. Y.), authorized
to be worn in attest of "Zeal, Devotion and Meritorious Services,"
of a Gold Medal, in 1852, from the FIELD and STAFF OFFICERS of his Command, 9th Brig., 3d Div., N. Y. S.
Troops, "In testimony of their Esteem and Appreciation of his Efforts towards
the Establishment of an efficient Militia," &c.
in 1870, of a Magnificent Badge, Medal and Clasps voted at the Annual Meeting of the Third Corps (Army of the
Potomac) Union held at Boston Mass., Thursday, May 5th, 1870, when
A Resolution was adopted to present a Gold Medal, of the value of $500, to Gen. J WATTS DE PEYSTER, of
New York, as a testimonial of the appreciation by the Corps of his eminent services in placing upon record
the true history of its achievements, and in defending its commanders and their men from written abuse and
misrepresentation:"
and of several other Badges, Medals, &c., for services in connection with the military service of the State of
New York.
HONORARY MEMBER of the NEW JERSEY and of the MINNESOTA HISTORICAL SOCIETIES, and of the
PHRENOKOSMIAN SOCIETY of PENNSYLVANIA COLLEGE, Gettysburg; of the PHILOSOPHIAN
SOCIETY, Missionary Institute, Selin's Grove, and of the EUTERPEAN SOCIETY,
Muhlenberg College. Allentown, Pennsylvania, and of the GASMAN LITER-
ARY SOCIETY, of Nebraska College, Nebraska City.
HONORARY MEMBER of the LYCEUM SOCIETY, in Cazenovia, Madison Co., N. Y.; and HONORARY MEM-
BER FOR LIFE of the AMERICAN RIFLE ASSOCIATION; to whom Gen. DE PEYSTER
presented the most original, exquisite and unique Gold Badge and Clasp, to be
shot for at the Annual Tests of Marksmanship.
HONORARY MEMBER of the N. Y. BURNS CLUB.
(BURNS was a member of the Dumfries Volunteers, of which Col. ARENT SCHUYLER DE PEYSTER, 8th or
King's Foot, B. A., was Colonel, to whom the "National Bard of Scotland" addressed
just before his death, in 1796, his " POEM ON LIFE,") and
LIFE MEMBER of the ST. NICHOLAS SOCIETY OF NEW YORK,
(of which city JOHANNES DE PEYSTER, first of the name in the New World, was Schepen, 1655, Alderman, 1666,
Burgomaster, 1673, Deputy Mayor, 1677. Mayoralty offered and refused).
MEMBER
of the NEW YORK, of the RHODE ISLAND (Newport) and of the PENNSYLVANIA HISTORICAL
SOCIETIES and of the MILITARY ASSOCIATION of the STATE of NEW YORK,
and of the CENTURY CLUB, New York City.
LIFE MEMBER
of the HISTORICAL SOCIETY of MICHIGAN, of the NEW YORK GALLERY OF FINE ARTS, of the ALUMNI
ASSOCIATION of COLUMBIA COLLEGE, in the City of New York, and Director of the N. Y.
INSTITUTION for the INSTRUCTION of the DEAF and DUMB, and of the
AMERICAN NUMISMATIC and ARCHÆOLOGICAL SOCIETY
of NEW YORK.
LIFE MEMBER or FELLOW of the AMERICAN GEOGRAPHICAL SOCIETY ; of the ROYAL HISTORICAL
SOCIETY OF GREAT BRITAIN ; of the NUMISMATIC AND ARCHÆOLOGICAL SOCIETY
of New York ; PATRON of the ASSOCIATION for the BENEFIT of COLORED
ORPHANS, and of the NEW YORK DISPENSARY; &c., &c., DI-
RECTOR of the AMERICAN TRACT and LIFE
MEMBER of the AMERICAN BIBLE SOCIETY, N. Y.
CORRESPONDING MEMBER
of the STATE HISTORICAL SOCIETIES of MAINE, of VERMONT, of RHODE ISLAND, (Providence,) of
CONNECTICUT, and of WISCONSIN ; of the LONG ISLAND, of BUFFALO, and of ONEIDA
COUNTY (S. N. Y.) HISTORICAL SOCIETIES ; of the NEW ENGLAND HISTORIC-
GENEALOGICAL SOCIETY ; of the QUEBEC LITERARY and HISTORI-
CAL SOCIETY ; of the NUMISMATIC and ANTIQUARIAN
SOCIETY of PHILADELPHIA, Pennsylvania;
etc., etc., etc.